New Interpretations in Naval History

Selected Papers from the
Fifteenth Naval History Symposium
Held at the United States Naval Academy
20–22 September 2007

Edited by Maochun Miles Yu

NAVAL INSTITUTE PRESS
Annapolis, Maryland

Naval Institute Press
291 Wood Road
Annapolis, MD 21402

© 2009 by the United States Naval Institute
All rights reserved. No part of this book may be reproduced or utilized in any form or by any means, electronic or mechanical, including photocopying and recording, or by any information storage and retrieval system, without permission in writing from the publisher.

Library of Congress Cataloging-in-Publication Data
United States Naval Academy History Symposium (15th : 2007)
 New interpretations in naval history : selected papers from the Fifteenth Naval History Symposium / edited by Maochun Yu.
   p. cm.
 Includes bibliographical references and index.
 ISBN 978-1-59114-983-5 (alk. paper)
 1. Naval art and science—History—Congresses. 2. Naval history—Congresses. I. Yu, Maochun, 1962– II. Title.
 V27. U55 2007
 359.009—dc22
                                                            2008054723

Printed in the United States of America on acid-free paper

14 13 12 11 10 09   9 8 7 6 5 4 3 2
First printing

Book layout and composition: David Alcorn, Alcorn Publication Design

Contents

Preface v

Part I. Ancient and Medieval Navies
Defending the Realm: Roman Naval Capabilities in Waters Beyond the Mediterranean, *by Jorit Wintjes* 1

The Naval Strategy of Roger II, King of Sicily, *by Chuck Stanton* 14

Part II. Canada
American Influence on Canadian Wartime Shipbuilding, *by Chris Madsen* 34

King, Canada, and the Convoys: A Reappraisal of Adm. Ernest King's Role in Operation Drumbeat, *by Kenneth P. Hansen* 57

Part III. China
Cutting Dwarf Pirates Down to Size: Amphibious Warfare in Sixteenth-Century East Asia, *by Kenneth M. Swope* 81

Training a Reluctant Ally: The U.S. Naval Advisory Mission to China, 1945–49, *by Katherine K. Reist* 108

Part IV. Europe
French Naval Intelligence during the American Civil War and the Mexican Expedition, 1861–67, *by Alexandre Sheldon-Duplaix* 129

The Strategic Plight of the Spanish Republican Navy in the Spanish Civil War, 1936–39, *by Willard C. Frank Jr.* 163

Part V. Latin America
The Allied Project to Liberate Cuba, 1866–67: Chile, Peru, and Colonel Barreda's Confederate Navy, *by David P. Werlich* 189

Part VI. Marines
A "Soldier of the Sea" in Sub-Saharan Africa: Brevet Maj. A. R. Chater, DSO, Royal Marines, of the Sudanese Camel Corps, 1921–31, *by Donald F. Bittner* 228

U.S. Marines' Counterinsurgency Campaigns in Nicaragua in the Early Twentieth Century, *by Charles Neimeyer* 247

Part VII. Social History
Hidden Lives: Elderly Cooks, Powder Boys, and Fugitive Slaves among
Eighteenth-Century Anglo-American Naval Crews,
by Charles R. Foy   266
Navy Women's Pioneering Experiences at Sea,
by Catherine A. Leahey   279

Preface

The Naval History Symposium as a scholarly enterprise of the U.S. Naval Academy History Department started in the early 1970s. Over the years it has become a hallmark of the History Department's commitment to the study of naval and maritime history. For nearly three decades this biannual event has been one of the most well-attended conferences in the world of its kind. Scholars from the United States and many countries have called the symposium home. The Fourteenth Naval History Symposium was scheduled to take place at the Naval Academy on 12 September 2001; the tragedies of the terrorist attacks on the United States the day before abruptly interrupted the course, and the event was promptly canceled owing to the new global war on international terrorism. Subsequently, issues of national security and international terrorism became the central subject matter of all major conferences and symposia at the Naval Academy. In late spring of 2005 the History Department convened a meeting to discuss the future of the symposium. The faculty voted overwhelmingly that the department should restore the event as a scholarly enterprise in its traditional format and with regular frequency. The 2007 Naval History Symposium, held in Annapolis on 20–22 September, thus marked the full resumption of this scholarly pursuit.

In 2007 we were fortunate to have the generous and enthusiastic support of the McMullen Seapower Fund, managed by the Naval Academy Foundation. This support enabled us to invite far more scholars to Annapolis for the event than originally planned. It also provided a significant number of travel stipends with which we could encourage scholars in financial need or young scholars in graduate schools to participate. Finally, this support permitted us to establish meaningful competition-based prizes for best essays.

Our call for essays in the fall of 2006 received an enthusiastic response from around the world. By mid-January 2007 more than 220 proposals from scholars in more than a dozen countries reached the committee. Those countries included Argentina, Australia, Austria, Canada, Chile, China, Denmark, Ecuador, France, Germany, Japan, the Netherlands, Peru, the United Kingdom, and the United States. Eventually about 110 essays were accepted into the program; they were then organized into thirty-six panels, the largest number so far of any Naval History Symposium.

The panels showed great diversity. Chronologically there were presentations on topics extending from ancient Greek navies to Operation Enduring Freedom. Topically they stretched from considerations of naval power in the Third Crusade to examinations of women's roles in the American Navy. In terms of institutions represented, scholars who were included in the final program came from various universities, research facilities, and government agencies in Argentina, Australia, Austria, Canada, Chile, Denmark, Ecuador, France, Germany, Japan, the Netherlands, Peru, and the United Kingdom. American scholars came from institutions ranging from Bates College, to Duke University, to the University of California–Berkeley, to Yale University, and various defense institutions such as the Marine Corps University, the National Geospatial Intelligence Agency, the Naval Historical Center, the Naval Post-Graduate School, and the Naval War College. Approximately three hundred scholars from various countries and institutions registered to attend the symposium.

Of the more than one hundred presentations at the symposium, the overwhelming majority were accompanied by written essays. Many of these essays represented the latest research on various aspects of naval and maritime history. The selection committee painstakingly valued the merit of each essay and selected the final thirteen essays included in this volume. In keeping with tradition, the 2007 Naval History Symposium decided against a particular theme or time period and regional restriction. As a result, the essays explored a wide range of topics. The current volume reflects this reality, covering a time span from antiquity to modern times, from different continents, and from different aspects of naval and maritime history. There are many more unselected essays that were exceptional, but the committee and the editor had to balance the high quality of these essays and the length requirements and theme groupings of the volume. Fortunately, Dr. Gary Weir, chief historian of the U.S. National Geospatial Intelligence Agency, suggested the brilliant idea of publishing some of the unselected yet worthy essays in the online *International Journal of Naval History* (www.ijnhonline.org).

Organizing a symposium of this nature and size requires a prolonged and collective effort. I would like to thank colleagues in the History Department who worked on the committee to make the 2007 Naval History Symposium a great success. Working on the committee were seven professors: Lori Bogle, Scott Harmon, Fred Harrod, Robert Love, Virginia Lunford, William McBride, and William Roberts; three U.S. Navy commanders: C. C. Felker, Mary Kelly, and Jeffery Macris; three U.S. Marine Corps majors: Shawn

Callahan, Mark Deets, and Brian Ross; and U.S. Navy Lt. Joseph Slaughter. Other colleagues not on the committee yet instrumental in the success of the symposium included Patrick Alfonso, Hayden Bellenoit, Barry Bradstreet, John Freyman, Keith Gibling, Daniel Masterson, Lee Pennington, Thomas Robertson, Richard Ruth, Thomas Sanders, and Ernest Tucker. Our department secretary, Mrs. Connie Grigor, processed seemingly endless paperwork with grace and efficiency. Without their tireless commitment to their assigned or voluntary tasks, the symposium would not have been run as smoothly as it was. To all of them I owe my primary gratitude.

Leadership support is crucial as well. The superintendent of the Naval Academy at the time, Vice Adm. Rodney Rempt, approved the symposium proposal with alacrity. The new superintendent, Vice Adm. Jeffrey Fowler, also gave his support to the project and graced the symposium with an opening speech. Col. David Mollahan, director of Social Sciences and Humanities of the Naval Academy, took a personal interest in how the preparation task was run and was greatly helpful. In particular, the symposium would also like to thank Vice Dean Michael Halbig for his crucial role in securing the financial support from the McMullen Seapower Fund. Finally, Professor David Peeler, chair of the history department, was supportive and involved throughout the entire process. The naval history community is deeply grateful for his enthusiastic support and commitment to resurrecting the symposium.

One particular point I would like to raise here is that the Naval History Symposium is truly an interdepartmental and interagency product. Throughout the two-year-long preparation and execution of our programs, various personalities from different organizations provided timely and important help. Dr. Sarandis Papadopoulos of the U.S. Naval Historical Center was immensely helpful in guiding me through various intricate webs of personalities and institutions within the naval history community and giving me a great amount of sage advice. Colleagues at the U.S. Naval Institute, especially Michael Collins, Tom Cutler, Laura Johnston, William Miller, Richard Russell, and Fred Schultz, collaborated with us on several aspects of the symposium with grace and generosity, including providing a lunch session for the program and advertising space in the *Proceedings* and *Naval History* periodicals. Dr. Scott Harmon, the director of the Naval Academy Museum, not only served as a member of the organizing committee, but also graciously provided the elegant exhibit hall of the museum as the venue for an evening reception. The artist Patrick O'Brien (www.patrickobrienstudio.com) of Baltimore gave us the right, free of charge, to use his majestic painting, *Victory at Trafalgar*, as our promotion and advertising image. Diana Green, the Naval Academy's resident art designer, helped put the poster and all the program materials together. To all these individuals, I offer my thanks.

Finally, as the editor of this volume, I would like to express my gratitude to all authors and our colleagues at the Naval Institute Press for working with me with such efficiency and good humor throughout the entire process.

Maochun Miles Yu
Director, 2007 Naval History Symposium
Professor of History, U.S. Naval Academy

PART I. ANCIENT AND MEDIEVAL NAVIES

Defending the Realm: Roman Naval Capabilities in Waters Beyond the Mediterranean

Jorit Wintjes

INTRODUCTION

The Roman army, probably the most professional fighting machine in classical antiquity, has always been an immensely popular subject among ancient military historians. Both traditional scholarship aimed at analyzing what the army did and contemporary interest in how the army operated are thriving. Events such as the annual Roman army school bring together archaeologists, ancient historians, and military professionals to share their insights into the ways of the Roman army.

In contrast, the Roman navy has not enjoyed nearly as much attention.[1] The navy certainly features in the context of Roman military operations during the Republic, when the Punic Wars, the expansion into the eastern Mediterranean, and the civil wars brought about large-scale naval activity. It is still rather common, however, to think of the Imperial Roman navy as some kind of second-class military establishment, useful primarily for providing seamen to work the awnings in the Coliseum or for allowing the rapid recruitment of army units in the event of an emergency.[2] Such an attitude toward the Roman navy is probably understandable since, with the end of the civil wars and the establishment of the principate, the Mediterranean was by and large a peaceful sea; only rarely, and then almost always in the context of civil wars, was the control the Roman navy exerted over the Mediterranean ever challenged. This general picture of Roman naval history is nevertheless wrong, though, primarily because it is far too focused on the Mediterranean.

There were, after all, other areas of intense naval activity outside the Mediterranean where Roman naval forces were almost constantly employed during imperial times. The advent of the empire saw not only the establishment of the imperial fleets in Misenum and Ravenna, but also the creation of standing provincial fleets on the frontiers: the *Classes Alexandrina* and *Syriaca* operated in the Mediterranean from their bases on the Levantine coast; the *Classis Pontica* was based on the northern coast of Asia Minor; the *Classes Moesica, Pannonica,* and *Germanica* worked the rivers Rhine and Danube; and the *Classis Britannica* was assigned to the waters off Gaul and Britain. All had important roles and provided the empire with crucial capabilities. They were indispensable in the ongoing tasks of patrolling and securing the borders, combating intruders, projecting power, and supporting large imperial expeditions. Although these provincial fleets regularly found themselves involved in important military activities, scholarly interest in them has been negligible, compared to the interest in the Roman army, and does not reflect the actual importance of these fleets.[3] While Roman naval activities along the frontiers of the empire were by no means confined to these standing fleets, it was their infrastructure and the nautical expertise concentrated in them that made it possible to increase Roman capabilities at fairly short notice.

The purpose of this essay is to take a closer look at Roman naval activities in order to highlight the importance of the provincial fleets in the overall context of Roman naval operations. As it is impossible to give a detailed analysis of all the operations in which Roman provincial fleets were involved, this essay will concentrate on a selected number of operations in northwestern Europe, most of them involving both naval and ground forces. These examples are not arranged chronologically, but rather have been sorted based on the complexity of the operation. This essay will focus on reconnaissance missions, transport operations, and amphibious assaults. This list of activities is by no means complete. Roman naval units were also tasked with logistical support for military installations, control of the coastline, and the fight against piracy. Concentration on the three types of operations mentioned above will yield useful results and allow some general conclusions regarding Roman naval warfare in northwestern Europe.

RECONNAISSANCE AND EXPLORATION

As far as complexity is concerned, reconnaissance and exploration missions rank among the simpler ones undertaken by the Romans, if only because—in many cases, as far as can be judged from the surviving sources—they involved naval forces alone. These were either employed in the collection of information that was of a tactical nature or used for expanding the overall knowledge of waterways and coastlines of what, for the Romans, was the northern ocean.

While Caesar's campaign against the Veneti in 56 BC, in which naval forces played a prominent role, must have seen reconnaissance operations of one kind or another, the first fact-finding mission of which surviving sources allow a fairly clear picture is set in the context of Caesar's first expedition to Britain the following year.[4] Having acquired enough information to get a general idea of the political situation in the southern part of Britain during the preparation for the expedition, Caesar sent one of his military tribunes, Caius Volusenus Quadratus, away on a scouting mission in a small, fast ship only days before the invasion fleet set sail.[5] His mission was simple yet important: he was to find suitable landing beaches for Caesar's forces. Volusenus spent four days at sea without making landfall, probably circumnavigating the Isle of Thanet in the process. Perhaps he penetrated even farther up the coast toward the Isle of Sheppey.

In his account of his first expedition Caesar put particular stress on Volusenus having kept away from the land.[6] These remarks have been interpreted as critical of Volusenus's decision to do so, yet there is nothing in the text justifying such an interpretation. That Volusenus avoided making landfall during these four days clearly shows that he and Caesar had a good understanding of how to run such a reconnaissance operation. In the run-up to the invasion, the information he collected on suitable landing beaches was much more valuable than anything he might have gained from going ashore, particularly because that would have brought with it the risk of being rendered incapable of returning the information to Caesar, if he had met with some unfriendly Briton.[7]

Around half a century later, Tiberius's campaign in Germany provides a good example for an operation with a much broader objective than that of Volusenus. In AD 5 a Roman fleet went on a strategic reconnaissance mission, exploring the coastlines of northern Germany and Jutland.[8] The Romans apparently circumnavigated Jutland, although it is not clear how far they eventually penetrated into the Baltic. While during Drusus's campaigns in Germany from 12 BC onward the Romans had already sailed along the North Sea coast, they had apparently never ventured beyond the Elbe estuary before AD 5.[9] Although little is known about operational details, it is clear that this mission must have differed markedly from that of Caius Volusenus and probably involved a sizeable naval force and included troop contingents to allow for minor landings.

This naval operation has been seen solely as a general part of Roman exploration. While one of its reasons may well have been a desire to get rid of blank spots on the maps, taking a closer look at the pattern of Roman operations in Germany in AD 5—or indeed from 12 BC onward—allows some further insight into exactly what the Romans were doing. During their campaigns in Germany, Roman commanders tended to lean rather heavily on naval support for logistical purposes. Both Drusus and Tiberius established bases close to navigable rivers, bases that were then used to support their troops. Compared to routes over land, waterways were much easier to control while conversely much more difficult for any enemy to cut off. Bases alongside rivers were therefore ideal both as staging areas at the beginning of a campaign season and as fallback lines at the end of the season or during a crisis. Roman camps found near the rivers Ems, Elbe, Lippe, and Main are testimony to this strategy.[10]

In AD 5 the Romans set out to eventually circumnavigate Jutland. It is obvious that, apart from generally broadening their geographical knowledge, they were specifically looking for points both at the coast and at the mouth of great rivers where bases could be established. Indeed, it is plausible that they also probed rivers and inlets for their navigability.[11] While it is impossible to say whether there were any plans to extend Roman control beyond the Elbe, it is safe to assume that, had the Romans indeed established provincial rule over Germany up to that river, the North Sea coast would have seen a considerable increase in naval activities.

Both Caius Volusenus's mission and the Tiberian expedition into the Baltic cannot be called *fleet operations* in the sense that they were undertaken by a provincial fleet. Volusenus's ship probably belonged to the Roman naval forces that had been established in the area prior to the campaign against the Veneti. Similarly, the forces involved in the Tiberian operation had been put together specifically for this mission. They show how, prior to the establishment of standing fleets, the Romans were able successfully to undertake naval missions in northern waters.

TRANSPORT OPERATIONS

From a modern point of view it is rather self-evident that, organizationally, troop transport is a considerable step up from reconnaissance missions. In contrast, ancient operations are often seen as involving little more than putting soldiers into ships. Particularly in the case of transport operations from Gaul to Britain, one is left with the impression that the Channel is seen as little more of an obstacle than transporting troops across the Rhine or the Danube.

In reality, putting any sizeable number of soldiers across open seas is inherently complicated. Quite apart from transporting the soldiers themselves, their personal kit and any equipment allotted to the units has to be shipped. And while one of the major advantages the Roman army enjoyed over its adversaries was a considerable self-sufficiency, this meant that the individual soldier's kit was substantial.[12]

To give a general idea of the complexity of such a transport operation, it is instructive to take a closer look at what it meant to transport just one cohort of infantrymen. In early imperial times one cohort comprised about 480 soldiers organized in six *centuriae* of eighty men, which were subdivided into eight-men tent sections called *contubernia*. Now, one might be tempted to cram all of these men into one ship—a tight fit perhaps, but theoretically possible with a big ship.[13] In reality, however, a number of factors made the task of transporting such a cohort much more difficult.

The first factor was the overall numerical strength of a cohort, which was beyond the 480 infantrymen themselves. Apart from command, staff, and administrative personnel—the latter probably even more numerous in auxiliary cohorts, because these were not integrated into legions and their administrative organization—noncombatants played an important role. Thus, one mule handler was assigned to each of the cohort's sixty *contubernia*, caring for the *contubernium*'s mule that carried the tent and the heavier pieces of equipment.[14] Also, one can assume that key command personnel had servants assigned to them as well. Although the overall total is difficult to judge with any certainty, around six hundred men is probably a conservative guess.[15]

The second important factor was the need to put horses and pack animals, such as the mules already mentioned, aboard as well. While an infantry cohort would be just that, an infantry formation, it would nevertheless employ a sizeable number of mules to carry not only the heavier parts of the soldiers' kit but also all the special equipment assigned to the unit, ranging from artillery pieces to any special amenities enjoyed by those in command. It is difficult to estimate the overall number of mules and horses employed by a cohort. With one mule assigned to each *contubernium*, however, this meant an absolute minimum of sixty mules for the cohort, although the total number might well have been around one hundred.[16]

Finally, the nature of the equipment further complicated the task of transporting a Roman cohort. Roman army equipment not directly used by the individual soldier was permanently assigned to a unit or subunit and was therefore normally not interchangeable between units. The tents are a good example here. Throughout their service life they were used and maintained by the same *contubernium*, which no doubt personalized it in one way or another.[17]

Taking these three factors together, a picture emerges of what must have been quite an involved exercise. If the cohort was to set out immediately, or even only soon from its disembarkation point, it needed to arrive at that point in a structurally intact way. It would thus have been highly desirable to avoid transporting men and their kit separately. Presumably the soldiers and their personal gear, including the *contubernium*'s tent, mule, and handler, were transported together, while heavy equipment assigned to the cohort probably traveled separately. This makes it very likely that under normal circumstances the cohort was split into its six *centuriae*, which were then embarked together with their kit, including at least the pack animals transporting the tents.[18] Heavy equipment needed by the cohort then had to travel separately, as had the command and administrative staff. Thus, putting a cohort across the sea required a transport capability for presumably around ten ships.

While ten ships may not sound like many, the troop numbers known from the ancient sources indicate that the Romans were capable of moving substantial numbers of troops across the sea. A brief look at the first decades of Roman rule in northwestern Europe will be sufficient to prove this. In AD 43 under Claudius, four legions (forty cohorts), as well as auxiliary forces of similar strength totaling perhaps forty thousand soldiers, were initially brought to Britain.[19] During the revolt of Boudicca, the Roman governor of Britain Suetonius Paulinus had his depleted forces bolstered with troops from Germany after his victory in AD 60, the reinforcements numbering around ten thousand soldiers, legionaries, and auxiliaries.[20] Then in AD 65 Nero had the Fourteenth Legion called back from Britain.[21] When Vitellius revolted in Germany against Galba after Nero's death, Vitellius began assembling detachments of the legions remaining in Britain totaling around eight thousand soldiers.[22] After his victory in the brief civil war following the death of Nero, Vitellius then sent the Fourteenth Legion back to Britain, although it was probably badly under strength at the time. The legion was supposed to stay in Britain for only about a year, to be ferried to the continent again in AD 70 for the campaign against Julius Civilis.[23] In AD 71 a newly established legion was sent to Britain in preparation for the campaigns of Cerialis and Agricola.[24]

The examples continue right up to the end of Roman rule, when the usurper Constantine III transferred as many as fifteen thousand men to the Continent in AD 406 or 407, showing that moving large bodies of troops, far from being an exception, was more likely a standard procedure for Roman naval forces. Here again the question arises as to whether all these transport operations were actually undertaken by the established fleets. Although in the case of Agricola's campaign in Scotland, during which naval units found widespread employment, Tacitus makes a clear distinction between soldiers and members of the fleet, it is doubtful, judging from the sheer size of the undertaking, that all the ships used by Agricola were permanently on strength with the *Classis Britannica*.[25] Instead, many would probably have been either commandeered or built specifically for the purpose of the campaign. Nevertheless, because these operations would have required careful planning and precise execution, it is highly plausible that for a Roman commander there were at least some persons available with suitable experience in planning and running such operations. In general, providing a core of experienced staff personnel able to organize large-scale operations at relatively short notice must be regarded as one of the main functions of the provincial fleets.

AMPHIBIOUS ASSAULT

Amphibious assaults no doubt rank among the more complex operations. In this context *amphibious assaults* can be defined as operations in which the Romans had to fight their way ashore or at least planned to do so. Certainly the best-documented example for such an operation is Caesar's first expedition to Britain in 55 BC. Unfortunately, this amphibious assault, being just one part of a larger operation that was not exactly graced with total success, has in the past suffered rather harsh judgement stemming from an overall assessment of the expedition as a whole. Thus, Frederick the Great, Napoleon, and J. F. C. Fuller, who called the whole undertaking "amateurish to the extreme," did not think very highly of this operation.[26] A closer look at the events, however, reveals that what happened during the actual landings displayed a surprising degree of professionalism on the part of the Roman invasion fleet.

Having arrived off the coast of Kent near Walmer, Caesar was confronted with the challenge of having the higher parts of the beach occupied by enemy forces trying to prevent the Romans from landing.[27] It is likely that such a situation was nowhere featured in the Roman military handbooks of the time. Caesar's account may provide us the first opportunity in Roman history to observe an actual amphibious assault. When hauling troops across the sea toward an enemy shore, the operational pattern was usually disembarkation, establishment of a camp, and only then setting out to confront the enemy. The Britons refused to play by the book, however, and tried to deny the Romans access to the beaches, resulting in the legionaries having to wade knee-deep in water while trying to battle their way onto firmer ground. Unit cohesion was apparently largely lost during this difficult process.[28]

According to Caesar's account, two things won the day for the Romans: a display of true Roman virtue and bravery, and the capability of the Roman war machine to coordinate land and naval forces. As to the former, according to Caesar it was mainly owing to the eagle bearer of his crack Tenth Legion that the soldiers still hesitating to join the fight jumped off the ships and eventually beat the Britons back up the beach. Needless to say, the historicity of this short episode, which so obviously serves as an example of true Roman *virtus* (valor), is debatable.[29] Much more interesting is how Caesar himself reacted to the unfolding crisis on the beach. Among his invasion fleet there were shallow-draught warships that he ordered to go closer inshore into a position flanking the enemy troops in order to provide direct fire support, both with archers or soldiers throwing javelins, and with onboard artillery. The latter proved particularly successful in clearing enemy warriors from the higher ground atop the beach.[30]

The way Caesar employed his ships in the fire support role is remarkable for a number of reasons. First, it is proof of the existence of working command and communication structures. Trivial as it may sound, Caesar must have been able to get at least a good general idea about what happened on the beach as well as among his fleet in the first place. Regardless of whether his flagship was positioned near the beach with unobstructed views of what happened on the beach, or was located farther behind among those warships not directly involved in off-loading troops, there must have been a constant stream of information reaching him. Moreover, it was apparently possible for him to give specific orders to a particular element of his fleet, orders that were directly related to what happened on the beach. Their execution, which was then somehow relayed back to Caesar, depended on the commanders of the respective ships having more or less the same general picture of the unfolding events as Caesar had. Though this may seem banal, the warships were about to use artillery at ranges probably well in excess of two hundred meters; information regarding the whereabouts of friendly and enemy troops was therefore vital to prevent casualties among the Roman troops. Since the invasion fleet numbered perhaps more than two hundred ships, such a working exchange of information is in itself no mean achievement.

It is also interesting to note that Caesar stresses the effectiveness of his naval artillery. A sizeable number of his warships obviously were equipped with artillery pieces, resulting in a considerable logistical effort and causing the need for diversifying the ship types in use because most of the ships involved in the bombardment had probably either been strengthened for putting artillery pieces on them or designed with the use of artillery in mind. In contrast, small and fast warships like the one Volusenus set out with were most likely unsuitable for artillery, particularly because the distances involved point at rather heavy artillery pieces.[31] It seems plausible that Roman shipwrights followed several different plans when constructing ships for the invasion fleet. That the Romans were able to adapt to different combat environments is amply shown by Caesar's decision to have shallow-draught, box-like landing barges built for his second expedition.[32] This type apparently entered the Roman inventory afterward, and was used again during Suetonius Paulinus's campaign in northwest Wales around AD 60.[33] The employment of artillery raises a host of other questions as well, though they are beyond the scope of this essay.

It is sufficient to say that the events surrounding Caesar's first expedition in 55 BC posed a considerable challenge. Compared to his second expedition or to the Claudian invasion in AD 43, the first landing was much more of an improvised operation. It was nevertheless a highly complex affair and its ultimate success depended both on Caesar's personal ability to coordinate land and ground forces and on the existence of structures allowing him to exert command over them in the first place.

CONCLUSIONS

Even a cursory look at the three different types of operations listed above produces a number of important results. It has been shown that the challenges the Romans faced were both considerable and multifaceted. Hauling a sizeable force across the ocean was in 55 BC as much of a logistical nightmare as it was in 1944 or in 1982—and it was a world apart from merely bridging a river. The embarkation and disembarkation of troops and equipment in an orderly fashion was of pivotal importance because it allowed Roman field commanders to make more or less immediate use of their troops. Here, careful planning was an absolute necessity.

Then, since the tasks of Roman naval forces in northern waters were diverse, so must have been the array of ship types employed by them. Though the archaeological record is dauntingly poor in that regard, it becomes clear from the pattern of Roman operations that they had a number of different ship types at their disposal, some of them highly specialized, like the landing crafts Caesar had had constructed for his second expedition to Britain.[34]

The sheer size of some of the amphibious operations described above highlights a third important point—communications. Coordinating a large number of ships of different types and different functions and keeping abreast of what happened on the ground must have posed a considerable problem to the Romans. While on a battlefield a commander might have tried to get a general picture of the action by simply heading for a higher vantage point, this was not possible at sea. Although one would assume that they leaned rather heavily on preset plans, it is clear from the historical record that Roman commanders were able to change plans while operations were under way, to react to unforeseen difficulties, and to exploit sudden turns of events to their advantage. This clearly shows that there must have been somewhat secure working lines of communication allowing the commander to exert at least some control over the overall operation.

Finally, taking this all together and looking specifically at the way the Romans undertook these operations—whether or not they were spectacularly successful—it becomes obvious that they must have had a very clear grasp of what they were actually doing. Although during his first expedition to Britain Caesar likely encountered a situation that most certainly was new to him and, as far as the historical record goes, new to the Romans in general, he nevertheless managed to bring his operation to a successful end. While it may be justifiable to ascribe some of that success to Caesar's fortune and military cunning—Caesar would certainly have done so—a sizeable amount of the praise must go to a command structure that allowed Caesar to put his generalship into effect.

Again, the available evidence is rather scanty here, particularly because our historical sources are much more interested in the action than in the preparations and staff work. Nevertheless, one has to assume that Roman commanders, when undertaking naval operations on a larger scale, were supported by staff officers who had experience in what they were doing. The Roman provincial fleets, apart from their involvement in day-to-day operations, can therefore be at least partly understood as instruments of preserving the expertise necessary to undertake large and complex operations. The fleets that accompanied the campaigns of Agricola and Septimius Severus certainly exceeded the peacetime strength of the *Classis Britannica* by a significant margin; many of the ships employed most probably were not formally integrated into the fleet. Much of the operational planning, though, must have been conducted by fleet personnel with suitable experience in operating naval forces.

In all, Roman naval operations outside the Mediterranean could be both as complex and as efficient as those of the army. Roman naval forces were an integral, and in northern waters indispensable, part of the Roman war machine. Thus, when dealing with the Roman military as such, the Roman navy deserves as much interest as the army already gets.

NOTES

1. Perhaps unsurprisingly, this is by no means a new phenomenon. In their 1928 standard introduction to ancient military history, Kromayer and Veith (J. Kromayer and K. G. Veith, *Heerwesen und Kriegsführung der Griechen und Römer* [Munich, Germany: Beck, 1928]) devoted more than 350 pages to the history of the Roman army and only 20 to the history of the Roman navy.
2. Nero drew soldiers from the imperial fleets (H. Heubner, *Cornelii Taciti Libri qui supersunt,* vol. II, 1, *Historiarum libri* [Stuttgart, Germany: Teubner, 1978], 1, 6. Throughout the notes abbreviations of ancient authors follow the lists in P. G. W. Glare, *Oxford Latin Dictionary* [Oxford: Oxford University Press, 1983], H. G. Liddell, R. Scott, H. S. Jones, *A Greek-English Lexicon* [Oxford: Oxford University Press, 1995] and G. W. H. Lampe, *A Patristic Greek Lexicon* [Oxford: Oxford University Press, 1969]), which were then under Galba officially established as the *legio I adiutrix* (M. Ihm, *Caius Suetonius Tranquillus: De vita Caesarum libri VIII* [Leipzig, Austria: Teubner, 1908]; see also Cl. Lindskog, K. Ziegler, H. Gärtner, *Plutarchi Vitae parallelae,* vol. III, 2 [Stuttgart, Germany: Teubner, 1973], 15). Similarly, Vespasian formed the *legio II adiutrix* in AD 70 from fleet personnel (D.C. 54.24.3).
3. Comprehensive overviews of the Roman provincial fleets in general are almost completely lacking, with only the brief sketches in Starr (C. G. Starr, *The Roman Imperial Navy 31 BC–AD 324* [Cambridge, MA: W. Heffer & Sons Ltd, 1960]), Kienast (D. Kienast, *Untersuchungen zu den Kriegsflotten der römischen Kaiserzeit* [Bonn, Germany: Habelt, 1966]), and Saddington (D. Saddington, "Classes: The Evolution of the Roman Imperial Fleets," in *A Companion to the Roman Army*, ed. P. Erkamp [Oxford: Oxford University Press, 2007] 201–217), available. The last, while only a brief introduction, is the first study on Roman imperial naval history to give the provincial fleets almost as much discussion as the imperial fleets. Similarly, only a small number of studies on the individual fleets are extant. For the Roman fleets operating on the Danube, see Bounegru and Zahariade (O. Bounegru and M. Zahariade, *Les Forces Navales du Bas Danube et de la Mer Noire aux Ier–VIeme Siècles* [Oxford: Oxbow, 1996]. For information on the *Classis Germanica*, see Konen (H. Konen, *Classis Germanica* [St. Katharinen, Germany: Scripta-Mercaturae-Verlag, 2000]); and for information on the *Classis Britannica*, see Mason (D. J. P. Mason, *Roman Britain and the Roman Navy* [Stroud, UK: Tempus, 2003]) and the brief overviews by Rankov (B. Rankov, "Roman Warships in the Mare Externum," *Mar Exterior: El Occidente Atlántico En Época Romana,* ed. M. Urteaga Artigas, [Rome: Escuela Española de Historia y Arqueología, 2005], 61–70), and Wintjes (J. Wintjes, "The Classis Britannica: Aspects of the History of Roman Naval Units in North Western Europe," *Hadrianic Society Bulletin* N.S. 2, (2007): 13–19).
4. W. Hering, *C. Iulii Caesaris commentarii rerum gestarum* (Leipzig, Austria: Teubner, 1987) 3.7–14, describes the campaign against the Veneti, which culminated in a sea battle (ibid., 3.14 sq). Caesar had a fleet built on the Loire for which crews were drawn together from as far as the southern coast of Gaul (ibid., 3.9). This fleet must have been substantial, as the Veneti were able to muster more than two hundred ships (ibid., 3.14).
5. Ibid., 4.21. Volusenus had already distinguished himself during the fighting around Octodurus in 57 BC (Ibid., 3.5).
6. "*Volusenus perspectis regionibus omnibus quantum ei facultatis dari potuit, qui navi egredi ac se barbaris committere non auderet, quinto die ad Caesarem revertitur quaeque ibi perspexisset renuntiat*" (ibid., 4.21.9).
7. Regarding the question of whether Caesar was satisfied with the way Volusenus had undertaken his mission, it is furthermore very telling that he continued to serve on special missions for Caesar (ibid., 6.41; 8.23; 8.48).

8. H. Volkmann, *Res gestae divi Avgvsti* (Berlin: De Gruyter, 1969), 26; W. S. Watt, *Vellei Paterculi historiarum ad M. Vinicium consulem libri duo* (Stuttgart, Germany: Teubner, 1998), 2.106.3; K. Mayhoff, *C. Plinii Secundi Naturalis historia, Libri XXXVII* (Leipzig, Austria: Teubner, 1892–1909), 2.167.
9. Drusus even had a canal built to facilitate easy movement of ships from the Rhine to the North Sea. See H. Heubner, *Cornelii Taciti Libri qui supersunt*, vol. I, *Ab excessu divi August* (Stuttgart, Germany: Teubner, 1994), 2.8.1.
10. D. Timpe, "Entdeckungsgeschichte," in *Reallexikon für Germanische Altertumskunde 7* (Berlin, Germany: De Gruyter, 1988), 358.
11. *Vellei Paterculi historiarum*, 2.106.2, who—as one would expect—is quite boastful about Tiberius's exploits, explicitly stating that the Roman fleet (apparently on their way back) went up the Elbe River.
12. For the most detailed surviving list of what the individual Roman soldier carried, see B. Niese, *Flavii Iosephi Opera omnia*, vol. 6, *de bello Judaico Libri VII* (Berlin: Weidmann, 1895), 3.5.5. M. Junkelmann, *Die Legionen des Augustus* (Mainz, Germany: Philipp von Zabern, 2003), 199, estimates the total weight at in excess of forty-five kilograms, depending on how many day rations were carried. For a detailed discussion of what the Roman soldier carried around see J. P. Roth, *The Logistics of the Roman Army at War (264 BC–AD 235)* (Leyden: Brill, 1990), 71–77.
13. B. Maurenbrecher, *C. Sallvsti Crispi Historiarvm reliqviae*, vol. I–II (Leipzig, Austria: Teubner, 1891–93), 3.8, mentions one cohort that was transported by one big ship.
14. Apart from the tent entrenching tools, the heavy equipment included stakes and a millstone, estimated by Junkelmann (*Die Legionen des Augustus*, 212) to have weighed around 140 kilograms, see also Roth, *The Logistics of the Roman Army at War*, 77–78.
15. Junkelmann, *Die Legionen des Augustus*, 94.
16. Unfortunately, mules and mule handlers seldom feature in ancient historiography. Hering, *C. Iulii Caesaris commentarii rerum gestarum*, 7.45.2, is one of the rare examples and therefore deserves to be mentioned here. During the siege of Gergovia, and in order to deceive the enemy into overestimating the Roman cavalry strength, Caesar ordered his mule handlers to don metal helmets and mount their mules.
17. Similarly, the stakes were apparently not interchangeable between units; surviving examples show unit markings; see Junkelmann, *Die Legionen des Augustus*, 205 sq., and Table 71b.
18. Alternatively, if larger ships were available one might consider splitting the cohort up into three pairs of *centuriae*.
19. The two main accounts (D.C., 60.19–22, and Suetonius Claudius, 17) do not give exact numbers, but the overall total is generally assumed to be around forty thousand; see Salway (P. Salway, *Roman Britain* [Oxford: Oxford University Press, 1981], 72–75). For an evaluation of the logistical challenges, see Peddie (J. Peddie, *Invasion: The Roman Conquest of Britain* [Stroud, UK: Sutton Publishing, 1987], 23–46).
20. *Cornelii Taciti Libri qui supersunt*, vol. I, 14.38.
21. Ibid., vol. II, 2.66.
22. Ibid., 2.57.
23. Ibid., 4.68.
24. Salway, *Roman Britain*, 1981, 136–139.
25. M. Winterbottom and R. M. Ogilvie, *Cornelii Taciti Opera minora* (Oxford: Oxford University Press, 1975), 25: "*Quae ab Agricola primum adsumpta in partem virium sequebatur egregia specie, cum simul terra, simul mari bellum impelleretur, ac saepe isdem castris pedes equesque et nauticus miles mixti copiis et laetitia sua quisque facta, suos casus attollerent.*"
26. J. F. C. Fuller, *Julius Caesar: Man, Soldier, Tyrant* (London: Eyre & Spottiswoode, 1965), 315; see also J. Wintjes, "From Capitano to Great Commander: The Military Reception of

Caesar from the Sixteenth to the Twentieth Centuries," in *Caesar and the Western World*, M. Wyke (ed.), London: Blackwell, 2006, 269–284; "The *Classis Brittanica*," 277.

27. Hering, *C. Iulii Caesaris commentarii rerum gestarum*, 4, 24, 3 sq.
28. Ibid. 4.26.1: "*Pugnatum est ab utrisque acriter. Nostri tamen, quod neque ordines servare neque firmiter insistere neque signa subsequi poterant atque alius alia ex navi quibuscumque signis occurrerat se adgregabat, magnopere perturbabantur.*"
29. Ibid., 4.25.3–6.
30. Ibid., 4.25.2.
31. Caesar calls his artillery pieces *tormenta* in ibid., 4.25.2, which on its own already hints at heavier pieces. The distances in question—which probably exceeded two hundred meters—were beyond what could comfortably be reached with smaller pieces issued to the cohorts of each legion. On Roman imperial artillery see E. W. Marsden, *Greek and Roman Artillery, Historical Development* (Oxford: Oxford University Press, 1969), 174–198.
32. Herring, *C. Iulii Caesaris commentarii rerum gestarum*, 5.1.1–4. Caesar evidently did not forget about the effectiveness of his shipborne artillery, either. During the battle for Alexandria he used artillery to clear some enemy positions (*B. Alex.* 19.3).
33. Heubner, *Cornelii Taciti Libri qui supersunt*, vol. I, 14.29.
34. The only Roman seagoing vessel in northwestern Europe of which substantial remains survive is the so-called Guernsey ship, which is dated to the third century AD and which fits quite well to Caesar's description of the Venetian ships. M. Rule, and J. Monaghan, *A Gallo-Roman Trading Vessel from Guernsey: The Excavation and Recovery of a Third Century Shipwreck* (Guernsey, UK: Guernsey Museums & Galleries, 1993).

The Naval Strategy of Roger II, King of Sicily

Chuck Stanton

Since before the time of Christ, control of the Mediterranean was the key to wealth and power in the Western world. This great watery arena was at the core of the Roman Empire, which made it the *mare nostrum* (our sea) of antiquity. Upon the fall of Rome, the Eastern Roman Empire under Byzantium inherited sway over the sea and struggled for centuries to maintain it against barbarian incursions and the onslaught of Islam. Sicily, in the center of the Mediterranean astride the east-west shipping channels, had long been the cornerstone to dominance of the "middle sea." The island's loss to the Aghlabids of North Africa terminated Byzantine hegemony forever and established what the great maritime historian, A. R. Lewis, termed "the Islamic Imperium."[1] The Byzantine Empire, the German Empire, and the Papacy all made attempts to recover the island, but failed. Arab pirates from North Africa took root in Calabria and Apulia, prompting the Arab chronicler Ibn Khaldūn to claim, "[T]he Muslims had gained control over the whole of the Mediterranean."[2] The Norman conquest of Sicily in the eleventh century under the relentless Hautevilles effectively ended that Arab suzerainty. The Norman knight chiefly responsible for that feat was Roger de Hauteville, who, with some initial help from his more famous brother, Robert Guiscard, managed to subdue the island after a dogged thirty-year campaign. It was Roger's son, Roger II, however, who subsequently turned the island into a bastion of unrivaled strategic importance that would help make Western naval power preeminent in the region throughout the remainder of the Middle Ages. It is the goal of this essay to explain how and why that occurred.

Curiously little has been written on the subject of Norman naval power in the Mediterranean, despite its inherent significance. The reason, of course, for the paltry coverage on the subject is that modern historians have been forced to rely in large measure on the chronicles of clerics such as William of Apulia,[3] Amatus of Montecassino,[4] and Geoffrey Malaterra,[5] all of whom possessed little knowledge of things nautical. There is a relative wealth of source material on the reign of Roger II, king of Sicily, for instance, but none that focuses directly on King Roger's use of sea power. The Latin chroniclers who dwelt on Roger's reign, such as Falco of Benevento,[6] Alexander of Telese,[7] and Romuald of Salerno,[8] concentrated almost exclusively on the king's struggles with Norman rebels—who were often allied with the pope—and his ongoing efforts to defend his kingdom against the intrusions of the German emperor. They paid little attention to the realm's maritime clashes with the Byzantine Empire and almost ignored Roger's bid to control the Maghrib coast of North Africa. Fortunately, we have recourse to Arab annalists such as Ibn al-Athir,[9] At Tigani,[10] and Ibn abi Dinar[11] for the latter campaigns, while Greek historians such as Anna Comnena,[12] John Kinnamos,[13] and Niketas Choniates[14] provide us with descriptions of those engagements involving the Greeks. The chroniclers of the Italian maritime powers such as Caffaro of Genoa,[15] Bernardo Maragone of Pisa,[16] and Andrea Dandolo of Venice[17] furnish another valuable, if slanted, layer of information on Norman maritime activities of the era. Finally, beginning at the turn of the twelfth century numerous charters and privileges, such as those contained in the royal registers of Erich Caspar[18] and Karl Kehr, started to appear, providing still more clues.[19] Thus far, only two modern historians have attempted to cobble the various pieces of the puzzle into a coherent picture of Norman naval history: Willy Cohn, who in 1910 wrote a 104-page booklet on the navies of Rogers I and II,[20] and Camillo Manfroni, who provided a few chapters on the subject in his *Storia della Marina Italiana*, published in 1899.[21] Unfortunately, both works are narrative in nature with only superficial analysis of King Roger's overall maritime strategy.

New avenues of research in the past twenty years, however, have made a fresh study of the topic more promising. Marine archeologists recently have made several crucial discoveries that have shed light on medieval ship architecture and operations. George Bass and Frederick van Doorninck, for instance, have produced extensive findings from Byzantine shipwrecks excavated at Yassi Ada[22] and Serçe Limani[23] on the southwest Turkish coast. Moreover, scholars such as John Pryor have recently investigated the effects of geography and weather patterns on the maritime technology of the day.[24] Finally, in 1987 the Hellenic Navy commissioned the reconstruction of an Athenian trireme, the *Olympias*, then conducted a series of sea trials that have revealed empirical data on maritime operations of the era.[25] The results of these exciting new approaches can now be applied directly to the Normans in order to present a more complete picture of their naval operations in the Mediterranean.

SICILY'S STRATEGIC SIGNIFICANCE

From the moment the Hautevilles seized Sicily and made it the core of their kingdom, it was the object of heated competition among the reigning powers of Christendom. Throughout the twelfth century a primary desideratum of imperial foreign policy, both Byzantine and German, was to wrest control of the Kingdom of Sicily from the Normans. A succession of Eastern and Western emperors, occasionally in collaboration with the papacy, attempted by all available means, military and diplomatic, to claim the crown for themselves. This was ostensibly because, as David Abulafia states in *Two Italies*, "the German and Byzantine emperors refused to recognize it as a kingdom at all, and regarded Roger II's coronation as the first king of Sicily in 1130 as an impudent usurpation of their own sovereign rights."[26] A more fundamental reason was the realm's dominance of the central Mediterranean, which brought the Kingdom of Sicily enormous wealth and power.

To grasp fully why Sicily was of such profound strategic significance, one must have an understanding of the naval technology of the era. Until the twelfth century the predominant warship of the medieval Mediterranean was the Byzantine *dromōn* (see figure 2.1). Variations of the *dromōn* were used by virtually all contemporary fleets, including those of Sicily, which was, until the Arab conquest, a major Byzantine naval theme. Additionally, marine archeology has determined that ship architecture improved little from the end of the Roman Empire to the early fourteenth century.[27] Roughly 115 feet long and about 14 feet of beam,[28] the *dromōn* carried an *ousia* (crew complement) of 108 men plus 30 to 40 marines and officers.[29] Because the oars had to be close to the waterline, it had a freeboard (the distance from the waterline to the deck) of a mere meter.[30] It also had a shallow keel so it could approach close to shore and be beached. All of this meant that it was susceptible to being swamped in foul weather. Contemporary chronicles are rife with tales of fleets decimated by storms, thus the *dromōn* needed easy access to safe havens and had to avoid the stormy winter months. Moreover, the primitive navigation of the time required these vessels to go under way only during daylight hours and to hug the shorelines.[31]

Whenever they could get under way they made achingly slow progress. Though they possessed two lateen sails, their low freeboard and shallow keel meant they could rarely use sails, and tacking into the wind was all but impossible. As a result, their normal cruising speed was around four knots.[32] Furthermore, we know from the journeys of Ibn Jubayr and other twelfth-century travelers that adverse weather conditions and other factors forced these vessels to average no more one and a half knots over the course of a

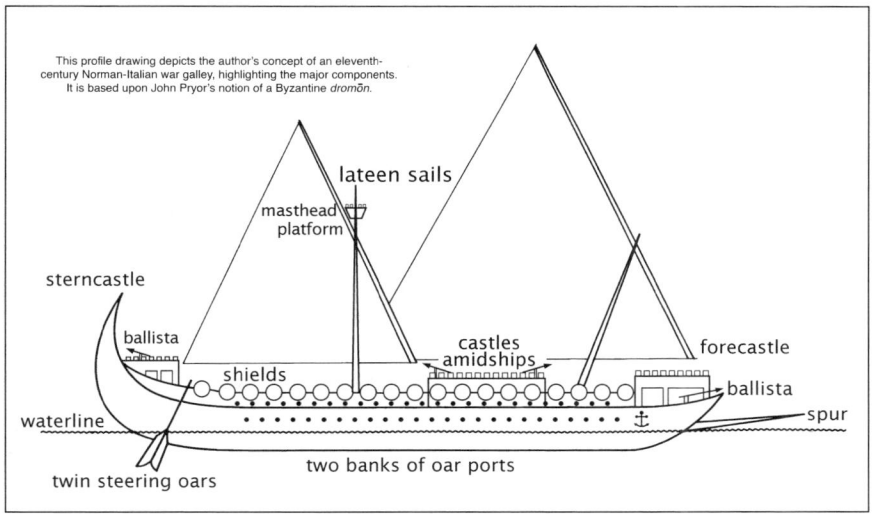

Fig. 2.1 *Norman-Italian War Galley of the Eleventh Century*

voyage. A speed of only three-quarters of a knot heading east to west, making a mere twenty miles a day, was not uncommon.[33]

The limitations on the galley crews were even more severe. Rowing was grueling work under the best of conditions. During prime sailing season in the summer months, when temperatures hovered around 100 degrees Fahrenheit, dehydration was an ever-present problem. Galley crews required enormous amounts of water. The sea trials of the *Olympias*, an exact replica of an Athenian trireme commissioned by the Hellenic Navy in 1987, revealed that each man required at least one liter of water per hour.[34] On top of that, their victuals consisted primarily of *biscotti*, at that time an awful, desiccated twice-baked concoction that required an abundance of water to digest.[35] All this meant that the average *dromōn* crew needed one thousand liters (one ton) of water per day, yet restricted cargo capacity limited onboard supplies to only a few days' worth.[36]

Consequently, galleys needed three things: (1) access to shelter from storms, (2) large quantities of fresh water, and (3) food, not to mention an occasional rest from exhausting labor. Accordingly, galleys put into shore almost daily. John Pryor said it nicely: "Control of the land meant control of the sea, because control of the land carried with it both control of the refuges to which all galley fleets had to have recourse in inclement weather and also control of the water supplies, without which no naval forces could operate for more than a few days."[37] Alfred Thayer Mahan's theories on asserting naval dominance by patrolling the sea-lanes had little applicability in the

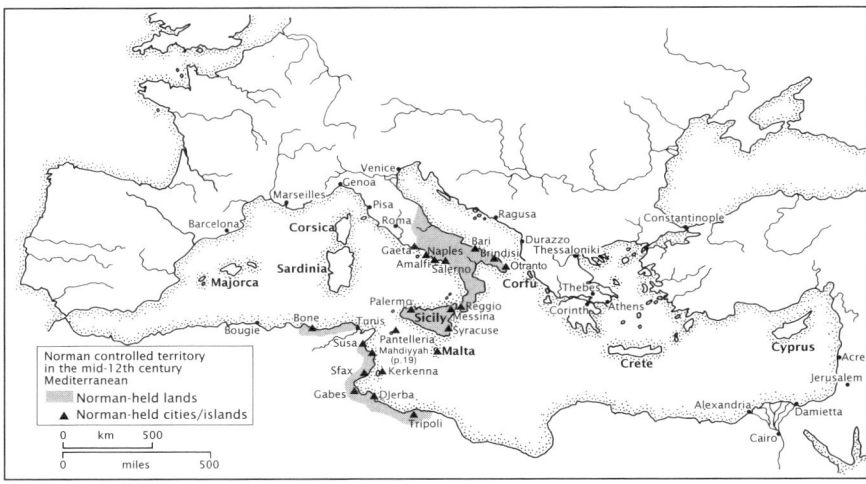

Fig. 2.2 *Norman Kingdom of Sicily ca. 1154*

twelfth century.[38] Moreover, the prevailing winds favored west-east travel while the shoals and the lack of safe havens along the south coasts of the Mediterranean meant that the northern shores were preferred.[39]

From the foregoing it can be deduced that the ultimate strategic advantage would be to control a platform with an unlimited supply of water and an abundance of food, located toward the north shores of the Mediterranean at approximately the center, astride the west-east shipping lanes. Sicily, by virtue of its fortuitous location, was the strategic linchpin of the Mediterranean (see figure 2.2). Whosoever held it held the key to east-west movement on the sea. It is thus no accident that the rise of West Italian sea power coincided with the Norman conquest of Sicily, and that the Norman Kingdom of Roger II became rich and powerful, and it is no wonder why all the other powers of the Mediterranean sought at one time or another to wrest control of that island from the Normans.

HISTORICAL BACKGROUND

Some historical narrative at this juncture will help put Roger's naval strategy in perspective. Sicily was largely the legacy of his father, Roger I, known as the Great Count of Sicily. The twelfth and last son of Tancred de Hauteville, a minor Norman noble, Roger de Hauteville had migrated to southern Italy in the middle of the eleventh century to join his brother, Robert, who bore the sobriquet Guiscard (old French for "the cunning"). Together they embarked upon the conquest of Calabria. Once that was completed with the taking of Reggio in 1060, the rapacious duo set their sights on Sicily.[40] They began with the seizure of Messina in 1061[41] and gradually worked their way west until they captured Palermo at the beginning of 1072.[42] Even then, it would be nearly a score of years before the conquest would be completed. In that time Roger was on his own, as Robert was distracted by numerous revolts of his Norman vassals in Apulia and his own ill-fated ambition to topple the throne of Byzantium. In point of fact, with the exception of the Messina and Palermo campaigns, Robert had participated little in the effort to subdue Sicily; after the fall of Palermo he never again set foot on the island. Roger had to do the rest himself with a handful of knights. In the process he became proficient in the use of sea power, gathering fleets to take Trapani (1077),[43] Taormina (1079),[44] and Siracusa (1085).[45] Noto, the last Saracen bastion in Sicily, submitted in 1091,[46] the same year Roger led a massive armada to cow Malta into obeisance.[47]

When Roger I, the feared and respected Great Count of Sicily, died in 1101,[48] his son, Roger II, was not even six years old.[49] Little is known about the regency of Roger II's mother, Adelaide, except that she was almost certainly responsible for her son's survival. She did the one thing that would enable him to mature and establish his power base in relative peace: she moved the comital household from Roger I's castle at Mileto in Calabria to Sicily, first to Messina then to Palermo.[50] This served to insulate Roger II from the fractious and dangerous Norman barony and taught him to rely on the Greek and Arabic advisers who would become the heart of his administration. More important, it gave him a bastion from which he was able to nurture his strategy to dominate the central Mediterranean.

Shortly after he began his majority as count of Sicily in 1112, George of Antioch, a financial administrator previously employed by the Zirid princes of Mahdiyyah, entered Roger's service.[51] This shrewd adviser undoubtedly apprised his new lord of the lucrative opportunities offered by North Africa. A few years later, in 1118, Roger II sent southward his first expedition, a fleet of twenty-four vessels in support of Rafi, governor of Gabes, who was attempting to break with Mahdiyyah.[52] The affair became a fiasco when the fleet of Prince Ali of Mahdiyyah surprised the Sicilian ships at Gabes and sent them scurrying home. But Roger did not desist. In 1123 he dispatched his chief minister, the Emir Christodoulos, along with George of Antioch at the head of a three-hundred-ship armada to take Mahdiyyah. This attempt also ended in a rout. The fleet was forced to abandon a garrison on the islet of ad-Dimas and to return home empty-handed.[53]

Roger most likely would have continued trying had not news of the death of Duke William of Apulia, his second cousin, intervened in 1127. Roger himself immediately proceeded north to Salerno with seven vessels in order to claim the duchy, which he believed was rightfully his. The citizens of the former Norman capital balked at first, but Roger eventually persuaded them with patient negotiation to submit. Amalfi and much of the rest of Calabria soon followed. Before the year was out, Roger was anointed duke of Apulia in Salerno by Alfano, bishop of Cappaccio.[54] His moment of triumph, however, was short lived. As soon as he had returned to Sicily, the rebellious barons of Apulia and Calabria rose in revolt, fomented in part by Pope Honorius II. The pope, however, was unable to hold his contentious alliance together and ended up being compelled to formally invest Roger as Duke of Apulia in 1128. The duke subsequently utilized an armada of forty to sixty vessels to besiege Bari, which capitulated, thereby ending the baronial revolt. Roger presided in triumph over the peace of Melfi a year later.[55]

Roger capitalized on this success by taking advantage of a schism in the papacy following the demise of Honorius II. In return for recognition as king of Sicily, he offered support to Anacletus II in his struggle with Innocent II for the papal throne. At the behest of Bernard of Clairvaux, King Lothair III of Germany declared his support for Innocent II, leaving Anacletus little choice but to accede to Roger's demand. Accordingly, in 1130 the papal pretender signed a bull declaring Roger king of Sicily. The latter was subsequently crowned on Christmas day in Palermo.[56] The new king knew that his coronation was likely to foster opposition, especially in Campania, so the following year he ordered George of Antioch to lead a fleet against Amalfi in order to preempt any resistance. George quickly occupied Capri, Trivento, Scala, and Ravello, thereby intimidating both Amalfi and Naples into submission.[57] The respite was only temporary, however. In 1132 rebellion erupted anew in Apulia and Calabria and was soon joined by Naples. Roger reacted by laying siege by land and sea to both Bari and Brindisi, eventually attaining their acquiescence.[58] Despite a land defeat at Nocera,[59] the king gained the upper hand in due course and cruelly subjugated most of Apulia.[60] He sought to end the insurgency in 1134 by hurling sixty *galee* (a *galea* was the primary Italian warship of the twelfth century) against Naples. Although initially repulsed, his forces soon compelled the port city to profess its loyalty once again.[61]

Roger must have felt he had some breathing space at this point to continue his African expansion plans because in 1135 he sent George of Antioch to capture the island of Djerba, a notorious enclave for Muslim pirates just off the coast of Tunisia.[62] News of his illness the same year, however, prompted rebellion to flare up yet again on the mainland.[63] Regaining his health, Roger once more rushed north with sixty *galee* to lay siege to Naples. This time, however, forty-six Pisan vessels—procured at some expense by Robert of Capua, a leader of the revolt—came to the aid of the rebels. The Pisans made a diversionary assault on Amalfi, mercilessly pillaging its old rival, but Roger surprised the Pisans while they were attacking nearby Fratta. He subjected them to a devastating defeat, compelling the entire force to withdraw to Pisa.[64] The king once more had the advantage.

The situation changed dramatically in 1137. Innocent II, seeking to remove the prime benefactor of his rival claimant for the papal throne, finally convinced German Emperor Lothair III to invade. The alliance included one hundred Pisan ships along with a contingent of Genoese vessels. A Sicilian fleet of thirty-three vessels was destroyed at Trani; twenty-five were captured at Brindisi. At this point Roger did the only sensible thing he could do: he retreated to fortress Sicily with the bulk of his naval and land forces. He was badly overmatched, but he knew his enemies well. The odd alliance of imperial forces, papal troops, and Norman rebels could not last. Roger managed to inveigle the Pisans into returning home by offering trade concessions. Without naval support, the invasion quickly foundered and fell apart in dissension. Lothair returned to the north, leaving Innocent II and the rebel leader Rainulf of Alife to their own devices.[65] Rainulf managed to hand Roger a setback at Rignano, but he suddenly died in 1139. In the same year Pope Innocent II was cornered at Galluccio near San Germano and forced to confirm Roger as king of Sicily while investing his son, also named Roger, with the duchy of Apulia and another son, Alfonso, with the principality of Capua.[66]

At last secure in his own domain, Roger directed his attention southward again. In 1142 he dispatched George of Antioch to raid Mahdiyyah with twenty-five ships. The admiral seized and burned many of the ships in port, thereby intimidating Prince Hassan to declare himself a vassal of King Roger.[67] The next year Roger sent George with an armada of three hundred ships to seize Tripoli. Unable to do so, the Sicilians instead sacked Djidjelli (Jijel), between Bougie and Bône.[68] The following year (1144) they conquered the small port of Bresk or Brashk, still farther west on the coast of modern-day Algeria.[69] In 1145 the Sicilians pillaged and occupied the island of Kerkenna, just opposite Sfax on the Tunisian coast.[70] Finally, in 1146 a fleet of two hundred ships commanded by George of Antioch managed to take advantage of some factional strife within the city of Tripoli to seize it for Roger's realm. By encouraging Western merchants with tariff exemptions, the king subsequently turned the city into a trading entrepôt.[71] A year later, Jusuf, governor of Gabes, gave Roger the opportunity to crown his African strategy. Jusuf rebelled against Zirid suzerainty and submitted to the Norman king. He was subsequently besieged at Gabes by Prince Hassan of Mahdiyyah and killed.⁷² Using the incident as a pretext, Roger then dispatched a fleet of 250 ships under George of Antioch, who subdued not only Mahdiyyah but also Susa and Sfax in rapid succession.⁷³

Sicilian successes in the central Mediterranean soon caused the Byzantine emperor grave concern. The attempts of John Comnenus and his successor, Manuel, to cobble together an anti-Sicilian league that included the German emperor and the Venetians eventually prompted Roger to take action.⁷⁴ He sent his great admiral on a preemptory raid of Greek lands. In 1147 a substantial fleet commanded by George of Antioch captured Corfu and plundered the Gulf of Corinth, sacking both Thebes and Corinth.⁷⁵ Emperor Manuel and his Venetian allies responded the next year by besieging the Norman garrison on Corfu. In order to draw pressure off his garrison, Roger once again dispatched his venerable admiral, this time with sixty *galee*, on a diversionary foray deeper into Byzantine territory. George penetrated all the way up the Dardanelles, eventually forcing his way into the port of Constantinople where he seized several ships and even had barrages of flaming arrows fired at the royal palace. In the course of the expedition, the admiral also engaged a Greek fleet off Cape Malea and managed to succor King Louis VII of France and his queen Eleanor of Aquitaine, who were returning from the Second Crusade. The Norman-held citadel on Corfu eventually fell, but Roger had made his point.⁷⁶ No Byzantine-led assault on Sicily ever took place.

According to Ibn al-Athir, George of Antioch, Roger's "emir of emirs" for most of his reign, succumbed to hemorrhoids and gallstones shortly afterward.⁷⁷ Roger attempted to replace him with a Muslim convert named Philip of Mahdiyyah, but the latter was burned at the stake as an apostate because of the leniency he demonstrated toward his former coreligionists following the capture of Bône in 1153.⁷⁸ Old and tired, bereft of the solace of his wife and the sagacious counsel of his great admiral, both of whom preceded him in death, King Roger himself passed away the next year.⁷⁹ He had, however, bequeathed to his son William a virtual maritime empire with a stranglehold on the central Mediterranean.

STRATEGY

The naval strategy by which Roger II established and maintained this maritime empire was composed of three closely related but distinct approaches: economic, diplomatic, and military. All three were based on his dominance of Sicily, perhaps the most strategic island in the Mediterranean. Since the island's wealth was the core of Roger's power and the basic reason why the other powers of the era coveted it, the discussion of strategy should begin with the economic approach.

ECONOMIC

A great deal of Roger's success in turning the island into the strategic bulwark of his kingdom and the primary source of his wealth has to do with simple geography. Sicily is situated almost in the center of the Mediterranean astride the east-west shipping lanes. Moreover, its proximity to the Italian peninsula and the Maghrib coast of North Africa enabled it to control the sea passages between the western Mediterranean (Tyrrhenian Sea) and the eastern Mediterranean (Ionian Sea). The Sicilian Channel between Mazara del Vallo in southwestern Sicily and Cape Bon of Tunisia, for instance, is barely one hundred miles wide. The Strait of Messina is less than five miles wide.[80] Furthermore, the maritime technology of the era meant that ships had to hug the coastlines for navigation purposes and for easy access to shelter in inclement weather.[81] All of this favored the northern shores of the Mediterranean because of the many treacherous rocks and shoals off the coast of North Africa.[82] The need for water also meant that vessels had to put into shore almost daily for replenishment. All of these factors, along with counterclockwise currents and prevailing northwest winds, made Sicily ideally located to control maritime traffic through the central Mediterranean.

The strategic significance of Sicily's geography could not have been lost on Roger II. After all, he had commissioned Ibn al-Idrisi, one of the greatest geographers of the Middle Ages, to produce the *Book of Roger*, a highly detailed textual description of the Mediterranean world based on eyewitness reports of observers dispatched from Sicily.[83] Moreover, Roger essentially owned the island. With the exception of a handful of trusted supporters and a few dozen ecclesiastical institutions under royal patronage, Sicily was the demesne of the Hauteville family. This meant that, with scant exception, Roger controlled every pasture, forest, town, and strip of coastline, along with the adjacent waters.[84] The royal registers of Karl Kehr and Erich Caspar are rife with diplomas showing that the king maintained a monopoly on virtually everything associated with this royal demesne, from pitch and lumber production to fishing and salt procurement.[85] It is clear from charter evidence that, unless specifically exempted, anyone using royal property for nearly anything had to pay a tax. Consequently, any merchant vessel that pulled into a Sicilian port had to pay an anchorage fee and a tariff on all its merchandise. There was even a duty on all trade goods transported on royal roads.[86] Once Roger had consolidated his power on the Italian mainland and conquered the adjacent coastlines of North Africa, hardly a vessel could move through the central Mediterranean without paying a fee to the king of Sicily. And George of Antioch, his shrewd and ever-reliable first minister, who had initially gained notoriety as an efficient collector of taxes for the Zirid princes, would have doubtless used the formidable Sicilian fleet to ensure that any merchant vessel paid dearly. Moreover, Roger's control of the North African coast assured him a portion of the profits from the caravan trade from sub-Saharan Africa, particularly in gold.[87] In other words, Roger II and George of Antioch most likely turned Sicily into a massive tollgate. No wonder the realm was legendary for its opulence—and, of course, that opulence was skillfully translated into power.

DIPLOMATIC
Sicily was not only Roger's principal source of wealth, but it was also his sanctuary from all the enemies of his rule; he was not above using that wealth to keep it as such. He knew that no power, no matter how strong militarily, could unseat him from his throne unless it possessed some sort of sea power. Since the two empires that coveted his kingdom both lacked sufficient maritime resources at the time, this meant they needed to effect some sort of alliance with the Italian maritime powers of the age, i.e., Genoa, Pisa, or Venice. Consequently, Roger's diplomacy consisted largely of detaching one or the other of these seafaring city-states from any imperially inspired anti-Norman league.

A prime example is revealed in the events of 1134. Robert of Capua, one of the leaders of the baronial revolt against King Roger, attempted to purchase the aid of both Genoa and Pisa with three thousand pounds of silver, ultimately winning the promise of one hundred vessels. Falco of Benevento notes that the doge of Venice may also have pledged support. But nothing happened. No fleet was sent that year from any of the maritime republics.[88] Two outraged letters from Bernard of Clairvaux, one to the citizens of Pisa and the other to those of Genoa, explain why. In these missives the anti-Norman cleric beseeches the Genoese and the Pisans not to be corrupted by Roger's enticements.[89] Clearly, the king of Sicily had suborned the profit-minded merchants of the two mercantile city-states with promises of largesse and commercial concessions. This would hardly be surprising, at least in the case of Genoa. It had enjoyed a small colony in Sicily since 1116, when Roger granted the Genoese consul Ogerius a plot of land near Messina.[90] Moreover, pacts of mutual maritime cooperation concluded in 1127–28 between the city of Savona, a Genoese protectorate, and the court of Palermo demonstrate ongoing amicable relations with the mariners of Liguria.[91] As for the seamen of Tuscany, Roger apparently succeeded in buying them off again during

Emperor Lothair's invasion of the kingdom in 1137. Roger capitalized on a falling-out between the Pisans and Lothair over the spoils of Salerno following its capitulation to lure the Pisans away with silver or trade concessions, or both. Whatever inducements were offered, they must have been sufficient, because the Pisans abandoned the imperial-papal coalition, which collapsed soon afterward.[92]

Roger also proved greed was a more powerful motivator than enmity with respect to the Venetians. Enraged over Sicilian pirate activity in the vicinity of Djerba, Venice and Constantinople formed an anti-Norman alliance and sent envoys to the German imperial court at Merseburg in 1136 to enlist Lothair.[93] Roger, however, had gotten wind of the negotiations and evidently managed to detach the Venetians from the proposed anti-Norman league by offering a trade deal that the merchants of the *Serenissima* could not refuse. Camillo Manfroni found references in an 1175 diploma of King William II to an 1136 concession of commercial privileges granted to the Venetians, supposedly in return for their neutrality in any war between the German crown and the throne of Palermo.[94] In any event, there is no evidence that Venice ever participated in the hostilities that followed. In point of fact, none of the Italian maritime powers were ever involved in an assault on Sicily during Roger's reign.

MILITARY

Roger II used military means to achieve his goals only when he felt there was no other practical alternative. Even then, he made the island of Sicily the flagship of his strategy. He had fortified his domains with a well-developed coastal watch, complete with towers manned through feudal obligation.[95] More important, he had made certain that command of his formidable fleet, based in Palermo and Messina, remained a primary duty of his first minister[96]—his *amiratus amiratorum* (admiral of admirals)[97] and his *maximus ammiratus* (highest admiral)[98] who for most of Roger's reign was none other than the gifted George of Antioch.[99] Defended by his well-led armada, Roger was virtually unassailable by either imperial forces or papal minions while he remained on Sicily. Thus, his basic tactic whenever threatened on the mainland by military might or recovering from a battlefield setback was to withdraw onto his nearly impregnable island, the flagship of his fleet, and wait until the inevitable dissension within the ranks of his enemies caused the collapse of their coalition. This was precisely how he dealt with the invasion of Emperor Lothair III in 1137.[100] He well understood the expeditionary nature of imperial incursions into southern Italy. Since the days of Charlemagne, no emperor had ever ventured into southern Italy and stayed. Roger knew that, sooner or later, imperial armies would always head north, leaving his papal enemies and rebellious nobles to deal with him alone. He also knew that any accommodation between his fractious nobles and the pope would also eventually break down, as it did under Pope Honorius II at Benevento in 1128.[101] All he had to do was wait.

Offensively, Roger used his redoubtable armada chiefly to strengthen his hold on the central Mediterranean. These aggressive efforts were mostly directed at North Africa. Almost from the inception of his majority until his death, he sought by a persistent campaign of conquest to secure the southern shore of the Sicilian Channel. Once he had done so, predominately through the victories of his brilliant admiral, he was able to take a sizable cut of east-west commerce while profiting from a hugely lucrative trade in Sicilian grain for ub-Saharan gold by virtue of his domination of the Maghrib coast.[102]

The fleet of war itself was no small part of Roger's success.[103] Many of the ships were, doubtless, procured through feudal obligation from subject port cities,[104] but a goodly number must also have come from the established royal arsenals in Palermo and Messina.[105] The ships were crewed primarily through the *datium marinariorum* (levy of sailors), which required lordships, abbeys, and townships to supply a specified number of mariners for the fleet.[106] According to the recent analysis of John Pryor, the fleet of war was most likely composed mainly of a distinctly Italian version of the *galea*, a swifter descendant of the *dromōn*. By closely examining the illuminations of Peter of Eboli's manuscript located at the Burgerbibliothek in Berne, Switzerland, he was able to determine that Norman vessels of the era probably employed the relatively efficient *alla sensile* oarage system. Instead of two or more decks of rowers, one above the other, stroking from a sitting position, Pryor believes that rowers on Sicilian galleys sat two per bench on the same deck, each manipulating his own oar in a stand-and-sit stroke fashion. This enabled greater power, resulting in greater speed, while allowing for greater load-carrying capacity below deck.[107] In other words, Roger's galleys were lighter and faster—ideal for interdiction at sea. Complaints of harassment by Norman warships contained in various Latin, Greek, and Arab annals seem to substantiate this.[108] In point of fact, although a certain amount of state-sponsored piracy probably occurred, Roger's fleets almost certainly fostered commercial activity through the central Mediterranean by quelling Arab piracy. It was in his best interest to do so.

Roger also used his fleets in an aggressive manner to keep his enemies at bay. Examples of this tactic were the raids against Greece conducted by George of Antioch in 1147 and 1149. Again, the fast *galea* was exemplary for such forays. It enabled George to strike whenever he wished and depart again before his adversaries could act. This was particularly true in 1149 during his audacious harassment of Constantinople and its environs.[109] In truth, Roger's fleets did not always prevail in engagements with enemy fleets, particularly with those of Pisa and Venice, but their performance was sufficient to discourage a full-scale assault on Sicily—that is, at least, while Roger sat on the throne.

IMPACT

By virtue of its fortuitous setting, Sicily was the strategic linchpin of the Mediterranean. Whosoever held it held the key to movement on the sea. Roger most certainly understood this, for he bolstered this advantage by strengthening his grip on the lands to the north and the south of the island and by developing a strong, swift fleet to protect it and control the adjacent straits. This enabled him to control both military and commercial traffic transiting the central Mediterranean, a development that, according to letters from the Cairo Geniza, may have produced lasting changes in trading patterns on the middle sea, particularly with respect to Muslim commerce.[110] This does not imply that he attempted to restrict the flow of commercial traffic in any way: it merely means that he did his best to route that traffic through Palermo and Messina so that he could take his cut, so to speak. In fact, Hubert Houben makes the argument that Roger's conquest of the Maghrib coast, including the islands of Djerba and Kerkenna, promoted trade by stemming Muslim piracy in the Sicilian Channel.[111] Roger thus became the envy of his world by parlaying Sicily's strategic advantage into enormous wealth and power. It was also was the key to the kingdom's survival against a host of adversaries until very nearly the end of the century. As long as his successors adhered to the principle of dominating the central Mediterranean while keeping their enemies off-balance and divided, the Norman Kingdom flourished. Once they strayed from that fundamental blueprint they, and the naval empire that Roger had founded, were doomed.

NOTES

1. A. R. Lewis, *Naval Power and Trade in the Mediterranean, AD 500 to 1100* (Princeton, NJ: Princeton University Press, 1951), 132.
2. Ibn Khaldōn, *The Muqaddimah, An Introduction to History*, trans., F. Rosenthal (Princeton, NJ: Princeton University Press, 1967), 210.
3. William of Apulia, *La Geste de Robert Guiscard*, trans M. Mathieu (Palermo, Italy: Istituto siciliano di studi bizantini e neoellenci, 1961).
4. Amatus of Montecassino, *History of the Normans*, trans. P. Dunbar (Woodbridge, UK: Boydell Press, 2004), Bk. VI, ch. 22, 159.
5. Geoffrey Malaterra, *The Deeds of Count Roger of Calabria and Sicily and of His Brother Duke Robert Guiscard*, trans. K. B. Wolf (Ann Arbor: University of Michigan Press, 2005); *De rebus gestis Rogerii Calabriae et Siciliae comitis et Roberti Guiscardi Ducis Fratris eius*, ed. E. Pontieri (Rerum Italicarum Scriptores, 2nd ed., Bologna, Italy: N. Zanichelli, 1928).
6. Falco of Benevento, *Chronicon Beneventanum*, ed. E. D'Angelo (Florence, Italy: Tavarnuzze, 1998).
7. Alexander of Telese, *Alexandri Telesini Abbatis Ystoria Rogerii Regis Sicilie, Calabria Atque Apulie*, ed. L. De Nava (Fonti per la Storia d'Italia, Rome: Istituto storico italiano per il Medio Evo, 1991).
8. Romuald of Salerno, *Romualdi Salernitani Chronicon*, ed. C. Garufi (Rerum Italicarum Scriptores, 2nd ed., vol. VII, Città di Castello, Italy: S. Lapi, 1935).
9. Ibn al-Athir, *Biblioteca Arabo-Sicula*, I, ed. M. Amari (2 vols., Turin, Italy: E. Loescher, 1881; reprint Bologna, Italy: Sala Bolognese, 1981), 353–507.
10. At Tigani, *Biblioteca Arabo-Sicula*, II, 41–81.
11. Ibn abi Dinar, *Biblioteca Arabo-Sicula*, II, 273–297.
12. Anna Comnena, *The Alexiad of Anna Comnena*, trans. E. Sewter (London: Penguin Books, 1969).
13. John Kinnamos, *Deeds of John and Manuel Comnenus*, trans. C. Brand (New York: Columbia University Press, 1976).
14. Niketas Choniates, *O City of Byzantium: Annals of Niketas Choniates*, trans. H. Magoulias (Detroit, MI: Wayne State University Press, 1984).
15. Caffaro, *Annali genovesi di Caffaro e de'suoi Continuatori dal MXCIX al MCCXCIII*, I, ed. L. Belgrano (Genoa, Italy: R. Istituto sordo-muti, 1890).
16. Bernardo Maragone, *Gli Annales Pisani di Bernardo Maragone*, ed. M. Gentile (Rerum Italicarum Scriptores, vol. VI, part II, Bologna, Italy: N. Zanichelli, 1936).
17. Andrea Dandolo, *Chronica per Extensum Descripta*, ed. E. Pastorello (Rerum Italicarum Scriptores, vol. XII, Bologna, Italy: N. Zanichelli, 1942).
18. E. Caspar, *Roger II und die Gründung der Normannisch-Sicilischen Monarchie* (Innsbruck, Austria: Wissenschaftliche Buchgesellschaft, 1904).
19. K. Kehr, *Die Urkunden der Normannisch-Sicilischen Könige* (Innsbruck, Austria: n.p., 1902).
20. Willy Cohn, *Die Geschite der Normannisch-Sicilischen Flotte Unter der Regierung Rogers I und Rogers II, 1060–1154* (Wroclaw, Poland: M. & H. Marcus, 1910).
21. C. Manfroni, *Storia della Marina Italiana dalle Invasioni Barbariche al Trattato di Ninfeo, Anni di C. 400–1261*, I (Livorno, Italy: n.p., 1899).
22. G. Bass and F. van Doorninck, *Yassi Ada: A Seventh-Century Byzantine Shipwreck* (College Station: Texas A&M University Press, 1982).
23. G. Bass and F. van Doorninck, *Serçe Limani: An Eleventh-Century Byzantine Shipwreck* (College Station: Texas A&M University Press, 2004).

24. J. Pryor, *Geography, Technology, and War: Studies in the Maritime History of the Mediterranean, 649–1571* (Cambridge: Cambridge University Press, 1988), 16–25.
25. J. Coates, J. Morrison, and N. Rankov, *The Athenian Trireme: The History and Reconstruction of an Ancient Greek Warship*, 2nd ed. (Cambridge: Cambridge University Press, 2000).
26. David Abulafia, *The Two Italies: Economic Relations Between the Norman Kingdom of Sicily and the Northern Communes* (Cambridge: Cambridge University Press, 1977), 32.
27. F. Hocker, "Late Roman, Byzantine, and Islamic Galleys and Fleets," in *The Age of the Galley, Mediterranean Oared Vessels Since Pre-Classical Times*, ed. R. Gardner and J. Morrison (London: Conway Maritime, 1995), 94–97.
28. Hocker, "Late Roman, Byzantine, and Islamic Galleys and Fleets," 94–97.
29. J. Pryor and E. Jeffreys, *The Age of the ΔPOMΩN: The Byzantine Navy, ca 500–1204* (Leiden, Netherlands: Brill, 2006), 255–256.
30. J. Pryor, "Byzantium and the Sea: Byzantine Fleets and the History of the Empire in the Age of the Macedonian Emperors, ca. 900–1025 CE," in *War at Sea in the Middle Ages and the Renaissance*, ed. J. Hattendorf and R. Unger (Woodbridge, UK: Boydell Press, 2003), 83–104, esp. 86–87.
31. Pryor, "From *Drom¯on* to Galea: Mediterranean Bireme Galleys AD 500–1300," 101–116.
32. Pryor and Jeffreys, *The Age of the ΔPOMΩN*, 255, 343.
33. Ibn Jubayr, *The Travels of Ibn Jubayr*, trans. Roland Broadhurst (London: Goodword Books, 1952), 26–29, 326–336.
34. J. Coates and J. Morrison, "The Sea Trials of the Reconstructed Athenian Trireme *Olympias*," *The Mariner's Mirror* 79 (1993): 131–141.
35. J. Guilmartin, *Gunpowder and Galleys: Changing Technology and Mediterranean Warfare at Sea in the Sixteenth Century* (Cambridge: Cambridge University Press, 1975), 54, note 26.
36. Coates and Morrison, "The Sea Trials of the Reconstructed Athenian Trireme *Olympias*," 131–141; Coates, Morrison, and Rankov, *Athenian Trireme*, 238.
37. Pryor, "Byzantium and the Sea," 99.
38. Guilmartin, *Gunpowder and Galleys*, 31–55.
39. Pryor, *Geography, Technology, and War*, 16–25.
40. Amatus, *History of the Normans*, Bk. IV, ch. 3, 112; Malaterra, *The Deeds of Count Roger*, Bk. 1, ch. 34–35, 74; *De rebus gestis Rogerii*, Bk. 1, ch. 34–35, 23.
41. Amatus, *History of the Normans*, Bk. V, ch. 10–12, 137–139; Malaterra, *The Deeds of Count Roger*, Bk. 2, ch.10, 91; *De rebus gestis Rogerii*, Bk 2, ch.10, 32.
42. Amatus, *History of the Normans*, Bk. VI, ch.13–19, 155–158; Malaterra, *The Deeds of Count Roger*, Bk. 2, ch. 45, 124–125; *De rebus gestis Rogerii*, Bk. 2 ch. 45, 52–53; William of Apulia, *La Geste de Robert Guiscard*, Bk. III, verses 187–337, 174–183.
43. Malaterra, *The Deeds of Count Roger*, Bk. 3, ch. 11, 140–142; *De rebus gestis Rogerii*, Bk. 3, ch. 11, 62–64.
44. Malaterra, *The Deeds of Count Roger*, Bk. 3, ch. 15–18, 146–149; *De rebus gestis Rogerii*, Bk. 3, ch. 15–18, 66–67.
45. Malaterra, *The Deeds of Count Roger*, Bk. 4, ch. 2, 177–179; *De rebus gestis Rogerii*, Bk. 4, ch. 2, 85–86.
46. Malaterra, *The Deeds of Count Roger*, Bk. 4, ch. 15, 190; *De rebus gestis Rogerii*, Bk. 4, ch. 15, 93.
47. Malaterra, *The Deeds of Count Roger*, Bk. 4, ch. 16, 192–194; *De rebus gestis Rogerii*, Bk. 4, ch. 16, 95.
48. Ibn al-Idrisi, *Biblioteca Arabo-Sicula*, I, 57; Caspar, *Roger II*, Regesten (Register), document no. G, 444.

49. Romuald of Salerno, *Romualdi Salernitani Chronicon*, 236.
50. Caspar, *Roger II*, Reg., no. G. and 1–25, 444–451; F. Chalandon, *Histoire de la Domination Normande en Italie et en Sicile* (2 vols., Paris: Librairie A. Picard, 1907), I, 357–359; H. Houben, *Roger II of Sicily: A Ruler Between East and West*, trans. G. Loud and D. Milburn (Cambridge: Cambridge University Press, 2002), 26–27.
51. Caspar, *Roger II*, Reg., no. 21, 449; At Tigani, *Biblioteca Arabo-Sicula*, II, 65–66; Ibn Haldun, *Biblioteca Arabo-Sicula*, II, 206.
52. An Nuwayri, *Biblioteca Arabo-Sicula*, II, 154; At Tigani, *Biblioteca Arabo-Sicula*, II, 66–67; Ibn abi Dinar, *Biblioteca Arabo-Sicula*, II, 289–290; Ibn al-Athir, *Biblioteca Arabo-Sicula*, I, 454–455; Ibn al-Athir, *The Chronicle of Ibn al-Athir for the Crusading Period from al-Kamil fi'l-Ta'rikh. Part I: The Years 491–541/1097–1146: The Coming of the Franks and the Muslim Response*, trans. D. Richards (Aldershot, UK: Ashgate, 2006), 185–186; Ibn Haldun, *Biblioteca Arabo-Sicula*, II, 204–205; Ibn Hamdis, *Biblioteca Arabo-Sicula*, II, 377–379.
53. Al Bayan, *Biblioteca Arabo-Sicula*, II, 34–36; At Tigani, *Biblioteca Arabo-Sicula*, II, 68–74; Ibn abi Dinar, *Biblioteca Arabo-Sicula*, II, 290; Ibn al-Athir, *Biblioteca Arabo-Sicula*, I, 455–458; Ibn al-Athir, *The Chronicle of Ibn al-Athir*, 245–246.
54. Alexander of Telese, *Ystoria Rogerii Regis Sicilie*, Bk. I, ch.4–7, 8–11; Falco of Benevento, *Chronicon Beneventanum*, 87–89; Romuald of Salerno, *Romualdi Salernitani Chronicon*, 213–214.
55. Alexander of Telese, *Ystoria Rogerii Regis Sicilie*, Bk. I, ch. 14–15, 14–15; Falco of Benevento, *Chronicon Beneventanum*, 100–102; Romuald of Salerno, *Romualdi Salernitani Chronicon*, 216–217.
56. Alexander of Telese, *Ystoria Rogerii Regis Sicilie*, Bk. II, ch. 2–4, 23–26; Caspar, *Roger II*, Reg., no. 65, 468–469; *Chronica ignoti monachi S. Mariae de Ferraria*, ed. Gaudenzi (Monumenti Storici, ser. I: Cronache; Naples, Italy: Società Napolitana di Storia Patria, 1888), 18; J. Deér, *Das Papsttum und die Süditalienischen Normannenstaaten, 1053–1212* (Göttengen, Germany: Vandenhoeck u. Ruprecht, 1969), 62; Falco of Benevento, *Chronicon Beneventanum*, 106–108; Houben, *Roger II of Sicily*, 50–56; *Regesta pontificum Romanorum ab condita ecclesia as annum post Christum natum MCXCVIII*, ed. Jaffé, S. Lowenfeld, F. Kaltenbrunner, and P. Ewald (2 vols., Leipzig, Germany: Veit, 1888), no. 8411; Romuald of Salerno, *Romualdi Salernitani Chronicon*, 220.
57. Alexander of Telese, *Ystoria Rogerii regis Sicilie*, Bk.II, ch. 8–12, 27–29; *Chronica ignoti monachi S. Mariae de Ferraria*, 18.
58. Alexander of Telese, *Ystoria Rogerii regis Sicilie*, Bk. II, ch. 18–21, 31–32; Falco of Benevento, *Chronicon Beneventanum*, 120.
59. Alexander of Telese, *Ystoria Rogerii regis Sicilie*, Bk. II, ch. 29–31, 31–32; Falco of Benevento, *Chronicon Beneventanum*, 130–132.
60. Alexander of Telese, *Ystoria Rogerii regis Sicilie*, Bk. II, ch. 36–53, 41–48; Falco of Benevento, *Chronicon Beneventanum*, 152–160.
61. Alexander of Telese, *Ystoria Rogerii regis Sicilie*, Bk. II, ch. 54–70, 48–57; *Chronica ignoti monachi S. Mariae de Ferraria*, 20; Falco of Benevento, *Chronicon Beneventanum*, 166–172.
62. Ibn abi Dinar, *Biblioteca Arabo-Sicula*, II, 291–292; Ibn al-Athir, *Biblioteca Arabo-Sicula*, I, 461; Ibn al-Athir, *The Chronicle of Ibn al-Athir*, 321–322.
63. Alexander of Telese, *Ystoria Rogerii regis Sicilie*, Bk. III, ch. 1–2, 59–60.
64. Ibid., Bk. III, ch. 3–28, 60–74; Falco of Benevento, *Chronicon Beneventanum*, 172–174; Maragone, *Gli annales Pisani*, anno 1136, 9–10; Romuald of Salerno, *Romualdi Salernitani Chronicon*, 221.
65. *Annales Cavenses*, a. 569–1315, ed. G. Pertz (*Monumenta Germaniae Historica, Scriptores*, XIX, Hanover, Germany: Impensis Bibliopolii Hahniani, 1839), anno 1137, 192; *Annalista*

Saxo, ed. G. Waitz (*Monumenta Germaniae Historica, Scriptores,* IV, Hanover, Germany: n.p., 1844), 772–775; *Chronica ignoti monachi S. Mariae de Ferraria,* 20; Falco of Benevento, *Chronicon Beneventanum,* 184–190; Maragone, *Gli annales Pisani,* anno 1137, 11; Romuald of Salerno, *Romualdi Salernitani Chronicon,* 221–224.

66. *Annales Casinenses,* annos 1000–1212, ed. G. Pertz (*Monumenta Germaniae Historica, Scriptores,* XIX, Hanover, Germany: Impensis Bibliopolii Hahniani, 1866), anno 1138, 309; *Annales Cavenses,* anno 1137, 192; *Chronica ignoti monachi S. Mariae de Ferraria,* 25; Falco of Benevento, *Chronicon Beneventanum,* 205–222; Romuald of Salerno, *Romualdi Salernitani Chronicon,* 225–226.
67. Al Bayan, *Biblioteca Arabo-Sicula,* II, 37; At Tigani, *Biblioteca Arabo-Sicula,* II, 75–76; Ibn abi Dinar, *Biblioteca Arabo-Sicula,* II, 292–293; Ibn al-Athir, *Biblioteca Arabo-Sicula,* I, 461–462; Ibn al-Athir, *The Chronicle of Ibn al-Athir,* 365.
68. *Chronica ignoti monachi S. Mariae de Ferraria,* 27; Ibn al-Idrisi, *Biblioteca Arabo-Sicula,* I, 131; Ibn abi Dinar, *Biblioteca Arabo-Sicula,* II, 293; Ibn al-Athir, *Biblioteca Arabo-Sicula,* I, 462–463; Ibn al-Athir, *The Chronicle of Ibn al-Athir,* 366–367; Ibn Haldun, *Biblioteca Arabo-Sicula,* II, 222–223.
69. Ibn al-Idrisi, *Biblioteca Arabo-Sicula,* I, 130–131; Ibn al-Athir, *Biblioteca Arabo-Sicula,* I, 463; Ibn al-Athir, *The Chronicle of Ibn al-Athir,* 375.
70. Ibn abi Dinar, *Biblioteca Arabo-Sicula,* II, 293; Ibn al-Athir, *Biblioteca Arabo-Sicula,* I, 464–465; Ibn al-Athir, *The Chronicle of Ibn al-Athir,* 378.
71. Albufeda, *Biblioteca Arabo-Sicula,* II, 100; An Nuwayri, *Biblioteca Arabo-Sicula,* II, 157–158; At Tigani, *Biblioteca Arabo-Sicula,* II, 60; *Chronica ignoti monachi S. Mariae de Ferraria,* 28; Ibn abi Dinar, *Biblioteca Arabo-Sicula,* II, 293; Ibn al-Athir, *Biblioteca Arabo-Sicula,* I, 465–466; Ibn al-Athir, *The Chronicle of Ibn al-Athir,* 380.
72. Ibn abi Dinar, *Biblioteca Arabo-Sicula,* II, 293–294; Ibn al-Athir, *Biblioteca Arabo-Sicula,* I, 466–468.
73. Albufeda, *Biblioteca Arabo-Sicula,* II, 101–102; Andrea Dandolo, *Chronica Per Extensum Descripta,* 243; At Tigani, *Biblioteca Arabo-Sicula,* II, 76–78; Ibn al-Idrisi, *Biblioteca Arabo-Sicula,* I, 131–132; Ibn abi Dinar, *Biblioteca Arabo-Sicula,* II, 294–296; Ibn al-Athir, *Biblioteca Arabo-Sicula,* I, 469–475.
74. *Annales Erphesfurtenses,* ed. O. Holder-Egger (*Monumenta Germaniae Historica, Scriptores Rerum Germanicarum,* 42, Hanover-Leipzig, Germany: Hahn, 1899), 42; Chalandon, II, 124–126; Houben, 78, 84; Otto of Freising, *Gesta Frederici,* ed. G. Waitz, (*Monumenta Germaniae Historica, Scriptores Rerum Germanicarum,* 42, Hanover-Leipzig, Germany: Hahn, 1912), I.24, 43–46; *The Deeds of Frederick Barbarossa,* trans. C. Mierow (New York: Columbia University Press, 1953), 56–57.
75. Andrea Dandolo, *Chronica Per Extensum Descripta,* 242; *Annales Cavenses,* anno 1147, 92; Niketas Choniates, *Historia,* ed. J. van Dieten (Corpus fontium historiae Byzantinae, 11, Berlin, Germany: W. de Gruyter, 1975), 72–73; Choniates, *O City of Byzantium!,* 43–45; John Kinnamos, *Epitome rerum ab Joanne et Alexio Comnenis gestarum,* ed. A. Meineke (Corpus scriptorum historiae byzantinae, 15, Bonn, Germany: E. Weber, 1836), 98–100; *Deeds of John and Manuel Comnenus,* 80–82; Romuald of Salerno, *Romualdi Salernitani Chronicon,* 227; Otto of Freising, *Gesta Frederici,* 1.33, 53; *The Deeds of Frederick Barbarossa,* 69–70.
76. Andrea Dandolo, *Chronica Per Extensum Descripta,* 242–244; Choniates, *Historia,* 82–89; Choniates, *O City of Byzantium,* 45–53; Ibn al-Athir, *Biblioteca Arabo-Sicula,* I, 476; Kinnamos, *Epitome rerum ab Joanne et Alexio Comnenis gestarum,* 100–105; *Deeds of John and Manuel Comnenus,* 78–82; Romuald of Salerno, *Romualdi Salernitani Chronicon,* 227.
77. Ibn al-Athir, *Biblioteca Arabo-Sicula,* I, 476.
78. Ibn al-Idrisi, *Biblioteca Arabo-Sicula,* I, 132; Ibn al-Athir, *Biblioteca Arabo-Sicula,* I, 476; Ibn Haldun, *Biblioteca Arabo-Sicula,* II, 229.

79. Romuald of Salerno, *Romualdi Salernitani Chronicon*, 236.
80. Pryor, *Geography, Technology, and War*, 6–7, 12–25, 92–93.
81. Pryor, "From Dromōn to Galea," 101–116.
82. Pryor, *Geography, Technology, and War*, 21–22.
83. Ibn al-Idrisi, *Biblioteca Arabo-Sicula*, I, 31–131.
84. David Abulafia, "Crown and the Economy under Roger II and His Successors," *Dumbarton Oaks Papers*, XXXVII (Washington, DC: Harvard University Press, 1983), 1–14, esp. 2–3.
85. Abulafia, "Crown and the Economy under Roger II and His Successors," 5–8; Caspar, *Roger II*, 443–541; K. Kehr, *Die Urkunden der Normannisch*, 407–502.
86. Abulafia, "Crown and the Economy under Roger II and His Successors," 8–11.
87. David Abulafia, "The Norman Kingdom of Africa and the Norman Expeditions to Majorca and the Muslim Mediterranean," *Anglo-Norman Studies*, VII (Woodbridge, UK: Boydell Press, 1985), 26–49, esp. 27–28.
88. Falco of Benevento, *Chronicon Beneventanum*, 162–170; W. Heywood, *A History of Pisa, Eleventh and Twelfth Centuries* (Cambridge: Cambridge University Press, 1921), 83–84.
89. Bernard of Clairvaux, *The Letters of St. Bernard of Clairvaux*, trans. B. James (London: AMS Press, 1953), nos. 131 and 132, 200–202.
90. Abulafia, *Two Italies*, 62–64.
91. Ibid., 65–68.
92. *Annales Cavenses*, anno 1137, 192; *Annalista Saxo*, 774–775; Heywood, *A History of Pisa*, 88. *Annales Pisani*, anno 1137, 11: *"Que per quindecim dies fortiter obsessa, cum manganis et castellis et gattis, tandem reddidit se imperatori Lotario et Pisani. Postea idem rex contristas est cum Pisanis; qui Pisani miserunt unam galeam com sapientibus et hoc fecerunt cum consilio sapientum regis Sicilie qui erant in Turri Maiore, et sic fecerunt pacem cum eo, postea Pisas reversi sunt XIII kal. octubris"*; Romuald of Salerno, *Romualdi Salernitani Chronicon*, 223: *"Unde Pisani in iram commoti ab imperatore, qui eis super hoc auxilium non prestiterat, recesserunt et postmodum sunt cum rege Roggerio concordati."*
93. *Annales Erphesfurtenses*, 42; *Annalista Saxo*, 769–770.
94. Manfroni, *Storia della Marina italiana*, 189–190.
95. *Catalogus Baronum*, ed. E. Jamison (Fonti per la storia d'Italia, 101, Rome: Istituto storico italiano per il Medio Evo, 1972), 33–34, 36–38; *Chronica ignoti monachi S. Mariae de Ferraria*, 26–27.
96. L. Mott, *Sea Power in the Medieval Mediterranean: The Catalan-Aragonese Fleet in the War of the Sicilian Vespers* (Gainesville: University Press of Florida, 2003), 54.
97. C. Brühl, *Rogerii II. Regis Diplomata Latina* (Codex Diplomaticus Regni Siciliae, Series I, Vol. II/1, Cologne, Germany: Böhlau, 1987), no. 24, 66–68.
98. Alexander of Telese, *Ystoria Rogerii regis Sicilie*, 27.
99. L. Ménager, *Amiratus: L'Émirat et les origines de l'amirauté, XIe–XIIIe siècles* (Paris: S.E.V.P.E.N., 1960), 44–54.
100. Romuald of Salerno, *Romualdi Salernitani Chronicon*, 222–223.
101. Alexander of Telese, *Ystoria Rogerii regis Sicilie*, Bk. I, ch.14–15, 14–15; Falco of Benevento, *Chronicon Beneventanum*, 100–102; Romuald of Salerno, *Romualdi Salernitani Chronicon*, 216–217.
102. Abulafia, "The Norman Kingdom of Africa and the Norman Expeditions to Majorca and the Muslim Mediterranean," 35–36.
103. Manfroni, *Storia della Marina italiana*, 182.
104. Mott, *Sea Power in the Medieval Mediterranean*, 56–57; H. Zielinski, ed., *Tancredi et Willelmi III Regum Diplomata* (Codex Diplomaticus Regni Siciliae, Series I, Vol. V, Cologne, Germany: Böhlau, 1982), no. 18, 42–46.
105. Ibn al-Idrisi, *Biblioteca Arabo-Sicula*, I, 60, 68.

106. Caspar, *Roger II*, Reg., no. 69, 472; R. Gregorio, *Considerazioni sopra la Storia di Sicilia* (Palermo, Sicily: n.p., 1805), II, 81–83; R. Pirro, *Sicilia sacra distinquisitionibus et nobitiis illustrata*, ed. A. Mongitore (2 vols., Palermo, Sicily: Apud haeredes Petri Coppulae, 1733), II, 999.
107. Pryor, *The Age of the ΔPOMΩN*, 423–444; Peter of Eboli, *Liber ad honorem August sive de rebus Siculis*, MS 120, folio 119r, (Burgerbibliothek, Berne); *De rebus Siculis carmen*, ed. E. Rota (Rerum Italicarum Scriptores, vol. 31, Città di Castello, Italy: S. Lapi, 1904), 100.
108. *Annales Erphesfurtenses*, 42; Ibn al-Athir, *Biblioteca Arabo-Sicula*, I, 461–462; Ibn al-Athir, *The Chronicle of Ibn al-Athir*, 365; Niketas Choniates, *Historia*, 100; Choniates, *O City of Byzantium*, 45.
109. Andrea Dandolo, *Chronica Per Extensum Descripta*, 242–244; Choniates, *Historia*, 82–89; Choniates, *O City of Byzantium*, 45–53; Ibn al-Athir, *Biblioteca Arabo-Sicula*, I, 476; Kinnamos, *Epitome rerum ab Joanne et Alexio Comnenis gestarum*, 100–105; Kinnamos, *Deeds of John and Manuel Comnenus*, 78–82; Romuald of Salerno, *Romualdi Salernitani Chronicon*, 227.
110. S. Goitein, *Letters of Medieval Jewish Traders* (Princeton, NJ: Princeton University Press, 1973), nos. 74 and 75, 323–330.
111. Houben, *Roger II of Sicily*, 83.

PART II. CANADA

American Influence on Canadian Wartime Shipbuilding

Chris Madsen

During the Second World War, North America led the world in production of emergency-type warships, merchant vessels, and landing craft for the Allied war effort. The tremendous wartime expansion of shipbuilding, second only to aircraft manufacturing in volume and numbers employed, resulted from the crucial combination of complex government financing, industrial capacity harnessed to war purposes, and mobilization of ready reserves of human power unaffected directly by the vagaries of war. The decision to pursue sea power was deliberate, growing from recognition of the strategic realization that safe transportation of matériel and troops across the oceans to active theaters of war in Europe, the Pacific, and South Asia required sufficient shipping and protection. The ability of Franklin Roosevelt's Arsenal of Democracy to build finished munitions and deliver them in a timely fashion underpinned evolving plans for taking the offensive to the Axis on land and at sea. Without the necessary ships, Allied strategy and the planning that derived from it were potentially delayed, and at worst upset.[1] If the scale of wartime shipbuilding in the United States easily surpassed most other countries, Canada ran a near third behind the United Kingdom, a maritime nation with a long shipbuilding tradition and a vested role in fighting a war on its doorstep. Geographical proximity, accelerated integration into a continent-wide economy, and shared outlook between the two countries ensured that American influence on Canadian efforts in wartime shipbuilding became hugely important. In fact, Canada's achievements in this field are hardly imaginable or explainable unless the United States is taken into account.

Canada boldly transitioned from lingering British attachments in favor of reinforcing the relationship with its American neighbor and closest ally, resulting in a country with a small population and uneven industrial makeup meeting a disproportionate share of the material burden in the worldwide conflict. William Lyon Mackenzie-King, Canada's wartime prime minister, was ever keen to limit the country's direct military involvement and to focus instead on in-country production that might benefit regional economic development and in turn the domestic political fortunes of the Liberal Party.[2] The Hyde Park Agreement, signed with President Roosevelt in 1941, gave Canadian manufacturers unfettered access to American sources of raw materials and supply. Steel, in particular, was an essential component of most major armaments such as tanks and ships; quantities of it were imported owing to limited blast furnace capacity in Canada. Government procurement officials, naval authorities, and leaders in private business identified shipbuilding as a key industry, one in which Canada could make a contribution on its own terms.[3] On the basis of initial contracts from the British Admiralty, shipyards expanded or opened facilities in certain parts of the country for the building of first warships, and then merchant vessels. Dedicated agencies came to exercise coordination and priority functions in overseeing Canada's shipbuilding effort, which was laid out as much as possible along mass production lines. Innovations such as prefabrication and welding were introduced and made standard to improve production. Cooperation from organized labor allowed the setting of fair wage rates and induction of new workers, especially large numbers of women, into the skilled metal trades associated with shipbuilding. In all three areas, American example and best practice were clearly evident.

MANAGEMENT STYLE

Canada entered the war sixteen months before the United States did with the barest foundation of industry and marine manufacturing dedicated to shipbuilding. The last major concerted attempt at steel shipbuilding had occurred during the First World War on behalf of the British-controlled Imperial Munitions Board. At the wartime industry's peak in 1918, tens of thousands of Canadian workers were employed in building freighters, primarily in the urban centers of Vancouver, Toronto, and Montreal.[4] In the intervening years, chasing too few contracts in a tight market forced a marginal existence on most remaining private companies, to the point where getting business usually entailed undercutting each other in bids and limited profits. Under the 1910 Dry Dock Subsidies Act, the federal Canadian government provided small, annual subsidies in return for construction and maintenance of commercial graving docks at strategic points across the country.⁵ A conglomeration of small shipyards in Ontario, operated locally and owned out of Montreal by John Wolvin, corporately maximized this type of government assistance. Other companies, such as Canadian Vickers and Yarrows, were loosely connected to British companies that had established a Canadian presence in anticipation of naval contracts that never materialized. The opening of a King George VI graving dock at Esquimalt in 1926, which was capable of taking Royal Navy capital ships and the largest passenger liners at the time, gave the latter a major commercial advantage. Canada's small navy relied primarily on hand-off British destroyers, however; steamship lines such as Canadian Pacific preferred to purchase overseas on the basis of price and quality. Burrard Dry Dock in North Vancouver may have proved convincingly, on rare occasions, that a capable Canadian company deserved a chance, but existing slipways were generally underutilized. The effects of the Great Depression further dampened orders for ships, commercial or otherwise, until limited rearmament began in 1937 with contracts for construction of steam-driven Fundy-class minesweepers.⁶ For the most part, the staple business of ship repair carried the prewar industry through to better times. The typical Canadian private shipyard was characteristically lean, frequently family owned or family managed, and geared toward economy to watch costs and maintain competitiveness.

At the outset of the war, management within the Canadian shipbuilding industry reflected a curious amalgam of foreign apprenticeship, with a tradition of pride in craft and novice opportunism attracted by the lure of fast profits. Responsible procurement officials believed that "the best results in the matter of producing completed ships, either naval or mercantile, can be obtained by concentrating on existing facilities rather than building new shipyards where organizations would lack the type of experience necessary to get good results."⁷ A significant proportion of established owners and operators came from British, more particularly Scottish, backgrounds. They had learned the trade and first gained experience in major and minor shipbuilding firms at such places as the Clyde, then settled directly in Canada or gravitated there through the United States as immigrants. Burrard's president, Clarence Wallace, casually referred to shipbuilding practice back in the United Kingdom and Scotland under the axiom of the Old Country and maintained regular contact with friends and business acquaintances there. Informal networks meant that supervisors, foremen, and often higher-skilled workers were likewise enticed from English and Scottish sources for employment in Canada's shipyards: the habit and ethic of hard work matched a predilection toward counting almost every penny. Since contracts were usually small, ships were customarily built in a semicraft fashion. Though looking to Great Britain for inspiration, these Canadian shipbuilders also remained intimately attuned to local and regional affairs, particularly in relation to suppliers and competitors across the border in the United States.[8] The war generally increased the size of contracts and, consequently, the need to look farther afield for assured sources of matériel and technical advice.

Various emergency-type shipyards also opened on a temporary wartime basis. In Toronto, James Franceschini, a wealthy self-made Italian immigrant with business interests in road paving and construction, established the Dufferin Shipbuilding Company; his facilities were in a space formerly occupied by a defunct shipbuilding enterprise. He secured early contracts for building minesweepers.[9] After Franceschini's internment as an enemy alien, the shipyard, now known as the Toronto Shipbuilding Company, reverted to government control, ran for a period of time under a mixed Canadian and American management team, and finally came under the agency of another prominent Toronto-area construction contractor, Clarence Redfern, on a fixed-fee basis. In June 1943 persistent production delays and labor troubles caused the federal government to amalgamate the activities of Morton Engineering and Dry Dock, George T. Davie and Sons, and the shipbuilding division of Anglo-Canadian Pulp and Paper into a crown corporation called Quebec Shipyards Limited. Such government intervention in wartime shipbuilding was rare and primarily signified a last resort, since well-run private enterprises were assured more than adequate returns. North Van Ship Repairs, a towing and salvage company relatively new to shipbuilding, accumulated ample wartime profits above the set margin of 5 percent by taking full advantage of favorable depreciation of added plant and equipment for tax purposes.[10] Managers Donald Service and Arthur Burdick were also astute enough to sell out to Clarence Wallace's Burrard Dry Dock by war's end at a hefty premium. West Coast Shipbuilders Limited, another wartime company affiliated with nearby steel fabricator Western Bridge, focused on volume production of merchant ships using management-focused industrial relations.[11] If wartime presented unrivalled business opportunities for all private operators in Canadian shipbuilding, the federal Canadian government assumed an ever-larger part in the coordination and direction of production efforts associated with broader Allied strategy in close consultation with similar agencies in the United States.

Once the initial period of extemporaneousness dissipated, the system of procurement underpinning wartime shipbuilding followed sounder organizational lines. A dedicated Department of Munitions and Supply was established in 1940 to take over the functions of several previous boards in placement and oversight of war-related government contracts, with federal cabinet heavyweight Clarence Howe as the responsible minister.[12] Since many early warship and naval armament contracts were actually British, the Canadians interacted extensively with an Admiralty technical mission based out of Ottawa that provided advice and inspection services in Canada and, to a limited extent, in the United States. Canada's entry into shipbuilding in a bigger way arose from two influential events in 1941: a personal visit by Howe to Great Britain during which his ship was sunk on the way by a German U-boat, and the signing of the Hyde Park Agreement. In London, the British encouraged the Canadians to build more warships and consider merchant ship construction in order to take some pressure off hard-pressed British shipyards, while the new financial arrangement with the Americans allowed ships destined for British usage to be built in Canada with U.S. engines and components against lend-lease funds rather than drawing upon slender reserves of U.S. dollars. For policy reasons, Canada chose not to accept lend-lease from the United States and tightly controlled foreign currency exchange expenditures south of the border.[13] A director of shipbuilding within the Department of Munitions and Supply was responsible for naval construction and made central purchases from American sources through a single-purpose crown company, Trafalgar Shipbuilding, in addition to normal requisitions through another crown agency, War Supplies Limited in Washington.[14] This arrangement effectively meant that individual shipyards were accorded necessary priority on the American side for timely delivery of components and materials.

For merchant ships, the crown corporation, Wartime Merchant Shipping Limited, came into existence and was headquartered in Montreal under the chairmanship of Harvey MacMillan. MacMillan was a well-known forester and businessman from British Columbia who had served as timber controller earlier in the war. He subsequently chaired the War Requirements Board, which, among other contentious issues, studied the troubled ship repair situation in the Maritime Provinces and its effect on Canada's prosecution of the sea war in the adjoining Atlantic. Consequently, MacMillan was already well versed in Canadian shipbuilding potential when he traveled to Washington the first week of June 1941 for discussions with the U.S. Maritime Commission. Out of this meeting came a commitment to build sixty-three 10,000-ton and ten 4,700-ton cargo vessels in Canada during the 1942 calendar year. Two weeks later, MacMillan advised the Admiralty's supply representative in Washington, Vice Adm. James Dorling, that sufficient capacity was available in Canadian shipyards for up to twenty twin-screw corvettes.[15] This combined program, roughly equivalent to the United Kingdom's scheduled production by tonnage, was very ambitious for a small country like Canada. Howe turned down a suggestion that Canadian shipyards might also build landing craft because existing capacity was by now filled by warships and merchant ships.[16] With little tradition in major steel shipbuilding, Canada's effort was admittedly modest compared to the large, twin programs of the U.S. Maritime Commission and Navy Department. To put it into perspective, MacMillan told a professional audience that Canada's shipbuilding contribution represented the crucial means to offset expected losses from a sustained submarine campaign, which British and American production alone were unable to replace.[17] Canada's ability to meet projected production targets depended entirely on the supply of steel and other materials being forthcoming, the availability of shipbuilding berths with adequate facilities, and the recruitment of sufficient workers capable of acquiring the necessary skills. Fortunately, the Americans assisted Canadian authorities as much as possible and, after the surprise Japanese attack on Pearl Harbor and entry of the United States into the war, in large part treated the program in Canada as an extension of their own gigantic wartime shipbuilding program.

Contacts between Canadian and American officials in the maritime procurement field at working levels grew exceedingly close during the war years. Although Canada was denied formal membership on allied bodies such as the Combined Munitions Assignment Board because the British objected, Canadians were equally represented with American counterparts on the Permanent Joint Board for Defence and the Combined Production and Resources Board, each of which served to put respective matters into a wider North American context. During regular visits, Howe and MacMillan established personal rapport with the individuals most directly involved with policy and decision making at the highest levels of war production in the United States. The retired admirals running the U.S. Maritime Commission, Emory Land and Howard Vickery, were known by first name. In turn, Canadian officials from the Department of Munitions and Supply resident in Washington and naval members of the Canadian Joint Staff frequently enjoyed direct access to relevant agencies and departments.[18] The Canadians seldom made tiresome demands as did the British, and geography accorded a certain degree of familiarity and association not shown the Europeans. The Joint War Production Committee, a forum for settling common problems facing the two countries in the munitions field, had active merchant shipbuilding and naval shipbuilding subcommittees on which Vickery and MacMillan (when he stepped down in 1944 and was replaced by Len Dewar) sat and conferred.[19] These face-to-face meetings solidified the existing relationship wherein answers were a simple phone call away.

The makeup of Wartime Merchant Shipping Limited, subsequently renamed Wartime Shipbuilding Limited and given purview over all merchant and naval shipbuilding in Canada, more and more resembled American agencies in style, with the Maritime Commission held up as a model of good government and business practice. MacMillan and Dewar went to the Americans first for advice and made sure any Canadian shipbuilding program corresponded with U.S. plans. The fact that the Canadians were still predominantly building ships for British end use, both cargo and conversion to naval auxiliaries destined for the Pacific and Indian oceans, was less significant than the virtually wholesale adoption of American management style and production practice.[20] Nonetheless, no Canadian shipbuilder ever gained the notoriety of Henry Kaiser, the quintessential American wartime industrialist of the era with a larger-than-life reputation for getting results in shipbuilding.

As an industry, the wartime experience and American example empowered those in Canada engaged in shipbuilding to seek higher visibility for achievements and greater association. In the United States, leaders in the Navy Department and Maritime Commission were keenly aware of the public relations value of tying the industrial home front to the war at sea. Production records in American shipyards and marine manufacturing firms were celebrated through elaborate ceremonies with high-ranking guest speakers and the presentation of awards, including the coveted Navy and Maritime Commission "E," which had been adapted from recognition of excellence in naval gunnery.[21] In the spirit of competition, so-honored plants and factories were allowed to fly "E"-emblazoned flags; corresponding designations were given prominence in corporate propaganda materials. For the vanity of industrialists such as Kaiser, the image was partly self-promotion, but was also the government's harnessing of private enterprise values for the war effort. Suggestions to set up a similar system of recognition and awards in Canada drew a decidedly lukewarm response from the deputy minister of naval services: "I don't like this kind of thing, on general principles, and feel that unless the Dept. of M[unitions] & S[upply] are anxious to originate and sponsor such a proposal,—and make it applicable to *all* manufacturers—the R.C.N. [Royal Canadian Navy] should keep out of it."[22] Thus, ship launchings and other suitable public events in Canada were customarily linked to broader war bond drives rather than the specific achievements of individual companies engaged in shipbuilding. Pressure from management to adopt more American-style recognition grew steadily, especially since some Canadian enterprises producing components for U.S. ships or affiliated as subsidiaries to American parent companies, and some Canadian companies received the Navy and Maritime Commission "E" in due course. The launching of the one-thousandth ship built in Canada, an Algerine minesweeper for the Royal Navy, took place to much fanfare, with Howe and his wife attending and Clarence Redfern playing host in Toronto.[23]

Most ship launchings in Canada, however, were much more subdued affairs than those in the United States, as the government behind MacMillan and his staff gave little encouragement on a sustained basis to the promotion of shipbuilding. Early on, boat builders in Ontario organized themselves collectively to build Fairmiles, wooden motor launches for antisubmarine and patrol duties, with designs from the United Kingdom and technical assistance from the United States, only to be left hanging when naval authorities decided not to pursue further contracts for this type of craft.[24] Despite such setbacks, makers of smaller boats persevered in efforts to organize an association encompassing all yards across Canada. Under the auspices of the Canadian Manufacturers Association, boat-builder owners and managers were invited to Vancouver in 1944 for this purpose.[25] For the first time, steel shipbuilders also organized via the Canadian Shipbuilding and Ship Repairing Association, comparable to the Shipbuilders Council of America, specifically to lobby government agencies to consider the industry's postwar prospects. Shipbuilders and their representatives looked toward leveraging considerable wartime investment and growth into a permanent economic sector employing upward of twenty thousand workers and attracting skilled professionals such as naval architects and marine engineers to Canada.[26] In addition to the federal Canadian government's underlying indifference to the basic idea, the chief obstacles were high production costs and inefficiencies relative to other existing shipbuilding countries. There was little support throughout parts of the country for the heavy subsidies demanded by Canadian shipbuilders.[27] Canada shared with the United States the problem of finding a sustainable basis to satisfy expectations raised for what ostensibly at heart was still a war industry.

PRODUCTION TECHNIQUE

Wartime shipbuilding in Canada, as in the United States, was essentially geared toward volume production of standard designs rather than high quality or craftsmanship. The object was to build the largest number of hulls on available berths in the shortest possible time and outfit them for acceptance by navies and merchant marines looking for immediate operational use. Emergency-type warships and merchant vessels were generally not designed to last lengthy periods and instead incorporated many new methods that eased and accelerated production.[28] Canadians closely followed the impressive numbers month after month at Kaiser's shipyards in Oregon and California. Through application of mass production techniques and extensive prefabrication of components, management and workers there decreased time from keel laying to hull launch, on several occasions to less than a few weeks. Kaiser and his son Edgar, the person primarily responsible for shipbuilding operations, defied opinion in other established shipyards and built ships faster than anyone else by drawing upon management and engineering experience in large capital projects such as dam building and highway construction.[29] True, Kaiser-built ships were known to develop structural cracks in war service and even break apart in some instances. Auditors and congressional inquiries were also critical of costs and allowed profit rates in Kaiser's shipyards. For his part, Admiral Land observed, "If you want fast ships, fast shipbuilding, fast women, or fast horses, you pay through the nose."[30]

Although the scale of Canadian shipbuilding was more akin to shipyards on the Gulf coast or eastern seaboard, MacMillan and Canadian officials consistently tried to follow and emulate Kaiser and his production efforts on the West Coast. From Howe downward, the Department of Munitions and Supply and its crown agencies were principally interested in numbers of ships delivered to set schedules. Procurement officials actively resisted alterations and additions requested by naval authorities in favor of uninterrupted production runs, and changes to facilities and productive techniques were explored to facilitate faster performance in construction. Canadians visited the large, expansive shipyards in Portland and the San Francisco Bay Area, while Americans were invited up to Canada. Vickery and Carl Flesher, the Maritime Commission's regional director based in Oakland, met with MacMillan and shipbuilders in Vancouver in July 1942 to discuss Canadian interest in continuous production and related matters.[31] The Kaiser yards were the first to implement this novel form of work organization, subsequently extended to thirteen out of fourteen U.S. shipyards along the Pacific Coast. Unfortunately, attempts to push through continuous production in western Canada with little explanation and eventually through legal means occasioned resistance. Once introduced, shipyards in British Columbia accounted for more than two-thirds of total ship production in Canada by tonnage. Unlike shipyards on the Canadian side of the Great Lakes and at Montreal and Quebec City on the St. Lawrence River, the West Coast was unaffected by winter freeze-up, and consequently yards operated year-round on a full basis. The wartime ships built in Canadian yards were of foreign rather than Canadian design.

Canada relied on plans and specifications from other Allies for the ship types produced because naval architectural and drawing capacity remained limited. The Admiralty's director of naval construction, Stanley Goodall, furnished working drawings and plans for the British warships selected, and the Canadian version of the slow EC-2 Liberty ship and improved Victory ship were based on Maritime Commission plans prepared in consultation with the British Merchant Shipping Mission. Plans and drawings, microfilmed or reduced for ease of transmission across the Atlantic, were often unreadable upon arrival and likewise required considerable reworking for conversion into North American standards of measurement. Lambert, German & Milne of Montreal, naval architects with a drawing office in existence since 1937, performed this work for the corvettes, minesweepers, and various other small craft started in Canada.[32] The firm also provided professional services; Harold Milne joined the Department of Munitions and Supply as a technical adviser to the director of shipbuilding. Pending the sort of central drawing office advocated by Milne, selected naval shipbuilders were grouped together with a lead-yard designated to handle plans and drawings with a requisite staff.[33] The practice was increasingly common on naval work in the United States but still quite new to Canada. Gibbs & Cox, a New York–based naval architectural firm boasting prewar experience with destroyers and cruisers, served as design agent for the Navy Department on many wartime ship classes, completed some early work for the Maritime Commission, and later provided direct consultation and purchasing services to individual shipyards.[34] Francis Gibbs, a senior partner in the firm, subsequently became technical adviser to the War Production Board's shipbuilding branch and chaired a committee appointed by the combined chiefs of staff in 1943 to study and make recommendations on effecting greater standardization in Allied ship production. The Combined Shipbuilding Committee (Standardization of Design) consisted of American, British, and Canadian representatives and considered the pressing issue of escorts, rationalization of merchant ship types, and the findings of consultation groups formed for specialized ships such as tugs and important marine components like engines and gears.[35] While the discussions generally resulted in many useful suggestions for improvement, the distinction between British and American warship types was essentially retained, and the Maritime Commission favored its own numbered merchant hull types at the expense of Gibbs' desire to concentrate on only one or two. Most significantly for Canada, the Royal Canadian Navy urged adoption of the Combined Shipbuilding Committee's revised frigate, citing better bridge arrangements and armament.[36] The design, an Americanized version of the original British twin-screw corvette or frigate suited to mass production methods, was sufficiently different to mark a significant departure for Canadian shipbuilding in terms of organization and production technique.

The revised prefabricated frigate turned the Canadians solidly away from British practices to wartime shipbuilding ways that were decidedly more American. Given its own scheduled program of two hundred Tacoma-class frigates, the Maritime Commission contracted Kaiser to establish a central engineering office in Oakland, called Kaiser Cargo Incorporated. It handled distribution of plans, engineering data, and issue of standard material lists along the same lines as Gibbs & Cox's arrangement with the Navy Department. Canadian authorities sent Kaiser Cargo a full set of frigate plans, which over the course of several months were completely redrawn to allow for all-welded construction and similar modifications to aid rapid construction.[37] Indeed, the Oakland office became, de facto, the central drawing office for this part of the Canadian shipbuilding program because these were the plans subsequently distributed to Canadian shipyards for building the new frigates. Wartime Shipbuilding Limited in turn assumed the limited functions of an American-like central engineering office by making common purchases of government-issued items, maintaining progress schedules, and expediting delivery of components from other contracted marine manufacturers [38] and Technical innovations pioneered and perfected in American shipyards migrated northward to Canada through official and unofficial channels. Welding, the joining of metal sheets or pieces by oxygen-assisted flame and heat, progressively supplanted traditional riveting in shipbuilding; the Americans were the first to use the method in any widespread fashion.[39] Given progress in the United States, the Department of Munitions and Supply's director of shipbuilding engaged a welding adviser in 1942 to study and report on opportunities for increased welding in Canadian shipyards.[40] Welding decreased the overall weight of steel used in overlapping plates and eliminated the weight of the rivets that would normally be used to join the plates. The process was dependent on the skill of the welder, and strength of the welds remained an issue. Thus, welding was used only in a limited fashion for minesweepers, corvettes, and earlier British-designed standardized North Sands cargo vessels, mostly in non-load-bearing areas such as superstructure. A British delegation touring North America in early 1943 observed that riveting was still predominant in Canada compared to shipyards visited in the United States.[41] Welding machines and equipment entailed additional capital investment. Canadian shipbuilders, accustomed to tried methods, were slow to undertake more welding until Wartime Shipbuilding Limited made it a condition for awarding further contracts and covered some of the costs. Fundamentally, welding entailed a completely new approach to shipbuilding, akin to assembly or fabrication, and was somehow forbidding to "men who were considered good shipbuilders in the days of riveted construction, and consequently know little or nothing with respect to the art and science of welding."[42] It is then no surprise that wartime procurement officials and naval authorities interested in speedier production pushed technical innovation. The revised frigates, the first ships in Canada to adopt a virtually all-welded design, required additional overseers at each shipyard to check on adherence to plans and quality of work.[43]

Spray painting, another innovation in wartime shipbuilding, met with similar acceptance. Instead of hand brush or roller methods, paint was applied uniformly under pressure through a nozzle. West Coast Shipbuilders Limited used gangs of painters in this fashion even before spray painting became standard practice in most Canadian shipyards. Industrial health problems associated with welding and spray painting without adequate safety measures were only partially understood at the time.[44] In Canada, as in the United States, prolonged exposure to confined spaces and environmental pathogens was a cause for later redress by those who worked in wartime shipyards. Technical innovations such as welding and spray painting, however, facilitated creation of new trades and entry of temporary workers into the shipbuilding industry under war conditions.

LABOR RELATIONS

In most large and many small shipyards in the United States and Canada, workers were organized into labor unions representing their collective interests with employers and reflective of individual trades. Bolstered by Roosevelt's New Deal policies and labor legislation such as the 1935 Wagner Act, the national labor movement in the United States was more developed than that in Canada. The international craft unions of the American Federation of Labor (AFL) held existing agreements with shipbuilders, while the expelled industrial unions of the rival Congress of Industrial Organizations (CIO) had made some headway with organizing and challenging the status quo in some individual shipyards, both in eastern and western Canada.[45] The Canadian labor scene was even more fragmented and complex, with the affiliates of the Canadian Congress of Labour squaring off against Canadian locals of AFL unions. Influential politicians such as Ontario Premier Mitchell Hepburn remained hardened in his "opinion of the C.I.O., and believe that, as a result of the activities of that organization in the United States, the war effort has been retarded more than by any other single factor."[46] Regardless, the CIO-backed Steel Workers of America made determined efforts to sign up workers and certify locals in Canadian wartime shipyards and marine manufacturing concerns. Representation of AFL boilermakers, machinists, painters, sheet metal workers, plumbers, stationary engineers, and electricians on metal trades councils reinforced a predominantly north-south orientation, with Vancouver and Victoria belonging to the Pacific Coast Metal Trades Council.[47] Canadian executive members were very aware of general labor conditions in the United States through personal friendships and travel to U.S.-hosted conventions.

The closed shop, a legal mechanism to designate a firm or workplace as being represented by a single union, was a natural point of confrontation between competing labor groupings. After electing a less-compromising leadership, the marine workers and boilermakers industrial union local in Vancouver, which represented a majority of shipyard workers, was dropped from the Canadian Congress of Labour in the midst of a concerted drive to get a closed shop recognized at West Coast Shipbuilders Limited.[48] No less than Kaiser had accepted the value of enforcing the closed shop. Jurisdictional disputes between unions were increasingly heard and settled through submission, either voluntarily or on a mandatory basis, to national and regional war labor boards on both sides of the border. Whatever the competing affiliation or union, locals in general expected adherence to existing agreements and allegiance from new workers entering the field of wartime shipbuilding.

Employment in shipbuilding grew tremendously during the war years. In September 1939 roughly 3,500 persons worked Canada-wide in the industry. At its peak in the summer of 1943 it counted some 126,000 employees nationally, with Vancouver and Montreal leading the way and Toronto, Victoria, and Halifax somewhat farther behind.[49] By contrast, Seattle, a shipbuilding center devoted mostly to warship construction and related naval work, alone employed about ninety thousand at its height, and the San Francisco Bay Area, by far the largest shipbuilding location in the United States, had hundreds of thousands of workers engaged in the shipbuilding industry. These numbers are important to keep Canada's relative effort in context on a North America basis: by population, Canadian cities were likely in the mid to lower range of average American employment in shipbuilding, though they faced many of the same challenges, such as massive rural-urban migration, overburdened transportation and municipal infrastructure, and acute housing shortages. To an almost unprecedented degree, the federal governments in both countries intervened with public monies to address these problems for the sake of uninterrupted war production.

Most persons coming into the shipyards were not only new to the locales, but also new to the type of the work they were called on to learn and do. Skilled metal trades related to shipbuilding usually entailed extensive apprenticeship and practical experience before full qualification. While a cadre of these skilled men was present for supervisory and other functions, the male and increasingly female workers hired by shipyards in the hundreds and thousands were mostly unskilled and were employed in tasks of a repetitive nature. All workers were required to join established unions and pay the requisite dues on a provisional basis for the duration of the war. These dues were sometimes collected directly off employer pay-stubs by prearranged check off. As in the United States, Canadian shipyards altered previous restrictions against employment of women, who made up about one-third of the available wartime workforce. The American Rosie the Riveter propaganda image was in turn adapted to Canadian sensibilities through posters and publicity efforts. In reality, most women found employment as assistants or hands in newer welding, painting, and assembly trades, or on tasks presumed suited to their gender such as precision machining and clerical office work.[50] To cater to women, shipyard management introduced suitably sized work clothing, separate washrooms, cafeterias serving hot meals, and day-care facilities, again following the lead of the United States. Canadian shipyards, on the whole, avoided the racial tensions associated with larger numbers of African American workers and the blatantly prejudiced stance of some AFL unions restricting membership and thus employment.[51] Depending on their experience and skill level in accepted trades, shipyard workers were paid according to uniform wage rates established across the industry for given geographical regions.

Wages in wartime shipbuilding were set on the basis of negotiated agreements between employers, trade unions, and government officials. Rates in Canadian shipyards and related metal trades were typically lower than in the United States by ten to fifteen cents per hour. Previously, locals of individual unions negotiated directly with company management for basic agreements covering a defined period. After the outbreak of war, trade union officials from several shipyard unions approached the Canadian Department of Labour about setting uniform wage rates for government war contracts in two zones dividing eastern and western Canada.[52] Shipyard wage rates in British Columbia were actually established from a board of conciliation decisions between Burrard Dry Dock and several AFL union locals in 1940 and were subsequently extended to all shipbuilders engaged in war work in the province. In the United States, on the other hand, shipbuilding wages had roughly corresponded to settlements that were given unions out of the Little Steel Companies standoff in the U.S. Midwest. At the insistence of President Roosevelt, a Shipbuilding Stabilization Committee was created in 1940 to examine the effect of increased numbers of contracts, mostly government related, on wage rates paid in shipyards across the nation and, if possible, to find means to keep them uniform and reasonable.[53] Spiralling shipyard wages had in part contributed to rampant inflation during the First World War, an experience politicians and government officials hoped to avoid this time around. In 1941 representatives from the shipbuilders, the Maritime

Commission, the Navy Department, and the AFL and CIO wings of organized labor signed a zone agreement covering the entire Pacific Coast at a basic mechanics wage of $1.12 per hour, followed by comparable zone agreements for the Great Lakes, eastern seaboard, and the Gulf Coast.[54] Within this overlying framework, implementation of exact terms was left to talks between shipyard management and union locals.

Canadian union locals, particularly the AFL, followed American developments very closely and pushed the Canadian government to match American terms. Though most shipbuilders in Canada accepted the idea for the sake of industrial harmony (increased labor costs were merely passed on to the government under existing war contracts), Minister of Labor Humphrey Mitchell decided to dictate wage rates to the unions after only perfunctory consultation. The main reason was the disparity of lower shipyard wages in eastern Canada, which were justified on the basis of different transportation and living costs. If American rates were to be paid in western Canada, pressure would mount among shipyard workers elsewhere to advance wages upward, or worse, to give cause for industrial action that might disrupt production. With no Canadian equivalent to the Wagner Act, government officials felt little need to appease unions and frequently used heavy-handed orders-in-council to enforce compliance. Some shipyard workers especially resented the loss of overtime pay and the customary day off on Sunday. Disgruntlement over pay and hours of work was the foremost inducement to strikes and similar occurrences in wartime shipyards.

Though comparatively rare, breaks in production owing to labor action were a constant worry under war conditions and were met with strong responses from government officials and national labor leaders. In a democracy, through their unions, workers retained the usual right to strike when certain conditions were met. Roosevelt was keen not to overturn existing arrangements and instead asked the labor movement to commit to support for national defense and the war effort. After the Japanese attack on Pearl Harbor, the AFL voluntarily pledged a no-strike policy for the duration of the conflict against fascism, and the Metal Trades Department in Washington, presided over by seasoned trade unionist John Frey, ensured individual unions and locals that fell under AFL jurisdiction in American and Canadian shipyards adhered unconditionally.[55] The upstart CIO, seeing the war as an opportunity for further recruitment and organization, never abandoned the threat of strike and left more discretion to lower levels. Admiral Land decried the small number of organizers and agitators who impeded production of ships and other armaments by causing unrest. In late 1942 he wrote, "I am against any one who puts his organization above his country in this great crisis."[56] Out of patriotic duty, responsible labor leaders actively partnered with shipbuilders and procurement officials while pressing for more representation for organized labor on government boards and agencies. During a major strike affecting shipyards in San Francisco, Frey personally escorted U.S. Navy trucks carrying fifteen thousand AFL workers through pickets set up by machinists and sympathetic CIO unions.[57] Canadian machinists in Vancouver from the same AFL union took lessons from this experience when they opposed Minister of Labor Mitchell's order-in-council, bringing into effect a continuous production plan. Striking in the summer of 1942, they simply stayed away from work, bringing all other trades to a standstill in the shipyards. The government was forced to back off and, after several months of inquiry by an appointed judge, brought in a scheme of hours and pay closely resembling those in the United States. Canadian shipbuilding also experienced a host of slowdowns and impromptu strikes lasting a few hours to a day, usually in response to some particular grievance. In Quebec, a large strike involving seven thousand workers caused the federal government to impose government ownership over two affected shipyards to keep the ships coming.[58] The U.S. Navy's takeover of the Brewster aircraft plant in the face of mismanagement and lagging production stands out as perhaps the closest American parallel. The top goal remained keeping the majority of workers satisfied and happy until the imperative of the wartime emergency had passed.

As incentives to good and constant work, shipyard employees made impressive gains prior to wholesale industry-wide reductions owing to changing strategic and operational needs in the war. Features of work and employment now taken for granted originated in wartime shipyards. Paid vacation time, for example, started as a measure to prevent growing absenteeism among shipyard workers. When demand for escorts and merchant ships ebbed, delivery schedules were extended and the pace of work slowed. Many workers decided personal time was more important on usual days off when they conflicted with shipyard schedules, or they stopped coming in to work altogether in favor of other employment. After a set period with no absences, workers received up to five days of paid vacation per year. Canadian authorities hurriedly implemented paid vacation and other incentives modeled on those in the United States. Moreover, many issues earlier referred by unions and employers to the National War Labour Board in Ottawa were being decided upon; shipyard workers received retroactive wage and cost-of-living increases as well as better conditions of employment. The irony was that these positive outcomes came just as wartime shipbuilding began to contract and the prospect of layoffs in the industry loomed. Newer and less-experienced workers were the first to go, since trade unions gave priority to long-standing members and those returning from military service. Women who had found easy industrial employment in the shipyards were expected to return home or go back to gender-specific jobs in the mainstream economy.[59] Shipyards in eastern Canada were naturally the first to feel the effects of cancelled escorts and minesweepers, and Howe pressured them to lay off workers quickly to cut costs to the government. In Toronto, Redfern Construction Company dismissed shipyard workers without complying with existing collective agreements.[60] The building of transport ferries and conversion work associated with naval auxiliaries for the Royal Navy's operations against Japan sustained employment in Montreal, Vancouver, and Victoria for a short time longer. On the American side, the entire West Coast had evolved into an important base and staging area for the conduct of operations across the Pacific Ocean, by virtue of its existing ship repair and production capacity.[61] The shipyard facilities at Vancouver and graving dock at Esquimalt were similarly included in the Royal Navy's fleet logistics plans for repair of battle-damaged capital ships and regular refit of warships up to and including cruisers. Japan's abrupt unconditional surrender in August 1945 removed any further rationale for the wartime shipbuilding industry and layoffs took place almost immediately.

CONCLUSION

American organization, methods, and practice exerted pervasive influence on Canada's shipbuilding efforts during the Second World War. Sharing a common continent, the United States and Canada grew closer together through greater economic integration and special arrangements for mutual consultation. The United States, the world's leading wartime producer of naval and merchant ships, set the standard for Canada to follow. Canada emerged from very modest beginnings to be ranked third among Allied countries in terms of wartime shipbuilding, slightly behind Great Britain. How this remarkable achievement came about can only be explained by American example and crucial assistance received from authorities in the United States. Management of shipyards transitioned from older British craft backgrounds to modern concepts of North American business practice. Canadian government procurement agencies involved with shipbuilding and the individuals who headed them dealt directly with American counterparts and emulated organizational styles found in the U.S. Maritime Commission. Under MacMillan, Wartime Merchant Shipping/Shipbuilding Limited became an adjunct of the massive American shipbuilding program, building ships under the Lend-Lease Act and often with American components and steel. Techniques of mass production, prefabrication, and project management, pioneered in Kaiser's shipyards on the West Coast and elsewhere, were eventually adopted outright in Canadian shipyards. Shipbuilders followed American-revised design plans and some of the features associated with a central engineering office in terms of consolidated purchasing and progress scheduling. Likewise, technical innovations such as welding and spray painting, introduced and perfected in the United States, greatly changed the nature of Canadian production. Moreover, workers who built the ships were either affiliated with Canadian locals of American craft and industrial unions or looked toward industrial relations in the United States for inspiration for wage improvements and better conditions of employment. American practices, such as the widespread entry of women into shipbuilding-related metal trades and incentives giving paid vacations, in due course, were instituted in Canadian shipyards.

However, those looking for a brighter future for putting a war industry onto a more permanent footing in Canada were largely disappointed. The federal Canadian government showed little encouragement, and layoffs from shipbuilding concerns proceeded apace before and after the end of the war. Perhaps the biggest mistake was not to adopt better-suited American-type ship designs that might have competed for postwar international markets and facilitated the Royal Canadian Navy's closer association with the U.S. Navy. Canada had the ability to produce almost any moderately technical item but proved too ready to back the wrong horse when natural affinities and North American industrial practices dictated otherwise. In the end, Canada proved willing to let the shipbuilding industry slide back to prewar norms of indifference and neglect.

NOTES

The following abbreviations are used in the notes:

BCA	British Columbia Archives, Victoria
LAC	Library and Archives Canada, Ottawa, ON
NARA-CP	National Archives and Records Administration, College Park
NMM	National Maritime Museum, Greenwich
NVMA	North Vancouver Museum and Archives, North Vancouver
TNA	The National Archives, Kew

1. Kevin Smith, *Conflict over Convoys: Anglo-American Logistics Diplomacy in the Second World War* (New York: Cambridge University Press, 1996).
2. Jack Granatstein, *Canada's War: The Politics of the Mackenzie King Government 1939–1945* (Toronto, ON: University of Toronto Press, 1990).

3. Michael Hennessy, "The Rise and Fall of a Canadian Maritime Policy 1939-1965: A Study of Industry Navalism and the State" (unpublished PhD dissertation, University of New Brunswick, Fredericton, 1995).
4. NVMA, Matthew T. Davie, Fonds 105, File 1C, Burrard Dry Dock Company Limited, "The Shipbuilding and Ship Repairing Industry in Canada and Its Relation to Unemployment" (corporate promotional material, n.d.).
5. LAC, Record Group 19, Vol. 528, File 131-5-0, letter from Alex Johnston to C. A. Dunning, 8 March 1939.
6. NVMA Versatile Pacific Shipyards, Fonds 27, Series 44, Box 210, File "Contract and Specifications of Minesweeper 1937," letter from Lambert & Milne Naval Architects to Burrard Dry Dock Company, "Minesweepers," 3 November 1937.
7. Marine Museum of the Great Lakes Kingston Canadian Steamship Line Corporate (Davie Shipyards), Series B-II Box 993.2.11, File "Davie Shipbuilding and Repair Company General 1940," letter from D. B. Carswell to David Craig, 19 March 1940.
8. LAC, RG 24, Series D-1-c, Vol. 8117, File 1280-325, letter from D. B. Carswell to K. S. MacLachlan, "Brief Summary of Shipbuilding Facilities in Canada," 25 November 1940.
9. "Sunk by Ceilingless Wages 21 Years Ago: Toronto's Ship Building Industry Revived," *Toronto Evening Telegram,* 1 November 1941; LAC, RG 28, Vol. 20, File 61, Draft "History of Toronto Shipbuilding Company Limited."
10. NVMA Versatile Pacific, Fonds 27, Series 53, Box 329, File "War Contracts Depreciation Board 1944," Certificate 1693 War Contracts Depreciation Board, 25 September 1944.
11. G. W. Taylor, *Shipyards of British Columbia: The Principal Companies* (Victoria, BC: Morriss Publishing, 1986); T. A. McLaren with Vicki Jensen, *Ships of Steel: A British Columbia Shipbuilder's Story* (Madeira Park, BC: Harbour Publishing, 2000), 54.
12. J. De N. Kennedy, *History of the Department of Munitions and Supply,* Vol. 1 (Ottawa, ON: Queen's Printer 1950), 5; Robert Bothwell and William Kilbourn, *C. D. Howe* (Toronto, ON: McClelland and Stewart, 1979), 128–129.
13. LAC, RG 19, Vol. 3991, File U-3-2-4-1, letter from James E. Coyne to W. C. Clark, 6 June 1941.
14. LAC, RG 28, Vol. 20, File 62, "Trafalgar Shipbuilding Co. Ltd.: Record of Development," 30 September 1943.
15. NMM, Vice Adm. James Wilfred Dorling, JOD/185/1 Diary, 18 June 1941. Wartime Merchant Shipping Limited undertook to build the twenty twin-screw corvettes: ten for the Royal Canadian Navy and ten for the Royal Navy under the Hyde Park Agreement for delivery by late 1942. LAC, RG 24, Series D-1-b, Vol. 3844, File 1017-10-38, K. S. MacLachlan, "Memorandum of Conversation with Mr. H.R. MacMillan Wednesday September 9th 1941," 10 September 1941.
16. LAC, Clarence Decatur Howe papers, MG 27 III B20, Vol. 42, File S-9-25(2), letter from C. D. Howe to C. A. Banks, "Landing Craft Required for Combined Operations," 19 June 1941.
17. University of British Columbia Library Special Collections Vancouver, Harvey Reginald MacMillan papers, Box 90, File 13, "Notes of Talk before the Cost & Management Institute Windsor Hotel October 3 1941," 3 October 1941.
18. Directorate of History and Heritage National Defence Headquarters, Ottawa, ON, Fonds 81/520/1550-157/1, Box 78, File 4, letter from Rear Adm. V. C. Brodeur to Vice Adm. P. W. Nelles, 26 October 1942.
19. NARA-CP, RG 178, Entry 28, Records of Commissioner H. L. Vickery, 1942–46 FRC, Box 158, File Joint War Production Committee, "Joint Meeting of the Naval Shipbuilding and

Merchant Shipbuilding Sub-Committees of the Joint War Production Committee Held in Room 4836 Department of Commerce Building at 2:30 PM Thursday March 2nd 1944"; University of British Columbia Library Special Collections Vancouver MacMillan papers, Box 113, File 6, letter from C. L. Dewar to H. R. MacMillan, 10 March 1944.

20. TNA, ADM 1/13030 Memorandum Director of Plans, "Co-ordination of Shipbuilding in U.K. and Canada: Fleet Minesweepers Frigates & Corvettes," 12 March 1943; TNA MT 9/3802, letter from C. A. Banks to Lord Leathers, 11 February 1944.

21. Robert Connery, *The Navy and Industrial Mobilization in World War II* (Princeton, NJ: Princeton University Press, 1951).

22. LAC, RG 24, Series D-1-a, Vol. 5652, File NSS 54-1-46, Memorandum Lieutenant A. C. Bethune to Acting Deputy Minister, "Proposal: Competitive Awards to Firms Producing R.C.N. Equipment," 15 January 1942.

23. "1000th Ship Launching and Military Parade Starts Loan Campaign," *Globe and Mail* 23 October 1944, 8; TNA ADM 1/16122, Message Admiralty to BATM 15 1805A, October 1944.

24. LAC, RG 24, Series D-1-a, Vol. 5609, File 29-27-1, Pt. 4, letter from D. A. Clarke to W. G. Mills, 14 November 1941; LAC, RG 28, Vol. 101, File 2-C-45, letter from D. A. Hunter to D. A. Clarke, 24 July 1942.

25. BCA Star Shipyards (Mercer's) Limited, Add. Mss. 448, Box 5, File "Canadian Manufacturers Association—Circular Letters," "A meeting of the Executive Committee of the Boat builders was held in the Board Room this afternoon May 19th 1944 at 4 PM," 20 May 1944.

26. Marine Museum of the Great Lakes Kingston Davie Shipyards, Series B-II, Box 993.2.22, File "Canadian Shipbuilding and Ship Repairing Association 1945," letter Angus McGugan to R. Brock Thomson, "Future of Shipbuilding—A Talk Given by Mr. Angus McGugan Manager Canadian Shipbuilding and Ship Repairing Association to the Foreign Service Officers (in training) Commercial Intelligence Service Department of Trade and Commerce, West Block, Ottawa, ON, May 15th 1945," 24 May 1945.

27. "Against Subsidies," *Winnipeg Free Press,* 13 April 1945. In fact, government officials had advocated consolidation and reduction of the entire industry. LAC, RG 28, Vol. 103, File 2-C-61, memorandum D. W. Ambridge to C. D. Howe, "Brief for Shipbuilding," 11 September 1944.

28. Christopher James Tassava, "Launching a Thousand Ships: Entrepreneurs War Workers and the State in American Shipbuilding 1940–1945" (unpublished PhD dissertation, Northwestern University, Chicago, 2003).

29. Stephen B. Adams, *Mr. Kaiser Goes to Washington: The Rise of a Government Entrepreneur* (Chapel Hill: University of North Carolina Press, 1997); Mark S. Foster, *Henry J. Kaiser: Builder in the Modern American West* (Austin: University of Texas Press, 1989).

30. Frederic C. Lane, *Ships for Victory: A History of Shipbuilding under the U.S. Maritime Commission in World War II* (Baltimore, MD: Johns Hopkins Press, 1951), vii; Emory Scott Land, *Winning the War with Ships* (New York: R. M. McBride, 1958).

31. Privately held West Coast Shipbuilders Limited, W. D. McLaren Diary, 18 July 1942. Flesher subsequently appeared as an expert witness before a royal commission into adoption of continuous production on the West Coast. LAC, RG 27, Reel T-10187, Vol. 269, File 6, "In the Matter of the 'Inquiries Act' and of a Royal Commission to Examine into and Report as to the Most Effective Means of Securing Maximum Production in the Shipyards of British Columbia: Proceedings of Inquiry," 7 August 1942, 1163–1170.

32. LAC, W. Harold Milne papers, MG 30 B121, File 1-9, Horace M. German to W. H. Milne, "Work Done by Lambert German & Milne for Dominion [Canadian] Government since

Outbreak of War until September 1942," 11 September 1942. The Canadian firm later proved unsuccessful in convincing Wartime Shipbuilding Limited that design business should be retained in Montreal rather than being given to design agents in New York. LAC, RG 28, Vol. 103, File 2-C-61, letter from C. L. Dewar to H. H. German, 13 October 1944.

33. LAC, RG 24, Series D-1-c, Acc. 1983–84/167, Vol. 3788, File 8200-6, Pt.1, "Summary of Meeting of Quebec Shipbuilders and Fitters with D. A. Clarke Esq. Director General of Shipbuilding Branch and His Department Heads Held at the Offices of Canadian Vickers Limited Montreal on December 18 1942 at 10 AM."

34. The Mariner's Museum Newport News, *Gibbs & Cox in World War II: Report to the Staff*, September 1945; NARA-CP, RG 178, Entry 5A, Miscellaneous Files of Adm. E. S. Land, 1937–45, Box 3, File "1943," memorandum E. S. Land for file, 26 January 1943.

35. TNA ADM 1/15477, Minutes 2nd Meeting Combined Shipbuilding Committee (Standardization of Design), 22 April 1943. MacMillan, one of two designated Canadian representatives, wrote in a letter, "I think we should keep in touch with this committee in order to be fully informed respecting trends in merchant shipbuilding in the United States." LAC, RG 28, Vol. 129, File 3-C-21, letter from H. R. MacMillan to G. K. Sheils, 5 March 1943.

36. LAC, RG 24, Series D-1-a, Vol. 5619, File NSS-30-1-3, memorandum from Acting Capt. A. R. Pressey to Assistant Chief of Naval Staff, 19 July 1943.

37. LAC, Milne papers MG 30 B121, File 1-3, memorandum from W. H. Milne to D.A. Clarke, "General Notes regarding our Naval Programme," 26 April 1943.

38. City of Toronto Archives, Toronto John Inglis Company, Fonds 1297, Series A5, Box 20 (196611), File "Thomas H. R. 1943," memorandum from H. R. Thomas to W. R. McLachlan, 1 September 1943.

39. LAC, RG 28, Vol. 162, File 3-S-15, "Minutes of the First Meeting of the Shipbuilding Co-ordinating Committee Which Met in Montreal December 31st 1943 at 11 AM in Room 65 Castle Building."

40. LAC, RG 24, Series D-1-a, Vol. 5601, File 29-1-1, pt. 3, letter from D. A. Clarke to Secretary Naval Board, "Welding Advisor—R. M. Gooderham," 15 April 1942.

41. LAC, Milne papers, MG 30 B121, File 2-1, "Report Submitted by Members of the Government Delegation Appointed by the British Ministry of Labour to Study the Methods of Ship Construction in United States," 14 December 1942–45 February 1943. A separate delegation of British shipbuilders and marine manufacturers also visited American shipyards. TNA ADM 1/12090 Message Admiralty to British Admiralty, Delegation 07, 1826A, October 1942.

42. Marine Museum of the Great Lakes Kingston Davie Shipyards, Series B-II, Box 993.2.17, File "Davie Shipbuilding and Ship Repairing Company—Plant Expansion 1943," "Erection and Welding Sequence as Applied to Welded Steel Hulls: A Lecture Given before the Los Angeles Section of the American Welding Society September 16 1943."

43. LAC, RG 24, Series D-1-a, Vol. 5619, File NSS 29-73-1, letter from Constructor Lt. Cdr. A. Annandale to Capt. A. N. Harrison, "Revised Frigates: Welding Construction," 8 December 1943.

44. Archives of Ontario Toronto, RG 7-12-0-792, Box 11, letter from J. R. Prain to J. S. Leitch, 15 September 1942.

45. David Palmer, *Organizing the Shipyards: Union Strategy in Three Northeast Ports 1933–1945* (Ithaca, NY: ILR, 1998). For the background of these developments, see Andrew E. Kersten, *Labor's Home Front: The American Federation of Labor during World War II* (New York: New York University Press, 2006).

46. Archives of Ontario Toronto RG 3-10-0-1190, Box 321, letter from Mitchell Hepburn to R. H. Gale, 14 January 1942.
47. City of Vancouver Archives, Vancouver Metal Trades Council, Add. Mss. 558 566-B-4, Vol. 2, Minutes Regular Meeting, 15 November 1939.
48. University of British Columbia Library, Special Collections, Vancouver Marine Workers and Boilermakers Industrial Union Local No. 1 Fonds, Box 1A, File 1, Minutes Regular Meeting 3, June 1943. LAC, Trades and Labor Congress, MG28 I103, Vol. 311, File 9, P. Conroy and J. E. McGuire, "Report of Commission Appointed by the Executive Council of the Canadian Congress of Labour at Its Sessions in Ottawa [ON] January 9 1943," 9 January 1943.
49. LAC, RG 28, Vol. 862, File "Canada's Industrial War Effort 1939–1945," Department of Reconstruction and Supply, "Canada's Industrial War Effort 1939–1945," 1947 Shipbuilding.
50. Deborah Hirshfield, "Rosie Also Welded: Women and Technology in Shipbuilding during World War II" (unpublished PhD dissertation, University of California–Irvine, 1987).
51. Josh Sides, "Battle on the Home Front: African American Shipyard Workers in World War II Los Angeles," *California History* 75 (1996): 250–263; Bruce Nelson, "Organized Labor and the Struggle for Black Equality in Mobile during the Second World War," *Journal of American History* 80 (1993): 952–988; Robin Dearman Jenkins, "Rivets and Rights: African-American Workers and Shipbuilding in the San Francisco Area 1890–1948" (unpublished PhD dissertation, Carnegie Mellon University, Pittsburgh, PA, 2004).
52. LAC, RG 27, Reel T-10092, Vol. 87, File 423.2:5, letter from E. Ingles to Gerald Brown, 7 November 1939. Department officials considered the proffered wage rates "ridiculous" and at least one shipbuilder considered setting up a company union. Marine Museum of the Great Lakes Kingson Davie Shipyards, Series B-II, Box 993.2.8, File "Davie Shipbuilding 1939," letter from R. B. Thomson to David Craig, 6 December 1939.
53. NARA-CP, RG 254, Entry 1, Classified Central Files 1940–47, Box 1, File SHPB.01/113, memorandum from J. A. Krug to Paul E. Porter, "Shipbuilding Stabilization Committee," 1 January 1945.
54. Library of Congress Manuscript Division, Washington, DC, John P. Frey papers, Box 14, File 199, letter from Chairman of Shipbuilding Stabilization Committee to Office of Production Management, Secretary of Navy, U.S. Maritime Commission, 2 April 1941; NARA-CP, RG 80; Entry 131I; correspondence of Joseph Powell, Navy Representative on the Shipbuilding Stabilization Committee, October 1940 to September 1941, Box 1, File "Shipbuilding Stabilization Committee 1940 to Feb 14 1941," memorandum from "Shipbuilding Stabilization—San Francisco Results," 13 February 1941.
55. Wisconsin State Historical Society, Madison, American Federation of Labor, U.S. Mss 117A, Series 11B, Box 9, Folder "World War II Policy—National War Labor Board," "Report of President Green to the Executive Council of the American Federation of Labor on the Conference of Labor and Industry Called by President Roosevelt."
56. Library of Congress Manuscript Division, Adm. Emory Scott Land Papers, Box 1, File "General Correspondence 1942," memorandum from Adm. Land, 21 October 1942.
57. LC, Frey papers, Box 26, Scrapbook, "Navy Trucks Carry Shipyard Men to Struck Plants Here," *Oakland Tribune,* 22 May 1941; Richard Boyden, "The San Francisco Machinists from Depression to Cold War 1930–1950" (unpublished PhD dissertaton, University of California–Berkeley, 1988).
58. LAC, RG 27, Reel T-3032, Vol. 429, File 211, Clipping, "Ottawa [ON] to Run Two Shipyards in Quebec Area," *Montreal Gazette,* 15 June 1943. The striking workers demanded a closed shop, which the companies flatly refused.

59. Amy Kesselman, *Fleeting Opportunities: Women Shipyard Workers in Portland and Vancouver during World War II and Reconversion* (Albany: State University of New York Press, 1990).
60. LAC, Toronto District Labour Council, Minute Books MG 28 I44, Reel M-2293, Minutes Regular Meeting, 21 December 1944.
61. NARA-CP, RG 178, Entry 5A, Miscellaneous Files of Adm. E. S. Land, 1937–45, Box 3, File "1944," "Memorandum with Reference to Ship Repairs and Conversions on the West Coast," 27 April 1944.

King, Canada, and the Convoys: A Reappraisal of Adm. Ernest King's Role in Operation Drumbeat

Kenneth P. Hansen

Adm. Ernest J. King was a titan of his era. His leadership of the United States Navy (USN) during the Second World War was instrumental to Allied victory. King's vision and guidance helped to create a world-class navy that possessed unparalleled combat power. However, a balanced assessment must also include a frank discussion of his personality traits.

Ernest King has been described as being abrupt to the point of rudeness, almost without a sense of humor, intolerant of lesser intellectuals, and completely averse to publicity.[1] It has been claimed that he was "a distinct Anglophobe."[2] Despite these drawbacks, King had the complete confidence of President Franklin Roosevelt and was able to work cooperatively with Army Chief of Staff Gen. George Marshall.

King's lack of tact caused dismay among British naval leaders and made him many enemies within the U.S. armed services. Among those people who it is claimed hated him were Secretary of War Henry Stimson, Prime Minister Winston Churchill, Chief of the Imperial General Staff Sir Alan Brooke, and First Sea Lord Adm. Sir Andrew Cunningham.[3] King's abrasiveness was a serious impediment to building effective working relationships with the other services and with the military leadership of Allied nations.

In fairness, Admiral of the Fleet Sir Dudley Pound, Cunningham's predecessor as first sea lord and King's counterpart, was just as difficult. Descriptions of him are similarly unflattering: "pig-headed; a hard-working plodder of limited intellectual ranges and interests; devoid of personal charisma; [possessing] a slow but good brain; and not a gentleman."[4] But while King was a consummate strategist who trusted his staff to deal with issues within their purview, Pound lacked strategic vision and was inclined to micromanage matters well below his direct responsibility. This combination of personalities could hardly have been worse and played a part in the sequence of events leading to Admiral King's only major failure.

KING AND THE CALAMITY OF OPERATION DRUMBEAT

It has been suggested that Admiral King's overconfidence and cultural bias led him to ignore advice from the Royal Navy (RN) on effective operational arrangements and tactical procedures for the protection of trade. Specifically, it has been charged that King failed utterly to remember the antisubmarine lessons of the Great War and that he learned nothing from the early experiences of the British in the Second World War. It is claimed that he made no preparations for the German submarine campaign (*Paukenschlag*, or Drumbeat) in American and Caribbean waters between January and July 1942. Once the German attack materialized, King resorted to offensive hunting groups that reputedly gave German submarine commanders no tactical difficulties whatever.[5] This was despite the fact that more than a month had elapsed between the Japanese attack at Pearl Harbor and the commencement of offensive operations by five German long-range Type IX submarines at midnight on the night of 11–12 January. By the end of the multiphased campaign, German U-boats had sunk 460 ships, which represented 83.3 percent of the 552 ships sunk in the North Atlantic.[6] Fifty-seven percent of these losses were tankers, which were already in short supply and were more costly and slower to build than dry cargo ships. It is claimed that King's lack of response in face of such losses "has vexed naval scholars ever since."[7]

The introduction of convoys along the American eastern seaboard in April and in the Caribbean in July 1942 ended the onslaught, and German submarines were withdrawn to operating areas closer to their support bases, but the damage had been done. The large number of tankers lost in this period contributed to a fuel shortage in the United Kingdom, which persisted practically until the end of the war.[8] Undoubtedly, Operation Drumbeat was a spectacular success for the *Kriegsmarine* (German navy), commanded by Grand Adm. Erich Raeder, and the U-boat force, commanded by Adm. Karl Doenitz.

How was it possible that a well-educated, experienced, and capable officer such as King could have committed such a major blunder? What factors influenced his decisions? Is it possible that perfect clarity of hindsight does not accurately represent the situation as he saw it in 1942?

This analysis will suggest that operational planning processes, logistical factors, and personalities lay at the center of this mystery. Both American and British planners lacked relevant intelligence, underappreciated important operational and tactical factors, and underestimated German determination and ingenuity. It appears that a complex interplay of factors— and not simply the intransigence of one person—resulted in the outcome of Operation Drumbeat.

In late 1941 Admiral King twice proposed a major reorganization to the Atlantic convoy system that could have significantly enhanced the operational and tactical effectiveness of Allied escort forces and increased the carrying capacity of the merchant ships. These plans, when coupled with King's statements before the USN's General Board about characteristics of future escort vessels as well as his personal strategic assessment of the situation in July 1941, show that he was aware of the theory and practice of trade warfare and that he was not insensitive to the plight of British and Canadian naval forces engaged in a desperate struggle. However, a fundamental difference in fleet operating practices led to divergent perceptions about how best to organize, conduct, and sustain escort of convoy operations.

Because the Royal Canadian Navy (RCN) was organized and equipped along British lines, it followed the RN's doctrine and tactical procedures. Although the USN proposed a workable solution, the RN rejected it and the RCN followed suit. Once the key leaders' personalities came into play, reconciliation became a practical impossibility.

The two navies remained diametrically opposed on many issues relating to escort of convoy operations: "The RN viewed the USN's anti-submarine tactics as immature while the USN thought the RN's doctrine was antiquated and obsolete."[9] Despite this impasse, King took many practical measures to prepare the USN for German attacks on trade in American waters. When considered in light of the USN's strategic and operational priorities, the intelligence available at the time, and the operational lessons being presented by contemporary RN-RCN actions, a new assessment of King's decisions in early 1942 becomes possible.

KING AND THE GENERAL BOARD

Admiral King was a member of the USN's General Board and chaired several sessions during the interwar period. His comments during hearings show that he understood very well what types of vessels were best suited for the protection of trade against submarine attack. His opinions were consistent with earlier testimonies that subsequently laid the groundwork for future American destroyer and cutter characteristics.

Numerous hearings on protection of trade operations already had been held before the end of the First World War. Testimonies in late 1917 and 1918 by USN escort commanders with recent experience in convoy operations established a clear relationship between warship endurance and tactical performance. Witnesses emphasized the absolute efficiency of the convoy system against attacks by individual submarines when adequate numbers of escorts were present. They also strongly criticized the British use of armed trawlers for convoy work because of to their low speed, poor equipment, and reservist crews, which rendered them practically ineffective. Above all, the importance of a great cruising radius was stressed by the witnesses Cdr. W. N. Vernou and Cdr. J. K. Taussig.[10]

By 1920 the board had approved a series of recommendations put before it to improve the performance of USN destroyers for escort work. They included a raised forecastle, greater flare to the bows, reduced turning circle, improved accommodations, increased bunkerage, higher endurance, and centerline placement of gun and torpedo mountings to make them more efficient in heavy weather.[11] A later report by Lt. Cdr. F. S. Craven proposed three types of destroyers: one of about 1,100 tons for day torpedo attack in good weather; one of about 2,200 tons for screening the main fleet against submarines and, secondarily, for making topedo attacks in bad weather; and one of about 4,400 tons that was commodious enough to carry range finders and the flotilla commander plus his staff. Their general characteristics included the greatest practicable range of speed at cruising power, sustained high speed in rough weather, great seaworthiness, stable platform (for combat functions), few and large boilers, and increased bunkerage. This document included the first recommendation to remove one boiler room from contemporary Wickes- and Clemson-class destroyers and to replace it with fuel tanks, which could raise endurance by 50 percent.[12]

With a large inventory of flush-deck destroyers left over from the First World War, the USN did not begin building destroyers again until 1934 and had little interest in smaller escort vessels. However, practically all of the recommendations made before the board were incorporated into new American destroyer designs. In particular, USN destroyers enjoyed significantly higher endurance than their British equivalents. This was owing to advanced propulsion systems with higher operating temperatures and pressures (six hundred versus three hundred pounds per square inch), turbines that were more efficient, and greater bunkerage. British systems and fuel capacities remained virtually unchanged since the standards were set in 1918.[13]

Critics of the USN's lack of interest in simple escorts fail to appreciate that the General Board addressed these issues when establishing the characteristics of cutters for the United States Coast Guard (USCG). By 1935 and while King was still a member of the General Board, the USCG was designing the 327-foot Secretary-class cutters. These ships were intended to meet new capability requirements in the post-Prohibition era, wherein the advent of maritime air travel and increased drug smuggling reemphasized high endurance and good seakeeping qualities. A detailed and extensive list of war tasks, which included convoy escort duties, was also presented.[14]

Although the new 327-foot cutters were only marginally larger than conventional destroyers, their actual endurance was an extraordinary 12,300 miles at eleven knots on 572 tons of fuel, which, although lower than anticipated, could not be matched by any contemporary destroyer. Being marginally slower than twenty knots and not armed with torpedoes, cutters were not governed by naval treaty limitations and were not accounted for within the aggregate destroyer tonnage allocation. The 327-foot cutters were renowned as excellent sea keepers, more sea kindly than destroyers, very commodious, and equipped with the most up-to-date communications facilities.[15] King expressed strong support for the 327-foot cutter and recommended its adoption by the USN as an escort vessel. Resistance from Rear Adm. Herbert Leary, head of the Fleet training office, was based on the established requirement for a minimum speed of twenty-five knots for an escort.[16] The board's reluctance to adopt cutters was likely based on the knowledge that a twenty-five–knot escort with improved endurance could be derived from the large number of decommissioned destroyers held in reserve. King expressed reservations about the performance limitations of converted flush-deckers. In retrospect, his error was that he did not emphasize the advantages of large cutters over old destroyers.

The General Board held hearings on the question of essential characteristics for future escort vessels between 6 September and 22 October 1940. Admiral King chaired most of these sessions. The board's evaluation process considered all the key factors (cost, speed, seaworthiness, maneuverability, acceleration, watertight subdivision, endurance, ASDIC [also known as sonar; developed through the work of the Anti-submarine Detection Investigation Committee] efficiency, rapidity of construction, and crew size) for three different proposals. An endurance of six thousand miles at cruising speed was specified, along with the bunkerage needed to satisfy the endurance figure. King insisted that the hull form be designed to optimize sea-keeping qualities and, in particular, to reduce pitching. The design was to be simple in order to make the ship suitable for construction in a large number of yards, and to make it suitable for operation by inexperienced sailors.[17]

The General Board heard that the key to effective convoying was adequate numbers of escorts. Rear Adm. Alexander Sharp, representing the Naval Districts Division, warned that small escorts suitable for coastal work would be ineffective in the event that convoys had to run elsewhere. King reiterated his contention that the new escort ships must be "exceptional sea boats" and urged the board to ensure that the Bureau of Ships paid particular attention to that feature.[18]

Rear Adm. Walton Sexton, chairman of the General Board, directed the final session on escort vessels. The three plans under consideration in the first two hearings were narrowed down to two: (1) a 1,175-ton model, and (2) an 875-ton version. While there were major differences in speed (twenty-four versus twenty-one and a half knots) and armament (four versus two 5-inch .38-caliber guns with a single director), the absolute minimum endurance for both ships was set at five thousand miles at fifteen knots.[19] Capt. James Irish, representing the Bureau of Ships, assured Admiral Sexton that they had heeded Admiral King's suggestions about sea-keeping characteristics: both were able to maintain speed in heavy weather, were stable in all conditions of loading, and were highly maneuverable. The result was two high-endurance escort vessels, each one optimized for antiair and antisubmarine warfare. It seemed that the USN would be well prepared for the demands of convoy operations. As events proved, war came unexpectedly early and building priorities placed escort vessels low on the list.

KING'S STRATEGIC ASSESSMENT

In July 1941, while he was commander in chief of the Atlantic Fleet, Admiral King sent a memorandum to the General Board in response to an oral request for a study on construction priorities arising from the Two-Ocean Navy Building Program. A typical example of the application of the estimate process, the report detailed all assumptions and factors, making the rationale for its deductions clear.[20] The report quantified the opposing forces, estimated building times for warship types, assessed the distances to the assumed theaters of operations (western Atlantic off Brazil and the South China Sea), determined the effect of distance on operating forces, assessed the likelihood of obtaining local bases for support and their effect on fleet forces, and established ratios between the resultant effective forces in both areas. While the rate of construction deemed "inadequate" for battleships and "wholly inadequate" for carriers, King recommended that submarines be given the highest priority, followed by destroyers. His reasoning was based on his appreciation of the enemy's vulnerability to interdiction along their lines of communication and America's vulnerability to the same type of attack. He identified the effectiveness of submarine attacks on Japanese merchant shipping, the large numbers of destroyers needed to protect both U.S. and British shipping, and the numbers of destroyers needed to screen the capital ships of the battle fleet.

The report established King's personal view of the entire naval situation, from strategic posture down to priority for tactical action. His assessment had the benefit of close observation of the early war years before direct American involvement and was consistent with the facts as he saw them developing. Far from not learning the lessons of the First World War and ignoring the events up to that point in the current conflict, King had written a report that set out a coherent vision of the problems and the actions necessary to deal with them. He was aware of the situation and knew the correct course of action to follow.

KING AND THE EARLY WAR YEARS

As an able logistician, King quickly identified one of the main limiting factors on RN-RCN escort effectiveness—low tactical endurance. British misunderstanding of German submarine endurance led to the conclusion that only the immediate vicinity of the British Isles, the Western Approaches, and the Mediterranean were within the radius of action of U-boats.[21] The principal open-ocean threat was viewed as being small groups or single warships plus armed merchant cruisers. As there was no submarine threat in the western Atlantic, RCN escort operations in 1939 and 1940 were measures to bolster the ocean escort against surface raiders while the convoy was in the vicinity of Halifax.

When France fell in June 1940 the situation in the eastern Atlantic became significantly more complicated. The threat from mines, shore-based artillery, aircraft, and minor warships made the English Channel, North Sea, and Western Approaches to the British Isles extremely hazardous.[22] Most ports in these areas were closed to merchant traffic. The concentration of shipping into convoys provided the strongest possible escort but increased round-trip voyage times. Diversion around known danger areas also added transit time. The Ministry of War transport reported that return transatlantic voyage times increased from about 90 days before France fell to about 122 days afterward.[23] The average increase in round-trip time was 35.5 percent. The one-way reduction in carrying capacity associated with the implementation of convoying was, therefore, between 15 and 20 percent even before problems of cargo unloading and handling ashore and losses owing to enemy action or marine accident were taken into account. The weakness of British and Canadian escort forces compounded the problem of reduced volumetric carrying capacity of the merchant fleet by making the likelihood of serious losses a distinct probability.

Admiralty guidelines for the minimum number of escorts required for the close escort of a convoy against attack by aircraft, light surface craft, or submarines were the number of ships in the convoy divided by ten plus three warships. By this formula, an average convoy of forty ships required an escort group of seven warships. If the threat of attack by heavy enemy surface units existed, attachments of capital ships to the convoy in sufficient numbers to at least deter the threat, if not defeat it outright, were required. Convoys of greater than sixty ships were forbidden.[24] Large concentrations of ships were regarded as exceedingly tempting targets, unmanageable to maneuver, and too great a burden for port facilities to off-load efficiently. Experience soon showed that double the theoretical number of escorts was required to ensure that the perimeter of a forty-ship convoy was adequately screened against a single attacking submarine.[25]

British estimates of German submarine endurance continued to be wildly inaccurate as Allied close escort of convoy operations was extended westward to cover attacks by submarines as The Allies shifted farther away to get beyond the zone of coverage. Moreover, multiple U-boat attacks against convoys began in the mid-Atlantic by December 1940.[26] By prosecuting a widely dispersed antimercantile war, the Germans intended to dilute British escort forces by creating danger areas over vast portions of the world's oceans.[27] These German initiatives forced Allied escort forces into a reactive posture. Now, however, low escort endurance limited their ability to respond effectively.

In reaction to widening German submarine operations, in mid-April 1941 the Admiralty extended convoy escort to 35 degrees west. To accomplish the tasks arising from this decision, three new escort groups were formed, based in Iceland. Their task was to provide continued protection from the point where Western Approaches local escort forces broke away from a westbound convoy out to the new western limit of close escort. The consequence of this move was the dilution of each escort group to half of the ideal strength of twelve ships. The revised and reduced escort groups usually comprised a mix of six destroyers, sloops, corvettes, and armed trawlers.[28] The nonhomogenous nature of the escort groups reduced the effective limit of their operations to the range of the ships with the lowest endurance.

From this point onward, escort fuel shortages played a major role in the conduct of convoy operations. The practical endurance of most British escorts was inadequate for transatlantic convoy work. To accommodate for this shortcoming, and to shorten the distance traveled by escorts into and out of Iceland for fuel, convoy routes were shifted six hundred miles northward from the Great Circle path. Accommodation also necessitated the institution of a complicated series of meeting points where escort groups exchanged convoys and commenced a return trip. While these adjustments saved fuel, they also added several days of extra steaming to a convoy's total traveling time, reduced the effective carrying capacity of the cargo ships, and limited flexibility for evasive routing.[29] The combination of added distance and British escort tactics soon created an operational fuel shortage crisis that made convoys more vulnerable everywhere. This was the exact opposite of the intended effect of extending escort coverage.

A study dated 16 April 1941 by Adm. Sir Percy Noble, commander in chief of the Western Approaches, examined the ineffectiveness of the new convoy arrangement. Admiral Noble noted the weakening of all escort groups that had occurred by basing newly formed groups in Iceland. He found the northern route past Iceland had limited opportunities for diversion and lamented that the low endurance of British escorts prohibited defensive maneuvering. Noble preferred a southern route that gave more room for evasive convoy tracks but knew that close escort could be accomplished in these waters only by *telescoping* (a one-way transit at economical speed to meet an inbound convoy or to return from escorting an outbound one), which he acknowledged was uneconomical. His final assessment was a chilling premonition of impending slaughter:

> It seems reasonable to conclude, therefore, that the use of the Icelandic route, combined with the operation of escorts based in Iceland, will prove no solution to the problem with which we may at any moment be faced. Indeed, by narrowing the front for the U-boats to cover outside the limits of westerly escort from Iceland, a zone of much greater potential danger has been created than existed previously. We certainly cannot count on the enemy failing to take advantage of the situation.[30]

Admiral King maintained a detailed and continuous correspondence with Rear Adm. Arthur Bristol, commander of the Atlantic Support Force based at Argentia, Newfoundland, throughout 1941. By 15 May losses to intercepted convoys often approached 20 percent and sometimes reached 25 percent. Admiral Noble's warning stated bluntly that the current arrangement threatened all convoys with the prospect of interception. To these devastating losses must be added the significant reduction in carrying capacity of the merchant fleet imposed by the introduction of convoying. Independently routed ships were suffering an average of 6.9 percent losses (13.8 percent on round-trips) and had the advantage of proceeding at their best speed and over shorter routes in southern areas where weather was better.[31] King assessed the numbers of British and Canadian escorts available to be "wholly inadequate."[32] The situation was so bad that King came to believe that a weak and poorly organized escort force could result in losses higher than those suffered among independently routed trade. Only signals intelligence allowed the employment of evasive routing around known submarine concentrations. Noble's prediction of German adjustments to take advantage of concentrated shipping was proving accurate. Further changes to the convoy plan became an urgent necessity.

KING'S PLAN FOR CONVOY REORGANIZATION

Before the attack on Pearl Harbor, Admiral King, then commander in chief of the Atlantic Fleet, sent a memorandum to Admiral Pound. King had been engaged in an active correspondence with Admiral Bristol during November about the problems of the current convoy arrangements.[33] Most of Bristol's recommendations for changes appeared unaltered in King's proposal.

King differentiated between three principal convoy routes across the Atlantic: (1) the Iceland Route, (2) the Great Circle Route, and (3) the Azores Route. He repeated Noble's earlier reservations about the northern route in winter weather and the all-too-evident German success against convoys passing through the narrow routing gate south of Iceland. He proposed shifting transoceanic convoys south, either to the Great Circle Route or the Azores Route. The Great Circle proposal entailed a telescoped eight hundred–mile transit by British and Canadian short-leg escorts with inbound or outbound convoys to augment through protection provided by long-leg American destroyers. For the Azores Route, owing to problems of Portuguese neutrality, King proposed stationing American oilers outside territorial waters to refuel passing escorts.[34]

The reply from the Admiralty entailed some frank admissions about the very limited endurance of British convoy escorts. It cited the following tactical endurance figures: high-endurance destroyers—1,800 to 2,400 miles; low endurance destroyers—1,200 to 1,600 miles; and corvettes—2,250 to 3,000 miles. It explained that 75 percent of British destroyers were short legged. The British reply was also somewhat incredulous at the American claim of being able to refuel at sea during winter, even in the relatively benign environs of the Azores.

Admiral Pound turned down both of King's proposals, but his reply to the Admiralty staff analysis focused on the suggestion of refueling at sea. He asked, "Have they any special arrangements for oiling their destroyers at sea which make them think they could do this in Atlantic winter weather?"[35] The files do not indicate that a convincing reply was received. Despite this rejection, a new American convoy routing proposal followed closely behind the first.

On 25 December 1941 Admiral King, now commander in chief of the U.S. Fleet, initiated another reorganization proposal. He succinctly tied together the problems of severe weather, enemy action, lengthy indirect northern routing, low numbers of American coastal escorts, and the lack of forward maintenance facilities, all of which were weakening the escort forces.[36] His plan advocated adopting direct through convoys along the Great Circle Course, then over the north coast of Ireland. The existing complicated series of five escort forces would be collapsed to three: short-radius Canadian forces operating from Halifax, long-radius Canadian and British escorts operating from St. John's, and short-radius British escorts operating from Ireland. Iceland would be used only as an emergency fuelling station. Long-radius American destroyers would base at their homeports of Boston or Casco Bay and join their convoy in Halifax. Long-radius British and Canadian escorts would join from either Sydney or, more probably, Newfoundland, and form a composite reinforced escort group for the transit across the Atlantic. King's first proposal for British short-radius escorts to accompany convoys on a telescoped one-way trip was reduced from a point eight hundred to seven hundred miles from Londonderry, where the RN-RCN Canadian ocean escorts would be relieved by a British local escort force for the remainder of the trip. The calculations were carefully worked out to include a five hundred–mile southward leg at economical speed from Sydney or St. John's, 1,200 to 1,300 miles in company with the convoy performing full escort duties, followed by six hundred to seven hundred miles at economical speed to Londonderry. The process worked in reverse on westbound convoy routes. The total distance of 2,300 to 2,400 miles, half of it at economical speed, made the plan feasible for both British and Canadian high-endurance destroyers and corvettes, if the endurance figures provided by the first sea lord were to be believed.

The study was another masterful example of the USN's estimate process. The advantages included better sailing conditions during winter months on southern routes. These measures would indirectly increase the effective carrying capacity of the cargo fleet by reducing transit times. The plan eliminated the requirement for layovers in navigationally insecure bases and anchorages in Newfoundland and Iceland. Bypassing Iceland reduced significantly the problems of providing logistical support. Above all, more USN forces would be readily available in American waters if a submarine offensive suddenly developed there; King clearly acknowledged there was a possiblity that such offensives could occur.[37]

The disadvantages of the new convoy plan also were clearly stated. First and foremost, it was obvious that in this arrangement escort forces would be weaker in the western local areas. Also, by providing through escorts for convoys, USN forces would be exposed to attack in UK waters, where the threat was the highest. Moreover, some short-radius escorts would be employed uneconomically during their transit time apart from a convoy. An important logistical consideration was that the concentration of higher numbers of escorts in the United Kingdom would increase the amount of fuel required at RN home bases. Finally, USN and RN-RCN units would be operating in mixed escort units. All of these factors merited careful consideration. King concluded that the advantages outweighed the disadvantages.

Admiral King's proposal recognized all the logistical and engineering factors that had plagued transoceanic convoy operations to that point and that would soon become critical. There was a pointed absence of commentary on convoy size, although the proposal to the first sea lord to change escort of convoy operations did include extensive analysis as to how escort numbers and effectiveness could be maximized. Above all, King himself, a supposed Anglophobe, was suggesting the formulation of mixed escort groups, something to which he was reputedly strongly opposed. Despite the clarity of purpose and practicality of the plan, the British remained unconvinced.

The British Joint Staff Mission in Washington prepared a review of King's second plan. The Mission's report to the Admiralty included a revealing observation: "We have pointed out verbally that units to the eastward of MOMP, whether British, Canadian, U.S. or mixed, must necessarily come under British operational control."[38] The staff review noted that the American force would probably constitute at least two or three destroyers and that "[their] Senior Officer would probably be senior to C.O. [commanding officer] of British escorts [normally a lieutenant commander]."[39] They also maintained that it was not possible for British escorts to reach a point seven hundred miles to the west of Londonderry. This assertion was made despite the fact that the misnamed Mid-Ocean Meeting Point for northern convoys lay exactly on that seven hundred–mile arc, and the southern route guaranteed better weather. The director of trade division, despite concerns over the security of such standard routes, supported the plan and recommended to the Admiralty that it be adopted.[40] Unfortunately, the files are incomplete and do not record the Admiralty's final response. Once again, neither of King's plans was accepted. All of the conditions that he forecasted, however, soon came to fruition.

On 8 January 1942 Admiral Bristol wrote to Adm. Royal Ingersol, now commander in chief of the Atlantic Fleet. Bristol outlined his ideas on the number of escorts for each group, the composition of groups, overhaul routines, escort cycles, and the effect of weather on escort operations. Bristol then described his ace in the hole to solving the problems of small escort groups and inadequate maintenance: He proposed lengthening the sailing interval between convoys from six to seven days. Convoy size, which averaged only forty ships, would be increased to forty-eight ships. Escort groups could be reduced in number but increased in size. Additionally, each group would gain a week in alongside time over the present cycle to provide rest for their crews and to conduct maintenance.[41] The idea was advanced to Admiral Ingersol for consideration but does not seem to have gained support. This failure to pursue enlarged convoys was truly unfortunate, because Bristol's basic ideas included many of those recommended in March 1943 by the renowned British operations research scientist P. M. S. Blackett.[42] By this point, the enemy was about to take the initiative by launching Operation Drumbeat.

KING AND OPERATION DRUMBEAT

Admiral King had anticipated that the *Kriegsmarine* might choose to attack shipping along the U.S. eastern seaboard when he made his suggestions for convoy reorganization. Having seen the development of the threat to this point, King had a good understanding of the complexity of convoy operations and of both its limitations and its advantages.

The Allies had a good appreciation of the numerical strength of the German and Italian submarine fleets. Based on their assessment of enemy endurance capabilities at that time, only twelve surviving Type IX U-boats had the range to operate off the American coast.[43] The two problems that could conceivably be faced, therefore, were either (1) an all-out assault of limited duration or (2) sustained operations by a lesser number of submarines in several waves. In the first case, the threat would be transitory, which would not necessitate permanent convoy arrangements and the attendant reduction in cargo-carrying capacity. In the second case, the best the Germans would be able to sustain would be three or four submarines along the entire coastline, either concentrated in one area or dispersed.[44] With the advantage of signals intelligence of the sort enjoyed up until that point in the war, adequate warnings could be issued for avoidance purposes, and the limited forces available directed onto the location of the enemy submarines for offensive patrols. With good locating information and so few submarines to be dealt with, offensive sweeps offered the prospect of achieving meaningful results by destroying relatively few submarines.

Whereas the theoretical maximum number of long-range submarines available was twelve, other factors caused it to drop substantially. German operational commitments in the Mediterranean reduced the number of boats available to six. This cut the threat of an all-out attack in half and reduced the threat of a sustained multiwave campaign to only two boats. Such threat levels would hardly justify the introduction of a convoy system that could reduce the effective volumetric capacity of the merchant fleet by 35 percent. In the event, U-128 was forced out of the first wave of attackers because of mechanical defects, which reduced the enemy force to only five submarines.

Allied intelligence provided detailed insights into the strength and deployment pattern of the German plan. With six Type IX boats already operating off the approaches to the Strait of Gibraltar, a warning that five boats would arrive off the American coast on 13 January to operate between New York and Portland, Maine, seemed to indicate the *Kriegsmarine* was surging all of its available long-range submarines.[45] So far, the threat estimate was proving accurate. Unfortunately for King, the assumptions on which the estimate was based were about to be invalidated.

Admiral Doenitz did not believe that operations by the medium-range Type VII boats in the far western Atlantic were possible.[46] However, German submariners displayed exceptional tactical innovation and were able to extend their range by converting some freshwater tanks to fuel and by packing every possible internal space with water and provisions. By strictly conserving fuel, the medium-range submarines were able to operate off the American coast for a few days. This totally unforeseen tactical development allowed the Germans to develop a sustained five-wave attack plan by interspersing Type VIIs for the second and fourth waves between the Type IXs that made up the first and third waves. The fifth wave was a mix of the two types. The number of submarines on patrol at any one time never exceeded eight, which was, nevertheless, two boats in excess of the anticipated maximum strength of a single-wave surge operation.[47]

Another altogether unforeseen development further enhanced the effectiveness of the German submarines. The introduction of operational replenishment for submarines by the *Kriegsmarine* was a world's first in naval warfare. The requisitioned ex-Turkish submarine U-A was reequipped as a supply submarine and deployed from Lorient on 14 March. She refueled two outbound submarines in the fourth wave and one homeward bound boat in the third wave (all Type VIIs), each receiving about twenty-five tons of fuel. The first purpose-built Type XIV supply submarine, U-459, sailed from Kiel, Germany, on 29 March, taking up her station north of Bermuda on 18 April. She carried five hundred tons of reserve fuel plus spare provisions and four spare torpedoes. By 2 May the U-459 had expended all stores to twelve Type VII boats and two Type IX boats in the fourth and fifth waves. On average, each submarine received thirty-five tons of fuel. U-116, a converted Type XB minelayer, refueled four Type VIIs and two

Type IXs in the fifth wave between 26 and 29 May, with each boat receiving about thirty-seven tons of fuel. These fuel transfers were sufficient to enable the Type VIIs to operate in the Caribbean, where convoying had yet to be instituted.[48]

The net operational effect of at-sea replenishment made torpedo capacity, rather than fuel supply, the limiting factor for U-boat operations.[49] The tactical effect of this new methodology was to extend the length of a patrol by a Type VII boat by as much as four weeks.[50] Effectively, there was no longer a distinction to be made based on endurance between the types of German submarines.

The strength and the duration of the German campaign could have come only as a severe shock to Admiral King and his planners. The initial onslaught seemed to indicate that the Germans had gone for a surge attack with all available long-range submarines. However, when that attack showed signs of sustained effectiveness long past the point where the first submarines would have had to leave the operating area, it was clear that a reassessment was in order. Unfortunately for the USN, Operation Drumbeat took place at the same time the Germans replaced the old three-rotor model of the Enigma encryption machine with a four-rotor type. The resulting cipher defeated British code-breakers and caused an intelligence blackout that remained in effect until December 1942.[51] Without the previous advantage of knowing the enemy's whereabouts and movements, convoying looked to be the only option left to deal with the situation.

An additional intelligence failure made it even more difficult for Admiral King to establish the source of the German's unexpectedly strong submarine campaign. The British Admiralty did not detect German development of supply submarines, nor did their surveillance methods discern additional submarine deployments to the American operating area. Increased volumes of radio traffic in the vicinity of U-459's rendezvous area were attributed to a number of causes, one of which did postulate refueling operations, but the possibility of such an activity was not connected to the strength and persistence of the German offensive. It was only in July 1942, after a medium-range Type VII boat was sunk off Cape Hatteras by a patrol aircraft and subsequently positively identified as such, that the endurance estimates for these submarines was raised to make it the equivalent of a long-range submarine. On 20 August the survivors from the supply submarine U-464, which was sunk southeast of Iceland by a USN patrol aircraft, provided the Allies with the first confirmation that the Germans were conducting refueling of U-boats at sea.[52] Aerial reconnaissance photographs taken at Lorient on 24 August showed a new and very large type of submarine, which confirmed the reports from the survivors of U-464.⁵³ By this time, Operation Drumbeat had concluded and the war had moved on to another phase.

There were two reasons for King's reluctance to order convoying: (1) the priority of his operational tasks, and (2) the obvious weakness of the Canadian coastal convoy system. The priority of tasks for Atlantic Fleet destroyers was clear: first, provide screening escorts to the battle fleet; second, provide escorts to the troopship convoys; third, provide destroyers to sustain the five American escort groups being run by Task Force 24 (formerly the Atlantic Support Force); and fourth, support the escort forces of the Eastern Sea Frontier.⁵⁴ The coastal escort forces of the Eastern Sea Frontier commander, Rear Adm. Adolphus Andrews, comprised only small low-endurance vessels that were "incapable of going to sea and maintaining a patrol."⁵⁵ These were hardly the type of forces needed for establishing an effective convoy system. The Canadian coastal convoy system at that time was run on an informal, ad hoc basis, with no timetable or schedule. This would have been a complete anathema to the meticulous King. Worse, the Canadian convoys sailed with only one or two warships to protect them, which King knew would be ineffective against a determined attacker. Without more information about enemy intentions and more escorts with which to furnish the local commander, King had every reason to believe that convoying would not work.

The only exception to this dubious Canadian situation was the institution of tanker convoys to Aruba during July to September. Four convoys were run under heavy close escort. Routing was deliberately set far off the coastal zones and away from straits where U-boats were known to be active.⁵⁶ Although the institution of tanker convoying caused significant fuel shortages in eastern Canada, no tankers were lost to enemy action and the slow increase in tanker numbers eventually rectified the supply situation.

KING AND THE VERDICT OF HISTORY

It has been argued that, once appointed chief of naval operations by President Roosevelt on 12 March, Admiral King had all of the command and administrative authority required to radically rearrange the USN's destroyer forces to permit institution of an effective coastal escort force and implement a coastal convoy system. It is true that King took several important organizational steps during this period: one example was the designation in March of Capt. Wilder Baker to run an antisubmarine section responsible for matériel, supply, development, and training as part of King's headquarters in Washington. King was undoubtedly a stubborn man and could only be forced to change his mind by pressure from the highest officials. Protestations from Admiral Pound carried no weight with King, since the reorganization plans he had proffered earlier had been rebuffed for little logical reason. Moreover, the problems that the mid-ocean escort groups had faced earlier continued with no solution in sight. Only once, when Prime Minister Churchill appealed directly to President Roosevelt in March over the alarming rate of loss in valuable tankers, did a serious discussion about substantive change in the American system of operations take place.

King did not know that Admiral Doenitz's operating philosophy was to attack shipping wherever it was left unescorted as a means of forcing the institution of convoying, which would stretch limited escort forces to the breaking point. In this endeavor, Doenitz was remarkably successful. The limited number of destroyers available to satisfy all demands forced King to make a most difficult decision and stand firm despite the carnage. He had every reason to believe that the German offensive could not be sustained.

King also could not have known of the tactical measures being taken to extend the endurance of the *Kriegsmarine*'s submarine fleet. Undoubtedly, once the submarine offensive began on what was assumed to be a surge basis, King expected the attacks to cease once the submarines exhausted their supplies of fuel and torpedoes, whichever came first. At that point, an operational pause would occur while the Germans prepared for their next undertaking, which could not be guaranteed to be in the same operating area. This pause in the offensive would allow more time for Allied reinforcements from new construction to arrive, which would strengthen the local defenses in the event that the second surge did happen to take place off the U.S. eastern seaboard.

The German offensive continued unabated, which must have caused a hectic reappraisal of all available intelligence about the German submarine fleet and its composition. However, try as they might neither the American nor the British staffs could determine how all of these long-range submarines has suddenly come into the *Kriegsmarine*'s order of battle. It was only the confirmed sinking of a Type VII submarine off Cape Hatteras in July that indicated that yet another miscalculation had been made about the endurance capabilities of German submarines. The fact that Admiral Raeder and Admiral Doenitz had achieved this miracle mainly through the use of operational sustainment did not become evident until after the campaign had concluded.

It is clear, therefore, that Admiral King's reluctance to impose a convoy system was based on more than just his conviction that the potential losses to a weakly escorted convoy were worse than those that would be suffered by independently routed shipping. King waited until he was sure beyond any reasonable doubt that the German surge attack could be sustained and that no letup in their attack would develop. He ordered the institution of convoys off the eastern seaboard in April, by which time the fifth wave of Type VII and Type IX boats had arrived and the Germans had begun to shift the focus of their operations to the Caribbean Sea. It is likely that only pressure from the highest political office would have had any effect on King, while he studied the situation and looked for conclusive evidence to indicate exactly what kind of situation was confronting him.

When Admiral Pound suggested in mid-March that the USN remove two of its five escort groups from the Atlantic Support Force to reinforce the Eastern Sea Frontier, King refused because it was not consistent with his task priorities. In mid-April, when Pound visited Washington, it was agreed that the two American escort groups would be taken from the Support Force and reassigned to troop convoy escort duties (two others had already been reassigned to other duties by this time), while the RN would reinforce the Mid-Atlantic Escort Force with destroyers. Although this move was consistent with the priority of King's operational tasks, he was reluctant to do so because of the low endurance of British destroyers and the obvious weakness of all RN-RCN mid-ocean escort groups. Only the endorsements of Admiral Ingersol and Admiral Bristol convinced King to accept the recommendation.[57]

Eventually, many of the recommendations Admiral King made in his earlier reports were implemented: the transatlantic convoy routes were shifted southward, Iceland was no longer used as an escort support base, the eastern meeting point was set about five hundred miles from Northern Ireland (22 degrees west), and a process of telescoping was adopted so that RN local escort groups could come out directly and take over the convoy from the mid-ocean escort group.[58] Escorts began to refuel at sea from commercial tankers in June 1942, but the process did not come into widespread use until March 1943. All of these measures could have been implemented far earlier if the leadership of the American and British navies had been in the hands of more conciliatory officers, and if they had expended the necessary personal energy to foster a trusting relationship. With King and Pound in the top positions, this was clearly impossible.

King's actions were entirely consistent with the views he expressed in the interwar period during his tenure with the General Board. His testimonies show that he was better aware of escort capabilities than were most of the design authorities planning escorts for the RN. King's support for the 327-foot cutters proved prescient: they became the most effective antisubmarine escort vessels of the war, largely owing to their impressive endurance.[59]

The recommendations Admiral King made for improving the convoy system and the escort organization provided practical, workable solutions to operational and tactical problems. Ever the strategist, King's recommendations also would have improved the ability of the merchant fleet to build and sustain combat power in the European theater of operation. That his plans were rejected for reasons that seemed to relate to the seniority of USN escort group commanders over RN ones, only to have the majority of his recommendations implemented soon afterward in any event, provides some justification for King's reputation as an Anglophobe.

There are many things for which Admiral King cannot be faulted. He reacted sensibly by waiting to see whether the German submarine attack would culminate and whether it would reappear in the same area after an operational pause. Based on what was known, in addition to the weakness of the escort forces, this course of action was a reasonable alternative to creating a major convoy system that might not be required beyond the immediate event. King also cannot be faulted for hesitating to implement convoying while an intelligence blackout deprived him of the invaluable information that had facilitated all Allied convoy evasive routing up to that point of the war.

Finally, King cannot be faulted for failing to foresee the German institution of operational logistics measures for their U-boat fleet through a groundbreaking innovation: U-boat tankers. The multiplication effect of these ships, based on their impact on the total tonnage of cargo ships sunk during their existence, has been estimated at an additional 10 percent, or one tanker being the equivalent of four additional attack submarines.[60] The supply submarines enabled sustained operations by medium-range submarines in areas that they would not otherwise have been able to reach and deprived the enemy of an operational pause that would have given them time to recuperate, reevaluate, and reorganize. Such an advantage was of inestimable value to the Germans, but in this case (admittedly in combination with a number of tactical factors) it allowed two and a half additional waves of submarines to operate off the U.S. eastern seaboard, and facilitated a two-phase campaign. In combination, the total effective multiplication is more than 100 percent, especially since some of the long-range Type IX boats also were replenished.

The one thing for which Admiral King could be taken to task is not making some provision for the safety of vital tanker traffic and the essential cargoes they carried. With limited resources and a threat of unknown dimensions and persistence, it would seem logical by today's standards that a list of critical vulnerabilities be generated, among which should certainly have been tankers and oil supply. For some reason, it appears that King viewed all merchant traffic uniformly. Is it possible that King's prodigious naval knowledge did not extend to maritime economics and trade patterns? If so, a potential deficiency in the naval education system of his day may have existed, making it a systemic weakness in the U.S. naval staff system.

It is known with certainty that the German naval staff system analyzed the vulnerability of its potential opponents to trade warfare and that its professional literature contained a lively debate in the interwar years about the relevance and methodologies of this form of warfare to the future of the *Kriegsmarine*. Task instructions to U-boat commanders taking part in Operation Drumbeat specifically identified the importance of sinking tankers. King's staff paper on shipbuilding priorities seems to indicate that he understood the vulnerability of Japan to trade warfare and that he also knew considerable effort had to be expended if American and British trade was to be protected from a similar threat. However, he did not distinguish between the importance of different types of merchant ships as targets. It seems that the low priority attached to the protection of trade in local areas, combined with the low level of perceived threat in that area, caused King to discard the premise entirely without due consideration of discriminating factors.

The Canadian example of tanker convoying in the same western Atlantic and Caribbean late in the campaign should have provided Admiral King and his staff with a concrete example of the correct methodologies and positive results that they produced. With the number of tankers sunk constituting such a high proportion of the total losses and the German tendency to abandon an area when escort operations appeared, it is conceivable that institution of a few American tanker convoys and a concentration of the few effective escorts available for their protection may have been enough to produce several results. Tactically, the few submarines on station would have failed to sink their preferred targets; operationally, an effective convoy operation could have been instituted simply by running only a few convoys on a simple schedule with a limited controlling organization. Strategically, the western Atlantic could have been made safe for independently routed dry-cargo merchant shipping to move at its most effective pace to sustain the war effort and the economy.

There were many areas of the world where convoying was never instituted, despite sporadic attacks by the enemy on merchant traffic. In January 1943, as the volume of Allied merchant shipping increased dramatically to support operations in the Pacific, Admiral King raised concerns with the RCN over the apparent weakness of Canadian escort forces on the West Coast. The director of plans, Capt. Harry DeWolf, conducted a staff estimate to assess the threat and examine possible courses of action.[61] He determined that the maximum sustained threat the Imperial Japanese Navy could mount in such a remote area of operations would be four long-range submarines, approximately the same anticipated threat as in January 1942 off the East Coast. Not surprisingly,

DeWolf recommended that convoying not be instituted, that air and surface local patrols be mounted only in the focal areas near ports and straits, and that evasive routing and air patrols in more distant areas were enough to provide a "reasonable degree of protection."[62] It is difficult to condemn Admiral King for not instituting a convoying scheme when only a year later Captain DeWolf reached the same conclusion in the face of the almost identical degree of threat. The danger to shipping was perceived to be too slight to merit institution of a system that would reduce the carrying capacity of shipping by 35 percent and instigate a plethora of other logistical problems.

Until the *Kriegsmarine* demonstrated an actual capability to conduct more than nuisance raids in American coastal waters, King's response was consistent with the measures taken by other Allied commanders throughout the war: tolerate the losses, take the necessary measures to recover, minimize the likelihood of reoccurrence, and carry on. That the Germans could generate the capacity to sustain the intensity of operations they attained surprised everyone at the time. In the absence of intelligence, it was reasonable for commanders to adopt a wait-and-see posture, at least for a while. When King finally did react, the measures taken were consistent with his other operational commitments and the priorities established between them.

Far from being unexplainable, Admiral King's response to Operation Drumbeat was consistent, measured, and, ultimately, effective. The only question that remains is whether the Canadian example of protecting critically vulnerable tankers could have been implemented earlier. It is unlikely that the answer is yes. With the RCN firmly in the camp of the RN and the Canadians adhering strongly to British naval doctrinal practices, it is highly unlikely King would have heeded the message from the "upstart" Canadians.

NOTES

The following abbreviations are used in the notes:

DHH   Directorate of History and Heritage
NARA-CP   National Archives and Records Administration, College Park, MD

1. Samuel Eliot Morison, *The Two-Ocean War: A Short History of the United States Navy in the Second World War* (Boston: Little, Brown and Co., 1963), 34–35, 102–103.
2. W. A. B. Douglas, Roger Sarty, Michael Whitby, Robert H. Caldwell, William Johnston, and William G. P. Rawling, *No Higher Purpose: The Official Operational History of the Royal Canadian Navy in the Second World War, 1939–1943*, Vol. II, Pt. I. (St. Catharines, ON: Vanwell, 2002), 172.
3. Morison, *The Two-Ocean War*, 34.

4. Correlli Barnett, *Engage the Enemy More Closely: The Royal Navy in the Second World War* (London-Penguin, 1991), 50–51.
5. Eliot Cohen and John Gooch, *Military Misfortunes: The Anatomy of Failure in War* (New York: Free Press, 1990), 59–94.
6. John F. White, *U Boat Tankers, 1941–45, Submarine Suppliers to Atlantic Wolf Packs* (Annapolis, MD: Naval Institute Press, 1998), 41–42.
7. Douglas et al., *No Higher Purpose*, 397.
8. D. J. Payton-Smith, *Oil: A Study of War-time Policy and Administration* (London: HMSO, 1971), 283, 302, 403–406.
9. Samuel Elliot Morison, *History of United States Naval Operations in World War II*, Vol. X (Boston: Little, Brown & Co. 1947), 17.
10. Minutes of Meeting, "Destroyer Operations Abroad," 17 December 1917, RG 80, M1493, Reel 4, *Proceedings and Hearings of the General Board of the U.S. Navy, 1900–1950*, NARA-CP.
11. Minutes of Meeting, "Destroyer Design," 17 September 1918, RG 80, M1493, Reel 4, NARA-CP.
12. The report identified the need for twelve types of destroyers, which Craven narrowed down to three by merging them "without any compromises of consequence." Discussions among the board members questioned whether plans for a 5,000-ton cruiser constituted a fourth type of destroyer. Minutes of Meeting, "Types and Characteristics of Surface Torpedo Vessels," 23 April 1920, RG 80, M1493, Reel 5, NARA-CP.
13. Barnett, *Engage the Enemy More Closely*, 481.
14. Minutes of Meeting, "Characteristics of Gunboats," 17 June 1932, RG80, M1493, Reel 8, NARA-CP.
15. Francis McMurtrie, ed., *Jane's Fighting Ships* (London: Janes, 1940), 505. See also Randolph W. King, ed., *Naval Engineering and American Seapower* (Baltimore, MD: Nautical and Aviation Publishing Company, 1989), 185–186.
16. Interview Notes, "Escort Ships," 27 November 1950, Manuscript 37, *Manuscript Collection: Admiral Ernest J. King Papers*, Box 7, Folder 16, U. S. Naval War College Archives.
17. Minutes of Meeting, "Escort Vessels of About 900 Tons Displacement," 6 September 1940, RG 80, M1493, Reel 24, NARA-CP.
18. Minutes of Meeting, "Escort Vessels and Net Layers," 24 September 1940, RG 80, M1493, Reel 24, NARA-CP.
19. Minutes of Meeting, "Escort Vessels," 22 October 1940, RG 80, M1493, Reel 9, NARA-CP.
20. Memorandum, Commander in Chief Lant Fleet to Chairman, General Board, "Priorities in 2-Ocean Navy Building Program," 30 July 1941, author's collection. Copy available upon request.
21. Martin Doughty, *Merchant Shipping and War: A Study in Defence Planning in Twentieth-Century Britain* (London: Swift Printers, 1982), 50–51.
22. Catherine B. A. Behrens, *Merchant Shipping and the Demands of War* (London: HMSO and Longmans, Green and Co., 1955), 126.
23. Ibid., 109, n. 3.
24. John Winton, *Convoy: The Defence of Sea Trade, 1890–1990* (London: Michael Josseph, 1983), 239–240.
25. Douglas et al., *No Higher Purpose*, 181.
26. HX-90 was attacked by five U-boats on the night of 1–2 December and lost ten ships, including the armed merchant cruiser HMS *Forfar* (ex-CNSS [Canadian National Steam

Ship] *Lady Somers*). Morison, *History of United States Naval Operations in World War II*, I. 24. See also Felicity Hannington, *The Lady Boats: The Life and Times of Canada's West Indies Merchant Fleet* (Halifax, NS: Canadian Marine Transportation Centre, Dalhousie University, 1980), A7, 166–167.

27. Clay Blair, *Hitler's U-Boat War*, Vol. I. *The Hunters, 1939–1942* (New York: Random House, 1996), 39–40.
28. Douglas et al., *No Higher Purpose*, 180–181.
29. Ibid., 180, 182.
30. Memorandum, Commander in Chief Western Approaches to Director of Anti-Submarine Warfare, "Protection of North Atlantic Shipping," 16 April 1941, File ADM 199/935, DHH.
31. S. W. Roskill, *The War at Sea, 1939–1945*, Vol. I (London: HMSO, 1954), Table 13, 458.
32. Morison, *History of United States Naval Operations in World War II*, I, 65.
33. U. S. Navy, *Administrative History of the U.S. Atlantic Fleet in World War II*, Vol. II, *Commander Task Force Twenty-Four* (Washington, DC: Comander in Chief, U. S. Atlantic Fleet, 1946).
34. Memorandum, Commander in Chief U.S. Atlantic Fleet to First Sea Lord, "North Atlantic Convoy Routes," undated, File ADM 199/935, DHH.
35. Minute Sheet, First Sea Lord, untitled, dated 29 October 1941, File ADM 199/1208, DHH.
36. Memorandum, Commander in Chief U.S. Atlantic Fleet to Chief of Naval Operations, "Escort-of-Convoy Operations—Changes in Current Methods," 25 December 1941, File ADM 199/1208, DHH.
37. Paragraph 11 of the proposal, which enumerated the advantages, listed as the second point: "(2) Destroyers will be more readily available for use in Western Atlantic waters if submarine concentrations suddenly develop there." Memorandum, commander in chief U.S. Atlantic Fleet to chief of naval operations, "Escort-of-Convoy Operations—changes in current methods," 25 December 1941, File ADM 199/1208, DHH.
38. Message, B.A.D. Washington to Admiralty (copied to NSHQ [Naval Staff Headquarters] Ottawa [ON] and FONF [Flag Officer Newfoundland] St. John's), 1341, 4 January 1942, untitled, File ADM 199/1208, DHH.
39. Naval "Cypher X" cable from British Admiralty Delegation, Washington, to British Admiralty, London, copied to Naval Staff Headquarters, Ottawa, and Flag Officer Newfoundland, St. John's, 5 January 1942, File ADM 199/1208, DHH.
40. Minute Sheet, Director of Trade Division to Secretary of the Admiralty, 28 January 1942, File ADM 199/1208, DHH.
41. U. S. Navy, *Administrative History of Task Force Twenty-Four*, II, 108.
42. Marc Milner, *North Atlantic Run: The Royal Canadian Navy and the Battle for the Convoys* (Toronto, ON: University of Toronto Press, 1985), 181.
43. Eleven of the *Kriegsmarine's* original fleet of twenty-five Type IXA, B, and early C submarines had been lost to this point in the war, mostly through misemployment in coastal areas. H. T. Lenton, *German Warships of the Second World War* (London: MacDonald and Jane's, 1975), 147–154.
44. This estimate is based on the standard "Rule of Thirds" that suggests one third of the fleet will be in the operating area, another will be in transit either to or from the area, and the final third will be at the sustaining base preparing to deploy or recovering from recent operations.
45. Douglas et al., *No Higher Purpose*, 380.

46. Roskill, *The War at Sea*, I, 95.
47. White, *U Boat Tankers*, 42–43.
48. Ibid., 45–46.
49. Roskill, *The War at Sea*, I, 100.
50. U-boat.net website, "Operations—Drumbeat," http://uboat.net/ops/drumbeat.htm (accessed 31 July 2007).
51. Douglas et al., *No Higher Purpose*, 394, 401–402.
52. U-boat.net website, "U-464," http://uboat.net/boats/u464.htm (accessed 31 July 2007).
53. White, *U Boat Tankers*, 78–79.
54. Douglas et al., *No Higher Purpose*, 401–403.
55. Ibid., 397.
56. Robert C. Fisher, "We'll Get Our Own: Canada and the Oil Shipping Crisis of 1942," *The Northern Mariner* 3 (1993): 33–39.
57. Douglas et al., *No Higher Purpose*, 397.
58. Morison, *The Two-Ocean War*, 104.
59. *University of Indiana Website*, "Performance: The ships-that-wouldn't-die!" http://www.indianna.edu/~r317doc/327/performa.html, accessed 13 September 2007.
60. White, *U Boat Tankers*, 223.
61. Later, vice admiral and chief of Canadian Naval Staff.
62. W. A. B. Douglas, Roger Sarty, Michael Whitby, Robert H. Caldwell, William Johnston, and William G. P. Rawling, *A Blue Water Navy: The Official Operational History of the Royal Canadian Navy in the Second World War, 1943–1945.* Vol. II, Pt. 2 (St. Catharines, ON: Vanwell, 2007), 503.

PART III. CHINA

Cutting Dwarf Pirates Down to Size: Amphibious Warfare in Sixteenth-Century East Asia

Kenneth M. Swope

> Offense lies within defense and defense is part of offense. If you attack without defending, then you have no root, but if you defend without attacking, then you have no trunk.
> —*Hu Zongxian and Zheng Ruozeng*[1]

> In sea battle there is no special trick. Larger ships defeat smaller ships. Larger guns defeat smaller guns. The side that has more ships defeats the side that has fewer. The side that has more guns defeats the side that has less.
> —*Yu Dayu*[2]

INTRODUCTION AND OVERVIEW

Perhaps one of the more surprising aspects of East Asian military history for comparative scholars is the relative paucity of large-scale naval operations prior to the nineteenth century. In spite of the facts that China has a massive coast, Korea is a peninsula, and Japan comprises many islands, there have been few major naval clashes between the states, with the notable exceptions of the Mongol invasions of Japan in the thirteenth century and the Japanese invasions of the mainland in the 1590s.[3] This record was not owing to a lack of technology, for the Chinese in particular were at the forefront of world naval technology, at least until the early fourteenth century, as demonstrated by the great Ming naval expeditions that have received so much international attention recently as a result of the controversial work of Gavin Menzies.[4]

But while there was a general lack of regular naval warfare for reasons particular to the histories of each of the regions under consideration, East Asia was by no means immune to periodic waves of piracy. Known as *wokou* (倭寇), which translates as *Japanese bandit* or *dwarf bandit* (which in this essay will be rendered simply as *pirate*), in China, bands of sea raiders plagued the coasts of East Asia intermittently from the thirteenth through the nineteenth centuries, though the exact nature of the piracy often changed.[5] Robert Antony suggests that both large-scale and small-scale piracy ebbed and flowed in patterns connected to the regular rhythms of climate, trade, and fishing seasons.[6] Piracy also could be tied to larger political developments. In many cases, most notably in the mid- to late-Ming period (1368–1644), piracy resulted from bans on regular maritime trade or restrictions on tribute trade with China, which was the recognized means of international intercourse in the era under consideration here.[7]

In other cases, piracy swelled in response to domestic unrest in China, Japan, or both. For example, in the formative years of the Ming dynasty (1368–98), as the new rulers were still consolidating their control over the remnants of the Mongol empire in China and the Japanese were emerging from their own nearly sixty-year period of civil war, there were some forty-four occurrences of piracy along the Chinese coast.[8] As Ming China's and Chosŏn Korea's authority and control waxed, incidents of piracy steadily declined until the mid-sixteenth century, when piratical activity in East Asia reached its apex in the premodern era.[9] Although they are generally referred to as "Japanese pirates" in the primary sources, in fact these buccaneers included many Chinese, Koreans, Southeast Asians, and even some European and African adventurers. Chinese officials of the time were not oblivious of this fact, noting that only 30 percent of the *wokou* were actually Japanese, though admitting that Japanese generally provided the military leadership and muscle for their operations while locals assisted as guides and fences.[10]

This essay focuses on amphibious warfare in sixteenth-century East Asia, particularly on strategy and tactics, while also considering the developments that led to the end of widespread piracy in East Asia toward the end of the century. Most significantly, I will examine the tactical innovations pioneered by the famous Ming general Qi Jiguang (1528–88),[11] whose methods became the blueprint for antipirate defenses throughout East Asia. Finally, we will consider the social, economic, and political ramifications of piracy within the larger context of late sixteenth-century East Asia, including how the experiences of the Chinese and Koreans in the middle of the century shaped their tactical responses to the Japanese invasion of the Asian mainland at the end of the century.[12]

THE UPSURGE OF PIRACY IN THE MID-SIXTEENTH CENTURY

There are a number of reasons for the upsurge in piracy in the mid-sixteenth century. Traditional Chinese sources suggest that the Japanese were upset that they had been officially barred from engaging in lucrative tribute trade with the Ming empire. This barring occurred as a result of a series of incidents including a brawl and fire in the Chinese port city of Ningbo in 1523, followed by shady dealings between Japanese would-be traders and unscrupulous Chinese eunuch port intendants.[13] Apparently, some Chinese traders became indebted to foreigners and then encouraged the emperor to more strictly enforce trade bans that had theretofore been largely ignored. Emperor Jiajing (ruled 1522–66) decided to follow their advice, thereby prompting the outbreak of what Robert Antony calls merchant-piracy and unwittingly criminalizing large segments of the maritime population in the process.[14] Faced with destitution and starvation, many locals threw their lot in with the pirates, some of whom, former merchants themselves, fled China to make their bases in an unstable Japan.[15] Aided by local families who profited greatly from smuggling activities, by the early 1550s pirate leaders such as Wang Zhi, Xu Hai, Chen Dong, and Ma Ye led fleets of several hundred against the coast, sacking and plundering local towns and even major cities, and prompting the Ming government to initiate substantial new defense measures that began with the appointment of a touring superintendant for military affairs (*xunfu tidu junwu*) for Zhejiang and Fujian provinces.[16]

There were both concrete military and more nebulous sociopolitical reasons for the success of these pirates. First, Ming military strength was at an all-time low. In theory, garrisons (*wei*) had a prescribed strength of 5,600 and each battalion (*suo*) had 1,120 men in the ranks. By the early 1500s, however, many units around the empire operated at around 10 percent of the prescribed levels and even these numbers could sometimes be reduced by the proliferation of local defense posts that drained men away from the originally established defense posts.[17] Such units were often required for simple defensive operations alone and therefore could not really be deployed to other areas.[18] These manpower deficiencies were exacerbated by the extent of coastline that needed to be defended. Even though Ming vessels were generally larger and better equipped than those of the pirates, the government lacked both the boats and the naval commanders to adequately patrol China's long coastline, although forward-thinking officials such as Yu Dayu proposed creating a large fleet of three hundred boats to intercept and crush the pirates at sea.[19]

Moreover, the pirate bases were often located in Japan, Taiwan, or the Ryukyu Islands, and the Ming were in no position to mount large overseas campaigns to formally integrate these regions into the empire. There was also the issue of local guides and conspirators. Suppressing pirates also involved cutting off these legs of support in China proper.[20] Finally, the considerable wealth and accessibility of south China made it a very attractive target for the pirates. Fair winds made the trip from Japan easy and the presence of many navigable waterways and excellent anchorages rendered the region a haven for amphibious raiders.[21]

In terms of strategy, it appears that pirate leaders initially hoped to force a Ming court already beset by Mongol threats from the northwest to lift its strict commercial bans by applying military pressure. Pirate leaders such as Xu Hai and Wang Zhi alternately ravaged large parts of the coast and held negotiations with Ming officials. The Chinese government even authorized the dispatch of Ming negotiators to Japan's Gotō archipelago. These maneuvers proved effective. When the pirates were eventually outfoxed and annihilated by Supreme Commander Hu Zongxian and his associates, broader strategic goals and leadership seem to have evaporated, and piracy degenerated into ill-coordinated but still often-devastating raids.[22]

Pirate tactics involved landing on the coast in ships that carried around a hundred men each, sometimes fewer. They would then rendezvous with their local guides and contacts and sometimes impress hapless villagers into service. They would even burn ships that could not be easily moored, assuming that new vessels would come the following raiding season, usually the following spring; the pirates often wintered in south China. The coast and interior areas would be systematically looted, the raiders taking items such as silk cocoons in addition to more traditional valuables like coins. They sometimes even built their own ships in China for return voyages to their offshore bases and employed locals in support activities like silk manufacture, demonstrating their awareness of international trade markets and a business savvy that belies the simple designation of pirate or raider.[23]

Their military strength lay in excellent discipline and teamwork in small unit tactics. The Japanese leaders dazzled local conscripts with their acumen with the twin swords used by the samurai and squad leaders and gave commands using drums, whistles, and fans. Japanese blades were sharper and more flexible than their Chinese counterparts and a skilled swordsman in action could supposedly cover an area eighteen feet in diameter. They also hurled javelins, plied long spears or pikes, and used Japanese longbows for ranged warfare. A favored pirate tactic was to engage government forces, feign a retreat into a narrow valley and then lure the enemy into a crippling ambush. The raiders made adept use of spies, created diversions, deployed in depth, and used captives as human shields to confuse Ming forces. These weapons and tactics initially proved quite intimidating for the Chinese peasant recruits that faced these marauders.[24] Interestingly enough, however, the pirates made little use of firearms, perhaps because they were either too unreliable or too cumbersome, though these would play a major role in the Japanese invasion of Korea in the 1590s.[25] The Chinese, conversely, would integrate firearms into their antipirate tactics, particularly on their boats.

At first the Ming government treated these pirates much like domestic peasant rebels. They assumed that the invaders could be overawed and intimidated by fierce aboriginal troops recruited from China's rugged frontiers, such as the Miao of Hunan and Sichuan provinces or the much-feared Wolf Troops of Guizhou.[26] They also attempted to recruit noted martial artists and acrobatic warriors, believing that individual skill alone could prevail. But experienced military commanders such as Yu Dayu and Qi Jiguang eventually came to the realization that discipline and teamwork rather than mere skill were the keys to pirate success. Qi realized that by standardizing training methods and weaponry and utilizing both in such a way that his troops would be comfortable he could beat the invaders at their own game.

THE TACTICS OF GENERAL QI JIGUANG

Qi based his approach on the use of small-group infantry tactics at first, later adapting these to both naval warfare and fighting on the northern steppe. He wrote two training manuals—*Jixiao xinshu* (*A New Manual for Training*), and *Lianbing shiji* (*A Veritable Record for Training Troops*)—in the 1560s that became the basis for military organization throughout the remainder of the Ming and beyond.[27] These manuals were later adopted by the Koreans in the 1590s, serving as the basis for Korea's military reorganization during the Imjin War, 1592–98.[28] In them Qi presents an interesting mix of the pragmatic and the mystical, including illustrations of weapons, battle formations, drilling forms, flags, banners, ships, and other equipment, while also explaining things in terms of traditional Chinese concepts such as yin and yang.[29]

Infantry squads of twelve men formed the root of his units. These units included four soldiers with shields in the front of the unit, followed by a pair carrying bamboo trees complete with branches to act as a protective screen for four lancers. The lances averaged about a dozen feet in length but could be longer. Behind the lancers were two rearguard men that carried trident-like weapons, which also could be rigged to fire arrows with small gunpowder charges. A squad leader, or corporal, and a porter completed the unit.[30]

Called the mandarin duck formation, this type of unit emphasized both offense and defense and placed a premium on teamwork. Because the lead shield-man on the right carried a larger shield, he was expected to dig in and hold the squad's advance position. The man on the left was to hurl javelins and lure the enemy into the open. The bamboo carriers were to pin the pirates down, allowing the lancers to attack more easily. Those in the rear were to defend the flanks and offer the potential of more striking power.[31] Mimicking their foes, squads were deployed in layers to create deception and enhance mobility.[32] Training was considered essential, as Qi believed that most men quailed in actual combat and that the best one could hope for was that soldiers would fight at perhaps 50 percent of their ability.[33] So he emphasized drills and repetition, devoting chapters of his manuals to training one's eyes and ears, stressing instantaneous reactions to audio and visual signals and so forth.[34] As Qi observed, "Training makes maneuvers easier and steels troops in the face of the enemy."[35] He also stressed, not unlike Miyamoto Musashi (1584–1643) in Japan,[36] that soldiers should train in a wide variety of weapons including bows, crossbows, firearms, polearms, spears, and clubs, recognizing that different situations called for different weapons.[37]

Iron discipline was also a hallmark of Qi's methods. Punishments and rewards were strict and were shared by the squad. Those who deserted in combat had their feet severed. Lesser infractions were typically punished by beatings with bamboo staves.[38] Commanders were responsible for their subordinates. Likewise, rewards were shared by the squad, including the standard reward of thirty ounces of silver per enemy head delivered after combat.[39] Such rewards could easily surpass a soldier's annual salary and constituted an important incentive for getting soldiers to join the ranks, though it admittedly sometimes led to abuses: soldiers might kill innocent villagers and attempt to present their heads as evidence of combat merit.

In terms of recruits, Qi Jiguang favored local peasant fighters rather than the aforementioned fierce aboriginals or specialists recruited from distant locales.[40] This was because Qi believed that locals were more apt to defend their home districts with vigor and that peasants took direction better than city folk. Those with bright eyes and clean looks were deemed most unsuitable for recruitment because these traits supposedly indicated craftiness and untrustworthiness.[41] In addition to believing that local recruits were more reliable, Qi stressed that they were cheaper to raise and maintain than professional mercenaries brought in from the frontier.[42] Indeed, Qi's tactical instructions reflect his preference for such recruits, particularly for land engagements, as evidenced by his observation that polearms were better than guns for such units because the latter were unreliable and unfamiliar to many rural recruits.[43]

Qi, in contravention of standard Ming practice, also forcefully advocated keeping commanders and troops together, rather than rotating commanders around the empire, recognizing that the longer commanders and their men worked together the more trusting they became of one another and the more effective they became on the battlefield. Qi, for example, developed such a good rapport with his men that they would drill for hours on end, even in the pouring rain.[44] Traditionally, Chinese empires had discouraged such arrangements on the grounds that they often led to the creation of challengers to the throne. But because Qi's methods were so successful and because he had powerful friends and patrons at the highest levels of government, he was allowed to take some of his men north with him in the late 1560s after the pirate threat was eradicated. This became somewhat standard practice, albeit with mixed results, through the rest of the Ming period, with commanders typically leading several hundred to a few thousand house stalwarts (*jia ding*) into battle all over the empire. Although they differed in some respects from the peasant youths favored by Qi, on the broader level it should also be noted in passing that these developments were related to the general commercialization of late Ming society that resulted in the creation of a more professionalized mercenary force out of the original hereditary military system of the Ming.[45]

Qi did not, however, reject the use of firearms entirely. In fact he strongly advocated their use on boats and in defensive positions on walls and in conjunction with war carts on the steppe against the Mongols. He particularly recommended the Portuguese gun (*folangji*) for naval warfare.[46] On Fujianese war junks Qi used five units of troops, with eleven men per unit: ten soldiers and one officer. Two of these units were arquebusiers. Two other units each manned the *folangji* cannon and used flamethrowers and primitive rockets. The last unit used other types of firearms.[47]

Qi's military reforms paid immediate dividends. From their inception in 1559 through the 1560s his forces enjoyed an unbroken string of victories over the pirates, smashing them in land engagements and even occasionally chasing them out to sea and wiping out their bases there. Contemporaries recognized that Qi's training methods were paramount in effecting this rapid reversal of Ming fortunes on the battlefield.[48] Throughout these engagements, Qi demonstrated an ability to see the big picture, and was willing to sustain heavy casualties in the pursuit of his objectives. Time and again the pirates were beaten, even when they had superior numbers; Ming forces captured weapons, boats, and provisions. The Ming state also adopted more proactive local defense measures, enlisting peasants, fishermen, traders, and even Buddhist monks in neighborhood watches and other activities.[49] Thus to some extent the very local interests that formerly facilitated piracy came to be turned to its eradication by dedicated officials. This resulted in a state of affairs where Zhejiang troops, formerly lightly regarded by the invaders, came to be "dreaded as if they were tigers" by the Japanese.[50] Ming vigilance and effectiveness continued for decades thereafter. Even as late as 1588 we read of a massive fleet of pirates being sunk off the coast of Zhejiang, with some 1,600 losing their lives in their rout at the hands of the Ming.[51]

The success of the antipirate measures introduced by Qi Jiguang and his contemporaries is attested to by the fact that in 1567, after more than a century of officially imposed isolation from maritime activities, the Ming state lifted the ban on overseas trade. This action is evidence that government authorities realized that the livelihood of coastal subjects was intimately tied to the sea and that if the people could be provided for, there would be less incentive for them to engage in piracy or to collaborate with pirates, an observation made by the compilers of the *Chouhai tubian* a few years before.[52] Additionally, one could argue that the Ming state was in fact seeking only to derive financial benefit from the vast new stores of wealth flowing into Asia from the Americas, particularly given that the Ming was in the process of shifting its taxation system to one based solely on cash.[53]

Notwithstanding these explanations, I would suggest that the lifting of the ban on maritime trade can also be viewed as a proclamation by the Ming court that pirate troubles of the preceding decades were over once and for all, and that the imperial state was now both willing and able to defend its maritime frontiers and interests. As noted above, even though piracy had been the bane of the Ming state for much of the sixteenth century, the realization that illicit trade could be curtailed by relaxing restrictions on licit trade, combined with a commitment to devising new antipirate strategies and bolstering coastal readiness paid serious dividends for the Ming, both literally and figuratively.[54] So in fact, when evaluated together, these measures signal a new resolve and adaptability on the part of an empire that just two decades before had appeared to be in serious trouble on a variety of fronts. The Chinese also increasingly realized where their military advantages lay. As a contemporary of Qi Jiguang, Huang Yuangong, remarked, "Our troops stand tall in naval warfare but are deficient in land warfare, whereas the Japanese excel in land warfare. Therefore we should intercept them at sea."[55] Huang recommended a system of coastal watchtowers and boats forming an interlocked defense, emphasizing the need for deploying adequate numbers of cannon on land and at sea.[56] One proposal even called for using the multioared centipede boats to hug the shallows in conjunction with runners on land to coordinate amphibious counterpirate measures.[57]

The movement toward greater military efficacy along all of China's frontiers was championed by the famous late Ming Grand Secretary Zhang Juzheng (1525–82) and continued by his protégé, Emperor Wanli (ruled 1573–1620).[58] Zhang supported Qi Jiguang throughout his career and was instrumental in bringing the general to the north. Though Qi later fell out of favor with the emperor because of his close association with the posthumously disgraced Zhang Juzheng, his training methods remained popular and soldiers who served with or under him were in high demand throughout the empire.[59] His son served in Korea in the 1590s, and many of the Ming commanders in that war had served alongside Qi.

Ming resolve would come to be seriously tested in the 1590s when Toyotomi Hideyoshi, unifier of Japan (and queller of piracy there), launched a massive invasion of Korea, with China as his primary objective. The assault on Korea touched off fears of Japanese invasion up and down the coast of China. Central and local officials alike made elaborate plans for the further bolstering of coastal defenses, many of which were obviously modeled after suggestions put forth in the 1560s. Contemporary accounts, including those left by Jesuit writers, are full of references to the paranoia and suspicion of foreigners engendered by these events.[60] In the rest of this essay we shall look at some of those plans and examine how they reflect lessons learned in amphibious warfare.[61] I will also consider these measures in light of the military revival then being experienced by the Ming state and tie them into the overall strategic goals of Emperor Wanli, who sought to reestablish the primacy of the Ming empire in East Asia against the upstart Hideyoshi.[62]

THE MING RESPONSE TO THE JAPANESE INVASION OF KOREA, 1592–98

The Chinese court first became aware of a possible Japanese invasion of the Asian mainland in late 1591.[63] Emperor Wanli was quick to respond to this news and issued general orders for the reinforcement of existing coastal defenses and the possible diversion of additional funds from government coffers for meeting this potential threat.[64] It is unclear exactly how far these measures went. Although the surviving Ming sources are very detailed with respect to proposals for bolstering coastal defenses, they are far less useful in determining the extent to which said proposals were adopted, though it seems that the use of firearms had remained important and most likely even proliferated. According to one Western observer, Ming cities were "walled about with stone walles and have ditches of water round about them for their securitie; they use no fortresse nor castles but only upon every gate of the towne they have strong towers wherein they place their ordnance for the defence of ye towne. They use all kinds of armes as calivers etc."[65] Despite this observation, the fact that commands were reiterated and further proposals put forth the following year when the anticipated Japanese invasion became a reality suggests that many of the early measures were not implemented. The fact that the Koreans, for various reasons, were loath to report all that they knew to the Ming court no doubt contributed to the general Ming laxity in responding to the court's initial directives.

In any case, when concrete news of an all-out Japanese invasion of the Korean peninsula reached Ming ears in the spring of 1592, the court acted quickly to gird itself for a possible invasion. The ministry of war immediately put Liaodong, Shandong, and all other coastal provinces on alert and ordered them to step up training and to repair existing defenses.[66] The Ming supreme commander of Jiliao asked that another commander be transferred to Tianjin, which guarded access to Beijing from the sea, so that their forces could be combined.[67] In the sixth month of 1592 requests were made for the shipment of sixty to seventy thousand *piculs* of grain to Tianjin to support the additional troops there.[68] Although an initial request for the dispatch of a high-ranking military censor from the capital to inspect local defenses in Shandong was turned down, local touring censors were dispatched to coastal areas to "soothe the hearts of the people."[69]

Moreover, the official who had originally reported on the Japanese situation was promoted and the emperor authorized the recruitment of local mercenaries and sending of funds from the Court of the Imperial Stud, which was an important branch of the Ministry of War charged with supplying funds for special military expeditions. Additionally, a request by the regional inspector of Shandong for forty thousand Chinese ounces (*taels*; each *tael* is equivalent to 1.327 ounces) for troop maintenance and defense upgrades was approved by the Ministry of Revenue.[70] Finally, although when the Japanese invaded the court was preoccupied with crushing a troop mutiny in the northwest border city of Ningxia, as soon as they realized the seriousness of the threat the emperor and his advisers began appointing some of the Ming empire's most prominent civil and military officials to key posts to deal with the Japanese.[71] For example, Chen Lin (unknown–1607), a noted firearms expert and a military officer with considerable experience battling pirates, was placed in charge of training the firearms divisions that were to be sent to Korea. He was subsequently promoted to the post of vice commander of the naval defenses of Jiliao, Baoding, and Shandong.[72] Chen would later serve with distinction alongside Korea's famed admiral, Yi Sunsin (1545–98).

We will now turn to some more specific directives and memorials pertaining to the plans for bolstering coastal defenses against the Japanese. These documents are taken from Song Yingchang's impressive collection of primary materials, the *Jinglue fuguo yaobian*, which can be translated as "Important Documents from the Military Commissioner's Restoration of the Country." Song Yingchang (1536–1606) was appointed military commissioner for Korean Affairs (*jinglue*) in late summer of 1592 by Emperor Wanli.[73] This compilation encompasses hundreds of official letters, imperial commands, directives to colleagues and subordinates, battle reports, censorial reports, and official communications between the Chinese, Japanese, and Koreans. The work's detail is invaluable in providing a picture of how central and local officials cooperated in defense matters during a time of national crisis.[74]

For example, a memorial on coastal defense, most notably the repair of walls and towers, begins with a discussion of Hideyoshi's overweening ambitions and the course of the first months of the war in Korea. Given the course of events to that point (the Korean king had already fled toward the Chinese border) and the strategic implications should the Japanese control the sea-lanes, Censor Peng Haogu of Shanxi, echoing the sentiments of Yu Dayu and Huang Yuangong decades earlier, noted that the best course of action was to stop the Japanese at sea before they reached China. Defending the coasts was second best, and waiting for them to disembark to fight them on land was equivalent to no plan at all.[75] Another memorialist from the Ministry of War warned that the Japanese were after the lucrative southeast coast of China and that if Korea fell China would be forced to spread its military forces thin. But simply recruiting mercenaries and bravos and deploying them along the coast would not be sufficient: many officials were unversed in warfare and, more important, would not know their own troops or their abilities.[76] Concerns such as these prompted some to stress defensive tactics.[77]

A recurring theme in the memorials is the desire to avoid the calamities of the mid-sixteenth century, and many writers recall the exploits of Hu Zongxian and Qi Jiguang in particular. Hideyoshi himself had used this historical example to embolden his men prior to their mobilization, and Ming officials frequently evoked the specter of the Japanese pirate to argue for strengthening the defenses of the southeast coast in particular. Some apparently feared that the Japanese might land in Fujian and cut their way north through the soft underbelly of China all the way to Beijing, even as the Chinese greatly strengthened their northern defenses to counter a push from Korea. In fact, some Japanese sources indicate that this very route had been proposed to Hideyoshi, who apparently rejected it on the grounds that supply lines would be too long. Yet still other officials invoked the successes of Qi Jiguang in arguing that southern Chinese troops were particularly adept at fighting the Japanese. Southern infantry units' use of large shields and hard, inflexible cudgels were supposedly quite effective against Japanese swords.[78] Consequently, southern troops would constitute an ever-increasing percentage of the Chinese forces in Korea proper as the war dragged on.[79]

As the military situation in Korea deteriorated, the Koreans dispatched a series of officials to the Ming, begging them for assistance and providing information on the military capabilities of the Japanese. The Japanese were said to be fearless and particularly adept in musketry, and—oddly enough—naval warfare, even though as of this early point there had been no purely naval clashes between the Japanese and the Koreans. This last point is also interesting in light of Ming estimations to the contrary and the fact that as the war progressed it became increasingly obvious that the area in which the Japanese were most clearly outclassed was naval warfare. For their part, Chinese officials bore a healthy respect for Japanese swordsmanship and musketry, as well as for their cavalry skills. In any case, being unable to devote their full attention to Korea until the mutiny in Ningxia was suppressed, the Ming urged the Koreans to strengthen their resolve and at the very least keep the Japanese from advancing across the Yalu on land or menacing Tianjin from the sea.[80]

A token Ming force was dispatched to attack Pyongyang in late summer 1592. Although it met with crushing defeat, it sent the necessary message to the Japanese. Shortly thereafter, in the ninth month of 1592, the Touring Pacification Commissioner of Zhejiang province, Chang Jujing, memorialized that some 82 boats, 1,500 troops, 3,600 assorted firearms and other weapons, 6,000 *catties* (*jin*) of incendiaries, and 8,200 Chinese ounces (*taels*, or *liang*) of cash and supplies were on the way north. Later that month, the first reports of Korea's naval victories over the Japanese reached the Ming, but these reports did not dissuade the Chinese from continuing their own defensive preparations.[81]

Military Storehouse Commissioner Liu Huangshang, who was in charge of coordinating defensive efforts along the northeast coast, put forth the following proposal in the autumn of 1592. Watchtowers would be erected every mile (three *li*; a *li* is about one-third of a mile) along the seacoast to guard against Japanese incursions. In the event that an enemy was spotted, smoke signals were to be used to communicate between towers. As most of these local towers were to be constructed of wood, local communities could assume the modest costs.[82] Each would have a platform capable of holding twenty men on top. Additionally, ten volunteers were to be recruited from the localities and put on regular patrol duty. Two thundering cannon (*hong lei pao*) were to be deployed per *li*, each with a company of men to guard and use it. Six men per squad of fifty were given cannon responsibilities. Others were tasked with maintaining equipment, signal fires, and the like. Firearms training and distribution were seen as critical. Ideally, as much as 50 percent of the defense forces were to be equipped with guns.[83] Attention was also paid to the placement of guns. Stoneworks were to be erected for more effective use of the cannon.[84] And while it was recognized that heavier firearms were not very mobile, they were more effective when used from elevated positions.

Another memorial on coastal defense stipulated that every circuit (roughly equivalent to a province) was to construct 1,670 large cannon, 60 military carts, 10,000 one-character small cannon (*yi zi xiao pao*), 333 small reliable cannon (*xiao xin pao*), 12,000 crossbows, 333 felt and 333 bamboo shields, 60,000 crossbow bolts, and an undetermined number of bullets for emergency use.[85] All these items were to be made to specific standards using specific materials. For example, elm, willow, and locust tree timber could be used for carts. The memorial even provides suggested plank widths and notes that all such carts should be iron plated, attesting to the wealth and sophistication of China at the time.[86] The same memorial gives instructions on the proper formula for gunpowder. The memorialist concludes with the observation that if all his suggestions are followed the Japanese will not dare invade because they will be cowed by China's superior coastal defenses.

Overall, the memorials contain an interesting mixture of pragmatic strategy and sound advice mixed with somewhat wishful thinking. For example, although one official reasoned that the Japanese would have a difficult time landing on northeast China's rocky coasts, China should still be sure to make extensive use of its superior firearms, such as the Grand General Cannon (*da jiangjun pao*), the Crouching Tiger (*hucun pao*), the Caitiff Exterminator (*mie lu pao*), and the Portuguese gun (*folangji*).[87] But because current defenses were not sufficient, production needed to be stepped up. This same official also called for hiring more mercenaries and deploying more mobile corps commanders in Liaodong province, north of the anticipated sea invasion route through Tianjin. These units could then cut off the tail of any Japanese armies that managed to penetrate China's outer defenses. However, while some officials championed the recruitment of stalwart mercenaries, people's militia being insufficient for the task of resisting the Japanese, others feared bringing in outsiders and believed that locals tended to be superior because they really had something to fight for.[88]

As noted above, Tianjin was considered the linchpin in China's coastal defenses because of its proximity to the capital. Therefore, the needs of officials in charge of defense matters in this region were given priority. Yang Hao, who would later earn notoriety for his mishandling of the siege of Ulsan in Korea in 1597–98, pledged to repair northeastern coastal defenses by early 1593 but emphasized the need for more horses to facilitate faster communications between defense locales.[89] Yang requested a total of two thousand additional mounts: six hundred were to be stationed in Jizhen and Tianjin, respectively, and another eight hundred were to be allocated between mobile corps commanders (one hundred for each of eight commanders) and commandants (one hundred for each of four commandants).[90] Yang also recommended fortifying offshore islands and arming peasant stalwarts with long spears. Again, the key, according to Yang, was for the Chinese to create an interlocking defense network that would thereby present a much more formidable defense than had been the case during the pirate troubles of the mid-sixteenth century.

Meanwhile, in his dispatches to Minister of War Shi Xing, Song Yingchang continued to express concerns that matters were not proceeding fast enough. Although mercenaries were arriving from all over the empire, Song complained that repair of existing defenses was going too slowly, in part because the various ministries concerned were slow to disperse funds.[91] New weapons still had not been manufactured and old ones seemed to be missing. Song noted that, according to existing regulations, all units were supposed to have firearms, gunpowder, and other advanced technology. "Yet why are supplies so low now?" he asked.[92]

The construction of boats—for both transportation and military purposes—was also emphasized. A letter from Song to Shi Xing dated 16 December concerned a request for boats to be assembled at Lushun, across the Yellow Sea from Korea and the surrounding islands.[93] All the islands within a five hundred–*li* radius north and south of Tianjin and Dagu were to erect defenses and keep watches. Likewise, the islands were to have extra boats for communication purposes. The commoners of the islands were supposed to till their fields during the day and keep watch by night. Each house was also to be furnished with a drum so that anyone in any village could call his compatriots to arms.[94] Each locale was entrusted with the task of selecting the most upright, brave, and trustworthy to act as squad commanders and lead the assembled stalwarts of the region.[95] As of late 1592, one estimate projected an assemblage of seven thousand marines and two hundred boats from various locales, and 950 sailors and eighty flat-bottomed (*shahu chuan*) boats from the Nanjing area.[96]

Some 1,535 troops were to be posted on various islands and furnished with small cannon.[97] Each such station was to possess several dozen torches to cast great light at night. They reasoned, "Once the Japanese realize how well-prepared we are, they won't dare to advance."[98] At the end of this report, Song Yingchang reiterated the importance of defending Tianjin and its environs and argued that successful naval preparations were essential to the positive and speedy resolution of the eastern expedition.

In another memorial on naval warfare dating from mid-December 1592, Song stressed that because the Japanese were not particularly adept at naval warfare, the Chinese should focus on building large warships and smashing the enemy at sea. Boats from Fujian were deemed superior, followed by pine boats (*cang chuan*) and then sand boats (*sha chuan*), which were flat-bottomed vessels. The ministry of war was instructed to bring all these kinds of vessels, as well as various other types, north at once. If they lacked sufficient ships, the ministry of works was to construct them in due haste.[99] Twenty *sha chuan* were to come from Zhejiang and another twenty from Nanzhili.[100] Various other locales were to furnish fifty to sixty more ordinary boats for conversion into war vessels. Song also called for Tianjin and other northern areas to supply one hundred salt transportation and fishing boats for government use.[101] Song noted that both these kinds of vessels and their crews could go about their normal business most days but serve as spy ships when needed. Between them Zhejiang and Nanzhili could supply one hundred more mid-sized galleys (*hu chuan*), while the ministry of works was asked to open the vaults to five- and eight-oared galleys (*ba la hu chuan*) to defend key points around Jizhen in the north.[102]

In addition to the boats already mentioned, the Ming possessed a wide variety of other vessels, many of which are described and depicted in the early seventeenth-century military manual, the *Wubei zhi*, compiled by Mao Yuanyi.[103] For example, the *you ting* was a small, fast, oared boat, useful in chasing pirates. The *meng chong* was a large warboat, heavily protected and equipped with powerful crossbows, while the *lou chuan* was a three-decked affair, similar in some ways to contemporary Japanese ships, but equipped with crossbows, cannon, and catapults.[104] The *shu jian* was another large warboat, and the *hai gu*, or sea partridge, was a large boat with a tall tail, resembling that of its namesake. Meanwhile, the *ying chuan*, or falcon boat, was a well-armed and reinforced vessel strikingly similar to Korea's turtle boats.[105] The smaller *gang suo chuan* often had two to three musketeers stationed in the front of the vessel. The centipede boat with many oars (hence its name) was a southern ship to which the Chinese added Portuguese cannon. It was designed for patrolling operations in shallows and rivers. The fancy red dragon boat supposedly fired rockets out of its mouth, again bringing to mind Korea's *kobokson*.[106]

As noted above, southern boats were considered the best. Guangdong vessels were supposedly better warships, but those from Fujian tended to be faster. The aforementioned oared galleys were generally manufactured in Zhejiang.[107] These southern boats were sturdily constructed of reinforced pine and ironwood and were equipped with cannon and small firearms, making them very effective in combat. Mao Yuanyi claims "there was nothing which could match them on the seas and the Japanese did not dare to take them on."[108] These boats also frequently carried Portuguese *folangji,* attesting to the oft-overlooked Ming willingness to adopt superior foreign military technologies when presented with the opportunity. Ironwood (*tie li mu*) was prized as a construction material and allowed Chinese captains to charge fearlessly into battle against ships made of more fragile woods. The larger Fujianese ships could carry upward of one hundred men; equipped with bows, catapults, and cannon, they were difficult for smaller boats to engage, though Qi Jiguang found them of limited use against smaller, faster craft, particularly in tight spots.[109]

Turning to the Korean side, the genius of the Korean turtleboat was that it was well-armed and well-protected and also very maneuverable. Yi Sunsin's nephew, Yi Pun, describes the turtle boat as follows:

> On its upper deck were driven iron spikes to pierce the feet of any enemy fighters jumping on it. The only opening was a narrow passage in the shape of a cross on the surface for its own crew to traverse freely. At the bow was a Dragon-head in whose mouth were the muzzles of guns and another gun was in the stern. There were six gun ports each, port and starboard, on the lower decks. Since it was built in the shape of a big sea-turtle, it was called *Kobokson* (Turtle ship). When engaging the enemy wooden vessels in a battle, the upper deck was covered with straw mats to conceal the spikes. It rode the waves swiftly in all winds and its cannon balls and fire arrows sent destruction to the enemy targets as it darted at the front, leading our fleet to victory in all battles.[110]

Making its appearance a few weeks after the beginning of the war in Korea, the turtle boat and its Chinese counterparts clearly demonstrate that the Chinese and Koreans learned from their mid-century encounters with

Japanese pirates. Both countries place a premium on superior firepower and maneuverability and emphasized the need to defeat the Japanese at a distance, fearing their swords and polearms at close quarters. Knowing that the Japanese favored high-decked vessels and liked to close and grapple, the allies realized that firepower could tilt the balance heavily in their favor. The addition of spikes to the top of the Korean turtle boats is further evidence of the countermeasures taken to negate perceived Japanese advantages. Throughout the war the prescience of these decisions to improve their naval capabilities would be manifested for the allies. They were eventually able to effectively cut Japanese supply lines around the Korean peninsula while maintaining their own naval supply lines from China to Korea. They also managed to keep the Chinese coast and the Yellow Sea relatively free from Japanese depredations even though the number of turtle boats probably never exceeded a dozen.

Nonetheless, Song Yingchang had reservations about having too many large ships, despite their general superiority to Japanese boats, because they were supposedly difficult to manage in high winds and rough seas.[111] Therefore, in his request to the Ministry of Works, Song asked for only fifteen large Fujianese vessels and eighty smaller pine boats, or mid-sized ships (*cang chuan*). All these boats could be outfitted with a dizzying array of weapons including bows and arrows, primitive hand grenades, three-eyed guns, rapid-fire guns, arquebuses, long spears, flying iron-tip spears, grappling hooks, swords, and *folangji* cannon. The larger boats could even handle more powerful cannon such as the Grand General and the Crouching Tiger.[112]

Despite the demonstrated superiority of the Chinese to the Japanese at sea, Song expressed some reservations about the hazards of naval warfare, perhaps reflecting the traditional land-oriented biases of Chinese elites. For example, he notes that high waters and rough seas tend to make fighting difficult and render sailors sick and dizzy. Dangerous currents can result in boats being smashed on shoals. In terms of dealing with the foe at hand, Song recommended the use of very long spears and tall bamboo screens to counter Japanese muskets and katana.[113] These were naval adaptations of the techniques used by Qi Jiguang on land. Smoke was to be used to confuse the enemy and to obscure volleys of fire arrows, regular arrows, and gunfire. As indicated above, ships were to be equipped with cannons that fired a wide variety of projectiles. The intent of having such craft was to overawe the enemy so that they would not even dare to engage Chinese ships, thereby saving valuable lives.[114] There were even suggestions that iron chains be strung underwater outside key ports to ensnare Japanese ship, a strategy used in some places in Korea.[115]

Song also did not fail to consider the possibility that China's initial defenses might still be breached. Although some officials advocated a frequently used strategy of moving coastal inhabitants 40–50 *li* inland, that was deemed both potentially too harmful to the people, possibly even provoking them to help would-be invaders, and dangerous from a military standpoint, particularly if wiping the Japanese out at sea was considered the preferred strategy. In the event the Japanese scaled the coastal stockade walls, iron caltrops and rows of wooden stakes were to be placed behind them. In fact, Song notes that he had already placed orders for caltrops, stakes, and saltpeter. Pit traps were to be set and ambushes prepared.[116] Song envisioned Ming defenses coordinating like the spokes of a wheel, funneling the invaders to a central location where they could be wiped out. In the north, both regular and peasant auxiliary units were to be deployed in both passive defense and active patrol. This striking power was deemed sufficient to deter nighttime Japanese raids. In Jiangnan and areas to the south, the primary preparation was the erection of many of watchtowers. Signal fires were to be kept burning at all times at these posts. Additionally, throughout China wherever possible, bamboo palisades were to be erected and existing walls and moats repaired. These efforts had the added benefit of providing protection against common marauders and mountain bandits.[117]

The most elaborate plan called for the construction of a wooden wall, about six feet (two *zhang*) high, stretching 180 *li* from Dagu to Zhengjiagou. Building a wall this size would require a force of thirty thousand men and take just one month.[118] It was envisioned that this structure could even augment the existing Great Wall in the northeast and would be a good plan for bolstering overall defenses in the long term. Again stressing the importance of active as well as passive defense, Song ordered the military commissioner of Shandong to station an assistant regional commander at the central location of Tangtou with three thousand to four thousand troops so they could respond quickly to an alert. Likewise, those in Liaodong were to be on constant watch for plunderers from Tsushima. The ultimate plan was to have forty thousand to fifty thousand troops guarding the port cities of the northeast alone, though it is highly unlikely that this number was ever attained.[119]

In terms of equipment, fire carts and defensive weapons were to be distributed among the common folk. Calling to mind the measures first adopted in the 1560s, villagers were told to store extra firewood and water within the safety of city walls. In case of trouble, villagers were to adopt the classic "clear the wilds and defend the city" strategy.[120] The ministry of works was to dispatch officials to tour and inspect defenses.

It is difficult to determine the degree to which these measures were implemented. Scholars have suggested that much of the Ming bureaucracy's work, like that of bureaucracies everywhere, consisted of little more than making reports and shuffling papers, with few actual results. Yet foreign observers noted that the Chinese coast was in a heightened state of preparation throughout the 1590s and that it was even more difficult than normal for foreigners to move about the empire owing to the widespread fear of Japanese spies. In any event, despite some proposals advocating an invasion of China rather than Korea, Hideyoshi persisted in sending his troops to the Korean peninsula to facilitate an overland assault on China, so the Ming defenses were never really tested. It is unclear whether the Japanese refrained from attacking the Chinese mainland because they had gotten word of China's defensive preparations, but I do not think that this was the case. It was simply much easier to ferry troops and supplies across the Tsushima Straits to Korea than hazard the perilous waters of the Yellow Sea, particularly given the mediocre quality of most Japanese ships. And given the problems the Japanese encountered even maintaining supply lines to Korea, extending them all the way to China was probably out of the question.

RESULTS OF THE ANTIPIRATE MEASURES

Nonetheless, I would still argue that Ming measures were not for naught. During the second phase of Hideyoshi's offensive operations (1597–98) in particular, the Chinese navy acquitted itself quite well, operating in conjunction with Korean units. If nothing else, the proposals put forth provide evidence of the depth and complexity of the Ming bureaucracy, as well as attesting to the overall wealth and resources of the Ming empire. They also reflect an aggressive and forward-thinking military policy on the part of the Ming monarch and his court. In contrast to his immediate forebears, Emperor Wanli was not reluctant to build up or deploy his army against those who challenged his suzerainty in Asia. The fact that he enthusiastically backed Song Yingchang, the architect of many of the measures discussed in this essay, attests to this observation.

With respect to the war in Korea, we can see much more obvious and concrete results. As noted above, the initial Ming expeditionary force of a few thousand had been massacred by the Japanese in Pyongyang in the summer of 1592, prompting the dispatch of a much larger force the following winter. They managed to recapture the walled Korean city of Pyongyang in just a day with vastly superior firepower. Upon hearing news of the allied victory, the Korean king, Sŏnjo (ruled 1567–1608) is alleged to have said, "Their army is said to have numbered 30,000. This is not a lot, but they know how to use them; this is military ability!"[121] The king then asked his ministers about Chinese firearms compared to those used by the Japanese. They replied, "When the Japanese fire their muskets, you can still hear, even if they fire from all sides. But when the Chinese fire their cannon, the sky and earth vibrate and the mountains and plains tremble and you can't even speak." The king responded, "With weapons like these, how can we not fight and win?"[122]

The Japanese concurred with this assessment of Ming firepower and military prowess. As one commander remarked, "We thought Korea was defeated but then the great Ming army came to the rescue."[123] The Japanese subsequently came to develop a healthy respect for Chinese cannons and Ming and Korean naval capabilities, eschewing large set-piece battles and naval confrontations when they could. They also started outfitting their own boats with more firearms, although they never acquired many large cannon, preferring to rely on arquebuses, to their own detriment.

In addition to Ming firepower, the Koreans were also very impressed with Chinese training and drilling methods. When the king asked the Ming commander Li Rusong (1549–97) about their methods, he said that they came from Qi Jiguang's *Jixiao xinshu*, explaining, "Previously we used the same techniques we employed against the Mongols [against the Japanese], but in the earlier battles, they were not successful. But recently we have used General Qi's *Jixiao xinshu*'s methods in combating the Japanese and we were therefore able to achieve a total victory."[124] Li then gave the king a copy of the book to peruse. Finding much of practical value therein, the king recommended it to his ministers and their military commanders asked their Ming counterparts for copies so that they could incorporate Qi's methods into their own training.[125]

From this point (early 1593) on, the Koreans asked for more and more Southern Chinese troops to be rotated into Korea to assist in offensive operations, active and passive defense, in training Korean units.[126] Most prized were units from Yiwu county in Zhejiang, where Qi had first implemented his methods.[127] As indicated above, soldiers with any connection at all to Qi himself also earned a considerable degree of respect. Liu Ting, for example, whose father Liu Xian had served alongside Qi, was brought to Korea to teach the Koreans field tactics and advanced maneuvers and to instruct them in bolstering basic defenses.[128] In reading the proposals presented to the Koreans, one is struck by how similar they are to the measures adopted in China earlier in the century. The Koreans were told to repair all city walls and erect new watchtowers. Narrow passes were to be fortified and garrisoned so they could be held with few men. Cannon were to be deployed wherever possible.[129] Other firearms, including muskets like those used by the Japanese, were also to be integrated into units in accordance with suggestions outlined by Qi Jiguang.[130]

By late 1593 serious peace negotiations were under way and the Ming decided to pull the majority of the troops out of Korea, leaving behind only about sixteen thousand southern troops to continue their training efforts and act in support roles. But before they pulled out, orders were issued for the dispatch of significant numbers of firearms to Korea, especially for defending the important cities of Seoul and Kaesŏng.[131] When the Koreans protested they needed more Ming troops to remain behind, the Ming tried to assuage them by pointing out that the troops left in Korea were Zhejiang men skilled in combating the Japanese. They also emphasized the importance of creating a multilayered defense network centered around strong points defended by firearms.[132]

The Chinese also pointed out shortcomings in Korean weaponry and tactics, noting that Korea's main difficulty in the early going of the war was that they had skill only in archery, whereas the Japanese used muskets, katana, and great pikes that the Koreans could not match.[133] Therefore, in addition to adopting the weapons and tactics used by southern Chinese, widespread manufacture and drilling with muskets was essential. The Ming estimated that Korea would need about 1,300 firearms specialists to train its entire army in a rotational system similar to that used by the Ming.[134] The Ming, not unlike the Americans in Iraq today, argued that once their superior training methods were systematically applied, the Koreans would be easily able to defend themselves from both internal and external threats and bring peace to their country.

While the long-term impact of the reforms introduced by Ming generals to Korea are still somewhat in question, they definitely paid short-term dividends.[135] After peace talks broke down and the Japanese launched another full-scale invasion in 1597, they were thwarted by the Sino-Korean allies south of Seoul and driven back to a string of heavily fortified bastions along Korea's southern and eastern coasts. The Japanese were never again able to mount any serious offensive thrusts and the Chinese and Koreans carried out joint amphibious operations that showcased their superior navies and firepower, culminating in the Battle of Noryang Straits in December 1598. The aftermath of this battle witnessed the Chinese admiral Chen Lin recapturing Korean islands and blowing Japanese stragglers out of caves all along Korea's south coast.[136] Combined with mop-up operations on land, the allies were able to secure Korea once and for all using amphibious methods pioneered several decades earlier.

In summation, it seems clear that despite some difficulties stemming from broader sociopolitical and institutional problems in Ming China and Chosen

Korea which are beyond the scope of this essay, early modern East Asian militaries could in fact learn from previous mistakes and devise clever solutions to vexing military problems. Leaders also had the ability to continue to adapt and modify techniques and tactics for application in different circumstances. We see this with Qi Jiguang's adoption of formations and tactics on war junks that mirrored those used by his land units. Given that the Ming (or the Koreans for that matter) did not have what we would call regular naval troops, keeping things as simple and familiar as possible made perfect sense. But the fact that Qi also decided to use more guns at sea because conditions were more favorable proves that he was pragmatic enough to maximize his potential for victory. Likewise once the Ming gained a sense of the Korean environment, they realized that southern troops and infantry tactics were more effective than northern troops and cavalry tactics, even if the former had to be transported to Korea by sea rather than overland. Finally, the fact that the Japanese came to respect and even fear the Chinese and Korean troops that they had run roughshod over just a generation before demonstrates that the mystique of the dwarf pirates had been shattered.

NOTES

I would like to thank the East Asian Studies Center of Indiana University for providing me with a travel grant to subsidize research conducted for this essay.

1. Taken from *Chouhai tubian* (ca. 1562) and cited in Fan Zhongyi, "Mingdai junshi sixiang jianlun," *Ming-Qing shi* 24 (1997)-43. Concerning the *Chouhai tubian,* it is a comprehensive illustrated manual of coastal defense prepared by one Zheng Ruozeng, a subordinate of the Ming Supreme Commander Hu Zongxian (1511–65). There are several editions of the work. For this essay, I consulted a 1624 edition held in the Lilly Library at Indiana University. Zheng was a subordinate of Hu; since Hu's descendants printed the 1624 edition, he is attributed authorship in this edition of the work. See Wolfgang Franke, *An Introduction to the Sources of Ming History* (Kuala Lumpur: University of Malaya Press, 1968), 223–224. This work's utility as a primary source is discussed in Wang Xiangrong, *Zhong-Ri guanxi wenxian lunkao* (Changsha, China: Yuelu shushe, 1985), 159–217. For a biography of Hu Zongxian in English, see L. Carrington Goodrich and Chaoying Fang, eds. *Dictionary of Ming Biography* (New York: Columbia University Press, 1976), 631–638.
2. Cited in Ray Huang, *1587: A Year of No Significance* (New Haven, CT: Yale University Press, 1981), 170.
3. For a recent reappraisal of these invasions, see Thomas D. Conlan, *In Little Need of Divine Intervention* (Ithaca, NY: Cornell University Press, 2001).
4. See Gavin Menzies, *1421: The Year China Discovered America* (New York: Perennial, 2003); and Menzies, *1434: The Year a Magificent Chinese Fleet Sailed to Italy and Ignited the Renaissance* (New York: William Morrow, 2008). For a scholarly rebuttal of Menzies that makes extensive use of Ming sources, see Edward Dreyer, *Zheng He: China and the Oceans in the Early Ming Dynasty* (New York: AB Longman, 2007). A discussion of the scholarly debate over Menzies' claims is beyond the scope of the present essay, but an incisive critique can be found in Robert Finlay, "How Not to (Re)Write World History: Gavin

Menzies and the Chinese Discovery of America," *Journal of World History* 15.2 (June 2004), 229–242.
5. The first pirates to be called "Japanese pirates" raided the coast of Korea in 1223. On the early years of pirates, see Benjamin H. Hazard, "The Formative Years of the Wakō," *Monumenta Nipponica* 22.3 (1967), 260–277.
6. Robert Antony, *Like Froth Floating on the Sea: The World of Pirates and Seafarers in Late Imperial South China* (Berkeley: University of California Press, 2003), 19.
7. Antony, *Like Froth Floating on the Sea*, 20; and Zhang Tingyu, et al., *Mingshi* (Taibei, China: Dingwen shuju, 1994), 8350.
8. Fan Zhongyi and Tong Xigang, *Mingdai wokou shilue* (Beijing: Zhonghua shuju, 2004), 18.
9. See Fan and Tong, *Mingdai wokou shilue*, 28–96, for an overview of the era from 1403–1522. The Koreans, incidentally, sometimes served as intermediaries between China and Japan, though there were occasional incidents, and a series of fights in Korean trading ports in 1510 caused serious strains in Korean-Japanese relations.
10. See Zhang et al., *Mingshi*, 8353.
11. For a brief biography of Qi, see Goodrich and Fang, *Dictionary of Ming Biography*, 220–224. For more thorough treatments of his life and military career, see the sources listed in notes 20 and 24 below.
12. The subject of piracy in sixteenth-century China is treated in a plethora of sources, including Kwan-wai So, *Japanese Piracy in Ming China During the Sixteenth Century* (Lansing: Michigan State University Press, 1975). In Chinese, see Fan and Tong, *Mingdai wokou shilue*. Zheng Liangsheng, *Mingdai Zhong-Ri guanxi yanjiu* (Taibei, China: Wenshizhe chubanshe, 1985), offers a thorough overview of Sino-Japanese relations in the Ming period. For more specialized looks at specific campaigns, see Charles O. Hucker, "Hu Tsung-hsien's Campaign against Hsü Hai, 1556," in *Chinese Ways in Warfare*, ed. Frank A. Kierman and John K. Fairbank (Cambridge: Harvard University Press, 1974), 273–307; and Huang, *1587: A Year of No Significance*, 159–166.
13. See Zhang et al., *Mingshi*, 8348–8351.
14. See So, *Japanese Piracy in Ming China*, 5; and Antony, *Like Froth Floating on the Sea*, 23.
15. See Merrilyn Fitzpatrick, "Local Interests and the Anti-Pirate Administration in China's Southeast, 1555–1565," *Ch'ing-shih wen-t'i* 4 (December 1979), 7–8.
16. Zhang et al., *Mingshi*, 8350–8352.
17. See *Chouhai tubian* (see n. 1), juan 4–5, for troop levels and garrison locations in Zhejiang and Fujian. Also see Fitzpatrick, "Local Interests and the Anti-Pirate Administration," 12.
18. Hucker, "Hu Tsung-hsien's Campaign Against Hsü Hai, 1556," 285–286.
19. *Chouhai tubian* 12, 5a. For Yu's biography, see Goodrich and Fang, *Dictionary of Ming Biography*, 1616–1618.
20. *Chouhai tubian* 11, 7a–7b; and Qi Jiguang, *Jixiao xinshu* (Taibei, China: Wuzhou chubanshe, 2000), 11.
21. Hucker, "Hu Tsung-hsien's Campaign Against Hsü Hai, 1556," 275–277.
22. On the defeat of Xu Hai, see *Chouhai tubian*, 9, 12a–20b; Zhang et al., *Mingshi*, 8353–8355; and Hucker, "Hu Tsung-hsien's Campaign Against Hsü Hai, 1556."
23. Huang, *1587: A Year of No Significance*, 164–165.
24. Qi, *Jixiao xinshu*, 12–13.
25. Huang, *1587: A Year of No Significance*, 165. That pirates used few firearms could also be tied to the fact that simply keeping adequate supplies of gunpowder dry and on hand was difficult for raiders seeking to maximize mobility. John Guilmartin has also suggested that the type of gunpowder used by the Japanese was very susceptible to the effects of saltwater and humidity, making its transports overseas difficult (personal communication). Also see John F. Guilmartin Jr., "The Earliest Shipboard Gunpowder Ordnance: An Analysis of its Technical Parameters and Tactical Capabilities," *The Journal of Military History*, 71.3 (July 2007), 649–670.

26. *Chouhai tubian*, 5, 25b.
27. See Qi Jiguang, *Jixiao xinshu*; and Qi, *Lianbing shiji* (Beijing: Zhonghua shuju, 2001).
28. See Han Myŏnggi, et al., *Imjin Waeran saryo ch'ongso* (Ming Foreign Relations section) (Chinju, Korea: Chinju National Museum, 2002), 2, 107–108.
29. See, for example, his discussion of spear forms in Qi, *Jixiao xinshu*, 172–179.
30. See ibid., 24–29, which also includes formation diagrams. Also see Fan and Tong, *Mingdai wokou shilue*, 261–264.
31. Huang, *1587: A Year of No Significance*, 169.
32. Qi Jiguang, *Lianbing shiji* (Beijing: Zhonghua shuju, 2001), 27–28.
33. Huang, *1587: A Year of No Significance*, 173.
34. Qi, *Lianbing shiji*, 78–86, 109–111; and Qi, *Jixiao xinshu*, 59.
35. *Chouhai tubian*, 11, 35a.
36. See Miyamoto Musashi, *A Book of Five Rings*, trans. Thomas Cleary (Boston: Shambala, 1994).
37. *Chouhai tubian*, 11, 38b.
38. Qi, *Jixiao xinshu*, 61.
39. Ibid., 41.
40. Hucker, "Hu Tsung-hsien's Campaign Against Hsü Hai, 1556," 287, suggests that southwestern aboriginals had not proved very reliable in combating pirate raiders. This may have been owing to their unfamiliarity with the terrain (including lack of experience in amphibious warfare) or the fact that Japanese may not have been intimidated by their reputation to the same degree that Chinese would have been. In one event a large contingent was slaughtered in an ambush, despite warnings from Supreme Commander Hu Zongxian (see Hucker, "Hu Tsung-hsien's Campaign Against Hsü Hai," 290). Incidentally, Xu Jie, onetime chief grand secretary and an official intimately involved with the piracy problem, also favored the recruitment of local forces over aboriginals because the latter were ill disciplined and unreliable. See So, *Japanese Piracy in Ming China*, 99–100.
41. See *Chouhai tubian*, 11, 24a; and Qi, *Jixiao xinshu*, 19.
42. See Qi Jiguang, *Qi shaobao zouyi* (Beijing: Zhonghua shuju, 2001), 65–66.
43. Qi, *Jixiao xinshu*, 18.
44. Zhang et al., *Mingshi*, 5610.
45. On these issues, see Kenneth M. Swope, "The Three Great Campaigns of the Wanli Emperor, 1592–1600: Court, Military, and Society in Late Sixteenth-Century China" (unpublished PhD dissertation, University of Michigan, Ann Arbor, 2001), chapter 2; and Kenneth Chase, *Firearms: A Global History to 1700* (Cambridge: Cambridge University Press, 2003), 166–171.
46. See Qi, *Jixiao xinshu*, 299–326; and *Lianbing shiji*, 310–318. An illustration of the war cart with the grand general cannon can be found on 311.
47. See So, *Japanese Piracy in Ming China*, 149; and Qi, *Jixiao xinshu*, 307–308, 325–326.
48. Gao Yangwen, et al., *Qi shaobao nianpu qibian* (Beijing: Zhonghua shuju, 2003), 56.
49. See Fan and Tong, *Mingdai wokou shilue*, 259–308, for a discussion of these antipirate measures.
50. Han et al., *Imjin Waeran saryo ch'ongso*, 2, 108.
51. Zhang et al., *Mingshi*, 8357.
52. See *Chouhai tubian*, 11, 1a–3a.
53. On the importance of the international silver trade for the late Ming economy, see William S. Atwell, "International Bullion Flows and the Chinese Economy," *Past and Present* 95 (May 1982), 68–90; and William S. Atwell, "Notes on Silver, Foreign Trade, and the Late Ming Economy," *Ch'ing shih wen-t'i* 3.8 (December, 1977), 1–33.
54. For a primary source pertaining to the initial establishment of these defenses, see *Chouhai tubian*, esp. *juan* 12.

55. *Chouhai tubian, juan* 12, 5b.
56. Ibid., 5b–6a.
57. Ibid., 14a.
58. See Fan Shuzhi, *Wan Ming shi* (Shanghai, China: Fudan daxue chubanshe, 2003), 1: 435. Professor Fan also takes up the issue of Ming China's involvement in the global economy, mentioned above, in the first section of this work, 1–187.
59. See Huang, *1587: A Year of No Significance*, 184–188.
60. See, for example, Matteo Ricci, *China in the Sixteenth Century: The Journals of Matthew Ricci: 1583–1610*, trans. Louis J. Gallagher (New York: Random House, 1953), 260, 300; and Michael Cooper, trans. and ed., *This Island of Japon: Joao Rodrigues's Account of Sixteenth-Century Japan* (Tokyo: Kodansha, 1973), 43, 76–78.
61. For the Japanese-Korean relationship, see Kenneth Robinson, "Centering the King of Chosŏn: Aspects of Korean Maritime Diplomacy, 1392–1592," *Journal of Asian Studies* 59.1 (February, 2000), 109–125; "Policies of Practicality: The Chosŏn Court's Regulation of Contact with Japanese and Jurchens, 1392–1580s" (unpublished PhD dissertation, University of Hawaii, Honolulu, 1997); and Etsuko Hae-Jin Kang, *Diplomacy and Ideology in Japanese-Korean Relations from the Fifteenth to the Eighteenth Century* (New York: St. Martin's Press, 1997).
62. For standard interpretations of Emperor Wanli's relationship with his civil officials, see Huang, *1587: A Year of No Significance*; and Jie Zhao "A Decade of Considerable Significance: Late-Ming Factionalism in the Making, 1583–1593," *T'oung Pao* 88 (2002), 112–150. For a more revisionist position, see Harry S. Miller, "State Versus Society in Late Imperial China, 1572–1644" (unpublished PhD dissertation, Columbia University, New York, 2001), 185–343.
63. See the discussion of sources and stories in Zheng, *Mingdai Zhong-Ri guanxi yanjiu*, 564–565.
64. See Zhang et al., *Mingshi*, 8357. Also see Li Guangtao, comp., *Chaoxian shiliao* (Taibei, China: Zhongyang yanjiuyuan lishi yuyan yanjiusuo, 1970), 1:1.
65. Cited in Joseph Needham, et al., *Science and Civilisation in China Volume 5, Part 7: Chemistry and Chemical Technology: The Gunpowder Epic* (Cambridge: Cambridge University Press, 1986), 390.
66. Qian Yiben, et al., *Wanli dichao* (Taibei, China: Zhengzhong shuju, 1982), 674. Also see Tan Qian, *Guoque* (Taibei, China: Dingwen shuju, 1978), 4681.
67. See Zheng Liangsheng, comp., *Mingdai wokou shiliao* (Taibei, China: Wenshizhe chubanshe, 1987), 475. The passages from this particular volume (Vol. 2) are all taken from the *Veritable Records of the Ming Dynasty*.
68. Ibid., 476.
69. Ibid., 477.
70. Ibid., 477.
71. See Qian, *Wanli dichao*, 692–693; and Zheng, *Mingdai wokou shiliao*, 477.
72. Tan, *Guoque*, 4691.
73. See Song Yingchang, comp., *Jinglue fuguo yaobian* (Taibei, China: Xuesheng shuju, 1986), 1. Also see Qian, *Wanli dichao*, 695.
74. On the utility of Song's work as a source for studying the war in Korea, also see Wang Xiangrong, *Zhong-Ri guanxi wenxian lunkao*, 264–288.
75. Song, *Jinglue fuguo yaobian*, 15.
76. Ibid., 16.
77. Zheng, *Mingdai wokou shiliao*, 479.
78. Song, *Jinglue fuguo yaobian*, 80.
79. On the supposed superiority of southern infantry versus northern cavalry in battling the Japanese, see Li Guangtao, *Chaoxian Renchen Wohuo yanjiu* (Taibei, China: Zhongyang

yanjiuyuan Lishi yuyan yanjiusuo, 1972), 103–108; and Li Guangtao, "Chaoxian Renchen Wohuo yu Li Rusong zhi dong zheng," *Lishi yuyan yanjiusuo jikan* 22 (1950), 290–292.
80. The Ningxia mutiny is fully discussed in Kenneth M. Swope, "All Men Are Not Brothers: Ethnic Identity and Dynastic Loyalty in the Ningxia Mutiny of 1592," *Late Imperial China* 24.1 (June 2003), 79–129.
81. Zheng, *Mingdai wokou shiliao*, 484.
82. Song, *Jinglue fuguo yaobian*, 49.
83. By contrast, a recent estimate suggests that perhaps 30 percent of Japanese fighters in Korea were equipped with firearms. See Samuel Hawley, *The Imjin War* (Seoul, Korea: Royal Asiatic Society, 2005), 102.
84. Song, *Jinglue fuguo yaobian*, 48.
85. Ibid., 52.
86. Ibid., 53.
87. Ibid., 59. For a more complete discussion of firearms used during the war, see Kenneth M. Swope, "Crouching Tigers, Secret Weapons: Military Technologies Employed During the Sino-Japanese-Korean War, 1592–1598," *Journal of Military History* 69.1 (January 2005), 11–42.
88. See the arguments in Song, *Jinglue fuguo yaobian*, 66, 74. In terms of cost, mercenaries were paid six *liang* a month, with an additional one *liang* eight cash (*qian*) provided for food. See Song, *Jinglue fuguo yaobian*, 77.
89. On the siege of Ulsan, see Kenneth M. Swope, "War and Remembrance: Yang Hao and the Siege of Ulsan of 1598," *Journal of Asian History* 42.2 (December 2008).
90. Song, *Jinglue fuguo yaobian*, 94–95.
91. Ibid., 103.
92. Ibid., 105. On the extensive Ming use of gunpowder weapons, see Peter Lorge, *War, Politics, and Society in Early Modern China, 900–1795* (London: Routledge, 2005), 125; and Chase, *Firearms*, 141–154.
93. Song, *Jinglue fuguo yaobian*, 167.
94. Ibid., 171.
95. This was actually an avenue for social mobility during the Ming. In fact the famed late-Ming commander Chen Lin, the most highly decorated veteran of the Ming intervention in Korea, had entered military service in just this fashion, answering a call to battle pirates in his native Guangdong. See Zhang et al., *Mingshi*, 6404.
96. Song, *Jinglue fuguo yaobian*, 171. It is not clear if those from Nanjing are included in the estimate of seven thousand troops.
97. Ibid., 172.
98. Ibid., 172.
99. Ibid., 174.
100. See Mao Yuanyi, comp., *Wubei zhi* (Taibei, China: Huashi chubanshe, 1987), 4806–4807.
101. Song, *Jinglue fuguo yaobian*, 174.
102. Ibid., 175.
103. Mao, *Wubei zhi*, Boats and naval defenses are covered in *juan* 116–117 in volume 11 of the modern reprint.
104. Ibid., 4760–4765.
105. See the illustration in Mao, *Wubei zhi*, 4797. For images of a Korean turtle boat, see Swope, "Crouching Tigers, Secret Weapons," 31.
106. Mao, *Wubei zhi*, 4821.
107. Ibid., 4783–4789.
108. Ibid., 4775.
109. Ibid., 4779.

110. See Adm. Yi Sunsin, *Imjin changch'o: Admiral Yi Sunsin's Memorials to Court*, trans Ha Tae-hung. (Seoul, Korea: Yonsei University Press, 1981), 210.
111. Song, *Jinglue fuguo yaobian*, 180.
112. Ibid., 180–181.
113. Ibid., p. 176.
114. Ibid., 176–177. The reference to saving lives is interesting because it is not particularly common. Officials often speak of preventing harm to the people, but they do not generally speak specifically of saving lives as an end in itself.
115. Song, *Jinglue fuguo yaobian*, 182.
116. Ibid., 178.
117. Ibid., 179.
118. Song, *Jinglue fuguo yaobian*, 185.
119. Ibid., 186–187.
120. Ibid., 179.
121. Cited in Zheng, *Mingdai Zhong-Ri guanxi yanjiu*, 597.
122. Ibid., 597.
123. Ibid., 599.
124. Fan Zhongyi, *Qi Jiguang zhuan*, Beijing (China: Zhonghua shuju, 2003), 579.
125. Ibid., 579–580.
126. Han et al., *Imjin Waeran saryo ch'ongso*, 1, 306.
127. So, *Japanese Piracy in Ming China*, 148.
128. Han et al., *Imjin Waeran saryo ch'ongso*, 1, 253. For a biography of Liu Ting, see Goodrich and Fang, *Dictionary of Ming Biography*, 964–968.
129. Han et al., *Imjin Waeran saryo ch'ongso*, 1, 253.
130. See Qi, *Lianbing shiji* 236–237, on the use of different firearms for different situations.
131. Han et al., *Imjin Waeran saryo ch'ongso*, 1, 338–339.
132. Ibid., 2, 72–74.
133. Ibid., 2, 131.
134. Ibid., 2, 132.
135. See Eugene Park, *Between Dreams and Reality: The Military Examination in Late Chosŏn Korea, 1600–1894* (Cambridge: Harvard University Press, 2007), 51–52.
136. Zhang et al., *Mingshi*, 6405. Incidentally, Liu Ting commanded the land operations in the war's climactic battle.

Training a Reluctant Ally: The U.S. Naval Advisory Mission to China, 1945–49

Katherine K. Reist

During World War II the American government attempted to support the Chinese government with aid, advisers, and training programs. Most notable were the training of Chinese air crews, particularly prior to the American declaration of war against Japan, and the training and equipping of Chinese ground forces, the so-called Alpha forces, planned for thirty-nine divisions. Yet it was the U.S. Navy that had, as Professor Maochun Yu has pointed out, the most successful mission during the war. Under the provisions of the Sino-American Special Technical Cooperative Organization (SACO), a combined intelligence and special operations alliance was formed among Lt. Gen. Dai Li, who was the head of the Military Bureau of Investigation and Statistics (an intelligence-gathering organization), and (then) Rear Adm. Milton E. "Mary" Miles, USN.[1]

THE END OF THE WAR

The war against Japan ended more quickly than had been anticipated, thus leaving those Americans in China with plans only somewhat formulated. The reality of the situation provided a challenge for the Chinese government, with the recognized Nationalist government in the southwest, the Communist forces controlling large population areas in north and central China, the Soviet military—under agreements reached at the Yalta Conference—occupying Manchuria and northern Korea, and Japanese and puppet or warlord forces occupying much of coastal China. American advisers attempted to moderate the government's immediate desire to regain control of all Chinese territory, especially the large cities of the coast, though U.S. air and naval resources were used to move Nationalist government personnel to the capital at Nanjing and military forces to the north and east.

The Americans wished to restructure the balance of power in East Asia by establishing a strong centralized democratic Chinese government, with a unified professional military. These developments would offset a defeated

Japan and an expanding Soviet presence in Asia. The Americans therefore tried to facilitate the repatriation of Japanese military and civilian personnel, a mission using the U.S. Seventh Fleet; used diplomatic pressure to control Soviet influence once the parameters of such influence had been ascertained; and then, through the Marshall mission to China, attempted to reconcile the various Chinese factions into an organized democratic government and professional military. Aid to China—financial, military, developmental, and other—would continue, but for the time being was controlled by George C. Marshall, who would later be appointed secretary of state.

The Chinese government was organized around the *Goumindang*, or Nationalist Party. The head of the party was also head of the government and head of the military. Although Chiang K'ai-shek had promised a constitution and a sharing of power once the period of tutelage had occurred, his major focus was not on government reorganization as the war ended. (The period of tutelage was a time for reducing the illiteracy rate in China and allowing the people to gradually understand the democratic process.) Instead, he was adamant in moving his government to Nanjing, the prewar capital of China, and regaining control of the country. His major challenger in this endeavor was the Chinese Communist Party, which demanded legal recognition and a share of the power.

In order to prevent the Communist forces from accepting Japanese surrender and Japanese weapons in north China, Chiang requested that five divisions of U.S. Marines be sent to hold the northern ports and their transportation links for the national government.[2] The American presence would perhaps prevent the spread of Soviet influence and forces, or at least would prevent the linking of Chinese Communist and Soviet interests in Manchuria. The 1st and 6th U.S. Marine Divisions (MarDivs) were dispatched to China. The 1st MarDiv was sent to Tianjin to control the coastal area south of the Great Wall and to guard the coal mines and other resources that would supply the cities of the area, while the 6th MarDiv was sent to Qingdao, a naval base in northeastern China, to secure the port and the coast.[3]

Meanwhile, the Chinese government moved to Nanjing, as did the U.S. Army and Army Air Corps advisory groups. The Naval Advisory Survey Board sent representatives there, as well. Under the president's wartime powers the various groups were reorganized as advisory missions to the Chinese government. But the original mission statement stipulated that any aid and advice would be for reorganization and modernization purposes only. Although the Marshall mission spent a year in intense and continuous negotiations, establishing several cease-fires between the Communist and Nationalist forces and reaching several tentative agreements regarding political reform, none held for more than a few months at best. Even with the establishment of the executive headquarters section in Beijing to monitor cease-fire violation charges by any of those concerned, using committees equally representing the Communists, Nationalists, and Americans, no permanent progress was made. Marshall returned to the United States in January 1947.

In the interim, the American military was demobilizing, downsizing not only its personnel but also its equipment. For the U.S. Navy, a number of ships, vessels, parts, and supplies were located in the Pacific and deemed surplus to needs of the postwar naval establishment. With the exception of a few river craft, the Chinese navy had been destroyed early in the Sino-Japanese War. The Americans offered advice and aid in rebuilding the service, which the Chinese accepted. The Administrative Survey Board, under Rear Adm. S. S. Murray, USN, was convened by direction of the chief of naval operations. The Board conducted preliminary surveys regarding the Chinese requirements for an appropriate naval establishment. They also recommended a format for a U.S. Naval Advisory Group. The Murray Board Report was submitted 5 December 1945.[4] The British also offered training and vessels, including a light cruiser, escort ships, and a few submarines. Thirty-four former Imperial Japanese Navy ships were available to the Chinese as well, most of them destroyers and smaller craft.[5] The Soviet Union, which recognized the Nationalist government while maintaining ties with the Chinese Communists, also offered aid and training, but more for the ground and air than for naval forces.

EARLY ADVISORY MISSIONS

Under presidential authority, the U.S. Naval Advisory Survey Board was established. It was to recommend to Congress the ships and supplies that would be needed for the establishment and training of a modern Chinese navy. The American naval personnel assigned would train the Chinese to operate only the American-supplied ships and vessels. Through negotiations with the Chinese government, Congress authorized a small naval training group and the transfer of up to 271 ships and craft to China. Restrictions on vessel size stipulated that the largest vessels to be so transferred were destroyer escorts; any larger ship was to have direct congressional approval. Sensitive documents, blueprints, and equipment were excluded from the aid package. Most of the vessels would be landing craft of one designation or another, or motor boats, or supply or repair vessels.[6]

During the war, Chinese naval personnel had either been retired or absorbed into the ground forces. Obviously, the training of naval officers, petty officers, technical ratings, and seamen would have first priority. Before that could occur, though, a naval mission was to be established, a plan for training produced and approved by both the American and Chinese authorities, sites for such training established, and facilities and training supplies designated and developed. All plans had to be written and approved by American authorities, then translated and further approved by the Chinese military bureaucracy. This process was, needless to report, very time consuming.

The United States desired that the Chinese military be sufficiently strong and well equipped to defend the country and fulfill its obligations under the United Nations. (As China held one of the permanent seats on the Security Council, she was tasked with maintaining peace and international security, along with the other permanent members.) For the Navy, the mission consisted of the ability to deal with piracy and smuggling, assisting the Maritime Customs Service, patrolling the major rivers, and defending the coast.[7] A request for training of a Chinese marine corps was also made.[8] The marines would be able to engage in amphibious landings, guard naval facilities, and enhance the government's ability to defend the country. The American assumption was that these goals could be accomplished under a unified government, in a period of rebuilding and restructuring the war-torn country. The reality would be otherwise.

First, the advisory groups had to be organized. The first proposal included a provision for a large number of personnel—one thousand officers and twenty-five hundred enlisted men—and a long list of guaranteed privileges. The State Department recognized the similarity to the Treaty Port privileges recently abrogated and, in conjunction with the Joint Chiefs of Staff, reduced the number of personnel to fewer than one thousand, with the naval contingent authorized at three hundred and the demands on the Chinese government to housing, support, and supplies.[9] Both the U.S. Army and Army Air Corps advisory groups and the U.S. Naval Advisory Survey Board began to operate in China. The initial estimate for the mission was for five years.

Legislation was sent to Congress to establish these groups in February 1946; Congress did not authorize either in the first year. In 1947 the Naval Advisory Group but not the Army Advisory Group was authorized, though the latter continued to function. Finally, in 1948 the organization including the Army, Navy, and Air Force missions was authorized as a Joint United States Military Advisory Mission (JUSMAG) to China.[10] The status of the groups in the intervening time was somewhat anomalous. Nonetheless, both groups established plans, inspected training sites, began to recruit instructors, and made contact with their opposite numbers within the Chinese government and military bureaucracy. The name of the naval group was changed to the Naval Advisory Group as the Chinese had not understood the previous nomenclature.[11] Furthermore, after November 1948 the group was no longer directly under the ambassador except for policy matters, but was instead under the Joint Chiefs of Staff for joint problems and under the Navy Department for strictly naval matters. Commander Forces Western Pacific (ComForWesPac) continued coordination and logistical support for the group. At the time the JUSMAG was established, the naval personnel in China numbered thirty-six officers and eighty-two enlisted men. The Joint Chiefs of Staff had authorized 165 naval and marine personnel and 750 members of the Army and Air Force.[12]

A further determination needed was for the position of the chief of the military advisory groups. Gen. David Barr, USA, chief of the Army Advisory Group (AAG), was initially appointed in order to facilitate the coordination of efforts and aid of the advisory groups. Later, under the JUSMAG, the position rotated among the senior members of the groups. Since appointment of the individual chiefs was staggered, senior officers of each service would fill the role in turn.[13]

AMERICAN GOALS AND CHINESE REALITY

Since the Chinese military and government had overlapping and interlinking elements that resulted in a less than transparent chain of command, a number of changes were needed at the government level before a modernized force could be organized. First, the Chinese military council needed to be restructured so that a more formal and recognized chain of command was established. A ministry of national defense was to be established, under but separate from the recognized government.[14] Beginning in July 1946 advisory group members, usually the senior members of the groups, would meet with the minister and other personnel within the ministry, although the formal naval headquarters organization was not approved until January 1947. An organization chart was established for the new ministry with links to the American joint staffs and secretariats, as combined units.[15] A series of plans for training and support of Chinese personnel were begun, including the training of a small number of Chinese officers in U.S. military schools.

Problems in this organization existed from the beginning. Since the Chinese military was dominated by the ground forces, many in the organization assumed that the same was true for the United States. Many complaints were recorded to the effect that naval matters were routinely routed through the Army group instead of directly to the Navy. One suggestion was to change the advisory group's name to the Military and Naval Advisory Group to emphasize the equality of the services. The suggestion went nowhere. The U.S. air advisers, separated from the Army in 1948, expressed similar frustration.[16] Many people seemed unaware that China had a navy or air force. Although both the U.S. naval and air missions were invited to send a few people to the meetings determining the organization and structure of the Ministry of National Defense, they found that the U.S. Army group had already been working on the plan with the Chinese for several months. Both U.S. Navy and U.S. Air Force expressed some reservations as to the functioning of the organization for their missions. The plan was submitted as written. The Chinese navy and air force felt strangled by the Army domination of all aspects of planning and requests for supplies.[17]

Other problems arose from the American demand that reforms accompany the aid and training provided. Many Chinese, particularly senior officers, were comfortable with or at least accustomed to the system as it existed. Areas of overlapping authority were common and lines of communication unclear. The American desire for a unified, professional military came into conflict with the reality of single-party domination, where loyalty to the party was paramount for position, and personal connection frequently more valued than professional qualification. Many of the attempted reforms were in appearance only, although many junior officers were found to be more amenable to the American system than to the established one. Several factors were responsible for these problems: The country was involved in a civil war where loyalty was stressed. The government was not as unified as it might appear to outsiders, with both political and military factions within the party, regional associations, warlords, and opportunists at many levels. Finally, many Chinese were wary of adopting a foreign system, given that circumstances, history, and other factors differed in development from country to country. Perhaps some aspects of the system might prove useful, but only with due deliberation and adaptation.

THE NAVAL ADVISORY MISSION

The primary mission for the naval group was to train crews for the American ships being turned over to the Chinese, the training to be conducted both ashore and under way; to provide technical advice for operations and maintenance of the ships; to improve navigation safety; to maintain established shipyards; and to provide advice to the Ministry of National Defense on naval matters. The American personnel were not to advise on missions related to the Chinese civil war. With four officers and eight enlisted men, Cdr. P. L. Carroll, USN, set up the initial shore establishment at the Chinese naval training center, which had been moved to Qingdao on 22 December 1945.[18] The training center was simultaneously commissioned as a base of operations by Rear Admiral Tang, Republic of China Navy. Naval units were also established at Shanghai to reorganize the Kiangnan Dockyard and at Canton as a small antipiracy, antismuggling base.[19]

The first program conducted at Qingdao by the Americans was for limited underway training aboard amphibious craft. The initial Amphibious Training Command, established in December 1945 at the suggestion of Admiral Kinkaid, commander of the Seventh Fleet, gave one-on-one training to a select group of Chinese. Six landing ship tanks (LSTs) were utilized for this purpose.[20] The trained crews would then be responsible for the repatriation of Japanese military and civilians still in China. Amphibious exercises were run by the Americans and observed closely by various Chinese officers and officials. The Americans also ferried ships from the U.S. naval base at Subic Bay in the Philippines to the training center. The initial trainees were to serve as instructors for subsequent groups, under American supervision. Meanwhile, schools were being organized ashore, with training aids and equipment from the decommissioned training center at Gulfport, Mississippi. The initial naval training group consisted of thirty-eight officers and ninety enlisted men, though obviously more Americans would be needed.[21] The senior member and staff of the Naval Advisory Survey Board were established in Nanjing in early 1946. With the senior member of the AAG, a joint advisory organization was available to the Chinese government. The senior members advised the generalissimo, the minister of national defense, the chief of the supreme staff, and the commander in chief of the Chinese navy directly. Political coordination was maintained with the American ambassador and the commander of the Seventh Fleet (later ComForWesPac). The Chinese maritime customs officials were also offered advice as to the kinds of craft available to fit their needs and were provided access to U.S. government agencies engaged in maritime affairs.[22] The senior naval member also terminated the SACO agreement and ended all flights of naval and marine corps troop transport aircraft for the Chinese government.

The naval staff also directed the naval communication center in the joint center and was responsible for the training personnel at Qingdao, Shanghai, and Canton. Naturally it was also responsible for the transfer of ships and other military aid, for processing Chinese crews to receive training in the United States, and for inspecting the various facilities. A series of lectures were held at the Republic of China Navy headquarters to increase morale and discipline. One problem identified in hindsight was that, owing to the initial lack of congressional authorization, most of the members of the original survey board were returned to the United States by February 1946.[23] In April of that year, many of the personnel assigned to the staff arrived in China. Those assigned to the Naval Advisory Group arrived in June. Also, because the initial amphibious training had not included maintenance, which was an obvious need, the establishment of rate schools had a high priority. The Chinese naval academy, having had many homes in the prewar era and having been established at Chungking in 1940, had been disbanded in the fall of 1946, and the midshipmen sent to sea. The new class for 1946 was sent to Shanghai, from which they were transferred in April 1947 to the reestablished naval academy at Qingdao. Included in the curriculum was a summer cruise.[24]

One of the problems at Qingdao and elsewhere for the advisers was the lack of adequate space and supplies for training purposes. At one point, Chinese officers were being trained in a facility designated for enlisted men, an "obviously undesirable" situation.[25] Construction began to remedy this situation. Training schedules were begun, modestly at first, then expanded as circumstances permitted. One major deficiency observed in the Chinese system was the lack of an organized supply and logistics service. A supply officers' school was begun in September 1946. A naval medical facility was organized in Shanghai and a training program for corpsmen was developed in Qingdao.[26]

As these programs were planned and established, a major problem came to light: the training and assignment of instructors. The first class at the reestablished naval academy began four weeks late owing to a lack of instructors.[27] Since the navy had ceased to exist during the war, many of those assigned to the Chinese navy lacked any naval knowledge or experience. Some civilian instructors were brought in from Shandong University, but their lack of naval perspective was less than acceptable, especially for the 293 fourth classmen. By October 1947 twenty naval and ten civilian instructors composed the faculty.[28] As an instructor's billet was not desirable for ambitious members of the service, few were willing to serve in this capacity. Such an assignment separated them from those in a position of influence and limited their service experience. Frequently, orders to such assignments were overturned by appeal to personal contacts outside the immediate chain of command. The inability to retain instructors hampered the establishment of the training curriculum, since sufficient staffing seemed to be something of an ongoing problem. Even in the spring of 1948 the superintendent of the Chinese naval training center, Commodore Wei, expressed some anxiety regarding the competency of replacement officers assigned as instructors. He reported that indiscriminate transfers hurt the efficiency of the program. Perhaps one aspect of the problem was the failure to establish a permanent billet for those so assigned.[29]

Another problem was that of lack of fitness for service. Some recruits were dismissed for chronic health problems, such as tuberculosis. Others were found to be illiterate, and so could be trained as sailors or firefighters but not as personnel with higher responsibility. An attempt was made to require a high school education for those sent to rate schools, but at least 10 percent of some classes were dismissed for an inability to read. Additionally, the problem associated with differing dialects made instruction difficult. Requests were made that Mandarin (*guo yu*) be required prior to enrollment in the training program.[30]

Camp Hank Gibbons had been set up in June of 1945 for the American advisers. The purpose of the camp was to indoctrinate all those serving in Naval Group China in the ways of life in China. Included in the course of acclimation was advice as to how to travel and obtain food and water. Sessions in understanding and cooperating with Chinese friends and allies were established. A suggestion was also made that Americans be required to learn the language, at least at the basic level. This instruction was provided at the camp, and further study was required while based in China. In the interim, a course in the proper use of interpreters was established for Americans assigned to training responsibilities. Explanations as to general communication and supply problems were also outlined. The organization tried to anticipate the postwar training needs for a continued role, although with a different mission.[31] As this program apparently died with the end of SACO, however, most Americans sent to China lacked language and cultural training, a significant problem with the training mission that should have been anticipated.

Once established—with an approved curriculum, translated instruction materials, and adequate facilities—a regular training cycle was instituted at Qingdao. For example, a training class for forty Chinese officers—twenty deck and twenty engineering—was being planned by the end of 1947, with anticipated classes for 1 May, 1 August, and 1 November 1948 and continuing into 1949. The agreement with the Chinese government for such training was signed 8 December 1947.[32] A report to the chief of naval operations detailed the enrollment of 348 newly enlisted personnel, with ninety-three to be assigned to the dockyards and the rest to be assigned to a course on advanced seamanship. Eighteen enlisted men were participating in the Radio School in Shanghai. Twelve people began a three-month hydrographic course.[33] A discussion was held with the AAG as to joint training of financial officers for all Chinese forces. Thus programs underway were expanded and others instituted, from basic training to a national defense university and national armed forces academy, in order to bring a truly professional military into being.

Chinese officers and government officials were invited to observe American naval exercises, both amphibious and those involving a cruiser and destroyers. There was, however, a delay in the delivery of the designated amphibious ships to China. The original schedule was reportedly too optimistic. This, coupled with the comment that, "We did not know nearly as much about the Chinese as we thought we did," meant that additional problems in the schedules for training existed.[34] Disagreements over funding, such as that over the Chinese desire that one year's supply of ammunition and parts be included gratis for each ship, are representative. Some of the lend-lease ships had been transferred with more than a year's supply of parts. With the end of this program, however, the Chinese government was to use loans and credits for such purchases. Subsequent ship transfers were to be released "where is, as is."[35] But the Chinese were taking more responsibility for the Qingdao base and training and improving discipline. A Chinese naval training activities command had been activated at Qingdao.

A great emphasis was placed on the rate training. One of the observed weaknesses of the Chinese military establishment was in the training of support and maintenance personnel. Supply and financial personnel in particular were needed. In addition, maintenance and repair facilities, from small electronics to the ships themselves, had to be organized and manned. One report noted the difficulty in translating the various supply terminologies into easily understood Chinese language terms. Classes ranged from sixteen to forty-four weeks depending on the specialty; ratings schools were one of the most frequently mentioned successes of the American naval training programs.[36]

ADDITIONAL MISSIONS

The Chinese government also requested the establishment of a marine corps for China in September 1946. An original estimate for a sixteen thousand–man service was later revised. Chinese marines would be assigned as garrison troops at naval shore facilities, or as a lightly equipped strike force. Originally no mention was made of a small close air support element, or a small fleet element; later these also were to be included.[37] This later request, however, did not include an estimate for the size of the force anticipated. Col. S. B. Griffith, United States Marine Corps (USMC), tasked with planning the training program, estimated that, if the Chinese provided a site with a base and reasonable facilities, a training program could be readily established, but first a school for Chinese officers and noncommissioned officers would be organized so that they could assist the American staff. Then an eight- to sixteen-week block training cycle could be instituted, with a new class beginning every two weeks to a month. Provision could also be made for training Chinese officers at USMC schools. The requirements would obviously include a good grasp of English and good health and education. One anticipated problem was that the Chinese would have to begin with the basic training course and then move into the more specialized training. All officers would then be assigned to the instructors orientation course. The number of personnel to be trained would be based on an estimated Chinese marine corps of forty thousand, and training could begin by November 1947.[38]

The training program for the entire Chinese marine corps was to begin by mid-March 1948 with 150 people. A suggestion was made that some of the SACO guerrilla-trained troops be sent to the marines.[39] There was reported to be a lack of necessary equipment and staff with naval experience, therefore the initial desire was for smaller classes. The first trainees appeared to be better fed and educated than those recruited for the Chinese army. At first, only physical training was begun, with an emphasis on ground fighting tactics. No formal classroom experience was yet provided.[40] A marine corps of 1,250 was authorized two months later. Training began slowly at Qingdao, as the facilities there were already strained. Chinese morale was low owing to low pay and a lack of disciplined leadership. Peak enrollment at the training facility reached 1,200 by July 1948.[41] The Chinese government anticipated that the new marine corps could engage in amphibious operations behind Communist lines while the Chinese navy blockaded the coast in Communist-held areas.

Secretary of State George C. Marshall wrote to Secretary of the Navy James Forrestal as to the desirability of postponing the initiation of a Chinese marine corps. He believed that diverting the limited financial and military resources for the establishment of the new service while the country was not unified would prove less than successful for the Chinese.[42] When the situation stabilized, a marine corps should be organized because it was not desirable to have American armed forces maintained ashore in any form of permanent assignment. Marshall's objections were obviously overridden.

Another group of officer and enlisted trainees arrived in the United States to begin familiarization with four of the six destroyer escorts to be turned over to the Chinese. These ships, based at Glen Cove Springs, Florida, composed the so-called Miami Squadron.[43] The idea was to train the crews while the ships were examined and supplied for their assignments in China. When the training was almost completed, the ships were towed to the Norfolk Naval Shipyard and turned over to the Chinese. They were to depart at the end of December 1948, to arrive in China in March 1949. One American liaison officer would sail with the squadron, with three American enlisted personnel aboard each ship.[44] A progress report on the status of the squadron was filed just before the ships were turned over to the Chinese. The liaison officer for Crews 1 and 2 reported that discipline was good, since the threat of being returned to China had worked well until the return itself had been scheduled. Morale, however, was affected by the news from China, which was not favorable to the Nationalist cause. The ships' inventories were at 90 percent, though looting of small portable instruments such as typewriters had occurred. Chinese officers were reported to lack discipline in spending, repeatedly requesting unnecessary and luxury items.[45] China's limited budget mandated that American loans and credits were necessary for the Chinese government to purchase supplies, so perhaps awareness that such supplies would be available only as long as there were American loans and credits motivated these requests for supplies.

ADDITIONAL PROBLEMS

As the American training system began to produce well-prepared personnel for the Chinese navy, the political, economic, and military situation in China was deteriorating. From June 1947 the military advisory group headquarters had estimated success for the various programs only after a period of six years from that date. Furthermore, the report stated that success could be assured only if certain fixed and variable factors were eliminated. The fixed group included the reorganization of the Ministry of National Defense, which was accomplished; the reorganization of the military advisory groups, which occurred; and the availability of established installations required for the military advisory groups, which continued to be a problem. Variables included the continued field operations of the Chinese armed forces, which drained the economy; the unstable national economy, which was threatened by military action; and the obstacles to industrial development and reconstruction efforts while the majority of the budget was allocated to the military. All these variable factors, as well as fixed factors, were influenced by postwar international relations, as well as by internal conditions.[46]

Chinese military organization, although somewhat streamlined on paper, continued to be less than transparent in reality. Overlapping allocations of functions and commands continued. Two naval captains, for example, had responsibility for the functioning of the shipyard at Qingdao. Neither accepted a particular area of responsibility and both tended to pass responsibility back and forth with the result that little was accomplished. A further example occurred when thefts of a considerable number of small arms was reported to Vice Adm. Kwei Yun-chin, the commander in chief of the Chinese navy, by the senior member of the Naval Advisory Survey Board, Rear Adm. H. R. Thurber, USN. Part of the reported problem was the unsatisfactory command relationship between the director of the Chinese naval training activities and the commanding officer of the guard battalion, over whom the director had no authority. The offenders were not punished. Admiral Kwei had graduated in the first class at Whampoa Academy, a group that was especially close to Chiang K'ai-shek. The admiral was reported to be friendly to Americans, to have a good grasp of English, and to be concerned with the efficiency of the navy. He was reported to be willing to fire those who proved unwilling or incapable of carrying out orders. American relations with him appear to have been not only professional, but friendly.[47]

An ongoing problem was the interference of the Nationalist Party in military affairs. Since the party controlled the military, party officers were assigned to all commands. A report to the senior member of the advisory group gave a heads up that the head of the Chinese naval training activities' politburo department, Major General Tau, had instructions from the Ministry of National Defense to set up a secret governing committee within the training authority to supervise policies, acting as a de facto superintendent of the Chinese naval training activities. It was known that the general had served in the army for twenty years, but according to the senior member, "He has never impressed me as being a man of great ability, force, or color."[48]

Obviously such party interference with personnel and policy matters did not allow a successful reform of many of the organizational problems. Especially noted were problems of personnel assignment. In addition, coordination between departments was often problematic. Orders might be issued for movement without any plans for the transportation of the forces to be transferred, yet the Chinese government was anxious to get as many ships under way as possible.

Success was reported in the breaking up of some of the provincial cliques that had dominated the nascent navy. One way in which this was accomplished was by recruiting from all areas of China to prevent one or two provinces from exercising virtual control of the service. These efforts improved morale, though a great many persons described as "deadwood" reportedly remained.[49] Accounts of such individuals assigned to the Chinese navy who were less than enthusiastic regarding their assignments were frequent. One report in 1947 stated that a Commander Lu had completed his second month of vacation with pay. He was ordered to Taiwan and instead went to Shanghai. He asserted that his ship needed a long list of repairs, but no one checked the request. He also requested a year's supply of ammunition for training purposes, although training was not conducted with ammunition. His relief was requested.[50]

As far as discipline problems were concerned, one commanding officer stated that he could discipline only enlisted personnel. He reported that many officers and petty officers requested leave and did not return. The leave was granted by persons in Nanjing, not within the chain of command in Qingdao. These problems complicated the running of the shipyard. For example, three merchant ships were reported grounded. Captain Liu stated that ships had been dispatched to rescue them, but no ships had left the dockyard and, on inquiry, none "was available."[51] When the officers left while repairs were being made, no one supervised the crew or, for that matter, the repairs and testing aboard ship. Frequently, as repairs were finished, further requests would be made for the same ship, even on the day the work was finished. One ship, the *Yung Ming*, was tied up for seven months. There was no prioritization of repairs nor adequate control of the process. When the shipyard tried to effect order, the ship's commanding officer would appeal to a contact in Nanjing and the shipyard would be overruled. Neither the captain nor the executive officer had reportedly ever been aboard a ship. Part of the problem was that three separate authorities shared responsibility for the ships.[52] Qingdao was home to the largest number of ships and was the second largest supply center in China. The opportunities for confusion abounded under these circumstances.

In addition to the interference by the Nationalist Party was the interference by the Chinese army. Not only were most of the senior naval officers transferred from the army, but most maintained their ties to those in positions of influence within the party and army. The Chinese army had plans for the navy, which included its use in the protection of its bases. It was therefore in the army's interest to maintain close personal relations with naval personnel. Such relationships frustrated the American advisers on many levels. One officer complained that as long as the Americans could not issue orders to the Chinese, the major reforms in the training and organization of the military forces would remain unresolved.[53] The Americans expected to have some control or at least supervision of the supplies and material sent to China, but the question of control in order to ensure that at least some reforms were instituted complicated United States–China relations.

A request from Admiral Kwei in June 1948 for the development of a naval base in southern China met with the response that the request would be studied. For the present, Admiral Thurber replied, men and funds would be allocated for the southern navy's needs. All major efforts would be directed to the problems in the north that were occurring because of the spread of the Communist forces and fighting in Shandong.[54]

ACCOMPLISHMENTS

Although conditions for the Naval Advisory Group were far from ideal, the group nonetheless accomplished a great deal in the short time that it operated in China. A survey of naval installations throughout China was conducted after the end of World War II and the results were reported to both governments concerned. Ships were transferred to the training center, with American training personnel to begin the reestablishment of a Chinese navy. Modern naval thought was introduced at both the administrative and ship's command levels, and the ministry of national defense and the Chinese naval headquarters were reorganized. More than forty-one formal studies of the major elements composing the Ministry of National Defense were completed and transmitted to the chief of the supreme staff.[55]

Elements of a supply system and a training program to support it were begun. The dockyards at Qingdao and Kiangnan were assisted with organization, technical advice, operations, and budgetary matters. Inspections were conducted on ships and craft transferred from the United States and a modern medical service established with a naval medical school at Qingdao. The training facility there began by training Chinese instructors. The training center graduated 327 officers and 3,074 enlisted men from whom crews were selected to operate the various naval vessels and facilities.[56] A rate school proved very successful; included were boatswain's mates, gunner's mates, quartermasters, signalmen, shipfitters, and more. One observer described the rate schools as the closest to a USN Class "A" facility. A four-year naval academy course was instituted with a student body of five hundred. A curriculum to train recruits was also developed. An underway program for familiarization was conducted for six weeks for small craft, and eight weeks for the larger vessels. The graduates manned those ships turned over to China, among them ten landing ships tank, eight landing ships medium, eight landing ships infantry, eight landing crafts tank, one tanker, one miscellaneous auxiliary, one small auxiliary floating drydock, two submarine chasers, and four destroyer escorts.[57]

The new Chinese navy stationed three ships and six patrol boats in the Bohai Gulf and near Qingdao; two ships and five patrol craft near Kiangsi, Fukien, and Chekiang, three ships and one patrol craft near Taiwan and Penghu; and nineteen ships and forty-one patrol boats in the Yangzi by May 1948.[58] The Chinese navy thus was patrolling along the entire coast, conducting some antismuggling efforts and patrolling the Yangzi River, where fighting between the Nationalist and Communist forces was observed.

Incomplete programs included the formation of an impartial system for promotion, a firm rating structure for enlisted men, the restructuring of courts martial, improved procedures for administrative personnel in specified fields, improved administration of subordinates in the field by the bureaucracy at the naval headquarters, various training manuals, and so on. Planned, but not yet begun, was a system of higher education for officers through postgraduate classes, fleet operational school, and a Chinese naval war college. A progressive education system for enlisted men had not been established. Plans to eliminate a large number of the Chinese army personnel positions and their personnel and to enunciate the qualities desirable for naval officers, presumably to preclude the reassignment of army personnel, were not yet developed. A system for a naval reserve component was not finalized, nor had budgetary control been established throughout the Navy (or the military, for that matter). A suggestion that civilian experts, particularly in finance and industrial development, be consulted if not employed on a quasipermanent basis was also indicated. In addition a number of other studies and programs were mentioned. Future recommendations included broadly based advice and assistance, contingent upon the acceptance and utilization of American advice and methods.[59]

END OF MISSION

The military advance of the Communist forces meant that, beginning in 1947 awareness of the ability or inability of the Nationalist government to protect American lives and property influenced or constrained the planning process. Since the Americans recognized the Nationalist government and all aid had been given to their forces, hostility on the part of the Communists was evident. Sabotage of ships was a possibility. Evacuation plans, in conjunction with ComForWesPac, were detailed. The American ambassador would determine when such plans would be put into effect; dependents and American nationals were encouraged to leave by the fall of 1948.[60] Preliminary steps for the reduction or suspension of JUSMAG were taken. By late November 1948 the JCS had directed the disposal of government property and the transfer of personnel. Naval advisory division activities were suspended in 1949: on 4 January at Canton, 24 January at Nanjing, 29 January at Shanghai, and on 3 February at Qingdao. Headquarters had already moved to Shanghai in November 1948 and to Tokyo in January 1949. The naval advisory mission to China formally ceased operations on 3 March 1949.[61]

As the position of the Nationalist government and military further deteriorated, desertions (sometimes described as massive desertions) from their forces occurred. Much equipment was captured by the Communists as well.

A CIA report gave the number of naval vessels captured or defected as sixty-three, including three of the destroyer escorts. China's navy still possessed 150 ships and harbor craft, but morale was reported as low, with crews and installations infiltrated by the Chinese Communist Party.[62]

ASSESSMENT

American plans for postwar China were founded on a number of assumptions. Among them was that peace would be established and political and economic reforms undertaken to develop a unified, stable, democratic country. Training plans were therefore developed with long-term goals, and a system established which by and large mimicked that of the U.S. military forces. With the optimism that accompanied the end of the Second World War, these plans were perhaps understandable. However, the reality of a one-party government, whose personnel also held military positions and which was not interested in a multiparty government or military, changed the circumstances of the mission. The Nationalist Party had been formed during the warlord era in China and organized as a revolutionary party by advisers from the Soviet Union. It had achieved success—unification (more or less) of the country, recognition by the major political powers, and alliances in the war against Japan. There was little incentive for the government to change, even absent the ongoing civil conflict with the Communists.

The Nationalist government also anticipated an armed conflict between the Soviet Union and the United States in which it would have a role similar to the one it had had during the war with Japan. In essence, the government would receive aid and advice but could accept the aid and ignore much of the advice. Most of the negative comments made by advisory personnel were focused on individuals who did not take responsibility for their positions. Many had less than clear lines of authority as many positions were shared among two or three officers. This personnel system was one of the areas mentioned most frequently as needing reform. Also mentioned was the accountability for supplies, again a problem demonstrating a lack of professionalism. Thus, although many junior officers and ratings and enlisted men had been trained in American naval thought and methodology, the senior officers and commanders were generally more comfortable with the system with which they were familiar and from which they benefited. Changes that occurred were at the surface of the organization, not at its core. Although a modern naval service had been created, the system remained personal, not professional.

Since the Americans could issue advice, but not orders, the Chinese could appear receptive yet fail to implement the advice. While the long-term goals of the two countries may have been the same, the short term goals were not. For the short term, the Chinese were reluctant to change their system. China was a U.S. ally, but one reluctant to adopt a foreign system, politically or militarily.

NOTES

The following abbreviations are used in the notes:

FRUS	*The Foreign Relations of the United States*
NAGSB	Naval Advisory Group Survey Board
NARA-CP	National Archives and Record Administration, College Park, MD
NARA-SF	National Archives and Record Administration, San Francisco
RG	Record Group

1. Maochun Yu, *The Dragon's War: Allied Operations and the Fate of China, 1937–1947* (Annapolis, MD: Naval Institute Press, 2006), 68. Their "navy" had one junk and a launch, but sizable ground forces engaged in intelligence and guerrilla operations. Biography File, Naval Group China Papers, Box 1, RG 38, NARA-CP.
2. Larry I. Bland, ed., *The Papers of George Catlett Marshall* (Baltimore, MD: Johns Hopkins University Press, 2003), 5:276, n. 1.
3. This was generally a two-year assignment. Most of the Marines were withdrawn by 1947, except for elements of the 6th Marine Division at Qingdao. E. B. Sledge, *China Marine* (Tuscaloosa: University of Alabama Press, 2002) xx; correspondance from G. C. Marshall to Col. M. S. Carter, 16 November 1946, FRUS 10: 883.
4. "Final Report," Naval Advisory Division, 16 February 1949, Political Relations File, Box 136, RG 334, NARA-SF.
5. Briefing of the Armed Services Committee, Naval Advisory Group Survey Board, Rear Adm. S. S. Murray, USN, 10 October 1947, A-7-1, Box 136, RG 334, NARA-SF.
6. These provisions were specified under (U.S.) Public Law 512, 16 July 1946; Briefing of the Armed Services Committee, Naval Advisory Group Survey Board, Rear Adm. S. S. Murray, USN, 10 October 1947, A-7-1, Box 136, RG 334, NARA-SF.
7. U.S. State Department, *The China White Paper, August 1949* (Stanford, CA: Stanford University Press, 1967) 1:341.
8. Correspondence from Col. S. B. Griffith, USMC, to Rear Adm. S. S. Murray, USN, "Training Chinese Officers as Marines at USMC Schools," A-3-1, Box 138, RG 334, NARA-SF.
9. Personnel and administrative advisory papers, 24 June 1946, Box 10, RG 334, NARA-SF; Bland, *The Papers of George Catlett Marshall*, 469, n. 1.
10. State Department, *The China White Paper*, 339.
11. Correspondence from from the chief of naval operations to the NAGSB, China, 1 July 1948, 001-2, RG 334, NARA-SF.
12. Enclosure "B," 27 March 1948, 1330/27, Box S 185, RG 334, NARA-SF.

13. Correspondence from from the ambassador in China (Stuart) to the Secretary of State, 11 July 1948, FRUS, 8: 266–267; memo of conversation betwen the chief of the division of Chinese affairs and an unnamed party, 15 June 1948, FRUS, 8: 256–257; Correspondence from from the ambassador in China (Stuart) to the Secretary of State, 11 July 1948, FRUS 8: 259–264.
14. State Department, *The China White Paper*, 341; the military advisory group in China, Political Relations File, Box 136, RG 334, NARA-SF.
15. Military advisory group: Combined and joint organization, Box 56, RG 334, NARA-CP.
16. Upgrading the Chinese army changed the power relationships within the government and military forces, especially with regard to training and supplies. Edward L. Dreyer, *China at War, 1901–1949* (New York: Longman, 1995), 260; correspondence from from commander of the Seventh Fleet to the chief of naval operations, "Report of the Activities of the Prospective NAG," 11 November 1946, A-7-1, Box 136, RG 334, NARA-SF.
17. Memo from the NAGSB to Rear Adm. H. R. Thurber, n.d., A-3-1, Box S 175, RG 334, NARA-SF.
18. Correspondence from from the commander, Qingdao Unit, Naval Advisory Division, JUSMAG, China, to the chief, Naval Advisory Division, "Final Report," 25 January 1949, 334.5.3, RG 334, NARA-SF.
19. Ibid.
20. NAGSB, China, Memorandum for Rear Adm. H. R. Thurber, USN. n.d., A-3-1, Box S 186, RG 334, NARA-SF.
21. "Final Report," 25 January 1949, 334.5.3, RG 334, NARA-SF.
22. Briefing of the Armed Services Committee, NAGSB, by Rear Adm. S. S. Murray, USN, 10 October 1947, A-7-1, Box 136, RG 334, NARA-SF.
23. "Final Report," Records of the Joint U.S. Military Advisory Group to the Republic of China, 16 February 1949, 334.5.3, Box 183, RG 334, NARA-SF.
24. "Final Report," Naval Advisory Division, 25 January 1949, Political Relations File, Box 136, RG 334, NARA-SF.
25. Ibid.
26. Ibid.
27. Correspondence from the senior member to the chief of naval operations, 1 November 1947, 043, Box 330, RG 313, NARA-SF.
28. Chinese Training Group, Tsingtao, 23 January 1948, JUSMAG 1947–49, RG334, NARA-SF.
29. Memorandum for Captain Nutting, "Procurement, Training and Distribution of Instructors for Officers Training Schools and Technical Rating Schools at CNTC," 24 May 1948, A-7-1, RG 334, NARA-SF.
30. Correspondence, 1 November 1947, 313.58.043, Box S 186, RG 334, NARA-SF.
31. "Proceedings of the Dedication of Camp Hank Gibbons," 15 June 1945, Miles Papers, Box 34, RG 38, NARA-CP.
32. General correspondence, "A" subjects, 15 December 1947, 313.59A, Box 330 RG 313, NARA-SF.
33. Correspondence from the senior member to the the chief of naval operations, 1 November 1947, 043, Box 330, RG 313, NARA-SF.
34. NAGSB memorandum for Rear Adm. H. R. Thurber, "General Information on the Background of the Prospective NAG, China," A-3-1, RG 334, NARA-SF.
35. Correspondence from the senior member to the the chief of naval operations, 1 November 1947, 043, Box 330, RG 313, NARA-SF; chief, Bureau of Supplies and Accounts to CNC

Pacific Fleet, Chinese Lend-Lease Program, 27 August 1946, A 16-4, Box 330, RG 313, NARA-SF.
36. Final Report, 25 January 1949, Records of the Joint U.S. Military Advisory Mission to the Republic of China, 334.5.3/ RG 334, NARA-SF.
37. "NAGSB Preliminary Proposal for the Organization of the Ministry of National Defense," 3 September 1946, 313–58, Box 173, RG 313, NARA-SF; Enclosure "F," A-8-2, Box S 181, RG 334, NARA-SF.
38. Memorandum to Rear Adm. S. S. Murray, USN, from Col. S. B. Griffith (USMC), "Basic Training of Chinese Marines," November 1946, A-3-1, RG 334, NARA-SF.
39. Enclosure "F," 22 April 1948, A-8-2, Box S 181, RG 334, NARA-SF.
40. Ibid.
41. "A" subjects, 18 June 1948, 0015, RG 334, NARA-SF.
42. Correspondence from Secretary of State G. C. Marshall to Secretary of the Navy James Forrestal, 23 July 1947, G-2/CICNFE, Box S185, RG 334, NARA-SF.
43. General correspondence, "A" Subjects, 15 December 1947, 313-58-1, Box 330, RG 313, NARA-SF; Progress Report from liaison officer with Chinese DE Crews 1 and 2 to chief, NAD, JUSMAG, China, 12 November 1948, "Progress Report," RG 313, NARA-SF.
44. "Report of Activities," December 1948, "A" subjects, Box 330, RG 313, NARA-SF.
45. Correspondence from liaison officer with Chinese DE Crews 1 & 2, Norfolk Naval Shipyard, Portsmouth, VA, "Progress Report," 12 November 1948, A-7-1 RG 334, NARA-SF.
46. Military advisory group (MAG), "The Office of the Chief: The Prospective MAG in China," 29 June 1947, A-7-1, Box 136, RG 334, NARA-SF.
47. Correspondence from Rear Adm. H. R. Thurber, USN, senior member, NAGSB, to Vice Adm. Kwei Yun-chin, CNC, CN, 22 March 1948, A-3-2, RG 334, NARA-SF.
48. Correspondence from the naval attaché, Nanking, Lt. Gen. Kuei Yung-ching, 23 September 1946, A-8, RG 334, NARA-SF.
49. Correspondence from commanding officer, Chinese training group, to senior member, NAGSB, 8 April 1948, A-7-1, RG 334, NARA-SF.
50. Briefing of the Armed Services Committee by Rear Adm. S. S. Murray.
51. A2-12, 13 February 1947, Box 186, RG 334, NARA-SF.
52. Memorandum for Rear Adm. S. S. Murray, USN, 24 February 1947, A 2-12, Box S 186, RG 334, NARA-SF.
53. Ibid.; memo 76, 26 May 1948, Box S 185, RG 334, NARA-SF.
54. Memorandum to Vice Adm. Kwei Yun-chin, acting commander, naval group, from Rear Adm. H. R. Thurber, USN, senior member NAGSB, 5 June 1948, 015-83, RG 334, NARA-SF.
55. Memorandum to Secretary of State re: State War and Navy Coordinating Committee, JCS 1330/18, RG 38, NARA-SF.
56. "Final Report," 25 January 1949.
57. State Department, *The China White Paper*, 342; "Final Report," 25 January 1949.
58. Correspondence from senior member to ComNavForWesPac, "Activities of the Chinese Navy," May 7–16, 1948, A-3.0016, Box S 186, RG 334, NARA-SF.
59. "Final Report," 25 January 1948.
60. Commander TG 70.4, USNavForWesPac, Operations Plan, 8 April 1947, 029-47, Box S 186, RG 334, NARA-SF; ComNavForWes Pac, Operation Plan 103, 10 April 1948, Box 59, RG 334, NARA-CP.
61. Records of the JUSMAF to the Republic of China, 17 September 1948, 334.5.3, Box S 185, RG 334, NARA-SF.

62. CIA analysis, China, CRE 45-48, 22 July 1948, https://www.cia.gov/library/center-for-the-study-of-intelligence/csi-publications/books-and-monographs/listing-of-declassified-national-intelligence-estimates-on-the-soviet-union-and-international-communism-1946-1984/1948.htm.

PART IV. EUROPE

French Naval Intelligence during the American Civil War and the Mexican Expedition, 1861–67

Alexandre Sheldon-Duplaix

From the beginning of the American Civil War in March 1861 to the departure of the last French troop from Mexico six years later, the relations between Paris and Washington were characterized by mutual suspicion over the possibility of a naval confrontation that could have been initiated either by France or by the United States. During nearly three years, Washington, weakened by the secession of the southern states, feared a French recognition of the Confederacy accompanied by a forceful lifting of the Union blockade to access the cotton very much needed by France's factories. From late 1863 to 1867, Paris was becoming more and more concerned over the increasing American support to its enemies in Mexico and the reaffirmation of the Monroe Doctrine.

The first phase of this Franco-American crisis (1861–63) coincided with the active role played by the French navy in American waters to monitor the effectiveness of the Union blockade and gather information on the revolutionary technological and tactical developments introduced by the Union and Confederate navies. The second phase (1864–65) was characterized by the embarrassing presence of the Confederate navy in French waters while the difficulties encountered by the French expeditionary force in Mexico made it likely that the Union could use the leverage of its attitude across the Rio Grande to check and balance France's neutrality policy toward Confederate ships. In a third phase, the aftermath of the Civil War (1865–67), the risks of an American intervention in Mexico seemed even more likely, contributing to the controversial decision to withdraw the expeditionary corps under the protection of the armored ships division.

Traditionally, captains and consuls were the two main sources for naval intelligence, forging a close cooperation between the foreign affairs and the marine ministries. Their correspondences illuminate the little-known role played by naval intelligence in support of French foreign policy during a period in which France had chosen a partnership with Britain departing from an earlier strategy to counterbalance British sea power with America's maritime might and prompting Russia to side with the Union. The correspondences also reveal the character of Rear Adm. Camille Clément de La Roncière Le Noury.[1] As director of the movements and operations and as the marine minister's chief of staff, he acquired an intimate knowledge of American affairs during the Civil War before commanding the armored ships division and the repatriation of the Mexican expedition.

MONITORING THE AMERICAN CIVIL WAR AND ITS IMPLICATIONS FOR FRENCH INTEREST

THE STRATEGIC AND INTELLIGENCE CHALLENGES

Historians Case and Spencer have shown that Emperor Napoleon III's first reaction to the American Civil War was toward strict neutrality since intervention would have favored the South—and slavery—antagonizing the liberal opposition at home. Secession could weaken the United States and open a new market for British and French industrial products in the South; it could also give birth to two aggressive competitors seeking expansion in Canada and Mexico, damaging British and French interests.[2] The idea of a foreign war suggested by William Seward, the Union secretary of state, was immediately rejected by President Abraham Lincoln, but soon the impact of the "cotton famine" on the French and British economies drove Paris and London to consider full recognition of the Confederate government and intervention to trade with the southern states.[3] For the North, French neutrality favored the South and Paris's alignment with London angered Seward.[4] But in November 1861 London and Washington were on the brink of war over the capture of the Confederate envoys to Europe onboard the British steamer *Trent*.[5] Paris pressed Washington to release the ministers, which avoided war. However, the sinking of a stone fleet to close the port of Charleston infuriated the emperor, who contemplated breaking the blockade to end the economic crisis at home.[6] In July 1862 Napoleon III was still toying with the idea of an Anglo-French mediation followed by a joint recognition of the Confederacy.[7] The Union victory at Antietam and Lincoln's Emancipation Proclamation drove the British government to withdraw its plan. France was forced to follow.[8]

FRENCH NAVAL INTELLIGENCE DURING THE AMERICAN CIVIL WAR AND THE MEXICAN EXPEDITION, 1861-67

France's Civil War diplomacy was complicated by its intervention in Mexico. Originally, Paris, London, and Madrid sought reparations from the Juarez government for the spoliations of their residents. The three powers had agreed on 31 October 1861 to send an expeditionary force. In January 1862 a French squadron[9] joined by British vessels arrived in Veracruz, where a Spanish expeditionary corps[10] had already been disembarked. Contrary to earlier expectations, the population did not welcome the invaders who were faced with the prospect of a military campaign.[11] As explained in an 1863 note, poor intelligence on the Mexican public opinion was to be blamed.[12] Paris also assumed that the Mexicans would readily accept any new government that would bring them stability and order and was willing to impose Maximilian of Austria as a new sovereign. Spain and England disagreed and withdrew their troops. France proceeded alone, taking control of Mexico City on 7 June 1863 after a one-year campaign.[13]

Still pressing the Union for an access to the southern ports, France was seen as the main adversary of the Union by Gideon Welles, the Union secretary of the navy.[14] On 25 September 1863 he remarked that France was becoming more threatening but that her policy was tied to Britain and that London was too scared by Union ironclads and cruisers to move while Adm. David Dixon Porter noted that "the Navy Department has kept France and England quiet, and got ahead of the whole world in offensive and defensive warfare."[15] A month earlier on 29 August 1863 de La Roncière Le Noury, the marine minister's chief of staff, had explained to his (La Roncière Le Noury's) wife how serious the situation was: "We have to discuss the recognition of the Confederacy. The Emperor is obsessed about it. . . . [The foreign affairs minister] is against. [The marine minister] does not dare to speak because of his personal interests in the South. This is a serious decision which could bring war with the North. But that would be a diversion to Poland; this is why [the foreign affairs minister] complains."[16] On 25 December Welles noted, "France was still an enemy of the USA but that fortunately the British were less and less bellicose."[17] For its part, Britain was very much afraid of a Union attack on Canada after the depredations committed by the Confederate cruisers built in British shipyards.[18] By 1864 the French efforts to intervene in the American Civil War had come to an end. Union victories, new sources of cotton, and a gradual decline of unemployment through retraining had removed the pressure on the imperial government to act forcefully.[19] Neither Paris nor London could find a mutually acceptable basis for joint intervention against a nation whose naval might seemed devastating and who could side with Russia in a European dispute.

In this context, naval intelligence was a key factor for the decision makers,[20] having always been at the core of the cooperation between the foreign affairs and the marine ministries. Orders of battle[21] were compiled by the foreign affairs' Bureau of Translations, which also deciphered diplomatic mail and dispatched agents abroad.[22] Technical intelligence was obtained by engineers traveling abroad.[23] On the operational side, the Depot of Charts and Plans at the Marine Ministry[24] collected foreign nautical instructions while the marine minister's cabinet oversaw intelligence and operations. Reconnaissance was conducted under the cover of fishery studies.[25] This system seemed to work if we accept this assessment made on the eve of the Crimean War: "[A]s to the Navy, we know that she has the most precise intelligence on the exact number of enemy ships; surveys . . . have been collected . . . long before the actual conflict."[26] Headed by Rear Adm. de La Roncière Le Noury,[27] during the entire American Civil War the Directorate for Fleet Movements and Military Operations[28] directed the French naval divisions posted on the North American coast, in the West Indies,[29] on the Gulf of Mexico,[30] and on the Pacific coast. The reports from the divisions' commanders were the main source of information for the decision makers in the marine and foreign affairs ministries.[31] These regular channels of information were supplemented by impressions collected by special envoys[32] and by personalities who visited America during the Civil War.[33]

ESTABLISHING COMMUNICATIONS AND ASSESSING THE BLOCKADE AND THE WAR

The mail took about two weeks across the Atlantic from New York or Halifax to Le Havre and Paris. Despite earlier attempts, the telegraph across the Atlantic did not become operational until 1866.[34] Communications with the consulates in the South was a problem. In Richmond and in Charleston, British and French consuls wanted a regular line of communications.[35] For this purpose, France and England established a continual naval presence on key stations: two French corvettes in New York, one of them rotating with a British vessel to visit Norfolk once a week.[36] The other corvette was moved permanently to Hampton Roads, where she maintained contact with the French consulates through a flag of truce arrangement.[37] Capt. Louis Raymond Montaignac, commanding the frigate *Pomone*, noted that both the North and the South benefited from that system and were extremely well informed on their enemy through the daily flow of "prisoners, ladies, foreign nationals, private letters, opened and read by both sides, newspapers and bottles of whisky" across the front line.[38]

Proclaimed on 19 April 1861, the blockade of the southern ports pressed France and England to decide whether or not they would accept the blockade.[39] By June they had agreed to recognize it if it was effective. By August,

French and British warships were covering the entire U.S. coast from the Gulf of Mexico to Hampton Roads.[40] On 25 July the *New York Times* published an article claiming that Adm. Alexander Milne,[41] the British naval division commander, considered the blockade inefficient.[42] Milne's words had been distorted. During his September visit to New Orleans, French commander Commo Amédée Ribourt called it a "a paper blockade": "the large vessels which block the main outlets [of the Mississippi] stay in their anchorages during the night. They can't see what's going by them even at a short distance because they have no dispatch vessels to connect them."[43] Ribourt had learned that the British steamer *Bermuda* had entered Savannah without having met a federal cruiser.[44] However, that same month Rear Adm. Aimé Reynaud noted, "The large ports such as Charleston and Savannah while not blockaded as tightly as possible nevertheless are effectively sealed off. However the smaller ports are not."[45] By October 1861 British Foreign Affairs Minister Earl Russel had decided to regard the blockade as generally effective.[46] France accepted the British view to continue England's common front with London although a loose blockade did not serve France's own interest should it be at war with Britain.[47] During the following months, conflicting reports gave a mixed picture. In February 1862 Ribourt noted that the fog enabled Confederate steamers loaded with cotton to evade the New Orleans blockade quite easily.[48] Touring the besieged Confederate port of Charleston, Montaignac remarked that the blockade was effective, the shops being empty and the imported goods sold at horrendous prices.[49] New Orleans was captured by Union forces in April 1862, Norfolk in May, Galveston temporarily in 1863, and Mobile in August 1864, reducing the blockade to four ports after that date.

In 1861–63 the visiting French naval officers tended to see no end to the war. Prince de Joinville was quoted by Gustavius V. Fox, the assistant secretary of the Union navy, as having divided the task confronting the Union into "three separate problems": "the first of those was to establish and maintain an effective blockade of the Southern coast; the second to divide the Confederacy in two by seizing the Mississippi river; the third, to defeat the Confederate Army in the field."[50] In February 1862 Ribourt in New Orleans concluded that the North would not be able to win through the blockade and that the South was acquiring new means of war, such as cruisers in European shipyards, that could prove effective.[51] That same month, Montaignac in Charleston noted that people hoped for a financial collapse of the North and a European intervention, the expensive Union army having already proved inefficient and unable to move. Montaignac expected a prolonged war: "[T]here can be no decisive battle. A position of lesser or greater significance will be conquered . . . but in this immense land . . . it is a war which would be endless."⁵² In March 1862 Lt. François Fabre concurred, noting, "[W]hatever are the successes of the Union Army, the men of the South are determined to fight to the end and ready to destroy towns and harvests when ill luck forces them to withdraw."⁵³ If Jean-Pierre Jurien de la Gravière had celebrated in May 1862 "a national war led with energy supported by heroic deeds and which gives a grand idea of the American sailors' spirit of enterprise," Capt. Jean-Charles Pigeard, touring the North from November 1863 to February 1864, was disenchanted: "[N]ever such corruption from top to bottom of the military has been seen . . . and this poor South which is being persecuted under this great principle [equality], if it ever collapses will be the victim of the North's greed."⁵⁴

EVALUATING THE COST OF INTERVENTION

In March 1861 the U.S. Navy consisted of seventy-six wooden ships, including forty-two in active service. Even then, the French navy was generally under the impression that American wooden frigates and corvettes were more powerful in gunnery and in construction than were their French and British counterparts.⁵⁵ In January 1862 a French commander had given the following estimate on Union frigates: "[I]n rough seas they would be superior to our frigates and ships of the line with their higher gun batteries 4–5 meters above water."⁵⁶ He also considered the "large British frigates that we have seen in Halifax to be inferior to American frigates in gunnery and in sea faring qualities."⁵⁷ This judgment was shared by the Royal Navy's controller, Adm. Spencer Robinson, who told Pigeard, the French naval attaché in London, that he feared "the outcome of isolated engagements between British vessels and the latest American corvettes which combined remarkable speeds with powerful Dahlgren guns."⁵⁸

On 24 January 1862 Montaignac toured Norfolk's Navy Yard, where he saw the *Merrimack*⁵⁹ being rebuilt by the Confederate as an armored ship.

> She measures 300 feet and can reach a top speed of 8 knots. She has been razed down to [the or lop] deck where a roof has been raised. This wall inclined by 35° is covered with steel bars (0,045 m x 0,12 m) disposed horizontally and vertically. This armor is pierced by 10 hatches on each side plus two more fore and aft for 9 inch guns. The Southern sailors hope to destroy the four frigates moored at Hampton and combine their operations with the army corps established at Yorktown to seize Fort Monroe and Newport News where 3000 Union troops are entrenched.⁶⁰

On 8 and 9 March the French frigate *Gassendi* was the only foreign vessel to witness the sinking of the *Cumberland* by the *Merrimack* and her subsequent engagement with the Union ironclad *Monitor*.[61] Ange Simon Gautier, her captain, praised the two ironclads, giving his preference to the *Merrimack*.[62] Lt. René Lefort estimated that the *Monitor*'s armor would not withstand rifled projectiles and advocated boarding her, tapping her exhausts, thus blocking her turret and asphyxiating the crew.[63] He learned that the tallow laid on the *Merrimack*'s inclined flanks to repel boarders had caused the shots to bounce off.[64] The French officers were even more impressed by the ramming of the *Cumberland*. Impacting at less than three knots, the *Merrimack* had ruptured the frigate's hull, opening a hole one meter by thirty centimeters.[65] All were astounded by the revolution they had witnessed, Lieutenant Fabre concluding, "Armored ships have proved their superiority over ordinary vessels and the ram has achieved the most spectacular results."[66] From Veracruz a Union officer reported to Fox, the assistant secretary of the Union navy, "the news of the fight between the Monitor and the Merrimack has created the most profound sensation amongst the professional men in the allied fleet here . . . the superb frigates and ships of the line, such as *Mersey*, *Massena*, *Donegal* and *Foudre* supposed capable a month ago to destroy anything afloat in half an hour . . . are very much diminished."[67] Visiting New York and Washington in May 1862, Adm. Jean-Pierre Jurien de la Gravière, the first commander of the Mexican expedition, urged Napoleon III to reconsider any plan to attack the Union: "Nothing as daring and as clever has been done in the naval field for the past forty years. . . . I would advise the Emperor to consider this side of the question. . . . I beg your Excellency to consider that if [intervention] were to happen, we would have to make a major effort. . . . [The Americans] have audacious ideas but to achieve their results they have captains and sailors even more audacious."[68] And in Paris, John Bigelow, the Union consul, reported to Secretary of State William Seward that this "event had done more to re establish us as a national power in Europe . . . than anything that has occurred since the Rebellion."[69]

The impact on France and Britain was indeed considerable. On 24 May 1862 Vice Adm. Louis Bouët Willaumez, port admiral in Toulon, ordered the study of a coastal armored ram for inshore defense.[70] Captain Pigeard, the naval attaché in London and best French expert on British armored ships and gunnery, was also ordered to go to America,[71] arriving in November 1863.[72] At that time, the Union navy numbered 588 vessels, including seventy-five armored ships.[73] Seven dockyards and twenty-eight private shipyards had produced this impressive fleet.[74] Pigeard first visited the Navy Yard in Washington and obtained from Alexander Dallas Bache, the chief hydrographer, a complete set of naval charts.[75] Then Pigeard toured the Midwest and Pittsburgh, known as the Iron City.[76] Back in New York in late January 1864, he met three times with the celebrated Swedish engineer John Ericsson[77] before visiting two dockyards and two foundries.[78] Having been denied the permission to cross into the Confederacy,[79] Pigeard met with the famed Adm. John A. Dahlgren[80] off Charleston.[81] After journeying to Key West and the Gulf of Mexico, Pigeard returned to Boston in March and to England the following month. The Union naval program seemed to him purely defensive: "[W]hy compete with Europe to build armored frigates? If the maritime nations were to attack America, their action would be restricted by the draught of their ships in many areas."[82] American ordnance was, in Pigeard's view, "the only one to be combat proven, capable of defeating French and British armor."[83] His American experience had convinced him that the casemate and the big guns were key to success. In July 1864 Pigeard advocated replacing "the 40 guns of our frigates by 20 capable of firing projectiles two or three times heavier."[84]

Two other naval dimensions of the Civil War caught the interest of the French navy: underwater defenses and commerce raiding.

During his visit to the blockading squadron off Charleston, Pigeard had been impressed by the Confederate underwater defenses, which in his view "would adjust the balance in favor of the smaller navies."[85] Lefort, who had met with Gen. Pierre Gustave Toutant-Beauregard, described to de La Roncière Le Noury the dispositions taken to protect that harbor.[86] Pigeard was later recalled to France, to direct the commission auditing the famous Mathew Fontaine Maury[87] on Confederate underwater defenses.[88] The commission for underwater defenses concluded in 1867 that the Confederate "torpedoes" had destroyed twenty-nine Union vessels and damaged fourteen others, having a decisive effect to prevent the capture from the sea of the ports of Charleston and Wilmington and delaying the operations against Mobile and Richmond.[89]

The Confederates had understood that the American merchant marine, the largest in the world, was the North's Achilles' heel. Stephen Mallory, the Confederate secretary of the navy,[90] deployed a total of nine cruisers and four converted prizes to attack Union trade and distract federal warships from their blockading duties.[91] Eight of these cruisers, including the famous or infamous *Alabama*, were built in Britain under the direction of John Bulloch, the main figure of the Confederate secret service in Europe.[92] Traveling around Britain, French naval engineer and future submarine designer Gustave Zédé noted on 2 June 1863 the local authorities' complacency before suggesting that France should build similar vessels to be used as raiders in wartime: "Our neighbors are not in a hurry to see the end of the American War; trade repays for the money lost for lack of cotton. That is why the government has never made any serious effort to stop Confederate shipbuilding on the British territory.... Just one vessel, CSS *Alabama*, was enough to obtain this considerable result of having the maritime trade changing hands."[93]

Last but not least, the French navy learned the Russian plans of operations should a war erupt with England and France over Poland. In September 1863 Reynaud and Milne, the French and British station commanders, were astonished to find six Russian warships[94] in the port of New York.[95] The local authorities had also been caught by surprise with the arrival of two British and French admirals, whereas the ongoing Russo-American public celebrations had a strong anti-British and anti-French character, Russia "being the only European power to have sided with them recognizing the rightness of their cause."[96] A well-known lawyer[97] spoke before an enthusiastic crowd: "[W]e complain about France and England, first because they declared their neutrality and then because they did not observe this neutrality.... The men from this generation whose hearts have bled with these insults will not rest until they have vengeance."[98] But then a former Russian naval officer of Polish ancestry, Zbyishevskii, whom Reynaud had known in China told him that Grand Duke Konstantin, the Russian navy minister, had asked separately for the opinion of three admirals as to the best way to fight the British and French fleets and that all three had come up with a similar plan to attack Britain's and France's possessions in the Pacific.[99] Zbyishevskii had fled Vladivostock to Japan, where he had already warned the British legation of the Russian plans to attack Australia, prompting a major effort to fortify the ports of the colony. Asked about the Russian larger crews, the fugitive added that they would staff two armored ships to be assembled in San Francisco for the defense of the Russian Pacific coast.[100]

American openness on their ironclads bemused the British,[101] but it served its purpose. Both France and Britain were convinced that lifting the blockade would not be an easy task.

NEUTRALITY ISSUES IN FRENCH AND MEXICAN WATERS, AND THEIR IMPLICATIONS (1863–APRIL 1865)

CONFEDERATE NAVAL ACTIVITIES IN FRANCE

After an earlier Confederate attempt to buy the frigate *Gloire*,[102] John Slidell, Richmond's representative, asked Napoleon III in October 1862 if ships could be built in France.[103] The emperor seemed to agree but failed to answer. When

Arman, the largest shipbuilder in France, offered a contract to the Confederates for four Alabama-type steamers, Slidell took the risk to accept it, later adding two ironclad rams,[104] this time after a verbal reassurance by Napoleon III.[105] But on 9 September a discontented employee from the office of Arman's associate[106] brought evidence to William Dayton and John Bigelow, the Union minister and consul in Paris, that the ships being built in Bordeaux and Nantes were for the Confederacy.[107] Until then, the Union minister had rejected reports referring to such a program.[108] While the French authorities were being confronted with these new evidences by the Union minister, another issue was just emerging. Between August and October 1863 three Confederate warships had suddenly entered French ports asking for urgent repairs. During the Civil War[109] Confederate cruisers made a total of twenty-five port calls in England, eleven in France, and seven each in Brazil and Spain.[110] But five Confederate cruisers spent more than nine hundred days in French ports making France the location of their longest stays, attracting five Union cruisers that in turn stayed around one hundred days. An unintended ambiguity in the French declaration of neutrality of 10 June 1861 was behind this preference. While the British declarations[111] prohibited a belligerent warship from spending more than twenty-four hours in a British port and making another visit before three months, the French declaration stated, "no privateers or naval ships of either belligerent could enter or stay in French ports with captured prizes for more than 24 hours except under stress of storms," implying that privateers or naval ships without prizes could enter and stay in French ports for more than twenty-four hours. Moreover, the French declaration did not put restrictions on coaling while the British declaration limited the amount of coal to the quantity needed to reach the belligerent's closest port. The neutrality rules of Spain and Brazil[112] were also more stringent on coaling.[113]

However less restrictive, French neutrality limitations needed to be enforced and the main purpose of the intelligence collected by the port authorities was to establish the conditions and characteristics of the visiting ships to make sure that these vessels would not increase their strength by procuring weapons or augmenting their crews. Commo. Raphael Semmes's three earlier visits to Cayenne[114] and Martinique in 1861–62[115] onboard CSS *Sumter* and CSS *Alabama* had already presented some difficulties for the French authorities. Coal was denied to him in Guyana, and the governor of Fort de France, Martinique, authorized local merchants to resupply the cruisers to support the French policy that coal should not be treated as contraband of war. On both occasions in the Martinique a confrontation had been narrowly avoided with two Union cruisers, USS *Iroquois* and USS *San Jacinto*.[116]

The successful escapes at night of the two Confederate cruisers led the Union commanders to unjustly suspect connivance between the governor and the Confederates. On both occasions, French warships[117] captured American merchantmen[118] who had signaled the Union cruisers, violating French neutrality. Later, the Imperial Navy had received occasional reports on American cruisers by French merchantmen stopped on the high seas,[119] but nothing indicated that in late 1863 three Confederate cruisers would choose the metropolitan ports of Brest, Cherbourg, and Calais to spend a total of 731 days, violating French neutrality in a number of ways. In needs of extensive repairs, the *Florida* elected Brest.[120] Having left Britain as a merchantman, the *Georgia* was secretly fitted as a warship off Belle Isle inside French territorial waters in April before seeking repairs in Cherbourg ten months later. To prevent her seizure by British authorities, the *Rappahannock*—a former *Royal Navy* gunboat[121]—escaped to Calais with British workers still onboard. The sudden arrival of three Confederate warships in French ports provoked the anger of Dayton, the Union minister, and the appearance of USS *Kearsarge* who visited Brest seven times during the 170 days of the *Florida*'s presence. Being able to communicate with the marine minister by telegraph, the port officials of Brest,[122] Cherbourg,[123] and Calais informed continuously the marine minister and acted on direct orders. As de La Roncière Le Noury wrote to his wife, "The *Florida* gives us much trouble. The [marine] Minister is confused. The Emperor has some scabrous plans. Drouyn De Lhuys does not say yes or no. Chasseloup says yes and no. I categorically say no even though I have more sympathies for the Confederates than for the Federals. But when we have trouble with them in Mexico, it is no time to create new problems. I prepare a note."[124] As a seasoned diplomat, Foreign Affairs Minister Édouard Drouyn de Lhuys steered French policies toward neutrality.[125] Coal would be granted as a matter of policy. Quoting the Brazilian precedent, Drouyn de Lhuys also authorized ship and engine repairs, the latter against the Union minister's demand.[126] As for the crew, Drouyn de Lhuys forbade any reinforcement but authorized the replacement of departing personnel provided that no Frenchmen were recruited. The presence of USS *Kearsarge* in or off Brest forced the Imperial Navy to prepare for action.[127]

French neutrality rules obviously favored the South, which needed the dockyards, while the *Kearsarge*'s visits were just a consequence of the Confederate presence. Therefore a fundamental misunderstanding altered the relations with the both Confederacy and the Union. Since the emperor had secretly approved the building of warships for the South, the Confederates were entitled to believe that they would get all the facilities they wanted, provided that they would pretend to be law abiding. They also took for granted their access to naval dockyards while in fact the *Florida* and *Georgia* were admitted because there were no similar private facilities in the ports of Brest and Cherbourg. Consequently, the Confederates were dismayed by the difficulties they subsequently met[128] while Dayton and Capt. John Winslow, the USS *Kearsarge*'s commander, were furious to see the Confederates admitted in naval dockyards. Having hired his own French pilot and maintained his ship under steam while in Brest, Winslow contemplated burning the *Florida* and escaping.[129]

WEAPONS SHIPMENTS TO MEXICO

Good intelligence was of paramount importance for the Imperial Navy to track down the weapons shipments to Mexican deposed leader Benito Juarez and his partisans. Since France was not at war with Mexico, a blockade could not be imposed. Nevertheless, the French vessels from the Gulf of Mexico and the Pacific divisions were tasked to intercept the vessels that carried weapons without stopping the regular trade.[130] This contraband was mainly sent to Tampico, which was briefly occupied,[131] and to Matamoros on the Rio Grande, where it was very difficult to tell the final destination of a war cargo, Juarez or the Confederates. Weapons were also being shipped through the Mexican ports of the Pacific coast, where the distances made it even harder to stop the flow.

In the gulf the Imperial Navy often met with vessels of the Union blockading squadron under Adm. David G. Farragut. As Secretary of the Navy Welles had explained to Farragut, the French naval presence had justified sending the large frigate *Colorado*: "The Colorado goes to you . . . the French are assembling a large force in the Gulf and your flagship ought to be the best in the service."[132] For Jurien de la Gravière, the attitude of the North was a constant concern. On 26 January 1863 he noted that the Union authorities were putting obstacles to the purchase of mules in New Orleans, fearing a secret understanding to assist Juarez and calling for the constitution of a "respectable military force in the Gulf" to address "the bad will of a great maritime power."[133] Instructed not to interfere with the military supplies being sent to the Confederates and confronted with American vessels that sometimes helped Juarez moving his troops on the river, Rear Adm. Auguste Bosse[134] Jurien's successor, felt powerless without good intelligence: "unless we have good intelligence, neutral vessels are almost completely out of our control."[135] Meanwhile, Juarez was collecting the custom taxes from the ports that were not under French occupation showing the weakness of the French plan. During June 1863 de La Roncière Le Noury listed the Mexican ports to blockade[136] and the forces required for that effort.[137] Through Eugène Rouher, the minister of commerce, de La Roncière Le Noury was getting intelligence from the Paris syndicate of traders and exporters and their representatives in Mexico.[138] On 6 September 1863 France finally proclaimed a formal blockade of the ports that were not occupied,[139] but again its enforcement was nearly impossible. A note for the marine minister dated 29 May 1864 criticized the fact that the Mexican ports were not occupied and, "the French Navy had not been used like the US Navy in the war of 1847 to accompany the Army alongside the coast."[140] On 24 December 1863 Seward had tried, with a veiled advice, to reassure Captain Pigeard, the French Navy special envoy to inspect Union ironclads, by denying any Union intention to act against France in Mexico: "[W]e have nothing to do in Mexico ... we believe that this is for the Mexicans to decide for themselves. ... If they want a Sovereign, it is up to them ... but we doubt so."[141] But on the Rio Grande, Admiral Bosse of France was confronted by Union forces. They had moved into Texas, mainly to prevent French forces from being in a position to help the Confederates.[142] The Union consul in Matamoros had provided a passport to a Mexican general[143] to go to New Orleans and purchase 15,000 rifles that, according to Bosse's intelligence, were to be delivered to the Mexicans by a Union gunboat.[144] Bosse also understood that the Juarists were being helped by the South,[145] writing, "I believe that there is an agreement between the Confederate general [Bee] and the Mexican authorities of Matamoros to deceive us."[146] On the Pacific coast, French forces were insufficient and it was first decided to block Acapulco and San Blas while waiting for additional forces to extend the blockade and then seize Acapulco, which became the main base of operations in this area.[147] In May 1864 Maximilian arrived in Veracruz, reaching Mexico on 12 June, but Matamoros remained a port of contraband with many Americans serving in the local garrison under Gen. Juan Cortina of Mexico.[148] In September Cortina's troops had moved across the Rio Grande to attack the Confederates. Bosse protested to the Union commander[149] while the Confederate commander[150] asked for French support.[151] On 21 July 1864 Maximilian ordered lifting the blockade, obliging the French navy to visit every ship that made it impossible. The occupation of Matamoros on 26 September 1864 by a Mexican general now rallied to Emperor Maximilian,[152] temporarily relieving the French navy on the Rio Grande. These difficulties clearly justified a revision of French neutrality rules to prevent the Confederates from using French ports in order to obtain Union cooperation on the Rio Grande and in the ports where the Mexicans were buying and shipping weapons.

INTELLIGENCE AND THE NEW FRENCH NEUTRALITY RULES
The Confederates' prolonged use of French ports and the indiscretion about their shipbuilding program led the Imperial government to reissue its rules of neutrality on 5 February 1864 and remove the original ambiguity on prizes, prohibiting clearly belligerent vessels from staying in port for more than twenty-four hours except for bad weather or urgent repairs.[153] The *Florida* and the *Georgia* were ordered to depart Brest and Cherbourg while the *Rappahannock*, initially summoned to leave, was detained after the Union minister had threatened to hold France responsible for the *Rappahannock*'s future actions. A month later, the *Georgia* dropped anchor near Bordeaux but was forced again to leave.[154] The foreign affairs minister admonished his marine colleague about the Arman contract,[155] and in May 1864 Chasseloup Laubat dispatched Captain Pierre to inspect Arman's steamers. His conclusions were unequivocal: "[T]hese are veritable ships of war and good ones . . . they cannot be used as commercial ships without extensive alterations." The fate of both the steamers and the rams seemed to be sealed. France would not deliver them to the South. Seward was very upset, though, planning to dispatch immediately the new armored ship *Dictator* across the Atlantic.[156] Meanwhile, he had blocked a shipment of coal purchased by France in New York and destined for Veracruz.[157]

But another incident was just waiting to happen. After a brief rest in the remote French colony of Pulo Condore off Indochina in December 1863, Commander Semmes of CSS *Alabama* sailed to Europe via the Cape, "for the purpose of . . . overhauling and repairing my ship."[158] Unaware of the new French neutrality rules, he reached Cherbourg in June 1864 asking to dock his ship in the naval base. The port admiral never really had an opportunity to tell Semmes that his minister had denied him access to the dockyard[159] because the Confederate captain withdrew his application to get ready and fight the *Kearsarge*, which had arrived in port. Again, the French navy had to watch both the *Kearsarge* and the *Alabama*, the first for sailing inside territorial waters,[160] and the second for wanting to chase France's foe, forcing the port admiral to order the frigate *Couronne* "to take some visible dispositions for getting under way."[161] French authorities were very upset with the perspective of a sea battle off Cherbourg and informed Semmes on the superiority of his opponent. The fact that the *Kearsarge*'s hull was armored with a chain was no secret. During his first visit to the port admiral in Brest,[162] Winslow had proudly invited the French admiral to come onboard and see his protection.[163] Augustin Dupuy, Cherbourg's port admiral, reported in a private letter to de La Roncière Le Noury that he had gone as far as to tell Semmes about the *Kearsarge*'s chain protection to discourage his sortie: "I have met Captain

Semmes onboard *Talisman*. He has asked details on the Kearsarge, refusing to admit that she had armor."[164] Lt. Arthur Sinclair from CSS *Alabama* also reported this meeting.[165] Semmes was determined to fight, probably because he felt that he stood better chances against a single cruiser or because he was eager to put an honorable end to his exhausting cruises and silence his critics who accused him of avoiding battle.[166] But Slidell, the Confederate minister, wanted to make the best of this tragic event. On the fateful day, he accused the French authorities of having compelled the *Alabama* to leave.[167] After having received the news of *Alabama*'s sinking, Slidell renewed his criticisms to Drouyn de Lhuys,[168] scoring a point. On the evening of the battle, Napoleon III telegraphed his marine minister that he "would regret the *Alabama*'s disaster if as it is rumored we had forced her to leave." De La Roncière Le Noury answered with these words: "[W]e have done everything that was possible to prevent the *Alabama-Kearsarge*'s battle. . . . Since *Kearsarge*'s arrival Mr De Chasseloup Laubat has tried to dissuade the Alabama from sailing out. We had no right to oppose by force the battle outside our territorial waters. Therefore I believe that we are in line regarding neutrality."[169] The other circumstance that the French navy did not assist in the rescue of *Alabama*'s survivors angered Napoleon III,[170] who summoned de La Roncière Le Noury to come to Fontainebleau and explain.[171] The intervention of the British yacht *Deerhound* also prompted an official investigation. She had assisted in picking up forty-two survivors before heading for England.[172] Was she an accomplice? The French navy was unable to establish that the two ships had communicated while in Cherbourg, although by a strange coincidence the *Deerhound* had been together in Gibraltar with Semmes' previous ship, CSS *Sumter*.[173] In the aftermath of the battle, the Imperial Navy collected detailed accounts of the engagement and the gunnery performance with the help of Cdr. Géo Sinclair, a Confederate officer posted in France. On 21 June 1864 he wrote to Dupuy that the two 11-inch Dahlgren guns had been decisive, extinguishing *Alabama*'s burners and damaging her engine and helm. Sinclair believed that if the Confederate cruiser had been able to close on her opponent her shots could have penetrated the chain armor and damaged the machine while *Kearsarge*'s projectiles would have transpierced *Alabama* without exploding. Again, Imperial naval authorities were under the impression that Union ships were far more powerful than their French equivalents. In his letter to de La Roncière Le Noury, Dupuy praised the *Kearsarge*'s two 27-centimeter Dahlgrens: "[T]wo or three of their shots weighting 130 pounds were just enough to decide the fate of the *Alabama*. During the two hours of the fight these two guns fired 29 shots. What could we oppose to such a ship? The *Talisman* would not stand half an hour in front of such an opponent."[174] One month later, the visit of Union corvette *Sacramento* in Cherbourg confirmed Dupuy's judgment. He noted that her speed and her powerful guns[175] allowed her to attack or to flee the enemy depending on the conditions. "In summary, the *Sacramento* is an extremely powerful 'aviso' both for her engine and her guns and I would not dare to compare her with any of our 'aviso.'"[176]

This success and the French enforcement of its neutrality eased the tensions with Washington.[177] During October 1864, when the issue of the French nationals blocked in the South[178] was raised, Seward authorized two French warships[179] to proceed on the James River in an attempt to evacuate them.[180]

Meanwhile, Arman, unable to deliver his ships to the Confederates, was looking for customers. One ram was sold to a Swedish banker allegedly for Denmark and the other to Prussia alongside two of the four steamers, the two remaining going to Peru. Having left Bordeaux on 15 October 1864 as the *Staerkodder*, the first ram, officially bound to Helsingborg, sailed to Copenhagen, where she was rejected by the Danish government, which no longer needed the ship after having lost its war against Prussia. Arman saw an opportunity and offered her to Bulloch. Under the new scheme the *Staerkodder* left Denmark in January 1865 to rendezvous off Belle Isle in Brittany with a steamer transporting her armament and a French tug loaded with supplies; she was commissioned as the CSS *Stonewall*.[181] On 23 January, five days before a formal Union protest, the marine minister had been informed that an unidentified foreign warship was off Palais. French authorities seemed genuinely unaware of these circumstances even though they took three days to order an investigation. Even Seward acknowledged it to his secretary of the navy: "[He] tells me he knows one of the French armed vessels recently sold is for Sweden . . . [and] that the French government is not deceitful in this matter."[182] However on 3 November 1864 a Danish telegraphic dispatch intercepted by the French foreign affairs ministry informed Drouyn and Chasseloup Laubat, "the negotiations were definitively broken with Arman."[183] However the foreign affairs and marine ministers had failed to realize that it referred to the *Staerkodder* and that this ship was therefore still under French ownership when she was handed over to the Confederates.

Intelligence was indeed a key factor in the neutrality policy. Without the documents sold to Dayton by a disloyal shipyard employee, the Union might not have been able to prevent the delivery of the little fleet under construction in Bordeaux and Nantes. These ships could have created trouble for the blockading squadron, threatening Northern ports and prolonging the devastating raids on Union trade while exposing France to later claims.

THE THREAT OF AN AMERICAN INTERVENTION IN MEXICO AND ITS AFTERMATH (APRIL 1865–67)

THE SPECTER OF THE MONROE DOCTRINE

On 9 April 1865 Gen. Robert E. Lee surrendered, ending the Civil War.[184] With the collapse of the South, France feared a reaffirmation of the Monroe Doctrine, for sometimes the intelligence received by the French commanders had been alarming. The previous October Rear Admiral Bosse had reported to his minister that four privateers were being readied in New Orleans and Key West to attack the packets from Saint-Nazaire,[185] prompting Rear Adm. Octave Didelot, his successor in the Gulf of Mexico, to suggest escorting them.[186] Calling at San Francisco just after Lincoln's death in April 1865, Rear Adm. Jean-Baptiste Mazères, the Pacific division commander, attended the mourning ceremonies. He was hosted by the French-speaking Commo. David MacDougal, who authorized the *Rhin*, one of Mazères's transports[187] to be repaired at Mare Island's dockyard.[188] Despite this friendliness, Mazères noted the hostility toward the French presence in Mexico. Weapons shipments to Juarez were however limited, "Mexican agents being short of cash and American traders delivering their cargo upon payment only."[189] Mazères's following reports were more worrisome: "I really wonder what would become of us if our relations were broken [with Washington]." But according to Mazères, the real effect was upon the morale of the Mexican population that was being manipulated by Juarez using rumors of an American intervention to undermine French authority.[190] In May the captain of *Phlégéton* had reported from New York, "American newspapers call people to join Juarez's army. They want to get rid of the soldiers who have been dismissed and to create problems for the Mexican Empire."[191] Gen. François Bazaine, the supreme commander, was keeping Mazères informed about a seven thousand–strong army under Gen. James Henry Carleton in New Mexico and two "filibustering expeditions" that were being readied to "throw the French into the sea." Bazaine's staff also provided intelligence on ships bound to Acapulco with guns or due to be fitted as privateer in the Chilean port of Valparaiso.[192] Immobilized by its repairs at Mare Island, the *Rhin* was concerned to hear about the Mexican efforts to raise money and purchase two ships and four guns[193] in order to attack the French warship, which had left her cannons at Mazatlan.[194] Meanwhile, the French consuls were providing an invaluable help to Mazères. Cayotte in San Francisco was successful in his requests to seize various vessels: a sailing ship about to depart to Mexico with four hundred volunteers, a cargo of weapons,[195] a brig, and a sloop also loaded with rifles.[196] The French consul kept Juarez's supporters meetings under surveillance, noting the participation of prominent military officials.[197] In Colon (Panama), an "Israelite spy" recruited by the French consul checked on the cargoes of steamers in transit for weapons and "torpedoes" allegedly purchased in New York by Juarez's supporters.[198]

Overstretched, Mazères's forces in the Pacific were insufficient for their multiple tasks.[199] However, acting upon his intelligence, Mazères ordered the frigate *Pallas* to patrol the Peruvian and Chilean coasts and seek the seizure of any Mexican privateer fitting out in Valparaiso. Action was to be taken if the authorities were to ignore his request.[200] From Callao, the *Pallas* sent back a detailed and precise report on the U.S. South Pacific naval squadron.[201] To appease the *Rhin*'s concern over Mexican privateers, Mazères also dispatched the *D'Assas* to San Francisco loaded with the *Rhin*'s guns, so that she could defend herself against any eventuality. Thanking again the American authorities for their cooperation, Mazères was told that any further assistance would have to be requested in Washington through the French legation.[202]

Despite the cordiality of Franco-American relations, the threat of a possible American intervention in Mexico was looming. In September, Rear Admiral Didelot in New York noted that the government's caution on the Mexican issue was owing to the state of the country, exhausted after a prolonged war, but that the current dispositions would not last given the deep popular hostility against U.S. presence in Mexico. Didelot added, "[W]e could rely on the neutrality [of the American government] until at least the first days of the coming year, when Congress would convene again."[203] The admiral noted the reinforcement of the San Francisco squadron with four warships, including the twin turret monitor *Monadnock*, officially "to deal with an independent minded State and repel the Indians but most likely to be able to address any complications over Mexico."[204] On the Rio Grande, incidents across the river were frequent.[205] In early May 1865 Captain Cloué left Veracruz, crossed the bar, and took four ships[206] up river to defend Matamoros against a Juarist general.[207] As Cloué was just about to take command of the Gulf of Mexico's naval station,[208] de La Roncière Le Noury listed two likely eventualities he would face: the necessity of an effective blockade (of the Mexican ports)[209] and the possibility of being attacked by privateers coming from the United States but flying the Mexican flag.[210] Taking very seriously this threat, the Gulf of Mexico's station obtained the armored frigate *Normandie*.[211] Facing the prospect of an American intervention, Bazaine ordered occupying Acapulco that was taken on 11 August 1865 while black troops subordinated to Gen. Godfrey Weitzel of the U.S. Army plundered the border town of Bagdad, which was reoccupied by Maximilian forces in January 1866. Weitzel was recalled as a sign of goodwill, and France also repatriated troops drawing later criticisms by the chief of the naval mission to Mexico, Lt. Pierre-Léonce Détroyat: "[W]e exhausted ourselves with bits and pieces instead of hitting hard and massively. We preferred to recall some troops instead of sending a lot more to finish it all at once."[212] But Capt. Georges Cloué was dissatisfied with his division's potential: "If we have to fight the Americans . . . I need better and faster ships."[213] On 30 November 1865 France proposed a defensive alliance to Britain should the United States attack either one of them. Having more to lose, London turned down the offer.[214]

THE DECISION TO WITHDRAW

The United States' mounting pressure as much as Napoleon III's worries about a rising Prussia led to his 22 January 1866 decision to withdraw the French expeditionary force from Mexico before the end of 1867, without having been able to extract concessions from Seward. In December Bigelow had been instructed to tell the emperor that the Franco-American friendship was in jeopardy. If General Grant was pressing for war, with motives that may have been to preserve an important military or to reunite the country, Secretary of State Seward thought rightly that diplomatic pressure would be enough.[215] On 1 February Bazaine gave his orders to repatriate the troops.[216] As Didelot wrote to de La Roncière Le Noury, this decision had removed for the time being the risk of a conflict with the United States: "[T]he crisis in Europe is far more serious than what we could fear from this side [of the Atlantic]; our concerns are secondary. The decision to withdraw our troops made publicly remove any character of gravity to the incidents which may occur with the United States." Lieutenant Détroyat, head of Maximilian's military mission, put the blame on the inferiority of the French ironclads but questioned the United States' will to go to war and criticized France's betrayal of Maximilian:

> [W]e have to avoid the war with the USA because we are not ready. . . . How right you were when you said that we should not let the United States force us to retreat. It is true that our Navy is not ready and as a sailor I regret it, blaming Admiral Ohier who celebrated our frigate *La Gloire*. Admiral Didelot showed me a sad letter from Admiral Paris about Admiral Bouët telling the truth at last on our armored ships. Nevertheless, America is vulnerable. She is broke. She does not want war. Her daring president wanted to scare. He succeeded. . . . We wrote bluntly to Maximilian: "we withdraw, we violate our treaties and promises." Is it fair?[217]

Didelot however did not see an end to the conflict with the United States over Mexico, also implying that France's withdrawal was related to the inferiority of its vessels: "We have about 18 months to two years ahead of us. But this question will surge again. Are we going to be in a position to face this quarrel which we lamentably declined because of our insufficient material?"[218]

Despite France's announcement, the United States did not relinquish its pressure. The French Gulf of Mexico's division was shadowed by two American double-enders gunboats, the *Paul Jones* and the *Mahasca*. In April 1866 the *Paul Jones* moved upriver, raising French suspicions as to its real motives in an area where Juarez's partisans were active. As General Doué reported to Captain Cloué, the new naval division commander in July, "[T]he US will do their best to harm us. Here is the end result. This is bad."[219] And de La Roncière even wrote to his wife that the United States might also side with Prussia because Napoleon III was trying to gain territorial compensations across the Rhine in the aftermath of Prussian victories over Denmark and Austria: "It is obvious that the war will break out in Germany. . . . I am afraid that the rest of Europe and the United States will get involved."[220] In September the *Phlégéton* noted the powerful armament of the *Paul Jones*[221] when she met her at Tampico. Writing to the French marine minister, Cloué,explained that in the eventuality of a confrontation "the division would be . . . reduced to the state of 'Turkish battleships,' as we say." In November the *Paul Jones* was again upriver provoking shows of support from the population on the Mexican bank,[222] and on 29 November the frigate *Susquehannah* carrying Gen. William T. Sherman and Minister Lewis Campbell arrived at Veracruz, seeking permission for the *Susquehannah*'s hosts to visit Mexico City. This move was accompanied by rumors about Emperor Maximilian's imminent abdication. On 2 December the *Susquehannah* departed, the emissaries having not been ashore.[223] As Cloué explained to de La Roncière, "[T]he State Council . . . had been conveyed by the Emperor at Oaxaca to receive his official abdication but the rumors about the coming of US Minister Campbell and General Sherman have agitated the Mexican leaders. They now realized a bit late that they will fell in the grasp of the Americans . . . [and] try to stop the collapse of the Empire that they have contributed to accelerate. A despicable people without political conviction or morals."[224] Meanwhile, American troops had briefly occupied Matamoros after a violent battle between the Juarists and a former supporter.[225] Having failed to withdraw the first contingent in November as previously announced, Napoleon III was given another warning by Seward through one of the first transatlantic cables. France answered, "[F]or military considerations it had decided to substitute a collective repatriation to one by divisions" and that its forces would be repatriated in the following March instead of November.[226]

A LAST SHOW OF FORCE AND AN INTELLIGENCE COUP

De La Roncière Le Noury was resentful about the United States' attitude that had precipitated the Mexican withdrawal and wrote a disheartened account of Adm. Louis M. Goldsborough's visit to Cherbourg in August 1866 that followed the news of peace among the German states:

> Boom, boom, guns, drums, clarions, guard, music, Reine-Hortense's anthem, flags, emotions, Champaign . . . silence . . . messieurs, gentlemen, we have just rejoiced at the peace that has been concluded between the belligerent parties in Germany, by the disinterested intervention, etc. . . . To Abraham Lincoln!!! A. Johnson! Great Admiral Goldsborough! Gallant Admiral . . . France has shed her blood for the US! Let's embrace! Boom, boom. US national anthem: half somniferous, half good for the bears to dance. Goldsborough answers. Nobody understands because he speaks too fast. Never mind. Night is falling.[227]

But on 21 December de La Roncière was ordered to rally Veracruz with the armored ships division to protect the evacuation of French forces. This symbolic gesture saved the honor of the flag, bringing the core of the French navy in American waters under the orders of the man who had masterminded French naval operations during the four years of the American Civil War and knew best the naval balance of the time. It may have been justified by the warning sent by Seward in November. It may also have reflected lasting fears of Mexican armored privateers. The instructions sent to de La Roncière Le Noury were posterior to the answer addressed to Seward. They required his ships to go directly to Veracruz and return immediately without calling in any other ports. They did not refer to a specific threat.[228] The Imperial Navy successfully completed the repatriation of the remaining twenty-six thousand men of its expeditionary corps in March. The confrontation with the United States was over. De La Roncière Le Noury blamed heavily Bazaine, saying "he is the main cause of our Mexican failure,"[229] and only had kind words for the water closets in the trains when he eventually visited the United States, "this weird country,"[230] on his way back. In July he was obliged to host another U.S. flag visit, in Cherbourg, this time by Admiral Farragut.[231] France was no longer in a position to defy the Monroe Doctrine, and when President Buenaventura Baez of the Dominican Republic suggested to a French officer that he would readily accept France's suzerainty over his country to resist American pressures to acquire the Bay of Samana, Adm. Eugène Mecquet, the new division commander, dismissed a prospect that would distract his country from North Africa and Indochina while endangering its relations with the United States: "I can't see why it would be our interest to prevent the United States from purchasing the Bay of Samana, reputedly very unhealthy."[232]

Despite common views that the War of 1870 had caught France by surprise, French naval intelligence scored a success, thanks to Britain, France's occasional strategic partner. On 18 April 1867 the French ambassador to Berlin was tipped by his British colleague about Prussia's plans to acquire American ironclads. On 25 April Paris telegraphed its consul in New York to buy the American warships on sale in order to prevent their acquisition by Prussia. On 30 April the consul was proud to answer, "[T]here were only two ironclads for sale . . . Prussia was about to conclude. I ruined this project by purchasing them."[233] As Secretary of the Navy Welles remembered, Seward was astonished by the news that the French were buying American warships. The purchase of the armored vessels *Onondaga* and *Dundenberg* was not made out of interest for American naval technology, considered though as superior by some in the Imperial Navy, but to prevent them from being acquired by Prussia.[234]

CONCLUSIONS

For a period of six years (1861–67), French sailors had to contemplate the possibility of a confrontation with the U.S. Navy despite the cordiality of their relations. Most in the Imperial Navy viewed American ships as more powerful than their French equivalents. This assessment was an important if not decisive factor to explain two decisions made by Napoleon III: nonintervention in the American Civil War despite his temptation to reestablish the cotton trade through recognition of the Confederacy (1862–63) and withdrawal from Mexico where the French Navy felt unable to confront the U.S. Navy (1865–67).

The naval lessons of the American Civil War prompted the French navy to adopt heavier guns and to favor the ram. A coastal defense ram was ordered as a consequence of the actions conducted by the *Merrimack*. Confederate raiders and underwater defenses were seen as having delayed the Union victory. They also inspired the French navy.

French naval intelligence was managed by the marine minister's cabinet in close cooperation with the foreign affairs minister, continuing a tradition that dated back to the Ancien Régime. Historians[235] have claimed that the intelligence "deuxième [second] bureaus" appeared as a consequence of the defeat in the 1870s. In fact the "deuxième bureau" (later renamed "première [first] section" and again "deuxième bureau") created in 1882[236] previously existed within the marine minister's cabinet where operations and intelligence matters were merged.

De La Roncière Le Noury, the marine minister's right-hand man for four years, was the de facto mastermind of French naval intelligence during the American Civil War and was the U.S. Navy's potential adversary in his following command of the armored ships division. Like Drouyn de Lhuys, the foreign affairs minister, he opposed recognition of the Confederacy and sought stricter neutrality in French harbors to avoid complication with the United States over Mexico. But his private letters also reveal a man who wanted to resist the Monroe Doctrine and not give in to American pressure in Mexico.

Franco-British naval cooperation was close. However, the Imperial Navy apparently did not share its reports on American ironclads, Russo-American secret naval cooperation, and Russia's war plans in the pacific. Later, the British were instrumental in helping France to prevent Prussia from acquiring American ironclads.

NOTES

The following abbreviations are used in the notes:

BB
GG
M   Marine
MAE   Archives of the Foreign Affairs Ministry, Paris
SHD   French Defense Historical Service

1. Camille Clément de La Roncière Le Noury (1813–81).
2. E. Laboulaye, *Les Etats-Unis et la France* (Paris, 1862), 72; L. Case and W. Spencer, *The United States and France: Civil War Diplomacy* (Philadelphia: University of Pennsylvania Press, 1968), 747.
3. C. Folhen, *L'industrie textile en france au temps du Second Empire* (Paris: Plon, 1956), 128.
4. The fear that privateers would attack merchant ships with little regard to their nationality never materialized. The United States had not ratified the 1856 Declaration of Paris banning privateering.
5. John Slidell and James M. Mason (Confederate envoys to Europe); D. Crook, *Diplomacy during the American Civil War* (New York: Wiley, 1975), 209; N. Ferris, *The Trent Affair: A Diplomatic Crisis* (Knoxville: University of Tennessee Press, 1977), 280.
6. Case and Spencer, *The United States and France*, 252.
7. Ibid., 594.

8. In late 1862 Paris renewed its offer of a joint mediation in the war, this time to England and Russia, without more success. Case and Spencer, *The United States and France*, 252.
9. One ship of the line, two frigates, two avisos, four transports, and 2,800 troops under Rear Adm. Jurien de la Gravière.
10. Seven thousand troops under General Prim.
11. Archives of SHD, M, Vincennes, SHD/M, BB4 819, December 1863. Note just dated December 1863 from the "bureau of movements and war operations" on the Mexican expedition.
12. "Assurances received on the favorable dispositions of the Mexicans had led us to believe that we would be able use the country's resources; this proved to be wrong" (SHD/M, BB4 819, December 1863).
13. An additional eight thousand troops were dispatched in March and June 1862 followed in August by twenty thousand troops under General Foray, who shared the command of the expedition with the Gulf of Mexico's division commander.
14. Gideon Welles (1802–78).
15. Correspondence from D. D. Porter to G. V. Fox, Mississippi Squadron, 6 December 1863 in G. V. Fox, *Confidential correspondence of Gustavius V. Fox, Assistance Secretary of the Navy, 1861–1865*, Volume II, 199.
16. SHD/M, GG2 17, de La Roncière Le Noury to the baronne, his wife, 29 August 1863.
17. Welles also wondered how France had perceived the Russian naval presence in New York and San Francisco a strategic move to allow the Russian fleet to attack British and French colonies and trade, should a war had broken out over Poland. G.Welles, *The Diary of Gideon Welles,* Volume I, *1861–63* (Boston Houghton Mifflin Company, 1911), 443.
18. Lord Richard Lyons, the British minister in Washington, wrote on 13 April 1863, "the State of things here so far as peace with us is concerned is more alarming than it has never been since the Trent affair." Quoted by R. A. Courtemanche, *No Need of Glory: The British Navy in American Waters, 1860–64* (Annapolis, MD: U.S. Naval Institute, 1977), 118.
19. Case and Spencer, *The United States and France*, 426.
20. Napoleon III, the emperor; Edouard Thouvenel (1818–66) and Edouard Drouyn De Lhuys (1805–81), the foreign affairs ministers; Henri Mercier and Alfred Paul, the French representatives in Washington and Richmond; Prosper Chasseloup Laubat (1805–73), the marine minister; and de La Roncière Le Noury, Laubat's chief of staff.
21. Napoleon had praised Talleyrand for "the work on enemy fleet's movements," later characterizing the consuls as "a chain of watchmen who tell everything that must be known." A. Sheldon-Duplaix, "Le renseignement naval français," in *Revue Historique des Armées*, April 2001 (Vincennes, France, October 2001).
22. Ibid.
23. French naval engineers traveled to America to study docking, shipbuilding, and wiring techniques, notably in 1824, 1839, and 1841. SHD(M), 6 DD1 Series; various reports.
24. P. Zanco, *Le ministère de la Marine sous le Second Empire* (Vincennes, France, 2003), 57–58.
25. Sheldon-Duplaix, *Le renseignement naval français*.
26. Ibid.
27. De La Roncière La Noury was a brilliant officer who had reported on steam propulsion developments in England before serving as a chief of staff for a previous marine minister, Théodore Ducos; having fought gallantly in Sebastopol, de La Roncière Le Noury had befriended with Prince Napoléon, the Emperor's cousin when he commanded the Imperial Yacht.

28. Zanco, *Le ministère de la Marine sous le Second Empire*, 95–96.
29. Rear Adm. Aimé Reynaud and Rear Adm. Auguste Bosse.
30. The following rear admirals: Jurien de la Gravière, Bosse, and Didelot; and Captain Cloué.
31. Rear Adm. Mazères.
32. His special envoy was Captain Pigeard, the first French naval attaché in London, sent to America from September 1863 to March 1864 to assess armor and gunnery developments.
33. Early in 1861 Prince Napoleon, a liberal, traveled extensively in the North and the South, voicing his support for the Union cause. Exiled in America, the Prince de Joinville, one of the most influential French naval thinkers, had a son serving as a cadet at the U.S. Naval Academy. He published a book about the Union and Confederate navies in 1865.

    D. B. Caroll, *Henry Mercier and the American Civil War* (Princeton, NJ: Princeton University Press, 1971), 86; Prince de Joinville, *La marine en France et aux Etats-Unis en 1865* (Paris: Revue des deux mondes, 1865). Prince de Joinville's son was assisted by a French naval officer as his personal tutor.
34. B. Dibner, *The Atlantic Cable* (Norwalk, CT: Burndy Library, Inc., 1959).
35. Paul, the French consul at Richmond, had been unable to forward his valuable information over a period of four months. Archives of the Foreign Affairs Ministry, Paris (Ministère des Affaires Etrangères), Affaires diverses politiques, Vol. 13, Montaignac to the marine minister, 7 February 1862.
36. The ships brought back the correspondence from the French and British consulates in the southern states; with the planned northern invasion of New Orleans in early 1862 one of the two French corvettes was detached to Havana to be able to communicate with the French community. Rear Admiral Milne, the British naval division commander, did not want not to have a ship where the French navy was present.
37. MAE, Affaires diverses politiques, Vol. 13, Montaignac de Chavance to Mercier, undated; Montaignac de Chavance, Louis (1811–91).
38. MAE, Affaires diverses politiques, Vol. 13, Montaignac de Chavance to the marine minister, 7 February 1862.
39. Effectiveness was a matter of debate. Did it mean that the 185 southern ports had to be blocked or just the seven largest trading ports of Norfolk, Wilmington, Charleston, Savannah, Mobile, New Orleans, and Galveston? That year, three flag officers—Samuel Dupont, Louis M. Goldsborough, and David Farragut—assumed command of the South Atlantic, the North Atlantic, and the Gulf of Mexico's blockading squadrons, respectively.
40. If the blockade was found deficient, French or British captains were to inform the closest Union blockading officer.
41. Alexander Milne (1806–96).
42. Ibid., 21.
43. MAE, Affaires diverses politiques, Vol. 13, Ribourt to the marine minister, 7 October 1861; Amédée Ribourt (1821–93).
44. It was loaded with thirty guns, eight thousand rifles, and forty thousand cartridges. Ibid.
45. MAE, Affaires diverses politiques, Vol.13, Reynaud to the marine minister, September 1861, quoted by Case and Spencer, *The United States and France*, 143. Aimé Reynaud (1808–76).
46. Russel remarked later, "British interests may profit to some extent by the imperfect manner in which the blockade may be maintained." Quoted by Courtemanche, *No Need of Glory*, 23.
47. Case and Spencer, *The United States and France*, 294; France later obtained from Washington the opening of three southern ports—Beaufort, Port Royal, and New Orleans—but the Confederates prevented France from getting cotton.

48. According to the Confederates, forty-nine vessels had reached Havana from southern ports since the beginning of the war and forty-six had completed successfully the opposite journey. MAE, Affaires diverses politiques, Vol.13, Ribourt to the marine minister, 19 February 1862.
49. Ibid.
50. Quoted by Rear Admiral Caspar F. Goodrich, in G. V. Fox, *Confidential correspondence of Gustavius V. Fox*, Volume II, xvi–xvii.
51. MAE, Affaires diverses politiques, Vol. 13, Ribourt to the marine minister, 19 February 1862.
52. MAE, Affaires diverses politiques, Vol. 13, Montaignac to the marine minister, 7 February 1862.
53. SHD/M, GG2 17, Fabre to the marine minister, New York, Catinat, 11 March 1862; Amédée Fabre (1832–unk).
54. Ibid.
55. In October 1856 Commo. Jean-Charles Pigeard, France's first naval attaché in Britain, had visited in Southampton the American frigate *Merrimack* and praised her strength. SHD/M, BB4 1041, Pigeard to the marine minister, London, 1 November 1856 SHD/M, BB4 1041.
56. SHD/M, BB4 1040, Fabre to the captain commanding the naval division of Terre Neuve, 16 January 1862.
57. Ibid.
58. SHD/M, 6DD1 30, Pigeard to the marine minister, London, 21 December 1861.
59. Renamed *Virginia*.
60. SHD/M, BB4 798. Gautier to the marine minister, Hampton Roads, 16 March 1862.
61. Ibid.
62. The *Monitor*'s apparent immunity to the twenty-three projectiles that had struck her did not impress Gautier, who believed that she could be disabled by concentrated fire on her turret.
63. Confidential information from Lieutenant Jones, CSN; SHD/M, GG2 17, Lefort to de La Roncière Le Noury, 8 December 1864.
64. Ibid.
65. Ibid.
66. Ibid.; Fabre to the marine minister, New York, Catinat, 15 March 1862.
67. Correspondence from L. M. Powell to G. V. Fox, Potomac, off Veracruz, 4 April 1862.
68. SHD/M, GG2 17, Jurien de la Gravière to the marine minister, Washington, 22 May 1862.
69. Correspondence from Bigelow to Seward, Paris, 4 April 1862, quoted by Case and Spencer, *The United States and France*, 267.
70. M. Battesti, *La Marine de Napoléon III* (Vincennes, France: Service historique de la Marine, 1998), 717; Louis Bouët Willaumez (1808–71).
71. From September to October 1862 the Admiralty dispatched Capt. J. Bythesea, who was allowed to tour extensively Union dockyards and private shipyards, even though he was prohibited to visit Boston's fortifications, Bythesea, according to the British war secretary. R. A. Courtemanche, *No Need of Glory*, 157.
72. Captain Bythesea's visit may perhaps explain why Pigeard's trip was delayed until November 1863. There is no evidence in Pigeard's correspondences, however, that Paris and London shared their intelligence on American armored ships. SHD/M, BB4 1041, Pigeard to the marine minister, London, 21 October 1862.
73. Forty-six for coastal defense and twenty-nine for riverine warfare. Joinville, *La marine en France et aux Etats-Unis en 1865*; D. McKay, *La marine des Etats-Unis avant la guerre et la marine actuelle* (Paris: Corréard, 1865), 14.

74. Dahlgren guns and steam engines were produced at the Washington Navy Yard. The Portsmouth Navy Yard and the Brooklyn Navy Yard were the two main shipbuilders, followed by the Boston Navy Yard. The Brooklyn Navy Yard was also the main repair facility for the North Atlantic blockading squadron, supplemented by the Philadelphia Navy Yard. Recaptured in May 1862, the Pensacola Navy Yard was supporting the West Gulf Blockading Squadron while Mare Island Navy Yard assisted the units stationed on the Pacific coast. Private yards were mainly located around New York, Philadelphia, and Baltimore (fourteen shipyards), in New England (eight shipyards), and in the Midwest (seven shipyards).
75. France had similarly obtained Russian charts before the beginning of the Crimean War.
76. Seeing four armored river vessels at St Louis (Missouri) and studying the fabrication of two-inch amour plates and 10- to 15-inch Dahlgren guns in Pittsburgh.
77. John Ericsson (1803–89).
78. The Parott foundry factory of West Point, the dockyards of Boston and Watertown, and the foundry Alger & Co. SHD/M, BB4 1041, Pigeard to the marine minister, New York, 9 February 1864.
79. Ibid., 22 January 1864.
80. John Dalhgren (1809–70).
81. Very upset after the sinking of the frigate USS *Housatonic* by the confederate submarine *Hunley*. SHD/M, BB4 1041, Pigeard to the marine minister, New Orleans, 5 March 1864.
82. Pigeard had catalogued Union armored vessels into two main categories: the coastal and river monitors (eight classes) and the experimental warships (six classes). The latter were of special interest since their seagoing capabilities could threaten a Franco-British squadron. He dismissed the *Roanoke* and the *New Ironsides*: the first for having "lesser speed and protection" than Coles' battery, the second for being "a poor imitation of the European types." The *Galena* and the *Keokuk* were ocean-going semiarmored ships. The *Stevens* battery was supposed to become the "most powerful warship afloat," while the *Dunderberg* combined the turret and the central battery. SHD/M, 6DD1 30, Pigeard to the marine minister, London, 2 July 1864.
83. Ibid.
84. Ibid.
85. Ibid.
86. "[N]ets and ropes were being disposed in the passes to engage the propellers while casks of powder were being laid on the ships' routes. Rumors were spread to the effect that the roads of Charleston were filled with infernal machines. Intimidated, the Federals withdrew after two hours and a half of battle after having lost the Keokuk and towing three monitors devastated." SHD/M, GG2 17, Lefort to de La Roncière Le Noury, 8 December 1864.
87. Mathew Fontaine Maury (1806–73). Pigeard audited Maury on 22–30 May 1866.
88. Maury had agreed to share his experience with France to be able to finance an education for his children. F. L. Williams, *Matthew Fontaine Maury, Scientist of the Sea* (New Brunswick, NJ: Rutgers University Press, 1963), 442–443; Battesti, *La Marine de Napoléon III*, 756.
89. "Rapport de la Commission des défenses sous-marines," 2 August 1867, quoted by Battesti, *La Marine de Napoléon III*, 251.
90. Stephen Mallory (1813–73).
91. Unwilling to fall into this trap, Welles, the secretary of the Union navy, reluctantly diverted a total of twenty warships, to chase Confederate cruisers and calm down the anger of the shipping business community.

92. Bulloch supervised the construction or acquisition of twenty-three vessels in Britain (four ironclads, sixteen commerce raiders, and three gunboats); the vigilance of C. F. Adams, the U.S. minister, prevented the delivery of all but eight vessels.
93. SHD/M, 6DD1 88, Zédé to the marine minister, Paris, 2 June 1863. Gustave Zédé (1825–91).
94. Under the command of Rear Adm. Lissovskiy.
95. Milne reported to Sir Frederick William Grey, the first sea lord, on 30 September, "I know nothing about them or even where they are from or where going." Quoted by Courtemanche, *No Need of Glory*, 120.
96. SHD/M, BB4 835, Reynaud to the marine minister, 1 October 1863.
97. David D. Field (1805–94).
98. SHD/M, BB4 835, Reynaud to the marine minister, 6 October 1863.
99. Australia, New Caledonia, New Zealand, and Tahiti had already been reconnoitred under the pretext of scientific expeditions. See V. Fitzhaurdinge, "Russian Naval Visitors to Australia, 1862–1888," *Journal of the Royal Australian Historical Society*, June 1966.
100. Six months before, de La Roncière Le Noury had drafted the French plans to attack the Gulf of Finland within six weeks of a decision to go to war. SHD/M, BB4 835, Reynaud to the marine minister, 30 October 1863; details on Zbyishevskii also appear in V. Fitzhaurdinge, "Russian Naval Visitors to Australia, 1862–1888."
101. Lyons commented to Russel on 3 October, "In military and naval affairs as well as in matters in general, the national tendency is toward publicity and men with competent professional knowledge, knowing how to observe have little difficulty in acquiring whatever information they may seek." Commander Lyons of the Royal Navy was authorized to visit the *Monitor* on 1 April 1862. Later that year, Captain Vansitart of HMS *Ariadne* wandered in the Brooklyn Navy Yard, getting onboard the *Keokuk* two days before her launch. From various talks with Union officers the British knew that the monitors was very unpopular because of their poor ventilation and therefore ill suited for any ocean service.
    Courtemanche, *No Need of Glory*, 157–159.
102. Made by Lieutenant North, CSN. Case and Spencer, *The United States and France*, 427.
103. And "if your Majesty could give some kind of verbal assurance that your police will not observe too closely when we wish to put onboard guns and men." Ibid., 429.
104. On 15 April and 16 July 1863. The guns were contracted to Armstrong at Elswick Works.
105. Case and Spencer, *The United States and France*, 433. The British naval attaché in Paris, Captaine Hore, visited "the vessels building for the CSA." Ibid., 434.
106. Trémont working as a clerk at Voruz in Nantes.
107. Paid fifteen thousand francs for his documents, the providential traitor helped establish that Arman had acted fraudulently but did not incriminate French officials.
108. From Confederate impoverished refugees. Case and Spencer, *The United States and France*.
109. Between August 1861 and June 1865.
110. And also two in Portugal and in the Netherlands and one in Venezuela.
111. On 13 May 1861. On 31 January 1862 the British authorities issued additional rules, prohibiting port calls in the Bahamas (except under stress of storm) and the use of British territory as a base, calling for enforcement of the twenty-four–hours rule and restricting the amount of coal delivered to the quantity needed to reach the closest belligerent's port. SHD/M, BB4 1345.
112. Respectively, of 17 June and 1 August 1861.
113. SHD/M, BB4 1345.

114. On 15 August 1861. R. Semmes, *Memoirs of Service Afloat* (Baltimore, MD: Kelly, Piet & Co, 1869), 195–196.
115. On 9–23 November 1861 and on 18–20 November 1862. Ibid., 233.
116. SHD/M, BB4 1345.
117. *Acheron* and *Tartare*.
118. *Winward* and *Hampden*.
119. On 4 April the *Mathilde* was visited by a Confederate cruiser off Brazil; six days later, the packet *Extramadura* was stopped by USS *Iroquois*. On 31 May the admiral commanding the French naval station in Brazil confirmed the presence of three Confederate cruisers, the *Florida*, the *Alabama,* and the *Georgia* in his area. In September, a fisherman from l'Île de Ré found a bottle with a year-old message from the *Alabama*, which was immediately forwarded to the marine and foreign affairs ministers though it had no operational value. BB4 829, Lafosse (commanding the *Extramadura*) to the admiral commanding the Brazil and Plata station, 23 April 1863; BB4 829, the admiral commanding the Brazil and Plata station to the marine minister, 31 May 1863; MAE, marine minister to the foreign affairs minister, 28 September 1863.
120. Because the British neutrality declaration prevented her from returning to England, where she had called in July.
121. *Victor* renamed *Scylla*.
122. Louis De Gueydon.
123. Octave De Chabannes Curton La Palisse.
124. SHD/M, GG2 17, from de La Roncière Le Noury to the Baronne, his wife, 28 August 1863.
125. Following two principles: "[A]bstain from actions immediately hostile" and "[G]ive or deny one what you give or deny the other." SHD/M, BB4 1345, from Drouyn de Lhuys to Chasseloup Laubat, Paris, 3 September 1863.
126. The case of the *Rappahannock* was very sensitive because this ship—who had never been formerly commissioned in the Confederate navy—was trying to complete her fitting out under the pretense of repairs.
127. Ships of the line *Ville de Lyon* and *Louis XIV* were instructed to prevent the *Kearsarge* and the *Florida* from leaving Brest at the same time and to prevent the former to cruise inside French territorial waters.
128. They were insulted when the *Florida* and later the *Rappahannock* were condemned in court for minor incidents.
129. J. M. Elicott, *The Life of John Ancrum Winslow, Rear Admiral, USN* (New York: G. P. Putnam, 1902), 123.
130. SHD/M, BB4 819, note from the "bureau of movements and war operations" on the Mexican expedition, December 1863.
131. Jean Jurien de la Gravière (1812–92). The Gulf of Mexico's division commander (November 1862–April 1863).
132. From G. V. Fox to D. G. Farragut, DC, 7 November 1862. G. V. Fox, *Confidential correspondence of Gustavius V. Fox*, 321.
133. SHD/M, BB4 826, Jurien de la Gravière to the marine minister, Sacrificios, 26 January 1863.
134. Auguste Bosse (1809–91). Gulf of Mexico's division commander, 15 May 1863–65.
135. SHD/M, BB4 830, Caillet to Bosse, 2 May 1863.
136. Matamoros, Tampico, Euxpan, Campeche, Alvarado, Goatzacoalcos, Tabasco, Carmen on the Gulf of Mexico.

137. Eight ocean-going and four riverine vessels in the Gulf of Mexico; four ocean-going vessels on the Pacific Coast; SHD/M, GG2 17, note, June 1863.
138. SHD/M, GG2 17, Note on Mexico from the Syndicat des négociants exportateurs de Paris, undated.
139. Tampico, Veracruz, Alvarado, Goatzacoalas, Tabasco, Carmen; SHD/MBB4 830.
140. SHD/M, GG2 17, E.de Mofras to the marine minister, 29 May 1864.
141. SHD/M, BB4 1041, Pigeard to the marine minister, New York, 27 January 1864.
142. D. B. Mahin, *One War at a Time: the International Dimensions of the American Civil War* (Washington, DC: Brassey's, 1999), 225–226.
143. Gen. Enrique Mejia.
144. SHD/M, BB4 830, Brizzon to Bosse.
145. Ibid., Bosse to the marine minister, 15 October 1863.
146. Ibid., Brizzon to Bosse.
147. SHD/M, BB4 819, December 1863, note from the "bureau of movements and war operations" on the Mexican expedition.
148. SHD/M, BB4 830, Bosse to Bazaine, 8 June 1864.
149. Colonel Day assured a skeptical Bosse that he would disarm the Mexicans and send them to New Orleans.
150. Col. John D. Ford urged Bosse to join him in fighting the Mexicans.
151. Two weeks later a reconnaissance on the Rio Grande showed that Cortina's forces had been permitted by the Union commander to return to Matamoros. Bosse retaliated by suspending his communications with the latter while Cortina accused the French and the Confederates to coordinate their actions, a claim that Bosse vigorously denied; SHD/M, BB4 830, Bosse to the marine minister, 11 September & 26 September 1864.
152. Mejia.
153. Citing a 1681 French law. SHD/M, BB4 1345. Quoted by Case and Spencer, *The United States and France*, 442.
154. To inspect the four Confederate warships being secretly built there. The Confederates intended to transfer her guns onboard the *Rappahannock*. The former was again forced to leave and both the *Georgia* and the *Rappahannock*—now detained in Calais—were sold, respectively, in April 1864 and June 1865.
155. I must regret . . . that your department did not consult with that of foreign affairs at the time it had to respond to the requests of Mr Arman." Quoted by Case and Spencer, *The United States and France*, 443.
156. Quoted by Ibid., 462.
157. SHD/M, BB4 835, Reynaud to the marine minister, 19 May 1864.
158. Semmes, *Memoirs of Service Afloat*, 704–705, 745.
159. SHD/M, BB4 1346., the marine minister to Dupuy, Paris, 15 June 1864.
160. Winslow, her captain, was for his part reminded by Union minister Dayton that the destruction of *Alabama* would take precedence over the respect of French neutrality: "[Y]ou avoid all unnecessary trouble with France, but if the Alabama can be taken without any rules of international law, and may be lost if such a principle is yielded, you know what the government would expect of you." ORN, 3:58. Dayton to Winslow, Paris, 16 June 1864. The letter is delivered to Winslow by Dayton's son on the 18 June. The *Kearsarge* had also been barred from taking the prisoners released by Semmes.
161. SHD/M, BB4 1345, Dupouy to the marine minister, Cherbourg, 15 June 1864.
162. De Gueydon, 15 October 1863.

163. "[H]e finally expressed the desire to see me onboard his ship where it is possible to observe new dispositions which are a consequence from the current war's experience. Indeed a S shaped chain protects the Kearsarge's engine; he [Winslow] claims that at a 60 meters distance, the shells fired by Mississipi's forts could not penetrate; he [Winslow] added that it was a quick way to armor a wooden vessel." Later, the port admiral visited the *Kearsarge* and reported to his minister on the protection he had seen: "The sides abeam of the machinery are armored down to the waterline by means of a chain as strong as the anchors' chain . . . planking covered the whole. I have not much confidence in this armor's resistance; however, the captain says that when a canon ball hits the links, it does not penetrate." SHD/M, BB4 1345, De Gueydon to the marine minister, 15 October 1863.
164. SHD/M, GG2 17, Dupuy to de La Roncière Le Noury, 22 June 1864. A. Sheldon-Duplaix, *Les escales américaines en France pendant la Guerre de Sécession, 1861–65* (Master's thesis, Sorbonne University, Paris, 1989).
165. "[T]he port-admiral manifested a fellow-feeling and interest in the lone, expatriated exponent of the Confederacy, by informing Semmes, a day or so before the fight that an officer detailed to visit the Kearsarge in the offing had reported the fact of the chain armor arranged on the ship and strongly advised Semmes not to engage her." U.S. Naval Institute reprint of Arthur Sinclair's *Two Years on the Alabama* (Annapolis, MD: U.S. Naval Institute, 1989). W. Still writes that Sinclair's position was supported by at least three other officers.
166. On 13 June Semmes wrote in his journal that he wanted to be relieved; R. Semmes, *Croisières du Sumter et de l'Alabama* (Paris: E. Dentu, 1864). Semmes later claimed that if he had known about the chain protection he would not have risked his valuable ship. In his *Memoirs of Service Afloat*, Semmes wrote that Winslow "did not show him a fair fight, for, as it afterwards turned out his ship was ironclad . . . if he had disclosed this fact to me and so prevented the engagement." For his part, 1st Lt. John McIntosh Kell, Alabama's executive officer, in his *Recollections of a Naval Life* (Washington, DC: Neale Company, 1900), claimed, "[H]ad we been in possession of this knowledge the unequal battle between the Alabama and the Kearsarge would never have been fought and the gallant little Alabama has been lost by an error."
167. "I went on the morning of the 19th to Fontainebleau, where the Emperor had been staying. . . . I took the occasion to inform . . . Mr de Persigny, and the Prince Murat of what was probably then going on near Cherbourg, and my apprehension of the result of a contest which had been in a great degree forced upon Captain Semmes by the manner in which he had been received here."
168. "I thought either his department or that of the Minister of Marine was mainly responsible for the loss of life and property which had occurred . . . even the neutrality which the Emperor had proclaimed was not observe towards us." Report of the CS commissioner to France to the Confederate secretary of state regarding interviews with French officials in the matter of the CSS steamer *Alabama* and *Rappahannock*, Paris, 30 June 1864; Official Records of the Union and Confederate Navies in the War of the Rebellion (ORN) Series 1: Volume 3, United States Naval War Records Office, Government Printing Office, Washington, 1896: 658–659.
169. De La Roncière Le Noury went to Fontainebleau on 21 June 1864 (and not Chasseloup Laubat as it is said in Case and Spencer, *The United States and France*, 512).
170. "[H]ow one of our warships was not ready to assist the defeated whoever he was."
171. In reality, the port admiral had instructed the frigate *Couronne* to escort the *Alabama* outside the territorial waters and then withdraw to avoid any risk of being involved in the

battle. Transport *Var* was dispatched by the port admiral to rescue the survivors but arrived too late. At that stage, the *Couronne* was no longer under steam and could not move in time to the battle scene. CG2 17.
172. It is generally acknowledged that *Alabama*'s crew numbered 149, including twenty-five officers. According to French archives, *Alabama*'s crew comprised only 147: twenty-six were killed on the *Alabama* or drowned, seventy (including seventeen injured and three mortally wounded) were rescued by the *Kearsarge*, forty-two were saved by the *Deerhound*, while nine escaped onboard two French pilot boats;. SHD/M, GG2 17.
173. Letter from Mr. Lancaster to the *London Daily News*, 27 June 1864; quoted in Elicott, *The Life of John Ancrum Winslow*, 224.
174. SHD/M, GG2 17, Dupuy to de La Roncière Le Noury, 1864.
175. Four Parott and six Dalghren guns.
176. SHD/M, GG2 17, Dupuy to the marine minister, 11 July 1864.
177. Welles, the Union secretary of the navy, noted in his diary, "Our Alabama news comes in opportunely to encourage and sustain the nation's heart. It does them as well as me good to dwell upon the subject and the discomfiture of the British and the Rebels. The perfidy of the former is as infamous as the treason of the latter." Welles, *The Diary of Gideon Welles, Volume II, 1864–65*, 70.
178. And forced to leave or to enlist.
179. *Phlégéton* and *Tisiphone*.
180. MAE, foreign affairs minister to the marine minister, 29 October 1863.
181. CSS *Stonewall* then sailed to Spain, Portugal, and Cuba, where she was disarmed. Union warships did not dare to engage her.
182. G.Welles, *Diary of Gideon Welles, Volume II*, 62.
183. SHD/M, GG2 17. The foreign affairs minister to the marine minister, 3 November 1864.
184. On 21 June 1865, Britain and France withdrew the belligerents' rights of the Confederacy.
185. SHD/M, BB4 830, Bosse to the marine minister, 14 October 1864.
186. Frigate *Themis*, SHD/M, BB4 850, Didelot to the marine minister, 21 July 1865.
187. *Rhin* was repaired at Mare Island over four months (May to August 1865).
188. De La Roncière Le Noury kept a detailed report from that visit to a key Union facility on the Pacific; SHD/M, GG2 17.
189. SHD/M, BB4 839, Mazères to the marine minister, San Francisco, 5 January 1865.
190. Ibid., Mazères to the marine minister, Mazatlan, 6 June and 15 June 1865.
191. Ibid. Commander Maudet of the *Phlégéton* to Rear Adm. Bosse, 15 May 1865.
192. Ibid., Bazaine to Mazères, 6 April 1865. The steamer *Ajar* left the New Orleans for Acapulco via Valparaiso to load a cargo of weapons; the steamers *Merrimack* and *Mississippi* also departed the same port. François Bazaine (1811–88).
193. Taken from the wreck of a Russian warship washed ashore in 1863.
194. SHD/M, BB4 839, Collos to Mazères, 27 June 1865.
195. Sailing vessel *Brontes*. Ibid., San Franciso consulate to Mazères, 24 May 1865.
196. Brig *San Diego* loaded with 4,992 rifles; sloop *Haze* loaded with 3,992 rifles; MAE, Vol.13, Affaires politiques, foreign affairs minister to the marine minister, 23 September 1864.
197. Like General Wright commanding the military district of California; SHD/M, BB4 839, San Franciso consulate, Cayotte to Mazères, 17 June 1865.
198. Ibid., Panama consulate to Mazères, 20 May 1865.
199. His chief of staff acknowledged that the division could no longer update the orders of battle of the other fleets and show the flag in South America. Ibid., 1 July 1865.

200. Ibid. Mazères to the marine minister, Mazatlan, 20 August 1865.
201. Comprising four vessels. Ibid., state of the U.S. naval squadron, 23 June 1865.
202. Ibid., letter to Mazères, Mare Island, 23 November 1865.
203. Ibid., Didelot to the marine minister, New York, 15 September, 20 September 1865.
204. Ibid., Didelot to the marine minister, New York, 28 September 1865.
205. Even though the neutral trade, mainly stimulated by the Confederate demand for war supplies, had now totally disappeared. SHD/M, BB4 863, Cloué to the marine minister, 12 May 1866.
206. *Magellan, Var, Tisiphone*, and *Adonis*.
207. Negrote. SHD/M, GG2 17 Note from the Cabinet, undated, 1865.
208. Frigate *Bellone*, four transports, two avisos, and three gunboats.
209. "[T]o face the first eventuality, we would need to add eight avisos to the station. Aside from Vera Cruz which is still occupied there are seven ports to block on the Mexican littoral: Matamoros, Tampico, Tuxsoan, Alvarado, Carmen, Campeche and Sisal. Seven vessels must station in front of these ports and be able to communicate." SHD/M, GG2 17 Note from the Cabinet, undated, 1865.
210. The United States had not signed the 1856 Paris convention banning privateering.
211. "If we have to confront, armored vessels, rams and privateers, we need an armored frigate and two fast frigates." SHD/M, GG2 17, note, undated.
212. Ibid., Détroyat to de La Roncière Le Noury, Mexico, 24 February 1866.
213. SHD/M, GG2 17, Cloué to de La Roncière Le Noury, Veracruz, 12 February 1866.
214. H. Blumenthal, *France and the United States: Their Diplomatic Relations, 1789–1914* (Chapel Hill: University of North Carolina Press, 1970), 113.
215. Mahin, *One War at a Time*, 269–285; D. Perkins, *The Monroe Doctrine, 1826–1867* (Baltimore: Hopkins, 1933), 464–548.
216. SHD/M, BB4 863, Cloué to the marine minister, 13 February 1867. The *Moniteur officiel* published the news in March.
217. SHD/M, GG2 17, Détroyat to de La Roncière Le Noury, Mexico, 24 February 1866.
218. Ibid. Didelot to de La Roncière Le Noury, Fort de France, 3 June 1866. Disillusioned, Didelot added, "Mexico is a wasted opportunity without any possible results. We made all the political and military mistakes one could imagine. At this stage, Marshall Foray's plan was the only one which would make sense. But given the situation in Europe and in the World, who would accept a permanent occupation, maybe for 20 years, taking over all the branches of the government and the administration?"
219. SHD/M, BB4 863, Doué to Cloué, Suttello, 7 September 1866.
220. SHD/M, GG2 17, de La Roncière Le Noury to the Baronne, his wife, 7 June 1866.
221. One 11-inch pivot gun, one 100-rifled Parrott gun; several 9-inch guns.
222. SHD/M, BB4 863, Cloué to the marine minister, 23 November 1866.
223. Ibid., 13 December 1866.
224. SHD/M, GG2 17, Cloué to de La Roncière Le Noury, Veracruz, 1 December 1866.
225. SHD/M, BB4 863, Wurtemberg to Cloué, Brownsville, 4 December 1866.
226. Quoted by Mahin, *One War at a Time*, 281.
227. SHD/M, GG2 17, de La Roncière Le Noury to the Baronne, his wife, Cherbourg, 16 August 1866.
228. Ibid., the marine minister to de La Roncière Le Noury, 15 December 1866.
229. Ibid., de La Roncière Le Noury to the Baronne, his wife, Magenta, Veracruz, 21 February 1867.

230. Ibid., 27 March 1867.
231. "[T]his has required a mass of salutes. I have my ears full of gun shots." Ibid., Cherbourg, Framce, 15 July 1867.
232. SHD/M BB4 877, Mecquet to the marine minister, *Semiramis*, St. Pierre, 23 April 1868.
233. MAE, Affaires diverses politiques, Vol. 13, French Consul, New York to the foreign affairs minister, 30 April 1867.
234. Costly refits improved the two vessels' performance raising the speed of the *Dundenberg*—renamed *Rochambeau* from eleven and a half to fifteen knots.
235. H. Navarre, *Le service de renseignement* (Paris: Plon, 1978) 15.
236. The U.S. Office of Naval Intelligence was created that same year.

The Strategic Plight of the Spanish Republican Navy in the Spanish Civil War, 1936–39

Willard C. Frank Jr.

A salient feature of the Spanish Civil War (1936–39) is the great material advantage of the Republican fleet in July 1936 and its control of the seas. Yet progressively and with relentless momentum the Nationalist rebels wrested control of the sea from the Republicans and built an effective naval force that by 1939 claimed complete victory at sea. What had happened to produce such a dramatic reversal of fortunes?

Conventional wisdom holds that the Republican navy lacked capable leaders and an offensive strategic sense and so became an inert mass while the real war swirled around it. The Nationalist navy, however, possessed leadership, aggressiveness, a strategic sense, and high morale. "Better to have men without ships than ships without men," has been the mantra in traditional Spanish naval culture ever since.[1] Several of the Nationalists' Civil War opponents, especially Capt. II Rank Nikolai G. Kuznetsov, the chief Soviet naval adviser in Spain from August 1936 until August 1937, largely agree.[2]

A common corollary to the central thesis of failed leadership depicts Soviet naval advisors, and especially Kuznetsov, imposing a limiting defensive strategy on the Republican navy, which led to inactivity, ineffective operations, and reduced morale.[3] This defamatory interpretation must be reevaluated in light of the wealth of evidence now available.

Further research leads me to conclude that such denigrating explanations, to which I had contributed, are insufficient and defective. Human failings abounded, but the ability of Republican sailors to make war greatly improved with time, while virtually insurmountable dilemmas constantly weighed it down. Even accomplished naval leaders would have been hard-pressed to meet the challenges of war to attain victory at sea. Perhaps the Republican navy performed as well as could have been expected.

CONDITION OF THE TWO FLEETS

The Spanish navy in 1936, relatively large and modern, was split by the military uprising of July 1936 and the sociopolitical revolution it triggered. At the outbreak of the Civil War, the large majority of the active fleet, including one older but operational battleship, three cruisers, twelve destroyers, and twelve submarines, remained loyal to the moderate leftist Republic. The few active warships under control of the Nationalist rebels, including one rundown battleship, one cruiser, and one destroyer, but no submarines, were no match for Republican forces. Yet with time the Nationalists, with advantages in shipyards, armament factories, bases, and foreign supply, completed two powerful cruisers, three minelayers, and one gunboat, and reconditioned one older cruiser, while the Republicans completed four destroyers then under construction. During the war Italy transferred to the Nationalists two submarines and four older destroyers, and Italy and Germany together transferred nine motor torpedo boats to the Nationalists, while the Republic gained from the Soviet Union only four motor torpedo boats. In the first months of war the Republic held the decided advantage in ships, after which, with wartime gains and losses, the Nationalists gained on and nearly captured the material advantage. The first months, therefore, were central to the Republic's opportunities for victory at sea.

A full evaluation of the course and outcome of the Civil War at sea must include the strengths of the Nationalist navy, its leadership, strategic orientation, geographical situation of coasts and bases, and the active participation of allied navies of the Axis powers, Fascist Italy and Nazi Germany. Nationalist officers exuded strong allegiance to their traditionalist cause and full confidence in victory. Under their leadership, most sailors, whatever their prewar political leanings, became disciplined and competent. The Nationalist navy did profit by a few competent, strategically minded, aggressive officers, preeminently Capt. (soon Vice Adm.) Francisco Moreno Fernández. A running conflict over operations and acceptable risks with his nominal chief, the more cautious Vice Adm. Juan Cervera Valderrama, chief of the naval staff, did not detract from Moreno's focus, allowed by favorable geostrategic circumstances, to deny control of maritime communications to the enemy as the first priority and ensure his own communications second.[4]

The Nationalists won the struggle for the sea, yet their real advantages do not alone account for their success. War is interactive. A full evaluation must include the significant dilemmas faced by those directing the Republican navy. Their problems were enormous and contradictions often intractable. Chance or genius might have resolved some of them in the Republic's favor to make the Republican navy a more effective fighting force in the Civil War, but those who found themselves directing Republican naval forces found the challenges they faced lacking perceptible resolution.

REVOLUTION

The first great challenge was revolution. The Nationalists from the beginning had the advantage in the human factor, as traditional interpretations attest. As the year 1936 advanced through spring and summer, and while people across Spain still went about normal routines of life and work, sociopolitical tensions mounted until an explosion of some sort seemed imminent. The attempted coup d'état of the generals on 17 July 1936 triggered an immediate and furious social revolution of the left, against the naval caste system and for the class struggle. The Spanish Civil War divided the larger Republican navy by the class struggle, while it united the smaller Nationalist navy under the authority of a unitary Spanish patriotism. A chasm opened up, extreme in the early months, between executive line officers on one side and machinist officers, most petty officers, and many seamen on the other side, ensuring that those officers who still served afloat were mistrusted, watched suspiciously, and at first allowed no authority, while elected ship command committees made administrative and operational decisions. Officers were afraid for their lives, while sailors, full of revolutionary enthusiasm, were slow to develop an effective participatory management of ships and were incapable of conducting a war.[5]

Most Spanish officers maintained an aristocratic bearing disdainful of the respect and concern owed the men under their authority, which only fed the class struggle. The chief of the Italian naval mission to the Nationalist navy, Capt. Giovanni Ferretti, labeled most Spanish officers as self-absorbed parasites. He reported that one sailor in the Nationalist navy confided to him that "if Spanish officers had been as you are, there would not now be a Red navy."[6]

The clash of caste and class and the purging of most officers did deprive the Republican navy of the best naval minds. Most who fell into the hands of leftist revolutionists were imprisoned and eventually shot. Kuznetsov, on arriving at the main base of Cartagena in September 1936, quickly saw the mass purges of officers as a great weakness to any Republican naval war effort. Kuznetsov, as the French naval attaché reported, surprised the central committee of the fleet by declaring, "[I]t is true that in August 1936 you committed the same folly that we did in March 1917: You got rid of the officers instead of using them. You will soon come to regret it, as we did."[7] However, the passions of July and August 1936 precluded a more accommodating attitude toward conservative officers.

The attitudes and actions of revolutionary petty officer leaders who rose to dominate the command committees, conventional wisdom maintains, ensured that the Republican navy would lack competent strategic and operational direction of the maritime war. It was a dilemma for the Republican navy that the social and psychological dynamics of revolution acted to impede and subvert the means to ensure its success. The disjunction between revolution and military effectiveness remained ever in tension throughout the Civil War. As revolutionary fervor faced the stark realities of war, however, the emphasis in the navy shifted from revolution to military effectiveness, with the anarchists always siding with revolution, the communists with discipline, and the socialists a bridge between. In the early months interminable internal debates eroded Republican unity and focus, as did later exhaustion and war weariness. Whereas the class struggle informed the Republican navy, patriotic unity informed the Nationalist navy, the distinction making a great difference in military effectiveness.

However, those who argue that the Republic lacked capable commanders miss the dynamics of change. In the first months revolutionary enthusiasm ran rampant, and the junior officers nominally in command of the ships lacked experience in ship handling and in leadership and were afraid for their lives. Yet this was just the time when the Republican navy had full command of the sea in the Mediterranean and in the critical Strait of Gibraltar. Later, Republican naval officers became much more capable in ship handling and combat, but only after developments from outside the naval service had impeded the effectiveness of the Republican navy and paved the way for the Nationalists to gain control of the strait and dispute control of the lines of communications in the Mediterranean Sea.

THE REPUBLIC'S EARLY STRATEGIC DILEMMAS

The second challenge to the Republican navy was how to respond to foreign interpositions affecting the pivotal control of communications.

At the outset the strategic instincts of José Giral, navy minister at the time of the uprising, and those who acted on their own to give orders from Madrid and to seize command of ships, were sound. Ordered from Madrid, the bulk of the petty officer–led Republican fleet gathered in the Strait of Gibraltar or off Melilla and blockaded Spanish Moroccan ports to ensure that the spearhead of the military rebellion, the powerful thirty-two thousand–man Army of Africa under the command of Gen. Francisco Franco, could not as planned cross the strait to quickly march on Madrid and depose the government. By the end of September only half of the Army of Africa had been introduced into the Iberian Peninsula, mostly by slow German airlift.[8] For more than two crucial months this naval blockade was highly effective, giving the beleaguered Republic time to allow spontaneous revolutionary activity to settle down and to gear for defense. The dogged focus on blockade prevented Franco from the timely employment of the forces that might have secured an early crushing of the Republic.

Nevertheless, the campaign for control of communications suffered from four major dilemmas for the Republican fleet born of foreign activity, especially in the strait. They were (1) how to respond to German and Italian air intervention in support of Franco; (2) how to respond to the refusal, by Britain and France as well as by Italy and Germany, to recognize the Republican declared blockade, thus depriving the Republic of the legal right of search and seizure; (3) how to respond to open intelligence gathering by German and Italian warships of Republican ship movements and logistic support; and (4) how to respond to the Non-Intervention Agreement, whereby the Republic was precluded from purchasing war supplies on the open market, while supplies surreptitiously flowed into Nationalist Spain.

As the first challenge, by the end of July German and Italian warplanes and transport aircraft operated with impunity and in increasing numbers to airlift troops to the peninsula and to bomb Republican warships trying to blockade Spanish Morocco. There was little coordination among Republican military aircraft dispersed around the country. Yet even if aircraft could have been concentrated to fight for control of the air over the strait—unlikely in the chaotic early weeks—to pit the Republic's inferior aircraft and less-capable pilots against the best of German and Italian air forces would have likely failed. Worse, Republican air attacks against German and Italian aircraft, given the character of their regimes where will and force ruled, would likely have provoked Italy and Germany to respond with greater determination to meet force with force. The Republic had no similar allies in its service to deter the Axis powers from doing so. Greater Axis deployments of aircraft to Spain, and the threat of direct action by their major warships in the region of the strait, which could have overpowered the Republican naval blockade, remained a continuing nightmare to Republican leaders.

Second, the Republic on 17 July 1936 imposed a de facto naval blockade on Spanish Morocco, and then on 9 August formally declared Spanish Morocco subject to blockade, which it expanded on 11 August to include rebel ports in the peninsula. On 20 August it reiterated to foreign governments that all rebel-held ports were in a war zone and under blockade and that foreign ships with cargoes that could help the rebels would not be allowed to enter rebel ports. However, by international law a blockade had to be recognized as belligerency, by concerned states, before it could have legal status and practical effect on the high seas. Significantly, Britain and France refused this recognition, foreseeing that a recognition of belligerency and the subsequent search and seizure operations in the strait and trade routes around and to Spain would disrupt the flow of commerce, widen the geographical scope of military action, perhaps lead to incidents with foreign navies, and threaten the vital geostrategic interests of both. Their refusal bolstered the Republic's status as the only legally constituted political entity in Spain, whereas a recognition of belligerency would have given increased legal standing to the Nationalists in international law. However, in the early months of war, the Anglo-French position on blockade operated against the Republic, since it did not allow the Republic to enforce its blockade against foreign ships, even against German and Italian ships bringing matériel into rebel ports.[9]

Thus when the Republic tried to act on its blockade, foreign warships, then teeming in Spanish waters, prevented its enforcement. On 18 August, for example, the German arms ship *Kamerun* was stopped by the cruiser *Libertad* and the destroyer *Almirante Valdés* and prevented from entering Cádiz, but it was quickly rescued by the German torpedo boat *Leopard*. The Spanish warships let the *Kamerun* go. Germany protested in strong terms, announcing, "German warships would use any means to protect German ships from any similar violations of international law in international waters." The Spanish Republic had no intention of getting into a shooting war with the German navy, which maintained significant forces in Spanish waters. When on 26 August a Republican submarine ordered the German steamer *Schleswig* leaving Ibiza to stop, the steamer ignored the order and the Spanish submarine could do nothing.[10] On 23 August when the Republican cruiser *Miguel de Cervantes* tried to prevent the British steamer *Gibel Zerjon* on its regular run from Gibraltar to Melilla from entering port, the British destroyer *Codrington,* backed up by the battlecruiser *Repulse*, intervened, forcing the *Miguel de Cervantes* to desist and to leave the area. *Gibel Zerjon* with the destroyer *Wolsey* in attendance entered Melilla unmolested on 25 August.[11] These incidents are illustrative of nine other occasions in July–August 1936 when Republican warships attempted to enforce the blockade against foreign vessels attempting to enter Nationalist ports. Yet, with international law on their side and their nation's warships nearby, they soon proceeded through the blockade into Nationalist ports. Not wanting to pick a fight with powerful foreign enemies and not wanting to alienate the democratic powers, by September the Republicans largely ceased to interfere with foreign ships entering or leaving Nationalist ports. Yet on 23 December 1936 Republican forces did seize the German steamer *Palos* and took it to Bilbao, where one passenger and some contraband cargo were landed. Germany reacted by seizing three Spanish steamers and threatening to seize more until the Republic relented. Germany released two captured steamers but handed one over to the Nationalists.[12] Thus thwarted, the Republic discontinued blockade efforts against non-Spanish ships as too risky.

Third, from the first days after the uprising, German and Italian warships in Spanish waters engaged in gathering intelligence, which they passed on to Nationalist authorities. Cloaked by their humanitarian activities to evacuate endangered nationals from Republican ports, and until Germany and Italy recognized Nationalist Spain in November, they entered Republican ports to gather data on deliveries of matériel. After November they continued to maneuver close to Republican ports to gather intelligence. German and Italian warships shadowed and reported the movements of Republican warships at sea. The Axis maintained reporting stations on the Turkish Straits. Italian destroyers patrolled the Sicilian Channel to report Spanish and Soviet merchant ships headed toward Spain.[13] Thus the Nationalists enjoyed an intelligence picture of Republican activities at sea that their opponents, with no pseudoneutral navies doing the same for them, could never begin to match. Any attempt to prevent or counter this reconnaissance activity risked a wider and open war at sea against the Axis partners, which the Republic without a powerful naval ally had to avoid.

The fourth dilemma was how to respond to the Non-Intervention Agreement. France had started to aid the Republic, but with the expanding intervention of Italy and Germany and political divisions at home, France drew back and with British urging proposed a Non-Intervention Agreement among the states of Europe. The intent was to curtail the expanding intervention and prevent the widening of the Spanish conflict. All twenty-seven nations of Europe eventually agreed not to export any matériel to either side in the Spanish conflict, and by early September the pact came legally into force. Many in Italy and Germany feared that the British and French would act to ensure that the agreement would be enforced, but it turned out to be very easy to violate at a cost of only Soviet accusations in the Non-Intervention Committee of ambassadors in London, with the British working to dampen the Soviet thrust. As a result, Italian and German aid flowed in a steady stream of ships in disguise on the last legs of their journeys they were escorted by units of the Italian and German navies. Meanwhile, Britain and the other neutral states of Europe, the main potential suppliers of matériel for the Republic, refused to sell the arms and supplies that would allow the Republic to defend itself.[14]

Thus the Republic in the first weeks of the Civil War faced a major dilemma of how to wage war against the Spanish rebels, significantly and increasingly aided by the Axis states, without provoking those states to escalate their military intervention to decisive proportions. Lopsided non-intervention compounded these challenges. The Republic was never able to solve these dilemmas diplomatically or militarily. They remained a wrenching and intractable problem for the duration of the war.

Compounding the challenges of revolution and foreign intervention were unsound strategic direction imposed by higher political authority. In August 1936 militia forces of Republican Capt. Alberto Bayo with naval support made an amphibious assault on the Nationalist-held island of Mallorca in the Balearic Islands. The intent was liberation, but Mallorca was strategically situated to command vital Republican sea lines of communications and ports in the Mediterranean. The expedition soon held a well-defended beachhead and probed for a breakthrough. With complete command of the sea, Bayo requested naval help and reinforcements for a new landing behind enemy lines. However, in expectation of an early victory and discounting Italian forces beginning to deploy to Mallorca, the dynamic and influential politician Indalecio Prieto argued strenuously that the expedition was a misuse of valuable militia forces and that a Nationalist Mallorca would be of no danger to the Republic. The central committee of the fleet agreed and, with its focus solely on the Strait of Gibraltar and seeing the Bayo expedition a distraction, removed naval support. Without other options, Bayo evacuated the island, and Italian naval and air forces, already moving in, expanded to occupation proportions in support of Italian strategic base interests and Nationalist operational goals.[15]

The abandonment of Mallorca was a major strategic error, for soon Nationalist and Italian forces based in Mallorca threatened Republican shipping and ports a landing of their own somewhere on the coast. Nearby Republican-held Menorca, far from being a formidable operating base, became an impotent target. This episode demonstrated the problem of strategy making by civilian authorities without a comprehensive strategic vision and assuming an early victory. It also highlighted the dilemma of neutralizing Italian naval and air intervention without provoking an even greater military intervention.

On 4 September, the same day as the evacuation of Mallorca, the new Largo Caballero government was formed in Madrid, and Indalecio Prieto attained the portfolio of navy minister. His first major decision as the civilian leader of the navy was to order the main body of the fleet to the Bay of Biscay in the north, where Nationalist troops were attacking from east and west, between which the available Nationalist warships, the cruiser *Almirante Cervera* and the battleship *España*, harassed coastal towns. Prieto, a moderate Socialist from Asturias who made his home in Bilbao, was personally and politically very attached to the region now under attack. The Basques were just forming an autonomous government under José Antonio de Aguirre, and keeping the loyalty and fighting spirit of the Basques enlisted for the Republican cause appeared a high priority.[16]

Prieto's motive in sending the fleet to the north was politically to retain the loyalty to the Republic of the peoples of the northern coast and militarily to impede the Nationalist advance ashore and to destroy any Nationalist naval forces encountered. He also employed the fleet to transport high-priority arms and supplies for the north.[17] By the presence of the fleet to demonstrate the government's commitment to the defense of the north was a valuable political goal, but in doing so Prieto, continuing to think that the war was almost won, ignored the threat to the all-important strait now guarded only by light forces.

Fleet commander Miguel Buiza y Fernández-Palacios, a lieutenant commander filling an admiral's role, listened quietly and played only a technical role as the central committee of the fleet—made up of petty officers and seamen who did not think beyond the assumption that the blockade of Spanish Morocco was a given. The committee after long debate decided, on comradely political grounds, to follow Prieto and take the fleet north.[18] Kuznetsov, who had just arrived, went along for the ride and soon realized the danger posed by inept command committees and by concentration of the fleet in a less significant theater while the essential Strait went almost unguarded. The risks of taking the main fleet to the north far outweighed the possible benefits.[19]

With the arrival of the Republican fleet in the north, Nationalist ships harassing the coast made a speedy departure for the fortified base at Ferrol, temporarily attaining much of Prieto's political goal. The Nationalists, however, in late September dispatched the new cruiser *Canarias* and the veteran cruiser *Almirante Cervera* to seize that critical waterway. On 29 September in the Encounter of Cape Spartel, they surprised in the trait the two Republican destroyers left on patrol, sinking one and forcing the other to flee heavily damaged.[20] From then on, Nationalist naval forces held control of the strait, which the Republicans hardly disputed. This naval battle was one of the most decisive battles of the entire Civil War, for it opened the floodgates to Nationalist reinforcement from Spanish North Africa for the entire war. Within a few days, the Nationalist cruisers now in command of the strait convoyed a further eight thousand troops of the Army of Africa across the strait fresh for the Battle of Madrid. These new forces were half the number that had previously taken three and a half months to cross, mostly by a slow airlift, owing to Republican warship patrols impeding a rapid crossing by sea. By offensive blockade operations, and despite international opposition, the Republican navy had given the Republic time to gather its strength for the land war, and now the Nationalist navy, taking advantage of Prieto's error, by its offensive had created the conditions for Franco to seriously challenge the Republic ashore. Naval operations made for a prolonged war ashore.

To gain political advantage in the regions of the north, Prieto had risked losing the entire Republican cause, including the hopes of the Basques and Asturians of the north. Prieto recognized his error too late, and after the Encounter of Cape Spartel ordered the fleet to return. The central committee of the fleet again debated the order at length but finally "decided" to obey. On the way back to the Mediterranean, when Nationalist forces were hunting for them in vain, the central committee stopped the entire fleet to drift off Oporto for six hours while it and ship committees debated what to do with some captured fishing boats. The Republican navy's command committees, despite the alarm bell of the Nationalist seizure of the strait, did not awaken from their dreamy assumptions in order to put their minds on the war.

STRATEGIC OFFENSE AS WELL AS DEFENSE

As Republican sailor committees drifted away from their early strategic focus on the strait, officers, aided by their Soviet advisers, started to think strategically. The realization sank in that victory would not be quick or easy. Through the autumn of 1936 the Republican navy lacked a functioning naval staff, avoided by petty officers in leadership positions out of lasting caste resentment against the haughty line officers. Nevertheless, officers began to fill the strategic gap with studies and proposals for offensive operations to attain strategic goals. The conventional assumption that the Republican navy did not ever think comprehensively or offensively is wrong.

Prieto, chastened by the disaster at Cape Spartel, allowed planners freer rein. They developed offensive amphibious operations to retake control of the region around Gibraltar, which would impede the dispatch of further elements of the Army of Africa to the Peninsula. With the return of the Republican fleet to Cartagena, and it being the more powerful force in the Western Mediterranean, the Nationalists were more cautious about risking their two active cruisers, especially at night when Republican destroyers would have the advantage in torpedo attacks. Nationalist ships largely remained in the strait or the Atlantic.[21] Nationalist caution gave the Republicans an opportunity. A project of 20 August 1936, likely the brainchild of Lt. Pedro Prado, the Communist chief of operations, envisioned a joint operation to seize Algeciras, and with it the region of Gibraltar. A far more wide-ranging plan of 13 November, in which Buiza and Kuznetsov likely had a major hand, aimed at descending on the Balearics again, this time with the full support of the fleet, a diversionary assault against Algeciras by land and that would close the strait, the mining of Spanish Moroccan embarkation ports, the bombardment of the disembarkation port of Cádiz, and air bombing of Nationalist and even German and Italian warships. The concept of intentionally bombing Axis warships was a repeated suggestion of Kuznetsov. He calculated that the Germans and Italians would remove their ships from Spanish waters rather than take aggressive countermeasures. His Spanish counterparts, however, dissented, justifiably fearing unrestrained Axis retaliation against the Republican fleet that would put it at great jeopardy. Still, the Nationalist chief of the naval staff, Adm. Juan Cervera, who gained intelligence on the November plan, deemed it quite feasible. Then on 2 January the newly formed naval staff under Lt. Cdr. Luis González de Ubieta produced a full study of the maritime situation that concluded with proposing a similar set of offensive operations.[22]

Despite Cervera's fears, none of these proposed offensive operations came to be. Several factors weighed against an early implementation of such plans: the lack of a joint army-navy-air force culture in the Spanish military, the unavailability of ground forces deemed more necessary for the defense of Madrid, the lack of reliable air support, and the lack of landing craft restricting amphibious landings to ports easily seized from the sea. Also, many ships required for such operations were in maintenance following the cruise to the north. Offensive operations, in any case, continued in Republican planning and increasingly in practice.

In October 1936 the strategic defense claimed top priority in Republican naval strategy to ensure the safe arrival of Soviet arms ships from the Black Sea to Spain. With the Non-Intervention Agreement a farce and German and Italian aid pouring into Nationalist Spain, and with the Republic until then having no major arms supplier, the priority was compelling. Prieto gave the order and Kuznetsov fully endorsed it. Now the Republic would receive the timely delivery of modern Soviet military equipment, including the best aircraft and tanks yet seen in Spain.[23]

Also in October, just as the Republic began to receive Soviet arms ships to Alicante and Cartagena, Italy and Germany decided to speed the victory of Franco by clandestine naval, and especially submarine, warfare. German and Italian aircraft had been bombing Republican ships and bases. Now, starting on 8 November Italian submarines and on 30 November German U-boats engaged in a clandestine hunt off the Republican coast. Prime targets were Republican warships, but also Republican and Soviet merchant ships if positive identification could be made. Since Soviet arms ships entered port only at night and did not fly flags or show navigation lights, the prowling submarines could not meet the rules of engagement and sank no Soviet arms ship. Nevertheless, the Italian *Torricelli* did torpedo and severely damage the cruiser *Miguel de Cervantes* anchored in the Cartagena roadstead on 22 November as a precaution against Axis air raids, and the German *U-34* did sink the surfaced submarine *C-3* off Málaga on 12 December. The shelling of Republican ports by Italian cruisers and submarines punctuated winter nights. Italian responsibility for their ravages was clear from torpedo and shell fragments, but secrecy and luck allowed the Germans to escape detection. These attacks culminated on 14 December 1936 when the Nationalist cruiser *Canarias* sunk the Soviet motorship *Komsomol*, a previous arms carrier, in broad daylight with impunity. Naval escort of Soviet arms ships now became an imperative.[24]

At first Soviet arms ships, called Igreks or "Y" ships, sailed alone without disguise or escort. The escalating war in the Mediterranean, however, required defensive measures to secure the Republican logistic lifeline to the east. The Igreks then disguised themselves by false appearances, names, flags, and radio call signs as ships of neutral countries, and steamed through the Sicilian Channel to confuse the Italian navy on patrol. They continued as innocent merchant ships on a course that would take them to Gibraltar, but once at a designated point off the Algerian coast they sharply turned to the north and headed straight for Cartagena. Thus revealed, and with enemy cruisers, submarines, and aircraft on the hunt, it was necessary to afford the Igreks strong naval protection. Often a full squadron of two cruisers and up to eight destroyers sortied to rendezvous with the Igreks and convoy them directly to Cartagena. On sixty-three occasions in the critical year between October 1936 and October 1937 did the Republican fleet escort supply ships to or from Republican ports, an average of one convoy mission, often lasting two or more days, every five to six days. On only two occasions, on 7 and 17 September 1937, did an escorted convoy not safely get through the Nationalist dragnet. These arms ships convoyed by the Republican fleet provided the material ability for the Republic to continue to wage war with some hope of victory.[25]

The Republic adopted a strategy that added practicable elements of sea denial to those of defense of sea lines of communications. The Republic had to weigh any offensive operations that seriously risked the loss of Republican ships against focusing the fleet on maintaining Republican supply lines. The defense of supply ships had to be top priority. Nevertheless, training exercises in the Republican fleet constantly prepared for nighttime destroyer offensive operations against Nationalist naval forces and convoys. Sorties to defend incoming Igreks were increasingly capable and ready to shift to the offense, should an encounter occur or other opportunity arise. Beyond the increasing ability to shift from the tactical defense to the tactical offense on convoy operations, from October 1936 to October 1937 the Republican fleet undertook twenty-three nonconvoy missions, including eight strictly offensive operations, especially nighttime seek-and-destroy forays against the Nationalist fleet, or an average of one every forty-five days.[26] Republican offensive operations kept Nationalist warships on guard and heavily protecting their convoys. Yet limited intelligence restricted Republican successes. Republican warships, when not undergoing needed maintenance and repair, were constantly at sea, on both defensive and offensive missions. In the process they gained greatly in ability and confidence.

Truly effective operations against Nationalist sea lines of communications, however, were beyond reach. By December 1936 Italy began sending full divisions, the *Corpo Truppe Volontarie*, to Spain in large troopships flying the Italian flag and escorted by Italian warships. Time after time these troopships brazenly steamed to Cádiz in front of Cartagena and in the face of the Republican fleet, with the Republicans having to bear the bald effrontery without being able to respond except by diplomatic protest. Furthermore, Italian supply ships, usually reflagged Spanish ships, constantly plied the routes between Italy and their Mallorca bases under Italian naval escort, entering Palma at night flying no flag but with navigation lights burning to signal their notional peaceful nature. German supply ships, after a brush with Republican blockade, unloaded at first in Lisbon and soon in Vigo as the regular port of destination. German warships escorted German arms ships, disguised as Panamanian steamers, on the last leg of their journey to Spain, because non-European ships and those under naval escort were exempt from non-intervention inspection. In all, some 160 German and about 290 Italian voyages of merchant ships with military personnel and supplies arrived in Nationalist ports during the Spanish Civil War, while U.S. firms shipped trucks and a steady stream of U.S. tankers with Texaco oil to Franco.[27]

In early 1937 military aid to the Republic crept up toward that coming to Franco, but thereafter the gap increasingly widened, with the greatest disparity in 1938. Overall, the balance of seaborne aid to the two sides, abetted by the non-intervention system and efforts to evade it, came greatly to favor the

Nationalists. An approximation accords overall military supply to the Republic of about 100 to 470 shiploads for the Nationalists, a disparity of one to five. To widen this indication of the supply gap, larger Italian and German aircraft flew to Spain, while much of the military equipment shipped to the Republic was of poor quality. Furthermore, Axis aid was regular and reliable, while aid to the Republic was irregular and unreliable, especially after August 1937 when Soviet aid via the Mediterranean was curtailed.[28]

FRUSTRATED HOPES FOR SOVIET NAVAL SURFACE AND AIR SUPPORT

One way to meet the dilemma of Italian and German maritime support without directly challenging the Axis could be a Soviet naval squadron in the Western Mediterranean providing low-profile, noncombat aid to the Republic. It could emulate the Axis by cooperating with the Non-Intervention Committee while supporting the Republic on the side. Republican sailors therefore asked, "Where is the Soviet fleet?" Reconnaissance of enemy activity at sea would be the safest and most legal of activities for Soviet warships. The Republican fleet, unlike their opponents, often went to sea blind, as the radio direction-finding system was defective and there were no allied nations with warships to report on Nationalist movements at sea. The Republican fleet needed the aid of friendly eyes at sea. Kuznetsov had repeatedly recommended to Moscow that the Soviet Union send a squadron of cruisers, destroyer leaders, and destroyers to Spain, with one primary function: to engage in reconnaissance, as the Fascist allies of the Nationalists were doing, to allow the Republic to gain operational intelligence of enemy ship movements.[29]

A suggestion in this direction came from diplomats. In February 1937 Soviet foreign minister Maksim Litvinov and the Soviet ambassador in London, Ivan Maiskii, requested Soviet warships for the Control Scheme of the Non-Intervention Committee, whereby naval patrols of the naval powers would monitor and report shipping carrying contraband to Spain, proposed Soviet naval participation on an equal basis as the other naval powers.[30] British Foreign Secretary Anthony Eden had not considered Soviet warships for non-intervention patrols, as he assumed the Soviet navy was too weak. To impress the British of the strength and reach of the Soviet navy as a step toward attracting Britain into an antifascist alliance, the Soviet navy prepared two cruisers, two destroyers, eight submarines, and a submarine tender to participate in the non-intervention patrol. However, Adm. V. M. Orlov, the chief of the Soviet navy, thought it inadvisable to operate at such a distance from Soviet bases, toyed with the idea of sending only a small contingent, and ended by heeding caution, sending none at all. There were too many replenishment problems so far from home, and there was too great a risk of an international incident without adequate support. He firmly rejected the idea of Maiskii that Soviet cruisers both participate in the non-intervention patrols and then by night secretly escort Soviet Igreks into Cartagena. With German and Italian warships prowling about, such activities would only make undesired incidents more probable.[31]

Without the aid of a Soviet squadron and to free valuable Republican warships, especially destroyers, for escort and offensive missions, Kuznetsov then requested the shipment of no fewer than sixteen Soviet motor torpedo boats for patrol duties at the harbor entrance of Cartagena. He received only four G-5-type motor torpedo boats, complete with Soviet crews, in May 1937. They were hardly seaworthy with any swell, but on patrol duty guarding against submarines and mines off Cartagena they freed the valuable destroyers to work with the fleet to ensure the safe arrival of the Igreks and for nighttime offensive missions. The motor torpedo boats undertook one major offensive mission against the Nationalist naval anchorage in Palma de Mallorca in March 1938, but they could not withstand the even moderate seas running, and the operation was canceled. The cruiser-destroyer force designated to support the motor torpedo boats that night nevertheless chanced on a Nationalist convoy off Cape Palos, whereupon the now combat-prepared destroyers sank the *Baleares*, the newest Nationalist cruiser. Motor torpedo boats were never employed in offensive operations again, but remained useful as escorts for short-run coastal convoys.[32]

Kuznetsov also sought and acquired aircraft for naval cooperation. The Spanish naval air arm had been disbanded with the onset of the Civil War, and so the Republican navy lacked any air support. German and Italian aircraft from Mallorca, however, were regularly flying reconnaissance missions over the western Mediterranean and frequently discovered an obvious Igrek. Buiza pleaded for help, seconded by Kuznetsov. Eventually Prieto, as navy and air minister, allowed a small detachment SB-2 "Katyusha" light bombers to be lent to the navy. Naval leaders wanted to use these aircraft for offensive missions. Soviet army aircrews, however, could not identify ships at sea or place bombs on a maneuvering warship, thus severely limiting their reconnaissance and attack roles. Bombing had to be restricted to warships in enemy harbors, with the assumption that such would be enemy.[33]

However, the SB-2s in May 1937 bombed and hit by mistake the Italian auxiliary cruiser *Barletta* in the roadstead of Palma and the German pocket battleship *Deutschland* at Ibiza, causing a major international crisis, and, in reprisal, a nearly implemented German naval bombardment of the Cartagena naval base and the actual bombardment of Almería.[34] Republican authorities then revoked permission to bomb ships in enemy ports. Kuznetsov objected to this restriction, as bombing of Nationalist ships put them out of action for some time, and he had noted that the bombing of the *Deutschland* led to German warships temporarily leaving the western Mediterranean, returning only after the Republicans had avoided bombing Palma for the next several months.[35] Nevertheless, Republican authorities considered the SB-2 detachment a political risk and an operational failure. They detached it from the fleet and sent it back to fight in the land war.

With time Kuznetsov's hopes that Soviet naval and air forces could materially help the Republic offset Axis naval help to the enemy vanished. No Soviet naval squadron appeared, and attempts to give the Republican fleet support by motor torpedo boats and naval-cooperation aircraft failed. Yet Italy and Germany increased their naval and naval air operations, leaving the Spanish Republic, loath to risk a confrontation it would lose, only to follow a fruitless diplomatic course in the Non-Intervention Committee and the League of Nations.

A STRATEGY OF PROLONGATION

The Republican government of Juan Negrín from mid-1937 onward shifted strategic priorities from defeating the enemy to persevering under increasingly adverse conditions long enough to allow diplomacy to end Non-Intervention or Hitler to provoke a European war, either eventuality giving the Republic an opportunity to prevail. To enhance these prospects, strategy should maximize defense, minimize risks, and do nothing to alienate the democracies or enrage the Axis dictators. Under the leadership of the Popular Army's military planner, Gen. Vicente Rojo, offensives in one sector served to divert Nationalist forces from operations of conquest in another, and thus buy time.

The Republican fleet, in line with the new strategy, prohibited the stopping and searching of any merchant ship at sea, a restriction Kuznetsov, more willing to take risks, opposed. Republican submarines under Soviet command, hampered by restrictive rules of engagement requiring positive identification of targets as Spanish and not Axis and unable to make positive identification because supply ships were darkened at night and using false flags by day, did avoid any further harmful international incidents but scored no success.[36] The requirements of the strategy of defense to prolong the war and avoid negative effects on foreign powers remained highly inhibiting to the Republican navy. Nevertheless, the fleet continued to operate both defensively and offensively, if more cautiously.

In August–September 1937 came a massive Nationalist-incited Italian submarine, surface, and air campaign against Republican and Soviet shipping throughout the Mediterranean. It was the second turning point in the war at sea (the first being the Encounter of Cape Spartel in September 1936). Of fourteen merchant ships sunk or captured by Italian forces, only six likely carried military-related cargoes, five were loaded tankers, and only one, which missed its rendezvous with the Republican fleet, was a major carrier of Soviet matériel.[37] Britain and France collaborated under the quickly agreed-upon Nyon Arrangement to destroy all predatory submarines in the Mediterranean, prompting Italian dictator Benito Mussolini to curtail his clandestine naval warfare, already exposed to the world as Italian. British and French warships patrolled prescribed routes with orders to sink any submerged submarine encountered. It was the only occasion before 1939 when Britain and France forcefully stood up to a Fascist dictator, but they then negated the political effect by inviting Italy to participate in the Nyon patrols. Italian foreign minister Galeazzo Ciano proclaimed it "a great victory. From accused torpedoers to Mediterranean policemen, with the exclusion of the Russians, whose ships have been sunk."[38] Italy continued its secret antishipping campaign through more cautious Italian "legionary" submarine and surface efforts until February 1938. More restrictive rules of engagement, however, allowed no significant results.

The Republican navy was unable to combat the submarine piracy in distant sectors of the Mediterranean Sea against fifty-two Italian submarines and forty-three surface warships actively preying on Republican and Soviet shipping. The Republican fleet, having limited resources and trying to avoid an all-out naval war with aggressive Italy and its powerful fleet, had to sit by as a passive bystander and allow the British and French to do the job for it through the Nyon antisubmarine patrols. A major part of the maritime war was out of Republican hands.

Worse was to come. Naval "piracy" had a tremendously damaging strategic effect on the Republican war effort. The Soviet Union was unable to protect its merchant shipping in the Mediterranean. Its freighters sunk by Italian torpedoes were not even carrying arms. Nationalist gunboats seized and confiscated nine more, accused of having carried contraband in the past, and added them to their own fleet as militarized transports. Stalin's plans for a powerful Soviet fleet, with which he might buy a British alliance against Germany, were slow to materialize. In the summer of 1937 he was unable to protect his own shipping or to have any confidence that the Republic could or would protect arms traffic. Resources that might go to Spain could also serve Soviet rearmament and a new commitment to supply China with arms to withstand Japanese aggression. In these conditions, to sustain a major supply effort to the beleaguered Spanish Republic under such risky conditions for what was looming as a lost cause put great pressure on Stalin to change course. There is as yet no direct documentary evidence available to detail Stalin's motives, but he did halt arms shipments through the Mediterranean just at this time, likely because of a combination of pressures. The Soviets only later restarted a much weaker, slower, and uncertain flow of aid from northern Soviet ports to French Atlantic ports and, when French politics allowed, overland to Republican Spain.[39] Stalin was in the process of abandoning the Spanish Republic, a step in the process of abandoning collective security, and a step toward the Nazi-Soviet Pact of 1939. With Nationalist arms supply completely outstripping that to the Republic, the curtailing of Soviet aid was a devastating blow to Republican chances of survival.

The "piracy" and Nyon affairs were a double blow to the Republic. Not only was Soviet aid cut, but also the Mediterranean in flames was a major factor in dashing the hope by Negrín that an early onset of a major European war would allow the Republic to ride the coattails of the democracies to victory. British prime minister Neville Chamberlain feared being drawn into a wider war, which would only encourage Germany or Japan to grab the opportunity for new conquests. Thus naval provocations stimulated Chamberlain to strengthen his determination to avoid war with Germany by diplomacy and to retain the non-intervention policy. As Chamberlain feared, Mediterranean troubles did propel Hitler to advance his plans for conquests in Central Europe, leading to the Czech crisis and the Munich agreement. The "piracy" campaign shattered Negrín's hopes for an end to non-intervention or an early European war. With the curtailing of Soviet aid, this delay in the onset of a major war was too great a span of time for the Republic to hold out and survive against relentless Nationalist advances.[40] The consequences of "piracy" proved a disaster for the Republic.

DEFEAT AND DEFEATISM

After their conquest of the north in October 1937, the Nationalists concentrated their naval forces in the Mediterranean to destroy the Republican fleet, ravage Republican supply lines, harass the Republican coast, and prepare amphibious operations. Their own disguised and protected supply lines were not in jeopardy: German and Italian warships continued to convoy their arms ships to just off Nationalist ports. In Republican ranks, however, defeat and frustration eroded morale. Nevertheless, Republican officers and crews were increasingly competent in naval combat, as Republican gunnery accuracy in the Battle of Cherchell on 7 September 1937 and the torpedo sinking of the *Baleares* in the Battle of Cape Palos on 6 March 1938 testify. Yet ships were wearing out, parts were in short supply, and air raids on Cartagena put the cruiser *Miguel de Cervantes*, having just emerged from repairs from the 1936 torpedo damage again out of commission.

In April 1938 the Nationalist land offensive had reached the Mediterranean, cutting the Republic in two and further hindering Soviet aid. A trickle of supplies still went by coastal steamer from Marseille and Sète to Barcelona and under attack by Nationalist naval and air forces, but for most of 1938 France denied transshipments, and arms supply to the Republic never again reached sufficient levels to sustain the war effort. All this added to the war weariness and defeatism enveloping the Republic, including its navy.

Yet even in this last discouraging phase of the war the Republican fleet did remain somewhat active, in accordance with the strategy to buy time. From November 1937 until the end, the Republican navy conducted twenty-nine successful coastal convoy operations, one every two weeks. Republican submarines under Soviet command continued to lie in wait off the busy Nationalist port of Palma and in the strait, but under restrictive rules of engagement produced only frustration and no success. Of fifteen offensive sorties of surface units against the Nationalist fleet, one was successful and resulted in the sinking of the *Baleares*.[41] Thereafter, with no hope in sight, fleet commander Ubieta saw more risks than benefits to further offensive actions, and acted to preserve the fleet and await developments.

Morale steadily declined. By the summer of 1937, concurrent with and even before the Italian naval "piracy," the nonappearance of a Soviet squadron, and the drastic cut in Soviet aid, tensions started to mount in the Republican fleet. The frightened junior officers of 1936 had by then gained experience and skill at handling their ships and tasks and were for awhile increasingly confident. Some of the petty officers and seamen thought officers were reverting to their prerevolutionary haughty culture and privileges that separated them from their men. With the war going poorly their former resentments and fears began to return, and sailors blamed officers when things went wrong. Mysterious cases of seeming sabotage increased. Republican crew members mumbled to each other that it would be better if the officers not executed in 1936 were now killed off. Officers whispered to each other that the war should end no matter who won. Defeatism was seeping in, and with it the return of caste and class resentments.[42]

These developments increasingly isolated the Soviet naval advisers. Spanish officers, who had earlier looked to their Soviet advisers for protection and expertise, now did not feel the need of such outside advice and increasingly resented their interference. Petty officers and seamen found less reason to show their former friendship for their Soviet partners. Newer Soviet advisers were fewer, more junior; some had less cultural sensitivity, and they worked in very difficult operational and social conditions. Sailors repeated to each other the overheard words of one insensitive Soviet adviser that undisciplined Spanish sailors should be ruled by the whip. Sailors now saw the Soviet navy and its advisers as arrogant imposters.[43]

The only offensive operation that the Republican navy planned in the last months of the war was a projected December 1938 amphibious assault on Motril, the last Nationalist coastal position east of Malaga. Its intent was to divert Nationalist troops poised for the last great offensive against Catalonia, and so prolong the war. The conquest of Catalonia would deprive a severely reduced Republic of its best industrial base and would seal it off from any further arms supply, a fatal prospect. With the coordination of a potent landing against defended territory, an extraordinarily difficult task at this late stage, given low morale and poor material readiness, and with a full moon threatening to remove surprise from the seaborne movement to the invasion site, Ubieta at the last minute canceled the operation.[44] The Republicans projected no other offensives.

By late 1938 the spirit of resistance was gone, both in the town of Cartagena and in the fleet. Sailors talked openly of surrendering, or taking their ships into exile. The morale of Soviet advisers declined with war weariness, defeatism, and the accusations of their Spanish colleagues. Soviet advisers were called home and not replaced. Sentiment in Cartagena progressively grew in intensity to be glad to see them gone, as their continued presence would only delay the coming of peace. A Nationalist coup attempt in March 1939 was crushed, but two days later the fleet, crammed with sailors, soldiers, Republican officials, their families, and some other refugees fleeing feared persecution at the hands of the Franco victors, sailed into exile in Tunisia. The war at sea was over.

CONCLUSION

I have suggested that traditional explanations for the failure of the Republican navy in the Spanish Civil War, the lack of capable leaders and a defensive passivity, are defective. The Republican navy, even had there not been the endemic conflict of caste and class, was beset with intractable strategic dilemmas that would have challenged even the best strategic minds: limited repair facilities, worn-out ships, and shortage of parts and munitions; international refusal to grant the Republic belligerent rights; the non-intervention system that Italy and Germany systematically and continuously evaded but that was applied to the Republic; brazen Axis submarine and air campaigns against Republican sea lines; bruising German retaliations for Republican blockade efforts and mistaken targeting; the refusal of the Soviet Union to send warships for low-profile missions while all other interested powers maintained squadrons in Spanish waters; the massive Italian sea denial campaign of 1937 that curbed Soviet supply efforts and prompted more-determined Western efforts to make peace with Germany and Italy. All these impeded an effective Republican strategy at sea.

Nevertheless, Republican naval strategy largely remained coherent and synchronous with shifts in conditions and policy aims, however. Coherence is clear in the early months, when the focus on controlling the strait and blockading Nationalist ports demonstrated strategic sense in an effort to crush the rebellion. The main strategic blunders in this early period, the abandonment of Mallorca and the removal of the fleet from the strait, were decisions imposed on the navy by its civilian chief. Coherence is also clear after mid-1937, when the national aim was to protract the war until an expected European war would give the Republic hope, a goal missed by only five months. In between, from late 1936 until mid-1937, the war was most in balance and thus Republican naval planners had open to them a wider range of options. During this period, defense of logistic support by sea had to be a top priority. Nevertheless, within this priority, offensive operations proliferated to weaken the enemy at sea, and at least had the effect of forcing the Nationalists to expend great effort in the defense of their own logistic sea lines of communication. The Republican navy found no good solution to the dilemmas imposed by circumstances, but probabilities among the unpleasant options available perhaps weighed in favor of the strategies the Republican navy adopted.

The assumption that Soviet advisers imposed a limiting strategic defense on a fleet capable of carrying the war to the enemy is wrong. Soviet naval advisers were mostly skilled professionals who did the best they could to help the Republican navy become an effective force at sea. The most respected and aggressive of these Soviet officers was Captain Kuznetsov, whose audacious offensive operational schemes against the Axis fleets his Spanish colleagues had to restrain as overly risky.

Internal human factors were of great significance, as traditional interpretations hold. Yet one should not assume that human factors alone account for the development and outcome of the war at sea. Intractable circumstances dire for the Republican navy also apply. Mental qualities and circumstances are not separable. Circumstances do affect such qualities as identity, group cohesion, morale, and will to persevere because these qualities also affect circumstances. Eventually, in the Republican fleet negative mental qualities and negative circumstances interacted to accelerate a downward spiral.

Despite defects and contradictions, the performance of the Republican navy in the Spanish Civil War under very difficult conditions was, in balance, creditable. In sum, the Republican fleet, its leaders, and its Soviet advisers deserve neither dismissal nor condemnation, but rather recognition for the dilemmas they faced defying resolution, and respect for conducting a war under appalling conditions as best as they knew how.

NOTES

The following abbreviations and foreign terms are used in these notes:

ADM	Admiralty
AGMAB	Archivo General de la Marina Alvaro de Bazán, El Viso del Marqués
AN	Archivo Nacional (apocryphal meaning)
AR	Archivo Rojo (apocryphal meaning)
BA-MA	Bundesarchiv-Militärarchiv, Freiburg im Breisgau
BB	French series designation. A-Z, AA-ZZ, each with subseries by superscript number.
busta, buste	Italian for bundle. Documents are located by busta.
CAB	Cabinet
Cmd.	Command
delo	Russian for file; the third level of filing of documents in a Russian archive
fond	Russian for source or archive; the first level of filing in a Russian archive
listy	Russian for sheets of paper (or pages within a delo)
MAE	Ministerio degli Affari Esteri, Rome
opis	Russian for inventory; the second level of filing in a Russian archive
RGAVMF	Rossiskii Gosudarstvennyi Arkhiv Voenno-Morskogo Flota (Russian State Naval Archive), St. Petersburg
RGVA	Rossiiskii Gosudarstvennyi Voennyi Arkhiv (Russian State Military Archive)
RM	Reichsmarine
SHEMA	Servicio Histórico del Estado Mayor de la Armada
TNA	The National Archives
TsKhIDK	Tsentr Khraneniya istoriko-dokumentalnykh kollektsii
US	Ufficio Spagna, a section of the MAE archive
USMM	Ufficio Storico della Marina Militare, Rome

1. For the failed leadership thesis, see Fernando, and Salvador Moreno de Alborán y de Reyna, *La guerra silenciosa y silenciada: Historia de la campaña naval durante la guerra de 1936–39*,

THE STRATEGIC PLIGHT OF THE SPANISH REPUBLICAN NAVY IN THE SPANISH CIVIL WAR, 1936–39

4 vols. (Madrid: Lormo, 1998), vol. 4, 2:3300–3339, and esp. 3334–3339; Ricardo Cerezo Martínez, *Armada española: Siglo XX*, 4 vols. (Madrid: Ponente, 1983), 3:21, 4:128–136; Michael Alpert, *La guerra civil española en el mar*, 2nd ed. (Barcelona: Crítica, 2008), 367; and Willard C. Frank Jr., "Naval Operations in the Spanish Civil War, 1936–1939," *Naval War College Review* 37 (1984): 46–47.

2. See Kuznetsov's official reports, "Doklad morskogo sovetnika glavnomu voennomu sovetniku," in fond 32082, opis 1, delo 23, listy 51–53 RGVA, Moscow; and "Obzor operatsii c momenta myatezha gen. Franko (18 iyulya 1936g.) do 1 iyulya 1937g.," in fond r.-1529, opis 1, delo 120, listy 138–149, RGAVMF. See also N. Nikolaev (pseud. of N. G. Kuznetsov), "Ispanskii flot v natsionalno-revolyutsionnoi voine, 1936–1939gg," in *Iz istorii osvoboditelnoi borby ispoanskogo naroda* (Moscow: Akademiia nauk SSSR, 1959), 52–54.
3. See Frank, "Naval Operations," 39–40; Moreno and Moreno, *La guerra silenciosa y silenciada*, vol. 4, 2:3304; and Cerezo, *Armada española*, 3:219–220.
4. For a summary of his strategic thought, see Francisco Moreno, "Importancia e influencia del poder marítimo durante la guerra nacionalista española," *Almanaque naval 1941 XIX* (Milan, Italy: Ministerio de la Marina de Italia, 1940), ix–xxi. See also Juan Cervera Valderrama, *Memorias de guerra* (Madrid: Editora Nacional, 1968).
5. Spanish archives are replete with testimony condemning the revolution in the fleet. See Expediente Nacional del 18 de Julio (Colomina), SHEMA, AN 94–2 & AR 94–1, 8921, AGMAB. Republican testimony, however, is sparse. Extensive reports by Soviet advisers on the evolving problems of leadership, discipline, and morale partially fill the gap. See Captain III Rank N. P. Annin, et al., "Operatsii voenno-morskogo flot Ispanskoi Respubliki: Obzor operatsii c momenta myatezha gen. Franko (18 iyulya 1936g.) do 1 iyulya 1937g.," fond r.-1529, opis 1, delo 120, listy 120–132, 137–149, RGAVMF.
6. Capt. Giovanni Ferretti, "Notizie e considerazioni sulla Marina spagnuola bianca," in busta 95, Ufficio Spagna, "Spagna, Fondo di Guerra," Archivo Storico-Diplomatico, MAE-US, 5.
7. Lt. Raymond] Moullec, "Intervention soviétique dans la guerre d'Espagne: Opinion des Espagnols sur la Marine russe" to Minister of Marine, Paris, No. L-118, 28 September 1938, fond 211, opis 1, delo 1048, listy 38–39, TsKhIDK, Moscow.
8. "Zu dem Stand der Beartetiung der Geschichte der Legion Condor: I. Das 'Unternehmen Feuerzauber,'" 8 March 1940, RL 2 IV/1 3187, BA-MA.
9. British Foreign Office and Admiralty papers are filled with concern to avoid recognizing a state of belligerency. For a summary of the law of belligerency and blockade as applied to the Spanish Civil War, see Norman J. Padelford, *International Law and Diplomacy in the Spanish Civil Strife* (New York: Macmillan, 1939), 3–12, 25–28.
10. Manfred Merkes, *Die deutsche Politik im spanischen Bürgerkrieg, 1936–1939*, 2nd ed. (Bonn, Germany: Röhrscheid, 1969), 166–167.
11. *Repulse* Letter of Proceedings, No. 191/2158, 29 August 1936, ADM 116/3051, TNA, London.
12. Merkes, *Die deutsche Politik*, 190–192.
13. The war diaries (*Kriegstagebucher*) of the German navy in BA-MA, the reports of Italian warships in USMM, and the records of the Nationalist navy in SHEMA are replete with evidence of such intelligence activities. See also Merkes, *Die deutsche Politik*, 147–148; Hans-Henning Abendroth, *Hitler in der spanischen Arena* (Paderborn, Germany: Schöningh, 1973), 58–59; and Franco Bargoni, *L'impegno navale italiano durante la guerra civile spagnola, 1936–1939* (Rome: USMM, 1992), 78–87, 124–128, 130–131.

14. There is no full study of the Non-Intervention Committee, but see John Bowyer Bell, "The Non-Intervention Committee and the Spanish Civil War, 1936–39" (unpublished PhD dissertation, Duke University, Durham, NC, 1958); and Padelford, *International Law and Diplomacy*, 53–120, and public documents on the establishment of the non-intervention system, 205–601. On the ease of Italian and German arms ships and troop transports slipping through the farce of the Non-Intervention Committee, see Willard C. Frank Jr., "Politico-Military Deception at Sea in the Spanish Civil War, 1936–39," *Intelligence and National Security* 5 (July 1990): esp. 93–95.
15. Alberto Bayo, *Mi desembarco en Mallorca* (Guadalajara, Mexico: Gráfica, 1944), 124–154; Josep Massot i Muntaner, *La Guerra Civil a Mallorca* (Montserrat, Spain: L'Abadia de Montserrat, 1976), 168–171; Ferdinando Pedriali, *Guerra di Spagna e aviazione italiana*, rev. ed. (Rome: Aeronautica Militare Italiana—USMM, 1992), 66–88; Bargoni, *L'impegno navale italiano*, 87–97.
16. José Carlos Gibaja Velázquez, *Indalecio Prieto y el socialismo español* (Madrid: Editorial Pablo Iglesias, 1995); Alfonso Carlos Saiz Valdivielso, *Indalecio Prieto y el nacionalismo vasco* (Bilbao, Spain: Laida, 1989).
17. Ordenes de Operaciones, 18–20 September 1936, SHEMA AR 25–13 (II), 9514, AGMAB.
18. For the voyage of the fleet to the north, see Captain III Rank N. P. Annin, report, 17 August 1937, in fond r.-1529, opis 1, d, 120, listy 1–15, RGAVMF.
19. N. G. Kuznetsov, *Na dalekom meridiane: Vospominaniya uchastnika natsionalno-revolyutsionnoi voiny v Ispanii*, 4th ed. (Moscow: Nauka, 2005), 74–82.
20. Parte de campaña no. 2, *Canarias*, 3 October 1936, SHEMA, AN, 25–13 (10), 9590, AGMAB.
21. Flota Nacional, Ordenes de Operaciones, SHEMA, AN 25–12 (2), 9479, AGMAB.
22. See "Proyecto de operación para ocupar Algeciras, 20 de agosto de 1936;" and "Estudio de la situación marítima actual presentada por el Estado Mayor Central, 2 de enero de 1937," SHEMA, AR 202–3 (capetas 8 and 30), 8921, AGMAB; Cervera, *Memorias*, 24–25. For Kuznetsov's offensive views, see, for example, N. G. Kuznetsov, "Doklad morskogo sovetnika glavnomu voennomu sovetniku," 30 August 1937, fond 35082, opis 1, delo 23, listy 47–51, RGVA.
23. Three important books drawn from Russian archival sources detail Soviet supply of matériel to the Republic: Gerald Howson, *Arms for Spain: The Untold Story of the Spanish Civil War* (London: Murray, 1998); Yurii Rybalkin, *Operatsiya "X": Sovetskaya voennaya pomoshch respublikanskoi Ispanii (1936–1939)* (Moscow: Airo-XX, 2000); and Daniel Kowalsky, *La Unión Soviética y la Guerra Civil Española: Una revisión crítica* (Barcelona, Spain: Crítica, 2004).
24. For clandestine submarine warfare, see cartella 3098, USMM, Rome; SHEMA AN, 25–13 (25), 9742 AGMAB; and "Ursula," RM 20/899, BA-MA. See also Bargoni, *L'impegno navale italiano*, 131–144, 185–186, 195–210; Frank, "Naval Operations, 33–37; and Willard C. Frank Jr., "German Clandestine Submarine Warfare in the Spanish Civil War, 1936," *New Interpretations in Naval History*, ed. William R. Roberts and Jack Sweetman (Annapolis, MD: Naval Institute Press, 1991), 107–123.
25. Republican defensive and offensive naval operations may be traced in "Instrucciones—Flota Republicana," and "Ordenes de Operaciones de la Flota Republicana," SHEMA AR 25–12 (I) and AR 25–13 (II), 9514 and 9515, AGMAB; and Annin report, 17 August 1937, fond r.-1529, opis 1, d, 120, listy 16–83, RGAVMF.
26. "Instrucciones," and "Ordenes de Operaciones," SHEMA AR 25–12 (I) and AR 25–13 (II), 9514, 9515, AGMAB.

27. A list of German supply ships with a summary of their cargoes is in Merkes, *Die deutsche Politik*, 373–379, and Italian supply ships and their cargoes may be found in buste 129–131, MAE-US. For the organization and dispatch of men and matériel, see "Tätigkeitsbericht der Schiffahrtsabteilung (O.K.M. A VI) im Dienste des Sonderstabes W während des Spanienkrieges, 26.7.1936 bis 1.6.1939," RM 20/1451, BA-MA; and buste 9–10, "Relazione finale sull'attività dell'Ufficio Spagna," MAE-US. Petroleum supply from the United States is summarized in Howson, *Arms for Spain*, 73–74.
28. The most thorough study, while incomplete, is Howson, *Arms for Spain*. To the data reported by Howson, I have added further certain and probable voyages.
29. Aside from a Soviet squadron, Kuznetsov's specific request was for no fewer than twelve submarines with Soviet crews, sixteen motor torpedo boats, no fewer than eighteen naval reconnaissance aircraft, and twelve bombers assigned to the navy. See N. G. Kuznetsov, "Doklad morskogo sovetnika glavnomu voennomu sovetniku," 30 August 1937, fond 35082, opis 1, delo 23, listy 51–52, RGVA.
30. Litvinov to Maiskii, 27 January 1937, *Dokumenty vneshnei politiki SSSR*, vol. 20 (1937) (Moscow: Izdalelstvo Politicheskoi Literatury, 1976), 60–61, 697; "Resolution Relating to the Scheme of Observation of the Spanish Frontiers by Land and Sea," *Parliamentary Paper, Spain No. 1 (1937)*, Cmd. 5399.
31. See correspondence in fond r.-1483, opis 3, delo 244, listy 1–85, RGAVMF.
32. Kuznetsov, *Na dalekom meridiane*, 187–191; N. Piterskii, "Pod voenno-morskim flagom ispanskoi respubliki," in *Problemy ispanskoi istorii*, ed. I. M. Maiskii (Moscow: "Nauka," 1971), 185–193; and Ubieta's after-action report, fond r.-1529, opis 1, delo 115, listy 363–366, RGAVMF.
33. Buiza report, 17 December 1936, SHEMA AN 202–3, 8921 AGMAB; Piterskii, "Pod voenno-morskim flagom," 190–211.
34. See Willard C. Frank Jr., "Cartagena en el punto de mira de la Alemania Nazi: El ataque al *Deutschland*," *Cartagena Histórica*, no. 6 (January–March 2004): 4–16.
35. Kuznetsov, "Doklad," 30 August 1937, fond 35082, opis 1, delo 23, l. 47, RGVA.
36. Ibid.; Reports of V. A. Egorov and S.G. Sapozhnikov in "Submarinos republicanos españoles bajo mando soviético (III)," *Revista de Historia Naval*, no. 70 (2000): 25–46.
37. For the official Italian report, see "Relazione finale," Allegati 31 & 41, b. 10, MAE-US. See also Bargoni, *L'impegno navale*, 280–342.
38. For Nyon conference minutes and British naval instructions, see ADM 116/3523, 3528, TNA, and for French naval instructions, see "Dispositif Spécial en Méditerranée," 18 September 1937, 1 BB^2 204, Service Historique de la Défense/Département Marine, Vincennes. See also Peter Gretton, "The Nyon Conference—The Naval Aspect," *The English Historical Review* 90 (1975): 103–112; and William C. Mills, "The Nyon Conference: Neville Chamberlain, Anthony Eden, and the Appeasement of Italy in 1937," *The International History Review* 15 (1993): 1–22. For the quote, see Galeazzo Ciano, *Diary, 1937–1943* (New York: Enigma, 2002), 10.
39. A fairly full account of Soviet aid shipments, although incomplete, showing the end of shipments by the Mediterranean coinciding with Italian submarine "piracy" is in Howson, *Arms for Spain*, 278–303. For possible factors other than the submarine campaign in the break in Soviet aid, see Kowalsky, *La Unión Soviética*, 225–228; and Rybalkin, *Operatsiya "X,"* 92.
40. For Chamberlain's fears, see Cabinet Conclusions, CAB 36(37)5, 6 October 1937, CAB 23/89, TNA. Hitler's use of the Mediterranean crisis to distract the democracies and speed

on the conquest of Austria and Czechoslovakia is detailed in the "Hossbach Conference" of 5 November 1937. See "Minutes of the Conference in the Reich Chancellery, Berlin, November 5, 1937," *Documents on German Foreign Policy, 1918–1945*, Series D, vol. 1 (Washington, DC: Government Printing Office, 1949), 29–39.

41. For Republican defensive and offensive naval operations, see "Ordenes de Operaciones de la Flota Republicana," AR 25-13 (II), and "Partes de Campaña de la Flota Republicana" and of individual ships, SHEMA, AR 25–14 (VI), 9514, 9516 AGMAB.

42. Soviet reports document these developments in detail, but they are hardly documented in Spanish naval records.

43. See, for example, V.A. Alafuzov, "Politiko-moralnoe sostoyanie respublikanskogo flota v Ispanii i drugie politicheskie voprosy," verified 10 March 1938, fond 33987, opis 3, delo 1149, listy 75–79, RGVA; and Moullec "Intervention soviétique dans la guerre d'Espagne," No. L–118, 28 September 1938, fond 211, opis 1, delo 1048, listy 38–46, TsKhIDK.

44. "Operaciones combinadas—Proyecto de Desembarco en Motril," SHEMA, AR 254–2, AGMAB; Moreno and Moreno, *La guerra silenciosa y silenciada*, vol. 4, 1:2597–2630.

PART V. LATIN AMERICA

The Allied Project to Liberate Cuba, 1866–67: Chile, Peru, and Colonel Barreda's Confederate Navy

David P. Werlich

In 1866 the allied republics of Peru and Chile contemplated a bold offensive in their war against Spain. In coordination with a revolution inside Cuba, they would dispatch an army, via Panama, to liberate that Spanish colony. The project had much to recommend it ideologically. The allied governments and those of many other Spanish-American nations believed that this conflict pitted republican independence against monarchical colonialism. Although modern scholarship suggests that the feckless government of Queen Isabella II aspired primarily to increased prestige and, perhaps, a leadership role among its former colonies, contemporaries believed that Spain wanted to restore its once vast empire in the New World, lost four decades earlier.[1] Madrid had not recognized the independence of several Spanish-American nations. In 1861 Spain reincorporated the Dominican Republic into its empire and joined a British and French blockade of Veracruz that prefaced Napoleon III's imposition of Austrian Archduke Maximilian on a Mexican throne.

These events evoked official protests from several Latin American capitals along with many popular demonstrations of anti-Spanish sentiment. Apprehension increased in 1862 with the dispatch of a Spanish scientific expedition to the Pacific coast of South America, accompanied by a flotilla of three warships. Madrid hoped that this show of naval power would engender respect for the persons and property of Spaniards in Latin America. But the opposite occurred in Peru, where attacks on Spanish immigrants led to an international crisis. To force reparations from Lima, Spain's reinforced Pacific

Squadron seized Peru's Chincha Islands, just offshore, the major source of guano that provided the bulk of Lima's public revenues. Although Peru initially surrendered to Madrid's demands and agreed to pay a large indemnity for the return of the Chinchas, Chile refused to allow the Spanish fleet to coal in that republic. Spain proclaimed a blockade of Chilean ports, and the government in Santiago responded with a declaration of war in September 1865. Two months later, a revolution in Peru brought a new regime to power that, on 5 December 1865, signed an agreement with Chile to prosecute a war against their common foe. Neighboring Ecuador and Bolivia later became junior partners in this quadruple alliance, called the American Union.[2]

At the onset of the war, Spain's fleet in the Pacific—spearheaded by five frigates and the huge ironclad *Numancia*—was far superior to the allied navies, which counted only three aging wooden warships and a few auxiliary vessels between them. Peru, however, anticipated the arrival of four new warships from Europe, including the potent ironclads *Huáscar* and *Independencia*. Until their arrival, however, the allies avoided open combat with the Spanish fleet. The Spaniards, meanwhile, hoped for a quick, decisive battle that would permit them to withdraw with honor from the distant enemy coast. Unable to force such a contest, the Spanish fleet bombarded the undefended Chilean port of Valparaiso on 31 March 1866,[3] and then steamed northward to attack Peru. On 2 May 1866 the Spanish fleet bombarded Callao, the contiguous port of Lima, in the face of fierce resistance from land batteries and gunboats. The Peruvian defenses also included mines and boats mounting spar torpedoes.[4]

Following the Battle of Callao, the Spanish fleet separated into a pair of squadrons. Several ships that had been seriously damaged sailed across the Pacific to Manila, in the Spanish Philippine Islands. The remaining vessels sailed around Cape Horn, anchoring at Montevideo and Rio de Janeiro. The *Huáscar* and *Independencia* joined the American Union fleet, anchored at Valparaiso in early June 1866, and the allies became anxious to mount an offensive against Spain. Several naval campaigns were discussed. The most favored, initially, was an attack on the Spanish squadron in the Philippines, where the allies hoped to surprise the enemy with some of its vessels in dry dock. Another option envisioned a thrust into the South Atlantic to challenge the Spanish squadron there. The allied force might then mount an attack on Cuba and, perhaps, even bombard ports in Spain.[5]

On 25 November 1865 thirty-four-year-old Benjamín Vicuña Mackenna arrived in New York City on a controversial ten-month mission as Chile's confidential agent.[6] Already a celebrated man of letters who would become one of his nation's more prolific historians, Vicuña Mackenna's most pressing task was to purchase ships and heavy guns. His instructions from Navy Minister J. Manuel Pinto, supplementing those from Foreign Minister Alvaro Covarrubias, authorized the agent to employ experienced military professionals—*hombres del arte* (men of the art of war) Vicuña Mackenna called them—to help him purchase war matériel and to get these elements to Chile. Santiago also envisioned sending armed cruisers—like the famed Confederate commerce destroyer *Alabama*—directly from the United States to prey upon Spanish shipping. Thus Vicuña Mackenna might offer temporary commissions in the Chilean navy to man these vessels.[7] The confidential agent soon learned that many *hombres del arte* were available for Chilean military service. Two weeks after arriving in New York, Vicuña Mackenna informed Covarrubias, "among the brilliant sailors of the extinguished Confederacy," Chile could obtain the best auxiliaries for the war against Spain. They were "valiant, knowledgeable men in an unfortunate position," which made them willing "to accept the modest wages which we can pay." The agent's impressive list of Confederate contacts already included Adm. Rafael Semmes of the *Alabama;* Commo. John Randolph Tucker, who had commanded the naval forces at Charleston, South Carolina; Cdr. John Taylor Wood, the "Sea Ghost of the Confederacy," famous for his daring raids; and ordnance expert Cdr. Catesby ap Roger Jones.[8]

Vicuña Mackenna's mission was greatly complicated by the neutrality laws of the United States, which barred the sale of weapons to belligerent nations. Although swarms of commission agents eagerly sought to sell arms to the allies, Washington carefully guarded its neutrality as it pursued the high-stakes *Alabama* claims against Great Britain. U.S. authorities were aided in their vigilance by Spanish operatives who hired spies in the New York City post office, customs house, and police department to report on the activities of Vicuña Mackenna and other allied agents.[9]

Vicuña Mackenna quickly discovered that ships expressly built for war, especially ironclads, were nearly impossible to obtain. Significant quantities of artillery could be secured from Robert Parrott's works, but only after considerable delay. Vicuña Mackenna ultimately acquired thirty-four heavy guns and four merchant steamers deemed suitable for conversion to naval service before his arrest on 6 February 1867 for violating U.S. neutrality laws.[10]

In the meantime, the Chilean agent's anguish about his nation's feeble defenses in the face of an imminent Spanish attack made him an early convert to the advantages of torpedo warfare. Among his first contacts in New York was former Lt. William T. Glassell—Commodore Tucker's torpedo expert from Charleston, admired for his attack on the formidable, iron-belted USS *New Ironsides* with the diminutive torpedo boat *David*. For the Confederates, spar torpedoes and mines (often called stationary torpedoes in that period) were "weapons of the weak" used to offset the superior naval power of the North, a disparity analogous to that between the South American allies and Spain. Three weeks after reaching New York, Vicuña Mackenna informed his foreign minister that he had hired a team of torpedo specialists (*torpedistas*), four men who knew "the most effective means to attack quickly the enemy's ships with the most formidable modern weapon," which had "revolutionized naval warfare the last four years." Led by former Confederate Lt. Edmund Gaines Read, this quartet departed for South American on 11 December 1865.[11]

Vicuña Mackenna had greatest enthusiasm for another aspect of his mission—that of political agitator and propagandist in support of the allied cause. Fluent in English, the erudite agent lobbied politicians, charmed other opinion leaders, lectured at public meetings, placed letters in major newspapers, and published his own Spanish-language journal, *La Voz de América* (*Voice of America*), whose first number appeared on 21 December 1865. Vicuña Mackenna informed his government that the primary objective of the *Voz* was to "agitate Cuba."[12]

Foreign Minister Covarrubias instructed Vicuña Mackenna to encourage unity among various Cuban exile groups in the United States, primarily so that they might finance and provide other assistance to privateers whom the Chileans hoped could be licensed to prey on Spanish shipping. But Vicuña Mackenna on 10 December 1865 informed his government that privateering—outlawed by most of the world's major nations in 1856—had "fallen into complete disuse and even universal discredit." So, the confidential agent conspired to foment revolution in Cuba. Initially, Vicuña Mackenna told his government that he advocated a Cuban insurrection because it would divert Spanish naval power away from the blockade of Chile. After Peru formally entered the war in mid-January 1866, however, and especially when it seemed likely that the Spanish fleet would soon abandon the Pacific coast, Vicuña Mackenna championed an allied invasion to liberate Spain's "Ever Faithful Isle."[13]

During his first week in the United States, the Chilean agent met with Juan Manuel Macías, an exiled Cuban merchant and leader of New York's small Republican Society of Cuba and Puerto Rico. The group's basic idea—a Cuban insurrection supported by an external invasion—was neither new nor unique. From the Soles y Rayos de Bolívar conspiracy of the mid-1820s (which proposed to use troops provided by Gran Colombia and Mexico), through the U.S.-based expeditions of Narciso López and other filibusters of the 1840s and 1850s, down to the 1961 Bay of Pigs invasion, this was the preferred pattern for regime change on the island. Macías and his cadre of revolutionaries quickly became major collaborators in the *Voz de América*. Vicuña Mackenna's editorial in the first issue of the newspaper was subtitled "The Liberty of Cuba and Puerto Rico."[14]

Vicuña Mackenna presented his ideas in a dispatch to his foreign minister dated 20 April 1866, and in a personal letter to Peru's President Mariano Ignacio Prado on 10 May. For the latter correspondent, Vicuña Mackenna supported his arguments with a report prepared by Macías.[15] Vicuña Mackenna had recently learned of the bombardment of Valparaiso and received erroneous intelligence that the enemy fleet was departing for home; word of the 2 May Battle of Callao, of course, had not reached him. Believing that the allies soon would want to take the offensive, Vicuña Mackenna discussed three possible targets—Manila, Spain's homeports, and Cuba—and succinctly argued against the first two. The Philippines, he wrote Covarrubias, had little commercial value and the population (being "almost entirely Asiatic") would be "hostile" to independence, an idea "incomprehensible" to them. Thus, an attack on Manila would have little political consequence and bring scant international prestige. The bombardment of ports in Spain, even poorly defended ones, would require much expense for additional ships, would be viewed as purely vengeful, and would gain Madrid the sympathy of the European nations.

An allied attack on Cuba in concert with an insurrection by the Cubans would cost less—only $500,000, he told Prado—and be much more rewarding. The prospect of victory was very high and would bring "glory and prestige" to the allies. They would liberate a people who wanted and were prepared for independence. Vicuña Mackenna asserted that all of Europe (especially England) and even the United States would be sympathetic to the cause, for the enterprise surely would bring the rapid and complete elimination of slavery on the island, accomplishing the emancipation that all Cubans believed inevitable without the race war that all Cubans feared.

Vicuña Mackenna proposed a joint Peruvian-Chilean expedition of two thousand men—500 Chileans and 1,500 Peruvians; dubiously, he believed the latter to be better suited to the Cuban climate. The allies would attack via the Pacific and the Panamanian isthmus, avoiding a long voyage around South America and possible interdiction by the Spanish fleet in Atlantic. Vicuña Mackenna asserted that by way of Panama, Callao was only ten days or less from Cuba. The allied troops might be carried to the isthmus on government vessels or, if necessary, as passengers on two or three of the large commercial steamers that regularly serviced the Pacific Coast. After an overland transit of the isthmus on the Panama railroad requiring as little as eight hours, the force would reembark on government transports, carrying all of the matériel for the campaign.

The allied invaders would face twenty thousand soldiers commanded by the captain general of Cuba; but this did not deter historian Vicuña Mackenna, who noted that Gen. José de San Martín's 1819 seaborne, liberating expedition to Peru numbered only four thousand men to challenge the Spanish viceroy's 23,000 troops. Like San Martín, the allies would carry sufficient arms (which Vicuña Mackenna earlier reported were abundant and cheap in the United States) to equip revolutionary volunteers—twenty thousand Cubans, in this instance.

Macías's report declared that Cubans of all colors and classes—slave and free—were united in their desire for independence and that at least five hundred volunteers would rise up with the initial allied landing. He deprecated the quality of the captain general's poorly motivated troops and their ability to take the field during the hot, rainy season from May to October, when yellow fever, malaria, and dysentery would debilitate them. Furthermore, Spain's military strength was highly concentrated in the western part of the island, near Havana. Macías recommended that the allies land at any of several southern ports to the east, which were poorly defended. He especially favored Cienfuegos for its large, pro-republican population, abundant agricultural resources, and good transport links to the rest of the island.

While Vicuña Mackenna pitched the proposal to his government pragmatically, in (for him) a largely dispassionate tone, the Chilean's appeal to his distinguished friend, Peru's thirty-nine-year-old President Prado, was pointed and emotional. The crusade to liberate Cuba would give the coup de grâce to the "infamous" Spaniards, for "without Cuba Spain perishes." With great possibility of success, this "glorious enterprise," would "immortalize" Prado's name. "Do not fail to take this matter into your hands. . . . Contemplate that Cuba is [only] ten days from Callao, and the great affairs of this world are reserved for faith, youth, and enthusiasm. You would deserve, my dear general," to be called "the second Bolívar."

Vicuña Mackenna was frustrated by his inability to obtain the true warships that his government wanted. Indeed, his high profile as an agitator contradicted his letterhead as Chile's confidential agent, undercutting Vicuña Mackenna's efforts to obtain war matériel. He was humiliated by his arrest for violation of U.S. neutrality laws, which he believed demonstrated the personal hostility of U.S. Secretary of State William H. Seward toward him and his country. Vicuña Mackenna's government replaced him on 31 May 1866, and he departed for home three weeks later. He expressed hope that allied efforts in the United States soon would produce better results under the leadership of Peru's Federico Barreda, who arrived in late April.[16]

Minister Plenipotentiary and Envoy Extraordinary Federico Luciano Barreda y Aguilar was a man of great energy and ability who had accomplished much during his thirty-eight years. The youngest child of a Spanish merchant who had immigrated to Peru about 1792 and who had returned to Spain during the Peruvian independence movement three decades later, Federico was the only one of his dozen siblings who had not been born in Peru. In 1840 at age thirteen Federico sailed for Lima to join his brother Felipe, twenty years his senior, who had returned to Lima in 1827. Following in his father's mercantile footsteps, Felipe already had become very wealthy by the time his youngest brother joined him. The Barreda brothers' success continued during the next decade with investments in many enterprises, most notably shipping and finance. In 1852 their partnership received the highly lucrative monopoly contract as Peru's guano consignee (shipping and sales agent) for the United States, and twenty-four-year-old Federico took up residence in Baltimore, Maryland, the principal port of entry for this valuable natural fertilizer.[17]

In March 1861 Peru appointed the well-connected businessman its confidential agent in the United States to resolve a claims dispute that had ruptured diplomatic relations between Lima and Washington two year's earlier. Skillfully accomplishing this task in Peru's favor, Barreda became minister to the new administration of Abraham Lincoln. From his post in Washington, Barreda also served as plenipotentiary in negotiations with Spain and Russia. In June 1862, as relations between Peru and Spain deteriorated, Barreda approached naval contractor John Ericsson about the purchase of two ironclad monitors, vessels that had proved their worth three months earlier at Hampton Roads. But the Union government prohibited the export of badly needed weapons, so Barreda's naval attaché was dispatched to Great Britain to initiate the construction of the ironclads *Huáscar* and *Independencia*. In mid-1864 Barreda went to Europe, where, assuming the duties of plenipotentiary to the courts of London and Paris, this one-man diplomatic corps secured the delivery of the two ironclads and purchased the new French-built wooden corvettes *América* and *Unión*. In recognition of his contributions to national defense, Barreda was named an honorary colonel.[18]

With his wife Matilde, Federico Barreda moved easily among the highest society of the eastern seaboard and in Washington's corridors of political power. He hired lobbyists before they were so-labeled in the United States, and used business deals to enhance his political influence. The young tycoon lavishly entertained important guests at his mansion on New York City's Madison Square and Beaulieu, his palatial estate at Newport, Rhode Island. While diplomats representing often-impecunious Latin American governments commonly suffered long delays in funding for even minor tasks, Barreda apparently dipped into his own pocket when necessary to act quickly. The young minister was the acknowledged leader among Latin American diplomats in the United States. Vicuña Mackenna deemed him the only Latin American minister who had the full respect of U.S. officials. In addition, he became a close personal friend and confidant of Secretary of State Seward and counterbalanced the influence of Spain's wily Gabriel García Tássara, the dean of the Washington diplomatic corps. The government in Lima, especially President Prado, had great confidence in Barreda's judgment and ability.[19]

An urgent task awaited Minister Barreda upon his return to Washington from London in late April 1866. Foreign Minister Toribio Pacheco ordered him to hire a commodore to command the Peruvian squadron. It seemed likely that this officer eventually would take charge of the combined fleet of Peru and Chile, as permitted under the treaty of alliance. The search for a foreign flag officer was prompted primarily to overcome hostility between the naval officers of Peru and Chile, traditional rivals on the Pacific coast. But the minister also needed to find a commodore familiar with modern naval technology and the distant seas where the allies might attack their enemy. Barreda initially hoped to find his man within the U.S. Navy but found that high-ranking officers of that service would not readily abandon their careers for an uncertain future in South America. The minister quickly turned to the roster of the defunct Confederate navy. After consulting with naval officials in Washington and Annapolis and former Confederate leaders, Barreda enlisted John Randolph Tucker, who became a rear admiral in Peru's navy.[20]

A fifty-four-year-old Virginian with a distinguished thirty-five-year career in the U.S. Navy before "going South" in 1861, Tucker had commanded the southern naval forces at Charleston, South Carolina—the showcase of Confederate contributions to naval technology. He had considerable experience with ironclad vessels and big guns and was a pioneer in torpedo warfare. Tucker also had cruised with U.S. squadrons in Asia, the Mediterranean, the South Atlantic and, especially, the Caribbean.[21]

Admiral Tucker and his personal staff of former Confederates—Lt. Walter Raleigh Butt and Lt. David Porter McCorkle—reached Lima in mid-June 1866. President Prado, his cabinet, and Peru's senior military leadership (including the navy director) welcomed Admiral Tucker enthusiastically, but the commanders and several other officers of the nation's major warships, anchored at Valparaiso, balked at serving under a foreign flag officer. Capt. Lizardo Montero, the squadron's controversial young commanding officer, vowed that his ships would not pass to Tucker's control. Ultimately, Premier Manuel Pardo arrived from Lima, arrested thirty-nine recalcitrant officers, and replaced them with men who were willing to serve under the former Confederate.[22]

Prior to his voyage home, Chile's Vicuña Mackenna and Minister Barreda discussed the former's proposed expedition to liberate Cuba. The Peruvian diplomat frankly expressed his doubts, which Vicuña Mackenna briefly noted in correspondence with his own government and with Peru's President Prado. Barreda detailed his reservations in a dispatch to Foreign Minister Pacheco on 10 May, the same day as the Chilean's missive to Prado. Unlike Vicuña Mackenna, the Peruvian minister questioned the universal desire of Cubans for independence and their ability to secure it. Many wealthy Cubans feared the loss of their slave-based fortunes, which would be jeopardized by an insurrection. Barreda believed the masses of poor Cubans to be in "an abject condition with not one noble instinct and completely subdued by the Spaniards." Their indifference to the prospect of independence had been demonstrated repeatedly by the failure of Narciso López's three expeditions and various domestic uprisings. Barreda also questioned the readiness of Afro-Cuban slaves to join the fight, for they were "less intelligent and civilized" than their counterparts in the United States. Barreda thought that a widespread revolt could not be sparked without confidence in eventual victory. An allied invasion might provide this impetus, but such an expedition would have no chance of success without naval support and a fortified base of operations in the Caribbean or Gulf of Mexico. Lacking this, an isolated force of three thousand allied troops (not the two thousand Vicuña Mackenna originally suggested) opposed by twenty thousand enemies would produce a "sterile sacrifice and give an easy triumph to Spain."

There was, Barreda thought, a more practical way to attack Cuba. "Send three or four well-armed, very fast ships" to the Caribbean to destroy Spain's commerce, disrupt her communications, and bombard Cuban ports. They might even make "temporary landings and provide arms" to Cubans in rebellion. All of the region's neutral ports could serve as refuges for these raiders, and they could avoid combat with Spanish warships unless they had the advantage. Vessels like Peru's corvette *América,* with double crews to take charge of prizes, could gain more "wealth and glory with less sacrifice" than Vicuña Mackenna's proposed expedition.[23]

On 9 June Barreda responded to a request from his government for information about conditions in Cuba and Puerto Rico, and the "possibility and consequences of an expedition against them." The inquiry was probably inspired by Vicuña Mackenna's earlier proposal. Barreda noted that he had become obsessed with this question since news had reached him about the bombardment of Valparaiso. He now had come to the conclusion that a "dignified and lasting peace" with Madrid could be secured only by an offensive against Cuba. Unlike an attack on Spain proper, in which neighboring governments would be prejudiced against the allies, an offensive in the Antilles would have the sympathy of "all of the peoples" of the Americas united by the "great idea of the emancipation of a race and the independence of a people."

Since his earlier critique of Vicuña Mackenna's proposal, Barreda had been in contact with many Cubans of "all classes and diverse opinions." He had lengthy meetings with Juan Manuel Macías and, most recently, with five wealthy Cubans, mainly slaveholders typical of the island's elite. Like Barreda, the latter group lacked confidence in the opinions of Macías and his clique, men with exaggerated ideas but limited resources and influence. Yet Barreda believed that both parties were essentially correct in their basic evaluation of Cuban affairs, differing mainly on the means to a common goal. In general, Cubans were dissatisfied with Spanish rule and wanted independence. But the failure of all previous efforts to achieve it had disheartened most of the people, especially the reluctant propertied class that had much to lose. Barreda's informants concurred that if Cuba were to receive significant outside assistance, republican leaders could quickly generate a major insurrection. Barreda's wealthy Cuban contacts believed that emancipation was the critical political issue. It must be proclaimed at the start of the uprising, leaving the thorny issues of compensation to slave owners and labor regulation among the manumitted to a national convention to be called after the success of the revolution.

Barreda outlined two broad strategies. The first was primarily a maritime campaign such as he suggested the previous month. This would be the safer way to "castigate" the Spaniards but would be less consequential. The second course would incorporate an invasion of the island in conjunction with a Cuban insurrection. It would be more difficult and dangerous—indeed, failure could be "calamitous." But it embodied "a great idea worthy of a free and energetic people" and, if "crowned by success," would "elevate our name and prestige in the world." The minister favored the second approach, on which he elaborated.

> The allies should send into the Caribbean their six best ships, including the *Independencia* and another ironclad which Barreda hoped to purchase. These vessels would carry the largest practicable number of sailors and marines who could be augmented by men recruited in the United States and elsewhere in the region. The fleet would congregate at Puerto Cabello, Venezuela, or another port in that nation. Barreda believed that the liberal Venezuelan regime of General Juan

Falcón could be persuaded to join the alliance or at least proclaim "positive neutrality." As the minister later explained the concept, positive neutrality would allow all of the belligerents—Spain as well as the allies—equal access to Venezuelan ports for shelter, supplies, and even to auction captured vessels. This "even-handed" posture, of course, would greatly favor the allies, whose home ports were very far away. Spain, therefore, might not respect this neutrality. To provide their fleet with minimal security in the event of an attack by a superior Spanish force, the allies needed to assist Venezuela in fortifying this base. Barreda asserted that he could quickly dispatch the necessary artillery from the United States. From this secure port, the allies would prey upon Spanish merchantmen and seek opportunities to battle, in detail, elements of the Spanish navy.

If the allies ascertained that an insurrection had begun in Cuba, they would rapidly dispatch an expeditionary force from Callao to Panama in government transports. It would number one thousand men organized into five battalions of two hundred men each, but with sufficient officers, sergeants, and corporals to expand these five units to one thousand men each. The expedition would be met with additional transports on the Caribbean side of the isthmus by the allied squadron. The weapons for these troops along with twenty-five or thirty thousand additional muskets could be carried by the squadron or dispatched from the United States, along with two or three batteries of light artillery.

The initial landing force would expand to no fewer than three thousand troops with the addition of the squadron's marines and men enlisted in Venezuela and other places. The expedition would land at a good, secure Cuban port in an area with a sympathetic population, and limit its operations to supporting Cuban rebel forces. Until the insurrection became generalized, the allies would only attack isolated enemy units and small garrisons. Barreda believed that the port of Nuevitas (on Cuba's north coast, some three hundred miles east of Havana) was the best place for a landing. It was located in the wider portion of the island with abundant resources and large forests ideal for guerrilla operations. The local population was very hostile to Spain, and would join the revolution in considerable numbers.

If the Cuban insurrection did not materialize, there would be no invasion. The allied squadron would limit itself to fighting the Spaniards under favorable conditions, destroying commerce, capturing merchant vessels, attacking the coasts, and "doing all the harm possible." Barreda lacked information about conditions in Puerto Rico, except that the people of this colony also suffered under Spanish rule. Furthermore, this smaller island was "so insignificant" that its "fate must follow" Cuba's.

Finally, Barreda briefly surveyed Cuban defenses: the distribution of 21,000 enemy troops, one-third of whom were native Cuban militia; the fortifications and artillery at various places; and the strength of the Spanish squadron in Cuban waters—naming five frigates mounting more than two hundred guns, along with various minimally armed coastal vessels. One month after relaying his first estimate of enemy strength, Barreda substantially revised his numbers based on new intelligence received from various informants. In the department of Havana—that is, the western part of the island—Spain had as many as thirty thousand men, including militia; six thousand troops were available in central Cuba, while the easternmost region had up to ten thousand defenders. Their arms, including artillery, were thought to be of poor quality.[24]

Over the next several months the two-option Barreda Plan—a naval campaign in the Caribbean, with or without an invasion of Cuba—seems to have been favored by the allies, with Peru's President Mariano Prado especially enthusiastic about the proposal. Under ideal circumstances and with optimum results, the Cuban project would cause most harm to the Spaniards, and provide greatest satisfaction to the allies. But innumerable vagaries of the real world haunted the complex, high-risk plan. It became an on-again, off-again venture, and secondary targets—notably Manila and the Spanish squadron in the South Atlantic—continued to be viable, competing alternatives.

Basic weather patterns provided one constant in allied planning. Seasons in the northern hemisphere are opposite those for the earth's southern half. Notwithstanding Juan Manuel Macías's assurances that Cuba's hot, rainy season from May to October would debilitate the Spanish defenders with malaria and yellow fever, the much smaller allied force seemed equally susceptible to these tropical diseases, as the U.S. Army would learn in 1898. More important, Cuba's heavy rains coincide with the hurricane season of the northern tropics. While disease and tropical storms would threaten an allied expedition between April and September, the passage around Cape Horn or through the Strait of Magellan during those same months would expose their vessels to freezing gales and pounding seas. Peru's new ironclads recently suffered significant damage in their voyage from Europe during the southern hemisphere winter of 1866.[25] Thus, the window of greatest opportunity for the Cuban offensive extended from October to May. Manila was the better option from June through September.

The allies also feared that Madrid might renew the attack in the Pacific, especially if the Caribbean option left the coasts of Peru and Chile poorly defended. In the months that followed, reports that the Spanish squadron had departed the Philippines for Tahiti (en route to South America) and of enemy movements from Rio de Janeiro and Montevideo brought indecision to the allied capitals. With their long coastline and closer proximity to the enemy in the South Atlantic, the Chileans were especially reluctant to see the allied fleet depart from its station at Valparaiso. Therefore, Minister Barreda hoped to send ships purchased in the United States to replace vessels dispatched from the Pacific, and his Caribbean plan posited leaving the powerful new ironclad *Huáscar* behind. Chile and Peru strengthened their defensive works at Valparaiso and Callao.[26]

Barreda hoped that the *Huáscar*'s place in Caribbean expedition would be filled by the ironclad ram *Dunderberg,* which many contemporaries believed to be the world's most formidable warship. Its very name—"Thunder Mountain" in German—evoked fear. The governments of Chile and Peru probably had their eyes on this monster even before the war with Spain began.

The U.S. Navy Department contracted for the *Dunderberg* in July 1862, with prominent New York shipbuilder William H. Webb. Responding to fears that Britain and France might intervene in the Civil War on behalf of the Confederacy, Navy Secretary Gideon Welles wanted to supplement the Union's low-riding monitors (largely confined to coastal waters) with powerful vessels capable of combat on open seas. The *New Ironsides,* ordered seven weeks after the *Dunderberg* was contracted, was rushed to completion in less than a year's time. Deficiencies discovered in the former vessel led to numerous modifications in the *Dunderberg*'s original design, increasing its cost and delaying its completion until August 1866. The ship made its first trial run the following month, September 1866. By that time, the Navy Department no longer needed the vessel and the government was reluctant to cover a cost overrun of perhaps $750,000 that Webb had incurred on the ship he originally agreed to build for $1.25 million. While Webb petitioned congress for relief, he sought to interest foreign buyers.

By 1866 a few recently completed European warships may have surpassed the *Dunderberg* in size or armament, but Webb's "Thunder Mountain" remained a formidable weapon. It was the largest armored ship built in the United States during the Civil War and would retain this distinction until the 1880s. Rated at seven thousand tons displacement, the ship was 377 feet long and 72 feet wide, but drew less than sixteen feet of water. Its armor was four and a half inches thick above the main deck, three and a half inches from that point to five feet below the waterline, and two and a half inches thick below that level. The *Dunderberg*'s elongated octagonal casemate (with sloping sides, like the Confederate rams) housed sixteen guns—four 15-inch and twelve 11-inch smooth-bore Dahlgrens. The fifty-foot-long ram was seven feet in diameter at the base. The vessel's two main engines, rated at five thousand horsepower, enabled the ship to achieve a speed of fifteen knots, remarkable for that period. Its design also incorporated many important technical innovations, including a double bottom and multiple, watertight bulkheads to keep the vessel afloat even if pierced in several places. Amenities for the crew included a galley that could serve four hundred men in one sitting, hydraulic toilets, and a "bathing apparatus."[27]

In a dispatch of 10 December 1865—his second after reaching New York City—Benjamín Vicuña Mackenna reported that he had been in regular contact with Webb about the *Dunderberg*. "It is a terrible machine of war," Vicuña Mackenna wrote, and "nothing can resist it." The builder was confident that he could quickly complete the vessel and rescind his contract with the U.S. government. For Vicuña Mackenna, "everything would be a question of money"—at least $1.5 million in gold. He hoped that his government would purchase the vessel with the proceeds of a loan under negotiation in London. But doubting the timely success of this transaction, Vicuña Mackenna urged President Mariano Prado to move quickly in obtaining the ship for Peru. During the next year, Chilean officials continued to consider purchasing the powerful warship, even as a joint venture with their ally.[28]

Peruvian special agent Mariano Alvarez apparently had begun discussions with William Webb about the *Dunderberg* in late 1865. On 13 March 1866 Peruvian Foreign Minister Pacheco ordered Federico Barreda to resume his post in Washington and to undertake the purchase of this vessel.[29]

Federico Barreda demonstrated his renowned abilities most clearly in his contributions to Peru's war effort, and his labor intensified with President Prado's enthusiastic endorsement of the minister's Caribbean proposal in mid-July 1866.[30] Barreda hired many consultants and agents to assist him in this large and complex enterprise. As Peru's highest diplomatic representative in the United States, Minister Barreda could not openly acquire war matériel in defiance of U.S. neutrality laws. And "Colonel" Barreda had little military expertise. So, like Chile's Vicuña Mackenna, Barreda mined the rosters of the Confederate officer corps. He wanted reliable, competent help and was willing to pay for it, offering substantial recruitment bonuses and salaries equal to those paid in the armed forces of the United States.

Barreda's most important military adviser and agent was former Cdr. Catesby ap Roger Jones. The scion of a prominent military family, Jones was best known to the public for his command of the CSS *Virginia* in combat with the USS *Monitor* at Hampton Roads, but his direction of the important gun foundry and ordnance works at Selma, Alabama, was more important to the

Confederacy.[31] Vicuña Mackenna initially hired Jones to inspect ships and artillery, and in January 1866 signed a contract with him to establish an ordnance works in Chile. On his journey to Santiago, Jones stopped at Lima and consulted with Peruvian officials about the defenses of Callao. With the consent of Chile's ambassador, the Peruvians hired Jones and sent him back to the United States as their naval agent.[32]

Jones consulted with Barreda on the hiring of Commodore Tucker, on the minister's proposed Caribbean offensive, and on the purchase of armaments. Jones inspected ships and guns, communicated with arms dealers, and sometimes negotiated contracts for Barreda. He was especially useful in arrangements with other former confederate ordnance specialists—notably his colleagues George M. Brooke (chief of naval ordnance) and Robert D. Minor (director of the Richmond ordnance works). Jones continued to provide limited advice about the defenses of Callao, producing diagrams for a system of armored turrets there. He admitted to limited knowledge in this field, however, so Barreda contacted Gen. Robert E. Lee in an effort to hire the chief engineer charged with the defensive works at Richmond and Petersburg.[33]

In preparation for the prospective Caribbean expedition, Barreda employed Capt. Walter J. Morris, the chief topographical engineer for the Confederate Army of Tennessee, to make a reconnaissance of Cuba. Morris completed his mission between September and December 1866. He returned with a recommendation that the allied expeditionary force land at Nuevitas, as Barreda originally suggested, and with military maps he had prepared for the operation.[34]

Barreda dispatched other specialists to recommend the placement of shore batteries at Puerto Cabello, Venezuela, the proposed allied naval base. While Peru's diplomats negotiated with the Venezuelans about joining the alliance or aiding it through a posture of positive neutrality, Barreda dispatched heavy guns to them. Barreda's agents made similar surveys of ports in Colombia, Nicaragua, and the Dominican Republic (which the Spaniards had abandoned in July 1865).[35]

The Peruvian minister also purchased small arms and other equipment for the allied expeditionary force that was to spearhead the Cuban invasion, and arranged for the arming of thirty thousand Cuban volunteers.[36] Like his Chilean colleague Benjamín Vicuña Mackenna, Federico Barreda had difficulty finding top-quality wooden warships. Catesby Jones asserted that they were unavailable at any price. Nevertheless, Barreda purchased four steamers deemed marginally suitable for military service. The best of these was the *Meteor,* a fast, long-range cruiser that had been constructed expressly to hunt the CSS *Alabama* but that now required extensive renovation.[37] And, of course, negotiations continued for the purchase of the *Dunderberg,* increasingly viewed as the key to an offensive in the Caribbean. Indeed, allied leaders believed that if their hopes for a full-scale campaign were denied, this monster supported by few auxiliary craft acquired in the United States, might raise havoc in Cuban waters.[38]

A new element in the Caribbean offensive emerged in September 1866 with a proposal from twenty-six year-old Edmund Gaines Read, the so-called torpedo specialist Vicuña Mackenna had dispatched to South America the previous December. At that time, Read and his team of former Confederate naval officers—Lt. Alexander McComb Mason, Lt. Daniel Trigg, and First Engineer Elias G. Hall—wanted to attack Spanish vessels blockading Valparaiso with spar torpedoes. An 1860 graduate of Annapolis, the Virginian Read, in fact, had limited credentials as a torpedo expert. Indeed, his colleagues—especially Mason, who had been Commodore Tucker's flag lieutenant at Charleston—had more experience with the weapon. But Read—an "enterprising fellow," noted Trigg—exuded confidence and was an effective salesman. The Read team arranged for a brief tutorial on torpedoes with Lt. William T. Glassell prior to their departure for Chile.

The men were to receive temporary commissions in the Chilean navy to protect them against charges of piracy, if captured by the enemy. In addition to their navy salaries, the former Confederates had been promised bounties for destroying Spanish vessels. Vicuña Mackenna did not provide specific amounts but indicated that his government would be liberal in its rewards. At the time, Stephen Rogers, the Chilean consul in New York, was spreading rumors that Santiago, with the backing of railroad impresario Henry Meiggs, would pay bounties as high as $1 million for the destruction of enemy warships.[39]

Once the Read party had reached Chile, however, the government objected to bounty payments and questioned the efficacy at that time of a lone torpedo attack on the entire Spanish fleet. On the eve of the bombardment of Valparaiso, Read volunteered to demonstrate his sincerity by sinking an enemy warship "for free," but his offer was rejected.[40]

The torpedo specialists departed for Callao, arriving at the Peruvian port a few days ahead of the Spanish fleet. Here—Daniel Trigg recalled—the young officers assisted in the last-minute placement of electrical mines. In the aftermath of the bombardment, a torpedo contractor (apparently John Louis Lay) asked them to join him in a nighttime attack on a Spanish warship with a boat mounting a "Cushing torpedo." The torpedo became entangled in its mounting apparatus, however, and the plan was aborted before the boat reached its target. Nevertheless, Read became a favorite of President Prado, who sent him home several weeks later with his recommendations.[41]

To Barreda, Read now proposed to raid Spanish merchant shipping in the Caribbean and, more important, to attack enemy warships with a fast, well-armed cruiser provided by the Peruvian government. In addition to the artillery needed for capturing merchantmen, this vessel would carry six steam launches fitted with spar torpedoes to sink major warships.[42] The latter concept was not new, and almost certainly was not of Read's invention. Perhaps Confederates bottled up in several southern ports during the Civil War had contemplated the efficacy of torpedo boats carried by mother ships into less-confined waters, where the enemy would be unprepared for torpedo attacks and less likely to protect their vessels.

Read may well have based his plan on the ideas of Cdr. Hunter Davidson, who was very much a torpedo expert. Davidson, a Marylander, had been the director of the Confederate Submarine Battery Service, succeeding the famous Matthew Fountain Maury in that post. He perfected the system of electrical mines protecting the James River. In April 1864 Davidson severely damaged the Union frigate *Minnesota* in the torpedo boat *Squibb* at Hampton Roads, earning a promotion to commander for gallant and meritorious conduct. Davidson and Read served together briefly on the blockade runner *Richmond* in the closing weeks of the war.[43]

In January 1866 Davidson and his partner Henry H. Doty (a shadowy civilian entrepreneur turned torpedo inventor) concluded a contract with Chilean confidential agent Ambrosio Rodríguez in London to attack Spanish warships off the Chilean coast with three torpedo-mounted steam launches carried on board the *Henrietta,* a fast, iron-hulled steamer. In addition to Chilean naval salaries, Rodríguez agreed to pay substantial bounties for the sinking of specific Spanish warships: $100,000 for the ironclad *Numancia,* $50,000 for each of six wooden frigates, and $10,000 to $15,000 for smaller vessels. Rodríguez confided to a friend his hope that the *Henrietta* expedition might "destroy the entire Spanish fleet in one month," giving Chile "revenge with much economy."[44]

In an early demonstration of Murphy's Law, however, everything that could go wrong did so, and the *Henrietta* would not reach Valparaiso until late July 1866, ten weeks after the departure of the Spanish fleet. Admiral Tucker failed in an effort to have Davidson appointed torpedo specialist for his fleet, but torpedo launches soon were placed on the major ships of the alliance. Cdr. Hunter Davidson returned to the United States in September 1866, about the same time as Read was making his proposal to Barreda. Davidson already had received approval in Lima for a raiding expedition, perhaps employing torpedo boats in the Pacific.[45]

Barreda consulted with Catesby Jones and other advisers about Read's proposal, and on 9 November informed his foreign minister that he had agreed to the venture. Peru would pay bounties—in bonds—for the "complete destruction" (demonstrated by sinking) of Spanish warships: $300,000 for ironclads of over two thousand tons displacement and $200,000 for smaller armored vessels. For wooden ships the bounties would be $150,000 for frigates and $100,000 for corvettes or gunboats of ten or more guns. The government would pay an "appropriate" sum for destroying smaller warships. Merchant vessels taken by Read were to be sold entirely for the benefit of the captors, with the proceeds distributed among the officers and men.

Salaries would be the same as those in the U.S. Navy, and each man would receive an enlistment bonus of three-months' pay. Barreda asked that expedition's instructions be drafted in conformity with the rules of the Ministry of War and Marine, permitting minor modifications justified by changing circumstances. As a safeguard against Spanish threats to treat foreign sailors as pirates, Read and his officers would be given commissions in the Peruvian navy; naturalization documents would give similar protection to the crew.[46]

With Catesby Jones's assistance, Read already had been searching for an appropriate ship—fast ("twelve knots with ease"), capable of mounting a respectable battery, and large enough to carry the torpedo boats, ample coal, and other supplies. In addition to surveying the market in the United States, Read sought help from Capt. James D. Bulloch, in Liverpool, the former Confederacy's principal purchasing agent for ships in Europe.[47]

By late October Read had identified the USS *R.R. Cuyler* as a likely candidate for his venture. A wooden screw-steamer built at New York in 1860, it had been chartered by the U.S. government in May 1861 and then purchased by the Navy three months later for $165,000. After modification and fitting with a battery of ten guns, it joined the Union blockading force on the Gulf Coast. The *Cuyler* was 237 feet long, with a beam of 33 feet. The vessel was reputedly fast, capable of fifteen knots. It had captured or destroyed fifteen enemy vessels, primarily blockade-runners, during the war.[48]

Barreda believed that ship broker Russell Sturgis, of New York, wanted too much money for the *Cuyler*. But Vernon H. Brown—the minister's trusted, longtime associate in the shipping business who now handled many of Barreda's confidential transactions—deemed the price appropriate. After inspecting the vessel, Catesby Jones assured the minister that with the modifications proposed by Read, it was the best ship available for his purposes. The *Cuyler*, he explained, could be "used as a cruiser alone, or in company with other vessels. Her power would enable her to tow the Dunderberg . . . in case of an accident. From all accounts she is the fastest vessel that can be purchased."[49]

In early November Barreda reached a preliminary agreement to buy the ship for $300,000 in Peruvian government bonds. Peru hoped to send the *Cuyler* (and, later, the *Dunderberg*) from New York fully armed and manned. This would guard against an easy capture by the enemy and permit the raider to undertake its mission without delay. To accomplish this in the face of the U.S. neutrality laws, Peru had signed a secret convention with neutral Colombia on 28 August 1866, under which the government in Bogota would purchase Peruvian warships in Colombia's name, but with funds provided by Lima.[50] The officers and crews would ship as Colombian naval personnel. Upon reaching Colombia, the vessels and their sailors would be transferred to Peruvian service. On 20 December 1866 Vernon H. Brown (Barreda's confidant) signed a purchase contract for the *R.R. Cuyler* with Russell Sturgis and Company on behalf of Gen. Eustorjio Salgar, Colombia's minister to the United States. Writing to President Prado about the acquisition, Barreda noted that the ship's name would be changed to the "*Rayo*" (Thunderbolt), "emblematic of the role" it would soon play.[51]

Barreda gave Captain Read carte blanche ("within reason") in preparing his vessel, securing arms and equipment, and recruiting men for the expedition. The minister did not want to give him "any excuse for failure." The *Rayo* would carry a battery of four 9-inch smooth-bore guns and two 30-pounder rifles on pivots, four pieces fewer than it had mounted during the Civil War. This reduction helped provide space for six large steam torpedo launches built in Virginia at a cost of $4,000 each. The specifications for these craft have not been located, but Read described them as "iron" vessels with roofs also of iron, to "shed bullets" as well as rain. He said they were large and powerful enough to tow harbor craft carrying supplies and troops, and in calm seas could travel between Colombian ports. After testing, the launches would be crated in sections and placed on board the *Rayo*.[52]

The torpedoes were manufactured according to plans provided by John M. Brooke, now a professor at the Virginia Military Institute. Brooke also provided instructions for them. Read contracted—cryptically—with Robert D. Minor to build the torpedoes, "eighty copper vessels of cylindrical shape . . . sufficient to . . . contain 100 pounds of Rice" plus five others large enough for "150 pounds of Rice." Minor also agreed to provide "per plan" one thousand fuse "tubes." Later, Read ordered an additional two hundred "leaden Tubes 3¼ inches long and ½ in inner diameter." Engineer Elias G. Hall, who had been a member of Read's earlier expedition to Chile and who would become the chief engineer on the *Rayo*, received a subcontract from Minor to supply the spars and mountings, including replacement parts. In addition to twelve 21-foot by 5-inch spruce spars for the torpedo boats, Hall was to build four "booms 30 feet long x 8 ½ in. in Diameter," probably to mount the larger torpedoes on the *Rayo* itself.[53]

By the time that Read had finished his requisitions for small arms, instruments, uniforms, provisions, stores for the medical and engineering departments, and a full bunker of coal, in addition to funds for enlistment bonuses and a $5,000 ship's reserve, Peru's investment in the expedition would surpass $470,000. Barreda told agent Vernon Brown to "see that [Read] brings down his pretensions to our standards as his, like all of these gentlemen, are always exaggerated and without regard to our scarcity of means." The minister asked Catesby Jones to review Read's shopping list and prune "all that will not impair the efficiency of the thing." Jones reported that, except for arms and munitions, the supplies ordered for various departments on the *Rayo* were below the standard specified for the U.S. Navy.[54]

Read apparently had no difficulty finding officers for the *Rayo*—two first lieutenants, four second lieutenants, a lieutenant of marines, two surgeons, a purser, a chief engineer, and six assistant engineers. All were former Confederates, and most had served with Read during the Civil War. The three senior line officers (1st Lt. George Borchert, 1st Lt. Thomas Dornin, and 2nd Lt. Francis Roby) had been Read's Annapolis classmates. Barreda wondered if Read had not enlisted an excessive number of officers, but Catesby Jones explained that each of the six torpedo boats required an officer and an engineer. As anticipated, the enlistment of able seamen was far more difficult. Read found some men in Charleston, South Carolina, and others in Washington, D.C. but a good number were hastily enrolled at New York City and had limited experience at sea. They enlisted for two years, "unless discharged sooner." The ship's petty officers were to be selected from among the able seamen after observing them during the initial voyage to Colombia. Read's 9 March 1867 list of the officers and crew of the *Rayo* contained 202 names. They received enlistment bonuses of three-months' pay and salaries at the rates for the U.S. Navy. The officers were to be commissioned for the duration of the war with Spain. The commission of "Capitán de Corbeta" (Lt. Cdr.) E. G. Read was to date from his service at the Battle of Callao—2 May 1866.[55]

Minister Barreda hoped to get the *Rayo* to sea by the end of December, but the late arrival of equipment and some personnel delayed the departure of the vessel for more than a month, much to Barreda's discomfort. The *New York Herald* had reported Colombia's purchase of the gunboat *Cuyler* soon after it occurred. Thereafter, numerous rumors that the heavily armed vessel was to become a Peruvian or Chilean corsair appeared in the city's newspapers.[56]

On 12 February 1867 U.S. Customs officials in New York impounded the *Cuyler* for violation of the neutrality acts. The Spanish embassy applauded the action; Colombia protested. Colombian Minister Salgar had notified the State Department of the impending purchase of the vessel on 7 December and no objection had been made at that time. Salgar now produced the signed contract that specified that Sturgis would retain ownership of the vessel until it was delivered, under the U.S. flag, to an unnamed Colombian port on the Atlantic. Ultimately, the State Department determined that the case against the vessel lacked sufficient merit to prevent its departure. It was allowed to sail about 2 March, after Sturgis and Company posted a $200,000 bond. Now transformed into the *Rayo*, the raider reached the Colombian port of Santa Marta (its secret destination) in only nine days, "demonstrating," noted Barreda with satisfaction, "that its name is not inappropriate."[57]

While the *Rayo* expedition prepared during the final months of 1866, Federico Barreda intensified his negotiations to purchase the *Dunderberg*. It was hoped that the secret convention with Colombia or a similar arrangement with Venezuela would suffice to skirt the neutrality laws and put this potent weapon, fully armed and manned, into the hands of the allies quickly. Financing continued to be a major impediment to the acquisition. Peru wanted to pay less than builder William Webb hoped to receive. And as with many of Barreda's larger military expenditures, the Peruvians wanted to pay in government bonds, which Webb resisted. The Lima government sought to raise more than $1 million in cash on the Paris market to cover the cost but could not find sufficient subscribers.[58]

In addition to funding, the allies faced a formidable challenge in providing personnel for the vessel. Barreda put the number at a minimum of 650 men; Vicuña Mackenna thought it would require sixty engineers and machinists, both of which were notoriously scarce in Latin American navies. Perhaps a few able seamen might be drawn from Chile, which had Latin America's largest merchant marine, but the two allies already faced a dearth of manpower in staffing the fleet at Valparaiso, and a shipload of Chilean sailors certainly would have seemed suspicious on a Colombian warship. So, the officers and crew would have to be recruited largely in the United States.[59]

Concerning command of the *Dunderberg*, Barreda asserted, Captain Jones was the "only man capable of handling this monster." In January, however, Barreda put the question directly to the ex-skipper of the *Virginia*, who refused the assignment. Jones explained that he had previously rejected several offers to enter the uniformed service of the allied nations (once, to become the commander of the Chilean squadron) because of likely objections by native officers. When Barreda had first told Jones about his "proposed plan of operations on this side" (i.e., in the Caribbean) and suggested that he might "take charge of it," the former Confederate was "tempted" by the offer. But his decision against accepting a naval commission was reinforced by the "troubles resulting from Tucker's appointment." Jones, however, believed that he could provide valuable advice if Peru "obtained the 'elephant'" as Barreda anticipated. With Jones unavailable to command the *Dunderberg,* Barreda now suggested the appointment of Hunter Davidson, whose proposed expedition had become untenable.[60]

By January 1867 Barreda and Webb had reached a preliminary understanding about the purchase of the *Dunderberg.* The latter had approached Navy Secretary Gideon Welles in September 1866 about the basic issue—the builder's repayment of some $1.1 million received in installments from the government, and the subsequent sale of the vessel to another nation. Welles privately discussed the matter several times with President Andrew Johnson and members of the cabinet. The latter body was divided on the issue, but Webb believed he could gain approval for the sale.

At Webb's request Secretary of State Seward on January 23 brought before the cabinet the sale of the *Dunderberg,* specifically to Colombia. Seward asserted that the transfer would not violate the neutrality laws, and Welles supported the proposal because it would help the depressed shipbuilding industry, but Secretary of War Edwin Stanton spoke forcefully against the proposal. The ship's menacing name alone was worth a million dollars, he declared. Action on Webb's proposal was postponed until 25 January, when the cabinet rejected it. Webb suggested to Barreda that the decision was likely made because of an "unwillingness to let another Govt possess such a forceful engine of war."[61]

The *Dunderberg* issue came briefly before the cabinet again on 8 February. The timing was most inauspicious for Barreda's cause. The meeting began with a lengthy discussion about the seizure of the *Cuyler* six days earlier for violation of the neutrality laws. Secretary of State Seward, who earlier had supported Webb's sale of the *Dunderberg* to Colombia, now condemned that nation's participation in a "fictitious cover," asserting, "the vessel . . . was to be converted into a privateer, or passed over to the Peruvians." Welles retorted that neutral Colombia had every right to purchase the *Cuyler* and that the vessel should be released. Secretary Stanton, however, pointedly compared the case of the *Cuyler* to that of the *Alabama.* "This was the very matter now in issue" with Great Britain, and the cabinet "must not embarrass the State Department . . . by committing a similar wrong."[62]

Four days later, at the urging of Attorney General Henry Stanbery, the cabinet supported the release of the *Cuyler,* under bond, for lack of evidence. But linkage had been established between the *Cuyler,* the *Dunderberg,* and the $15 million *Alabama* claims. Furthermore, Seward had forcefully impugned the integrity of the Colombian government and its minister, General Salgar—"a weak man" who "can easily be imposed upon." Legislation secured in early March, as Barreda was preparing to leave his post, permitted Webb to repay the government for the *Dunderberg* and sell it to another customer. Barreda instructed Francisco Agudela, Colombia's consul general who had replaced the discredited Salgar in the negotiations, to present Webb a draft contract for $2.2 million. Although it was less than the builder wanted, Barreda thought it an acceptable offer. But Webb waited for a better price from a more credible buyer likely to gain approval from the government. Anticipating a war with Prussia, France purchased Barreda's monster in May 1867 for $2.5 million. The French navy rechristened it the *Rochambeau*.[63]

The speedy voyage of the *Rayo* to Colombia was the last good news that Barreda would hear about that vessel. Flying the U.S. flag, the *Rayo* had sailed from New York with most of its officers and crew on board, bound for an unnamed Colombian port under the command of Captain Dollard, a civilian employee of ship seller Russell Sturgis. Dollard's sealed instructions—opened only after leaving U.S. waters—directed him to deliver the vessel to Colombian customs agents at the port of Santa Marta and obtain signed receipts to fulfill Sturgis's sales contract and the terms of the U.S. Customs bond. For reasons of secrecy, Captain Read, Lt. William Murdaugh, and Surgeon Robert Powell, departed 11 March on a merchant steamer bound for Panama and continued on to Santa Marta.

Read's party also included young 2nd Lt. Carlos Corpancho of the Peruvian navy who carried the sensitive documents pertaining to the nationality of the *Rayo* and its sailors, as well as dispatches for the Peruvian minister in Bogota, Col. Manuel Freyre. Barreda's orders to Read and Corpancho directed them, upon reaching Santa Marta, to obtain further instructions from Minister Freyre in the Colombian capital or, more expeditiously, from an agent the minister might have dispatched to the port.[64] But Read found no instructions from Freyre awaiting him in Santa Marta, so he and Corpancho made the difficult three hundred–mile journey (which usually required ten days) by boat and rugged trail up the Magdalena River Valley to Bogota.

Barreda had periodically apprised Freyre about the progress of Read's expedition since its approval in November. But Freyre claimed to be unprepared for Read's arrival on 19 April because he had been incommunicado with both the United States and Peru for many weeks; bad weather and an uprising in the Magdalena Valley had halted mail service. The documents expected from Lima—additional officers' commissions duly signed by the minister of war and marine, a patent for the *Rayo,* and instructions for Read—had not arrived. Corpancho's dispatches from Barreda to Freyre detailed Read's mission and the assistance needed from Freyre and included copies of Barreda's instructions to Read and five blank commissions. But Freyre declined to provide Read any direction until the minister received further instructions from Lima, expected to arrive in perhaps two weeks. Similarly, Freyre refused to execute the blank commissions or provide a temporary document identifying the *Rayo* as a Peruvian warship because the moment was most inopportune for the host government of Gen. Tomás Cipriano de Mosquera.[65]

Barreda and Salgar apparently had agreed on a formula for transferring the *Rayo* from Colombia to Peru without it seeming to be an egregious violation of U.S. neutrality. Colonel Freyre was to present Colombian authorities a bill for the $420,000 cost of the warship and its armament. It was anticipated that Colombia would refuse to pay, and the *Rayo* would revert to its underwriter—Peru. Until this scenario played out, however, Read was instructed to maintain the putative status of a Colombian officer, commanding a Colombian warship, and subject to the orders of the Colombian government. After his meeting with Colonel Freyre, Read briefly visited with Mosquera, exchanged courtesies, and placed himself at the president's orders. But Mosquera did not have instructions for him and requested that Read keep the entire *Rayo* matter secret.[66]

Known as the grand general, the aged Mosquera was a former dictator-president within a centralized political system that by 1863 had become a very loose confederation of nine highly autonomous states, each with its own president. This fragmented political structure complemented Colombia's fractured geography and diverse regional cultures. But Mosquera chafed under his anemic authority as president of the now misnamed "United States of Colombia." He wanted to assist the allies in their war with Spain and even, perhaps, join the alliance. His secret agreement to purchase the *Rayo* on behalf of Peru had been made without the knowledge of his congress.

A few days before Read's arrival in Santa Marta, an uprising occurred in the important coastal state of Magdalena that threatened to engulf the rest of the nation. Meanwhile, a New York City newspaper reached the capital with a report that Mosquera had secretly purchased the warship *Cuyler* from the United States for the Colombian navy. Responding to a congressional demand for information, Mosquera initially denied that he had purchased the ship, which would have required congressional authorization. Then rumors spread about the secret convention with Peru for the purchase of the warship, and discussions focused on the serious ramifications of such a transaction for Colombia's relations with Spain and the United States. Several days later, the beleaguered Mosquera would claim that, indeed, he had purchased the *Cuyler*—but with his own personal funds. After Mosquera failed in an attempt to suppress the hostile legislature, congress arrested him and named a new president who renounced the secret convention with Peru. The turmoil would develop into a full-scale civil war. The transfer of the *Rayo* from Colombia to Peru did not occur. Read later asserted that he "never rec'd a word of instruction or advice" from Mosquera or Freyre in Bogota—or from Lima, either.[67]

Read correctly suspected that Minister Freyre was not being candid with him. Although mail service between the coast and Bogota was problematic, the ministers of the United States and Britain did receive their dispatches, via diplomatic courier, notwithstanding bad weather and rebels. And Freyre's diplomatic dispatches to Lima demonstrate that he had received most of Barreda's correspondence about Read's expedition as well as pertinent information from Lima and Colombian officials, too. But Freyre opposed the venture. In a dispatch of 30 April 1867 (no. 175), after meeting with Read and Corpancho, he opined that the *Rayo* expedition was ill advised. He thought the transfer of the *Rayo* to Peru would result in a war between Spain and Colombia for which the latter country was unprepared and from which Peru would receive no benefit. Freyre considered Read's objective unrealizable. The wooden *Rayo* would be no match for a vessel such as Spain's *Tetuán*, a fast new armored frigate posted at Havana. The *Rayo*'s sailors had been shipped under false pretenses and might mutiny upon learning the expedition's true nature. And the loyalty of Captain Read and his officers—all North Americans—could not be guaranteed. Thus, Peru's substantial investment in the warship would likely be lost. Freyre recommended that fifty men from the Peruvian navy be dispatched by way of Panama to take the ship, under Colombian flag, to Peru. Although Barreda and the foreign minister had emphasized to Freyre that the success of Read's mission would depend on getting the *Rayo* to sea without delay, Freyre informed his government that he was withholding the documents Read needed until further instructions arrived from Lima.[68]

On his return journey to the coast, Captain Read learned that a disaster had befallen the *Rayo*. Before leaving Santa Marta for Bogota, he had acceded to a request from Gen. Luís Level de Gorda, President Mosquera's regional military commander, to transport troops to a nearby district threatened by rebels. In compensation, the general's order provided that at the conclusion of this task the *Rayo* should proceed to Cartagena, Colombia's largest port, and fill its bunkers with free coal. On 21 April, without challenge from local authorities, the forty-eight-gun Spanish frigate *Navas de Tolosas* entered Cartagena harbor and accosted the *Rayo*. Although the latter vessel was flying the Colombian flag, the Spanish captain challenged its nationality.

He supported his charge with a copy of Colombia's official gazette containing President Mosquera's letter to congress denying that he had acquired the *Cuyler/Rayo*. The Spaniard threatened to take the ship and the "pirates" manning it to Havana unless documents were produced in two hours demonstrating that the vessel was not and would not soon become an enemy warship. Read's executive officer, Lt. George Borchert, and local Colombian officials negotiated a forty-day reprieve to produce the required documentation, by allowing the Spaniards to disable the ship. Sailors from the frigate removed a crucial valve from the engine and also carried off the ship's condenser, used for distilling fresh drinking water from the sea. Meanwhile the *Navas* stood guard over the *Rayo*.[69]

Captain Read's *Rayo* could not resist this indignity because the "Thunderbolt" lacked its deadly charge. Soon after the vessel arrived in Santa Marta, Lieutenant Borchert discovered key omissions in the vessel's armament. The fuses for the torpedoes were missing, and so were those for the 9-inch guns. Gone, too, were the elevating screws needed to operate the thirty-pounder rifled guns. Read had personally inspected the torpedo tubes some weeks before the departure of the expedition and had had them delivered to Vernon Brown's warehouse along with the other armaments. Nobody connected with the enterprise had been aware of problems with the guns and their munitions, which Catesby Jones and his agents had inspected. As the anticipated day of departure approached, Barreda ordered Vernon Brown to be certain that the guns would be ready and on board.[70]

Greater damage to the *Rayo*'s mission could not have been inflicted by the enemy itself. Read later lamented that the most unfortunate oversight had been the absence of the torpedo fuses. Two of the torpedo boats were complete, and if Lieutenant Borchert had had the fuses, asserted Read with characteristic exaggeration, he would have been the master of the situation. Risking a diagnosis of historian's paranoia, we must consider the strong possibility of sabotage, skillfully accomplished with surgical precision. Spanish agents were aware of the *Cuyler*'s objectives long before its departure from New York. Spanish Minister Tássara seems to have instigated the seizure of the vessel there, which was done without authorization from Washington. The impounded ship and its cargo were in the hands of customs officials for eight days. A year earlier Tássara had reported to the captain general of Cuba on the efforts of his operatives to prevent the departure of allied cruisers from New York: "To frustrate them we have at our disposition all of the employees of the customs house."[71]

Captain Read and his men had contemplated only a brief stay in Colombia. According to Barreda's provisional instructions, Read was to proceed to the Azores as soon as the *Rayo* was transferred to the Peruvian flag. At the port of Fayal he was to receive from allied agents intelligence about the departure of Spanish vessels from the ports of Cadiz and El Ferrol. Barreda provided Read with an expanded version of their original agreement regarding the expedition. Its primary focus continued to be torpedo attacks on enemy warships, with the substantial bounties promised earlier. The financial stipulations for captured merchant vessels were also the same: all proceeds were to go to the officers and men; but the instructions now included provisions for the safety of passengers and crews, for disposing of the prizes in neutral ports, and for communicating with allied authorities. Intriguingly, Read's orders also included procedures for converting captured enemy vessels into additional Peruvian corsairs and appointing officers for them.[72]

While a series of heavily armed Spanish warships continued to guard the disabled *Rayo* (even after a gale blew the vessel onto a reef in mid-September), Read attempted to extricate his ship from enemy control. He urged Colombian authorities to provide the documentation demanded by the Spaniards—demonstrating that it was a neutral, Colombian vessel. They delayed doing so for several weeks; and once the documents arrived from Bogota, the Spanish commander challenged their validity and sent them to Havana for review. Read craftily arranged an intervention on his behalf by the U.S. and British consuls at Cartagena as well as the commander of a U.S. warship in port, only to have his effort fail owing to a lack of timely cooperation by the state president. He also contemplated using force against the *Rayo*'s captors—an unattractive as well as dangerous option that might have resulted in war between Spain and Colombia.

Read's men smuggled several torpedoes off the *Rayo,* and Chief Engineer Elias Hall was dispatched to Panama and beyond in search of fuses or materials to make them. Unfortunately, two fully assembled torpedo launches had been left behind in Santa Marta and were now unavailable. With the endorsement of local Colombian officials, Read asked the Spanish commander for permission to remove one of the launches from the *Rayo* so that it could be used to open the Magdalena River for communications with Bogota. The Spaniard refused, perhaps suspecting (correctly) that Read might try to torpedo his frigate.[73]

Read also wrote to Vernon Brown, Barreda's agent, imploring him to send more fuses. Although Minister Barreda had resigned his post and Brown's agency for Peru would soon end, he purchased as many as fifty tubes from Robert Minor in late April, and perhaps obtained new elevating screws for the two pivot rifles, too. These items may well have been delivered to Cartagena by a new, late-arriving member of the *Rayo* expedition, whom Captain Read probably recruited earlier.

First Lieutenant Charles W. Read, from Mississippi, was not related to Edmund Gaines Read. They had been classmates at Annapolis, where Charles's accomplishments in French class were limited to his mastery of the word *savez,* which he used at every opportunity. Leaving the Naval Academy for the Confederate service in February 1861, "Savez" Read became famous for his audacity, ingenuity, and courage in a series of exploits that well-recommend him for the *Rayo*'s mission. As a junior officer on the Confederate raider *Florida* in 1862, he took charge of a prize off the coast of Brazil. With only one boat howitzer and some dummy guns, he cruised up the East Coast of the United States as far as Portland, Maine, transferring his flag to four different vessels in the process of capturing or destroying twenty-one ships. In the closing months of the war, Savez succeeded Hunter Davidson as commander of the torpedo-boat squadron on the James River.[74]

Savez Read probably reached Cartagena in mid-May. With the Spaniard's threatened removal of the *Rayo* to Havana looming at the end of the month, the two Reads became desperate. They planned to attack the Spanish frigate *Virgen del Carmen* with a torpedo mounted on the Colombian gunboat *Colombia;* two smaller enemy escort vessels were to be torpedoed in rowboats. If successful, they hoped to take the *Rayo,* flying the Colombian flag, to Kingston, Jamaica, under sail where the ship's engine might be repaired. The plan was aborted, apparently when the vessel's documents, though suspect, arrived from Bogotá.[75]

Although the imminent threat of enemy seizure passed, the expedition's circumstances continued to deteriorate. Many of the ship's enlisted men, unpaid and hungry, appealed to the U.S. consul for release from their contracts on the grounds that they had enlisted under false pretenses. A majority of them soon left the vessel and were provided passage home. By 1 June the ship's meager cash reserve was exhausted, and so were most of the provisions. For a while officials in Cartagena provided a minimal allowance for food and freshwater, exacting in return the temporary assignment of parties from Read's ship for service on the gunboat *Colombia*. On 1 July all provisioning ceased, and Read reported that the *Rayo*'s contingent had been reduced to a half-dozen officers and some twenty-five sailors. Most of the men moved on shore, leaving behind a few sailors to look after the vessel; soon this vigilance declined, with only occasional visits to *Rayo*. The men took with them their personal possessions and small arms. Read removed the ship's documents along with the valuable chronometers and some other instruments, hoping that the latter items might secure a loan of perhaps $500. When this effort failed he put them in storage. The derelict ship was soon looted—primarily by Colombian officials and soldiers, Read claimed. He continued to appeal for assistance and instructions from Bogota and Lima, but received neither. In his dispatches to Lima, Minister Freyre continued to claim that he had only sporadic communication with coast; but he did pass along rumors and information provided by a Colombian colonel who recently returned from the region.[76]

The men of the *Rayo* hoped to avoid being drawn into Colombia's civil war. Orphaned by Minister Freyre and Colombian authorities in Bogota, and immobilized by the Spaniards, they navigated erratically through the shoals of local politics on the Caribbean coast. "I could only drift along with the current of events," noted Read. Ultimately, he and his colleagues "made many enemies and no friends." The remaining story of the *Rayo* expedition is convoluted, with conflicting accounts and significant gaps in the documentation.[77]

From the time of their arrival in Colombia, Read and his men had identified with the regime of President Mosquera, Peru's collaborator. His opponents, favoring neutrality in the war, were later said to be supported by the Spaniards holding the *Rayo*. As the civil war engulfed the entire Caribbean coast, the political lines became blurred. The state of Magdalena (with its port, Santa Marta) fell to Mosquera's enemies, while the state of Bolívar (with its port, Cartagena) continued its nominal allegiance to the Mosquera party. From its station in Cartagena, the gunboat *Colombia,* increasingly supplied with officers and men from the *Rayo,* maintained a very leaky blockade of Santa Marta. By mid-July, the anti-Mosquera party had achieved the upper hand in the conflict, and the national leadership of both sides proclaimed an end to the fighting. But the *Colombia* continued to harass shipping at Santa Marta. After appeals from the foreign consuls there, that vessel's commander (Lt. William Bradford—another ex-Confederate) took his ship back to Cartagena and declared his neutrality. Promising to pay the back wages due the men of the *Rayo,* the president of Bolívar State induced Captain Read to seize the *Colombia* and reestablish the blockade of Santa Marta. Read and his men took the ship without bloodshed. But Read determined that the struggle was futile and that it was politic to realign his party with the victors. So, he brought the *Colombia* into the harbor at Santa Marta under a flag of truce. With the assistance of the foreign consuls there, he reached an agreement with representatives of the new government. He surrendered control of the *Colombia*. They promised to pay the wages due to Read's men and offered them a new contract for their continued service.[78]

In August Captain Read sent Savez Read to Lima. The captain believed that his many reports to Peru's capital had been intercepted by the postmaster in the Colombian State of Panama. In addition to delivering copies of these errant documents, Savez was authorized to speak for Captain Read, explaining all of his actions. The two Reads also were anxious to resume the *Rayo's* mission with another vessel. Savez was cordially greeted by officials in Lima, including President Prado. They seemed unaware of the details concerning the fiasco in Colombia. Savez initially requested the assignment of the corvettes *América* or *Unión* to their expedition, but then shifted his attention to the recently arrived *Meteor,* built to hunt down the *Alabama.* Savez reported that President Prado's friendly attitude suddenly cooled. The Reads assumed that he had received damaging reports about their conduct in Colombia. Indeed, Minister Freyre had asked his friend Manuel José Anaya, who was traveling to the coast on his way to Europe, to send a report to Lima about the *Rayo* and its men. Anaya's letter to Lima, sent from Cartagena on 24 July, quoted local government documents and other information published in a Cartagena newspaper, claiming that Read and his men had stripped and abandoned their vessel. They had "seized by surprise the *Colombia*" and had since engaged in "scandalous acts of piracy." Freyre, himself, repeated the charges in less inflammatory terms and noted that the local population considered the men of the *Rayo* "pirates."[79]

On 1 September 1867 four of Captain Read's officers returned to Cartagena from Santa Marta by coastal steamer to retrieve personal property left behind in that city. They were soon surrounded by a hostile mob of civilians and soldiers who denounced them as "pirates." Lt. George Borchert and Lt. William Murdaugh were murdered—allegedly by a soldier using a Spencer rifle taken off the *Rayo.* Lt. Thomas Dornin, though badly wounded, managed to escape with Lt. Philip Smith. They found a place to hide and were later rescued by U.S. Consul Augustine Hannabergh, who spirited them away to a steamer in the harbor. Fortunately, Read's agreement with Colombian government officials was honored. The men of the *Rayo* received $22,000 of back pay, in three installments, with drafts against customs receipts in August, September, and October. Edmund Gaines Read returned to the United States in late October 1867.[80]

As the *Rayo* expedition languished in Colombia, the allied coalition and the Peruvian administration of President Prado crumbled. The allies had accepted an offer by the United States to mediate an end to the war. The proposal did not require an armistice, so Prado continued to press his allies for an offensive against Spain; but in February 1867 the Chilean government retreated from a planned expedition to the Caribbean that it had approved the previous month. The Lima government briefly resolved to continue the fight alone, and rancorous negotiations followed for the separation of the allied fleet. The wartime solidarity of Peru and Chile soon receded into their traditional rivalry.[81]

The Prado regime's abandonment of the Caribbean offensive became manifest with the publication on 27 March 1867 of Admiral Tucker's resignation. The Prado administration considered Tucker's leadership indispensable to a successful campaign. The admiral had endured considerable personal embarrassment in recent weeks. He had been locked in a nagging war of salutes with the commander of the U.S. South Pacific Squadron, Adm. John A. Dahlgren, who rigidly refused to exchange traditional naval courtesies with the "unpardoned rebel," which, in practical application, extended to the allied fleet he commanded. In early February and with much public celebration, a court martial exonerated and ordered back to active duty the naval officers led by Capt. Lizardo Montero who had rejected Tucker's command of the Peruvian squadron. The admiral hoped to lead his fleet into battle. He likely would not have resigned (and Prado probably would not have accepted his resignation) if a reasonable prospect for an offensive had remained. Thereafter, the ill-fated *Rayo* expedition—languishing in Colombia—was the regime's last hope for significant blow against the enemy.[82] By late 1866 a widening rebellion in the provinces and financial scandal gravely weakened the regime. Scurrilous accusations of fraud in the complicated transactions related to the war brought the resignations of key members of the administration—Premier and Finance Minister Manuel Pardo, Foreign Minister Toribio Pacheco, and, finally, Federico Barreda. Peru's extraordinary envoy submitted his resignation three times before finally leaving his post after the departure of the *Rayo* and his failure to purchase the *Dunderberg*. In January 1868 the beleaguered Mariano Prado resigned the presidency and left Peru.[83]

The following October Cubans rose in rebellion—the onset of the bloody Ten Years' War. Although hindsight suggests failure, we cannot know what might have happened if the insurrection had begun one year earlier in combination with the proposed liberating expedition of Chile and Peru. And we can only ruminate on Cuba's different future if independence had come with the aid of the Andean allies (perhaps in 1870), rather than the fettered autonomy imposed by the United States under the Platt Amendment in the wake of the Spanish-Cuban-American War of 1895–98. The allied project envisioned by Benjamín Vicuña Mackenna and Federico Barreda (and their Cuban contacts) was inspired by worthy ideals—"the emancipation of a race and the independence of a people."[84] But the venture was quixotic—unrealistic given the enormity and complexity of the task and the limited economic and institutional resources of the allies.

NOTES

The following abbreviations are used in the notes:

AGMREP	Archivo General del Ministerio de Relaciones Exteriores del Perú, Torre Tagle Palace, Lima
Barreda Papers, SIUC	Federico L. Barreda Papers, Special Collections, Morris Library, Southern Illinois University, Carbondale
MRE, ANCH	Ministerio de Relaciones Exteriores, Archivo Nacional de Chile, Santiago
State Department, Consular Records	U.S. Department of State, Records of the Foreign Service Posts of the Department of State, Record Group 84, Consular Records, Cartagena, Colombia, 1863–69, U.S. National Archives, Washington, DC

1. The standard work in English is William Columbus Davis, *The Last Conquistadors: The Spanish Intervention in Peru and Chile, 1863–1866* (Athens: University of Georgia Press, 1950). Davis adopts the traditional view and stops his coverage at the 2 May 1866 Battle of Callao. For the modern interpretation, see James W. Cortada, *Spain and the American Civil War, 1855–1869,* Transactions of the American Philosophical Society, n.s., vol. 70, pt. 4 (Philadelphia, PA: American Philosophical Society, 1980).
2. Alberto Wagner de Reyna, *Las relaciones diplomáticas entre el Perú y Chile durante el conflicto con España, 1864–1867* (Lima, Peru: Ediciones del Sol, 1963), is an excellent treatment of the subject.
3. Davis, *The Last Conquistadors,* 291–320.
4. Fernando Romero Pintado, *Historia marítima del Perú: La república, 1850 a 1870,* 3 vols. (Lima, Peru: Instituto de Estudios Marítimos del Perú, 1984–85), 2:583–697.
5. Ibid., 2:697–701.
6. The confidential agent recounted his activities in Benjamín Vicuña Mackenna, *Diez meses de misiónma los Estados Unidos de Norte América como cajente confidencial de Chile,* 2 vols. in 1 (Santiago, Chile: Imprenta de la Libertad, 1867), which includes much of his private correspondence as well as extracts of his official reports. See also David P. Werlich, "Those 'Confederates' at Callao: The Participation of North American Sailors of Fortune in the War of Chile and Peru against Spain to June 1866," *Actas del Primer Simposio de Historia Marítima y Naval Iberoamericana (Callao, 5 al 7 de noviembre de 1991),* ed. Jorge Ortiz Sotelo (Lima, Peru: Instituto de Estudios Históricos Marítimos del Perú, 1993), 413–436. A Spanish translation of the latter is in the *Revista Frontera* (Temuco, Chile) (nos. 9–10, 1990–91), 109–122.
7. J. Manuel Pinto, "Instrucciones que deben server de guía de comisionado de gobierno de Chile para la compra, equipo y envio de buques de Guerra" (octubre 9 de 1865) in *Chile, Ministerio de Marina, Memoria que el ministro de estado en el Departamento de Marina presenta al Congreso Nacional de 1866* (Santiago, Chile: Imprenta Nacional, 1866), 66–67; Alvaro Covarrubias to Vicuña Mackenna, 1 October 1865, in Vicuña Mackenna, *Diez meses,* 1:12–14.
8. Vicuña Mackenna to Covarrubias, 10 December 1865, Misión confidencial de Chile en Estados Unidos de Norte América, 1865–1866, vol. 127, MRE, ANCH.
9. Chile, *Ministerio de Marina, 1866,* 13; Vicuña Mackenna to encargado de negocios, 8 January 1866; Vicuña Mackenna to Covarrubias, 20 and 28 February 1866, Misión

confidencial, vol. 127, MRE, ANCH; Vicuña Mackenna to Señor Administrador de Correos de Nueva York, 8 February 1866, in *Diez meses,* 2:11; Eustorjio Salgar, *El ministro colombiano en Washington i la adquisición del vapor "Rayo"* (Bogota, Colombia: Imprenta de Gaitán, 1867), 11; Tássara to Captain General of Cuba, 13 February 1866, in Spain, Museo Naval, Madrid, Archivo Alvaro de Bazán, *Documentos relativos de la campaña del Pacífico, 1863–1867,* ed. Ana María Vigón and María del Carmen García Sotoca, 2 vols. (Madrid: Museo Naval, 1966), 1:399.

10. Vicuña Mackenna, *Diez meses,* 2:249–253.
11. Ibid., 1:326; Vicuña Mackenna to Covarrubias, 10 December 1865, Misión confidencial, vol. 127, MRE, ANCH.
12. Cristián Guerrero Yoacham, "La misión de Vicuña Mackenna a los Estados Unidos (1865–1866)," *Atenea* (nos. 453–454, 1986), 239–275; Eugenio Orrego Vicuña, *Vicuña Mackenna y la independencia de Cuba* (Havana, Cuba: Imprenta "El Siglo XX," 1951), 17–36; Vicuña Mackenna to Covarrubias, 10, 20, and 29 December 1866, Misión confidencial, vol. 127, MRE, ANCH. Vicuña Mackenna provides a synopsis of the nineteen numbers of the *Voz de América* in *Diez meses,* 2:128–138.
13. Covarrubias to Vicuña Mackenna, 15 October 1865, in Vicuña Mackenna, *Diez meses,* 1:13–14; Vicuña Mackenna to Covarrubias, 10 December 1865, and 20 April 1866; Vicuña Mackenna to encargado de negocios, 8 January 1866, Misión confidencial, vol. 127, MRE, ANCH.
14. Vicuña Mackenna to Covarrubias, 10 December 1865, Misión confidencial, vol. 127, MRE, ANCH; Orrego Vicuña, *Vicuña Mackenna y la independencia de Cuba,* 18–19.
15. Vicuña Mackenna to Covarrubias, 20 April 1866, Misión confidencial, vol. 127, MRE, ANCH; Vicuña Mackenna to President Prado, 10 May 1866, with enclosure, J. M. Macías, Informe que presenta el señor Juan Manuel Macías al señor Benjamín Vicuña Mackenna . . . sobre una expedición militar para hostilizar a España en sus colonias . . . [30 April 1866], Misión confidencial, vol. 127, MRE, ANCH. The letter to Prado also appears in *Diez meses,* 2:79–82.
16. Mario Barros Van Buren, *Chile y la Guerra de Secesión: La misión Astaburuaga a los Estados Unidos* (Santiago, Chile: Editorial Universitaria, 1992), 194–218, provides a critical appraisal of Vicuña Mackenna's mission and of Chile's participation in the war. Vicuña Mackenna to Covarrubias, 18 April and 10 June 1866, Misión confidencial, vol. 127, MRE, ANCH.
17. Barreda's story, with emphasis on his private life and social activities, is told gracefully by his grandson, in Frederick Barreda Sherman, *From the Guadalquivir to the Golden Gate by Way of Lima, Baltimore, New York, Newport, Washington, London, Paris, and Cuajiniquilpa* (Mill Valley, CA: Hill and Smith Co., 1977).
18. For key episodes in Barreda's diplomatic career, see Rosa Garibaldi, *La política exterior del Perú en la era de Ramón Castilla: Defensa hemisférica y defensa de la jurisdicción nacional* (Lima, Peru: Fondo Editorial Fundación Académica Diplomática del Perú, 2003), 121–128, 291–294, and 366–369; Sherman, *From the Guadalquivir to the Golden Gate,* 70–79, 84–124, passim, 159, 167–181. See Sherman, *From the Guadalquivir to the Golden Gate,* 102–103, for "Colonel" Barreda.
19. Sherman, *From the Guadalquivir to the Golden Gate,* passim; Vicuña Mackenna, *Diez meses,* 2:100, 272; Vicuña Mackenna to José Gálvez, 10 March 1866, in *Diez meses:*272–273; Vicuña Mackenna to Covarrubias, 10 April and 10 June, 1866, Misión confidencial, vol. 127, MRE, ANCH; Pacheco to Barreda (personal), 27 March 1866, Barreda Papers, SIUC.
20. David P. Werlich, *Admiral of the Amazon: John Randolph Tucker, His Confederate Colleagues, and Peru* (Charlottesville: University Press of Virginia, 1990), 86–88.

21. Werlich, *Admiral of the Amazon,* 1–77.
22. Ibid., 88–107.
23. Barreda to Pacheco, no. 25, May 10, 1865, Libro copiador de las comunicaciones entre el Ministerio de Relaciones Exteriores del Perú y su legación en los Estados Unidos de América entre los años 1863 y 1866, tomo 68-A, 325–329, AGMREP.
24. Barreda to Pacheco, no. 51, 9 June 1866, Libro copiador, tomo 68-A, 374–389, AGMREP; also, Barreda to Pacheco, no. 76, 9 July 1866, and no. 105, 9 August 1866, Ibid., 434–437, 477–478. On the concept of positive neutrality, see Barreda to Juan V. Camacho, 13 June 1866, Libro copiador de las comunicaciones entre Perú y su legación en los EEUU de América, no. 62A, correspondencia a los años 1862–1866, 398, AGMREP.
25. Pacheco to Barreda (personal), 13, 21, and 27 July, and 13 September 1866, Barreda Papers, SIUC; Werlich, *Admiral of the Amazon,* 102–104.
26. Barreda to Pacheco, no. 112, 9 August 1866 and no. 118, 18 August 1866, Libro copiador, tomo 68-A, 485–490, 497–498, AGMREP; Pacheco to Barreda (personal) 21 and 27 August, and 13 September 1866, Barreda Papers, SIUC.
27. William H. Roberts, "'Thunder Mountain': The Ironclad Ram *Dunderberg,*" *Warship International* 30 (1993): 363–400.
28. Vicuña Mackenna to Covarrubias, 10 Decececember 1865, Misión confidencial, vol. 127, MRE, ANCH; Pacheco to Barreda (personal), 21 July and 21 September 1866, and Prado to Barreda (personal), 21 October 1866, Barreda Papers, SIUC.
29. Vicuña Mackenna to Covarrubias, 19 January 1866, Misión confidencial, vol. 127, MRE, ANCH; Pacheco to Barreda (personal), 13 March 1866, Barreda Papers, SIUC.
30. Prado to Barreda (personal), 10 and 21 July 1866, and Pacheco to Barreda (personal), 13 and 21 July 1866, Barreda Papers, SIUC.
31. Norman C. Delaney, "Jones, Catesby ap Roger," in *American National Biography,* ed. John H. Garaty and Mark C. Carnes, 24 vols. (New York: Oxford University Press, 1999), 12:186–187.
32. Vicuña Mackenna, *Diez meses,* 1:328–331; Barreda to Pacheco, no. 36, 30 May 1866, Libro copiador, tomo 68-A, p. 350, AGMREP; Werlich, "Those 'Confederates' at Callao," 420, 428.
33. For examples, see Barreda to Jones, 16 August 1866, and Barreda to V. H. Brown, 16 August 1866, Libro copiador, no. 62A, 440, 441, AGMREP; Barreda to Pacheco, no. 97, 1866, Libro copiador, tomo 68-A, 470–471; Jones to Barreda, 17 December 1866, Barreda Papers, SIUC; and Barreda to Pacheco, 10 September 1866, letterbook 3:498v, Barreda Papers, SIUC. About correspondence with General Lee, see Barreda to Prado, 20 and 29 June, and 31 August 1866, letterbook 3:240r–242r, 286v–284v, and 457v–471v, Barreda Papers, SIUC.
34. Barreda to Prado, 30 September and 30 December 1866, letterbook 6: 101v–102v, 339v–338r, Barreda Papers, SIUC; entry for Morris, 24 December 1866, Libro de cuentas de la legación del Perú en los Estados Unidos de América para los años 1866 y 1867, tomo 98-A, 21–22, AGMREP.
35. Prado to Barreda (personal), 6 August 1866, J. V. Camacho to Barreda, 7 September 1866, and V. Brown [memorandum concerning Parrott guns], April 1867, Barreda Papers, SIUC.
36. Prado to Barreda (personal), 21 July 1866, Barreda Papers, SIUC; Barreda to Jones, 16 August and Barreda to V. Brown, 16 August 1866, Libro copiador, no. 62A, 440, 441, AGMREP.
37. Barreda to Prado, 19 September 1866, letterbook 4:180v–174v, and Jones to V. Brown, 27 February 1867, Barreda Papers, SIUC.

38. Barreda to Pacheco, no. 112, 9 August 1866, Libro copiador, tomo 68-A, 485–490, AGMREP; Barreda to Prado, 9 December 1866, letterbook 6:241v-238r, and Pacheco to Barreda (personal), 27 September 1866, Barreda Papers, SIUC.
39. Vicuña Mackenna to Covarrubias, 10 December 1865, Misión confidencial, vol. 127, MRE, ANCH; Vicuña Mackenna, *Diez meses,* 1:319–322, 444–45; Werlich, "Those 'Confederates' at Callao," 420–423; Angela Trigg, "A Romantic Adventurer Comes of Age: The Life of Daniel Trigg of Abingdon, Virginia" (master's thesis, Georgia State University, Atlanta, 1997), 56, 71–83. Trigg's thesis is particularly valuable for the Read Expedition because she utilized the "Journal of Daniel Trigg" and also his brief autobiography "The Life of Daniel Trigg, C.S.N.," which were unpublished manuscripts in her possession.
40. Werlich, "Those 'Confederates' at Callao," 423, 429–431; Daniel Trigg, "Journal of Daniel Trigg," entry for "11th May 1866 'Lima,'" and Daniel Trigg, "The Life of Daniel Trigg, C.S.N.," unpaginated.
41. Werlich, "Those 'Confederates' at Callao," 434–435; Trigg, "The Life of Daniel Trigg, C.S.N."; Vicuña Mackenna, *Diez meses,* 1:321, fn 1. Lay provided the torpedo that Union navy Lt. William B. Cushing used to sink the Confederate ironclad ram *Albemarle,* in October 1864.
42. Jones to Barreda, 14 September 1866, Read to Barreda, 25 September 1866, and Barreda to Pacheco, no. 216, 9 November 1866, Barreda Papers, SIUC.
43. Werlich, "Those 'Confederates' at Callao," 424.
44. Ibid., 425; Rodríguez to Antonio Varas, 17 December 1865 and 1 January 1866, with enclosed undated contract between Rodríguez and Doty, in Miguel Varas Velásquez, ed., "Algunos cartas y documentos sobre la Guerra entre Chile-Perú y España," *Revista Chilena,* año 12 (1928): 531, 534–538.
45. Werlich, "Those 'Confederates' at Callao," 425–427; Werlich, *Admiral of the Amazon,* 104–106; Pacheco to Barreda (personal), 27 September 1866, Barreda Papers, SIUC; Davidson to Barreda, 19 December 1866, receipt for documents for proposed expedition, enclosed with Barreda to Pacheco, no. 255, 19 December 1866, Oficios de la legación del Perú en los Estados Unidos de América dirigida a Lima, 1866, segunda semester, carpeta 5–3, AGMREP.
46. Barreda to Pacheco (personal), 10 September 1866, letterbook 4:139v–134v, and Barreda to Pacheco, no. 216, 9 November 1866, Barreda Papers, SIUC; on the piracy issue, see Tássara to Seward, 5 March 1866, U.S. Department of State, Notes from Foreign Legations in the United States to the Department of State, Spain, 1790–1906, microcopy M–59, roll 19, record group 59, U.S. National Archives, Washington.
47. Jones to Barreda, 2 November 1866, and James D. Bullock to Read, 30 October 1866, Barreda Papers, SIUC.
48. "The *R.R. Cuyler,*" Ships File, Ships History Branch, U. S. Naval Historical Center, Washington, DC.
49. Jones to Barreda, 2 November 1866, and Sturgis to Brown, 13 September 1866, Barreda Papers, SIUC; Barreda to Prado, 20 November 1866, letterbook 6:199v–197v, Barreda Papers, SIUC.
50. Barreda to Pacheco, no. 216, 9 November 1866, Barreda Papers, SIUC; Barreda to Manuel Freyre, 9 November 1866, and Barreda to Prado, 20 November 1866, letterbook 6:171v–168v, 199r-197v, Barreda Papers, SIUC; Entry for *R.R. Cuyler,* in "Cuento general del costo del vapor 'R. R. Cuyler' y los artículos á su bordo," 33v-33r, Libro de cuentas, tomo 98-A, AGMREP; Manuel Matta, *Documentos para un capítulo de la historia diplomática de Chile en su última Guerra con España* (Santiago, Chile: Imprenta Ferrocarril, 1872), 216–219.

51. Salgar, *El ministro colombiano en Washington*, 9–10; Barreda to Prado, 30 December 1866, letterbook 6:339v-338r, Barreda Papers, SIUC.
52. Barreda to Prado, 20 November and 9 December 1866, letterbook 6:199v-197v, and 239v, Barreda Papers, SIUC; Augustine Hannabergh to [commander of any U.S. Navy vessel], 30 April 1867, Letters Sent, 1863–69, copybook, 241, State Department, Consular Records; Barreda to Brown, December 18, 1866, and Barreda to Pacheco, 30 December 1866, letterbook 6:286v-283r and 344r; Read to Salgar, 5 February 1867, Barreda Papers, SIUC.
53. Accounts numbered 1, 2, and 3 for *R. R. Cuyler*, its equipment and other expenses, Libro de cuentas, tomo 98-A, AGMREP; contracts between E. G. Read and R. D. Minor, 16 October and 22 November 1866, and between R. D. Minor and E. G. Hall, 11 December 1866, Minor Family Papers, Virginia Historical Society, Richmond.
54. No. 3, "Cuenta general de costo del vapor 'R. R. Cuyler' y los artículos á su bordo," 28 February 1867, Libro de cuentas, tomo 98-A, AGMREP; Barreda to Brown, 26 December 1866, letterbook 6:330v–328v, and Jones to Barreda, 28 January 1867, Barreda Papers, SIUC.
55. U.S. Navy, Office of Naval Records and Library, *Register of the Officers of the Confederate States Navy, 1861–1865*, rev. ed. (Washington, DC: GPO, 1931), passim; Barreda to Ministro de Relaciones Exteriores, no. 341, letterbook 7:28v-26v; Barreda to Brown, 18 December 1866, letterbook 6: 286v-283r, Barreda Papers, SIUC; Read to [Barreda] no. 9, 9 March 1867, and enclosed "Lista de los oficiales y tripulación del 'Rayo,'" both with Barreda to Ministro de Relaciones Exteriores, 10 March 1867, Oficios de la legación del Perú en los Estados Unidos de América dirigida a Lima, 1867, carpeta 5-3, AGMREP.
56. Barreda to Brown, 9, 18, and 26 December 1866, letterbook 6:242v, 286v-283r, and 330v-328v, Barreda Papers, SIUC; Salgar, *El ministro colombiano en Washington*, 11 and 13. The *New York Times*, 13 February 1867, 1, reported rumors under the item "An Alleged Privateer Seized," which, in fact, included much correct information on the *Cuyler*—"staunch and very fast," with crated torpedo boats, 4–9" Dahlgrens and two pivot rifles.
57. Salgar, *El ministro colombiano en Washington*, 11–13; Barreda to Ministro de Relaciones Exteriores, no. 356, 23 March 1867, letterbook 7: 91v-90r, Barreda Papers, SIUC.
58. J. V. Camacho to Barreda, 7 September 1866, Barreda Papers, SIUC; Barreda to Pacheco, no. 112, 9 August 1866, Libro copiador, tomo 68-A, 455–489, AGMREP; Prado to Barreda (personal) 10 September 1866, Pacheco to Barreda (personal) 13 September 1866, and Webb to Barreda, 5 and 14 December 1866, Barreda Papers, SIUC.
59. Barreda to Pacheco, 10 September 1866, letterbook 4:136, Barreda Papers, SIUC; Vicuña Mackenna, *Diez meses*, 1:230; Werlich, *Admiral of the Amazon*, 107; Pacheco to Barreda (personal), 13 September 1866, and Prado to Barreda (personal), 10 September and 13 October 1866, Barreda Papers, SIUC.
60. Barreda to Prado, 19 September 1866, letterbook 4:175r–176v; Barreda to Blest Gana, 23 February 1867, letterbook 6:588r–589v; Jones to Barreda, 9 January 1867; Barreda to Davidson, 25 January 1867; Barreda Papers, SIUC.
61. Roberts, "'Thunder Mountain,'" 383–385; Webb to Barreda, 25 and 29 January 1867, Barreda Papers, SIUC; Gideon Welles, *The Diary of Gideon Welles*, ed. E.T. Welles, 3 vols. (Boston: Houton Mifflin Co., 1911), 3:27–29.
62. Roberts, "'Thunder Mountain,'" 383–385; Welles, *Diary*, 3:38–40, 41.
63. Roberts, "'Thunder Mountain,'" 384–385; Welles, *Diary*, 3:38; Barreda to Agudela, 20 March 1867, letterbook 7:59r–60v, Barreda Papers, SIUC.
64. Salgar to V. Brown, 15 January 1867, enclosure no. 3; Brown to Lt. George A. Borchert, 25 February 1867, enclosure no. 8; Barreda to E. G. Read, 15 January 1867, enclosure no. 5,

and Barreda to Carlos Corpancho, 10 March 1867, all enclosed with Barreda to Ministro de Relaciones Exteriores, no. 335, 10 March 1867, Oficios de la legación del Perú en los Estados Unidos, 1867, carpeta 5-3, AGMREP. Barreda had requested the assignment of the English-speaking Corpancho, who was probably the son or nephew of Manuel Nicolás Corpancho, Peru's distinguished minister to the Juárez government of Mexico.

65. Barreda to Manuel Freyre, 9 November 1866, 29 January and 19 February 1867, letterbook 6:171v-168r, 501v-498v, 577v-576r, Barreda Papers, SIUC; Freyre to Ministro de Relaciones Exteriores, no. 175, 30 April 1867, Servicio diplomático del Peru, legación en Colombia, 1867, código 5-8, AGMREP; Read to Minister of War and Marine, 1 October 1867, Barreda Papers, SIUC.

66. Barreda to Read, no. 5, 15 January 1867, and Barreda to Freyre, 10 March 1867, both enclosed with Barreda to Ministro de Relaciones Exteriores, no. 335, 10 March 1867, Oficios de la legación del Perú en los Estados Unidos, 1867, carpeta 5-3, AGMREP; Read to Barreda, June 4, 1868, with enclosed copy of Read to Minister of War and Marine, 1 October 1867, Barreda Papers, SIUC.

67. James William Park, *Rafael Núñez and the Politics of Colombian Regionalism, 1863–1886* (Baton Rouge: Louisiana State University Press, 1985), 48–50, and passim; Germán Cavelier, *La política internacional de Colombia,* 4 vols. (Bogota,Colombia: Editorial Iqueima, 1959), 2:25–29; Freyre to Ministro de Relaciones Exteriores, no. 48, 16 June 1866; no 177, 30 April 1867; and no. 188, 1 June 1867, Servicio diplomático del Perú, legación en Colombia, 1867, código 5-8, AGMREP.

68. Read to Barreda, 4 June 1868, Barreda Papers, SIUC; Freyre to Ministro de Relaciones Exteriores, no. 135, 17 December 1866; no. 147, 19 February 1867; no. 165, 5 April 1867; and no. 175, 30 April 1867, Servicio diplomático del Perú, legación en Colombia, 1866 and 1867, código 5-8, AGMREP.

69. Read to Barreda, 4 June 1868, with enclosure, Read to Minister of War and Marine, 1 October 1867, Barreda Papers, SIUC; Freyre to Ministro de Relaciones Exteriores, no. 180, 16 May 1867, and no. 192, 1 July 1867, Servicio diplomático del Perú, legación en Colombia, 1867, código 5-8, AGMREP; Hannabergh to [commander of any vessel of the U.S. Navy], 30 April 1867, Letters sent, 1863–69, copybook, 241–46, State, Consular Records, Cartagena, Colombia, 1863–69.

70. Read to Ministro de Guerra y Marina, 20 April 1867, enclosed with Freyre to Ministro de Relaciones Exteriores, no. 176, 30 April 1867, Servicio diplomático del Perú, legación en Colombia, 1867, código 5-8, AGMREP; Read to Minister of War and Marine, 1 October 1867, copy enclosed with Read to Barreda, 4 June 1868; Jones to Barreda, 17 December 1866, Barreda Papers, SIUC; Jones to Brown, 26 December 1867, Comunicaciones entre la legación peruana en los Estados Unidos de América y la cancillería peruana en 1866 y 1867, tomo 96-A, 46-48, AGMREP.

71. Read to Minister of War and Marine, 1 October 1867, enclosed with Read to Barreda, 4 June 1868, Barreda Papers, SIUC; Tássara to Seward, no. 9, 1867, U.S. Department of State, Notes from the Spanish Legation in the United States to the Department of State, 1790–1906, microcopy M-59, roll 20, U.S. National Archives, Washington; Seward to Tássara, 14 February 1867, U.S. Department of State, *Papers Relating to Foreign Affairs, 1868,* 2 vols. (Washington, DC: GPO, 1869), 2:26; Salgar, *El Ministro Colombiano en Washington,* 12; Tássara to Captain General of Cuba, 13 February 1866, in Spain, Museo Naval, Madrid, Archivo Alvaro de Bazán, *Documentos relativos de la campaña del Pacífico, 1863–1867,* 1:399.

72. Barreda to Read, no. 5, 15 January 1867, and [Barreda] to Read, undated Spanish translation of Read's instructions for a cruise against Spanish shipping, included in Barreda to Ministro de Relaciones Exteriores, no. 335, 10 March 1867, Oficios de la legación del perú en los Estados Unidos, 1867, carpeta 5-3, AGMREP. For the intelligence operation, see also Barreda to Francisco de Rivero, 6 November 1866, letterbook 6:161v-158r, Barreda Papers, SIUC.
73. Hannabergh to Sullivan, 14 September 1867, and ca. 21–25 May 1867 State, Consular Records, Cartagena, Colombia, Letters Sent, 1863–1869, copybook, 326, 262; Read to [Barreda] copy, 1 June 1867, and Read to Mr. B[rown], 1 June 1867; Read to Barreda, 4 June 1868, with the enclosed Read to Minister of War and Marine, 1 October 1867, Barreda Papers, SIUC; Freyre to Ministro de Relaciones Exteriores, no. 192, 1 July 1867, and no. 204, 31 July 1867, Servicio diplomático del Perú, legación en Colombia, 1867, código 5-8, AGMREP.
74. Entries for payments by Vernon Brown to Minor, 30 April 1867, C. Knap, 10 April 1867, and to C.W. Read, 18 April 1867, Libro de cuentas, tomo 98-A, 42 AGMREP. For a good, succinct biography of Savez Read, see the essay by William R. Robinson Jr., in *Dictionary of American Biography,* ed. Allen Johnson and Dumas Malone, 21 vols. (New York: Charles Scribner's Sons, 1928) svv, "Read, Charles William." Robinson believes that Savez's "brilliant record was unsurpassed by any other officer of his rank in either the Union or Confederate Navies."
75. Read to Mr. B[rown], 1 and 12 June 1867; Read to Minister of War and Marine, 1 October 1867, copy enclosed with Read to Barreda, 4 June 1868, Barreda Papers, SIUC; Freyre to Ministro de Relaciones Exteriores, no. 192, 1 July 1867, Servicio diplomático del Péru, legación en Colombia, 1867, código 5-8, AGMREP.
76. Read to Minister of War and Marine, 1 June 1867; Read to Barreda, 4 June 1868, with enclosed Read to Minister of War and Marine, 1 October 1867, Barreda Papers, SIUC. Freyre to Ministro de Relaciones Exteriores, 1 June, and 1, 2, and 31 July 1867; Manuel José Anaya to Ministro de Relaciones Exteriores, 24 July 1867, Servicio diplomático del Perú, legación en Colombia, 1867, código 5-8, AGMREP.
77. Read to Barreda, 4 June 1867, Barreda Papers, SIUC; Read to Hannabergh, 27 October 1867, State, Consular Records, Cartagena, Colombia, Letters Received.
78. Read to [Minister of War and Marine] copy, 1 June 1867; Read to Brown, 12 June 1867; Read to Barreda, 4 June 1868, and enclosed Read to Minister of War and Marine, 1 October 1867, Barreda Papers, SIUC; Read to Hannabergh, 27 October 1867, State, Consular Records, Cartagena, Colombia, Letters Received.
79. Cornejo to Ministro de Hacienda, 21 August 1867, Minsterio de Guerra y Marina, March–October, 1867, paq. 0.1867.1, Archivo Histórico-Militar del Perú, Centro de Estudios Históricos Militares del Peru, Lima; Read to Barreda, 4 June 1867, Barreda Papers, SIUC; Freyre to Ministro de Relaciones Exteriores (no. 195) 2 July and (no. 204) 31 July; Manuel José Anaya to Ministro de Relaciones Exteriores, 24 July 1867, servicio diplomático del Perú, legación en Colombia, código 5-8, AGMREP. E. G. Read (in Read to Barreda, 4 June 1867, Barreda Papers, SIUC), suspected that false reports from the xenophobic Capt. Lizardo Montero who had been sent to Colombia poisoned the atmosphere in Lima.
80. Hannabergh to E. P. Pellet, 2 September 1867; Hannabergh to Sullivan, 2 September 1867; Hannabergh to E.G. Read, 5 September 1867, State, Consular Records, Cartagena, Colombia, Letters Sent, copybook, p. 311, 313–15, 319–24. Manuel Dávila to E. G. Read, July, 1867, no. 38, State, Notes from the Colombian Legation in the United States to the Department of State, 1810–1906, microcopy M-51, roll 6, U.S. National Archives, Washington. E.

G. Read returned home in straitened financial circumstances. He borrowed money from friends, which he was able to repay in April 1869, when he accepted a consultantship with the Japanese navy. He died at New York City on 21 December 1872, at age thirty-four. Read to Robert Minor, 25 March 1869, Minor Family Papers; his obituary appears in the *Army and Navy Journal* 10 (4 January 1873).
81. Wagner de Reyna, *Las Relaciones diplomáticas entre el Perú y Chile durante el conflicto con España,* 302–307; Werlich, *Admiral of the Amazon,* 111, 129–130.
82. Werlich, *Admiral of the Amazon,* 112–133.
83. Jorge Basadre, *Historia de la república del Perú,* 5th ed., 10 vols. (Lima, Peru: Ediciones "Historia," 1961) 4: chaps. 67, 69, 71.
84. Barreda to Pacheco, no. 51, 9 June 1866, Libro copiador, tomo 68-A, 375, AGMREP.

PART VI. MARINES

A "Soldier of the Sea" in Sub-Saharan Africa: Brevet Maj. A. R. Chater, DSO, Royal Marines, of the Sudanese Camel Corps, 1921–31

Donald F. Bittner

Overseas expansion and the ability to command the seas, to conquer other peoples and then to run colonies require a sophisticated knowledge of the world, an officer class that is well-versed in the ways of the world, newspapers that can inform, universities that can train, a culture that can sustain.[1]

BRIEF CAREER SUMMARY

Major Gen. Arthur R. Chater, CB, DSO, CVO, OBE, of the Royal Marines, had a distinguished career in Britain's Royal Marines from 1913 to 1948. A veteran of World War I, he saw combat ashore at Antwerp (1914), Gallipoli (1915), and Zeebrugge (1918) and served four times as adjutant of the Royal Marine Brigade of the Royal Marine Division, twice at the Royal Marine Corps depot at Deal, and once for 4 Royal Marine Battalion. During World War II he planned and then initially implemented the defense of the protectorate of British Somaliland (1938–40); after its reconquest he served as its military governor (1941–43). He later supervised the training of British forces for Operation Husky, the Allied invasion of Sicily (1943); commanded Eastney barracks and the defenses around Portsmouth; and landed at Normandy (1944). Chater then served simultaneously (1944–45) as the director of combined operations for the commander in chief, India, and for the supreme Allied commander, Southeast Asia command. After the war he was chief of staff to the commandant general, Royal Marines. In his final posting he served as commanding general, Chatham Group, supervising young marine and officer training for an amphibious Royal Marine Corps and helping shift it from a traditional seagoing service with ad hoc landing force operations to one with an institutionalized commando mission and capabilities.[2] For the era, Chater's career was thus most unusual for a "Soldier of the Sea." He had limited sea duty (one tour in World War I and two in the 1930s) and, more atypical, was on detached service from his corps—serving in Egypt and the Sudan from 1922 to 1931 with the Sudanese Camel Corps, which he eventually commanded.

OFF TO AFRICA, 1921

With the end of the Great War, contraction of an expanded wartime Royal Marine Corps and declining numbers of recruits entering it, the routine of peacetime duty loomed before Chater. As he wrote, "My job [as adjutant at Deal] became a shadow of what it had been. I began to look for new adventures." For him, the goal became service in the Egyptian army, "in which some of the best RM [Royal Marines] officers had served."[3] The latter statement is somewhat of an exaggeration, but it is certain he served with officers who had colonial constabulary duties and heard officers lecture and discuss such postings.

Thus he sought the assignment and in September 1920 submitted the appropriate application to the adjutant general, Royal Marines. A routine official response ensued: The Royal Marine Corps had no objection, and his name was noted for such employment. On 26 October the War Office officially applied for his services and inquired of his availability and medical fitness. By 24 November his selection was confirmed and he was provided guidance on travel and other matters, such as bringing firearms and ammunition. In January Chater was detached from his assignment as the adjutant at Deal. He was booked to sail for Egypt from Liverpool on 3 February 1921 and on that date ceased drawing pay from the Royal Marine Corps.[4]

There was, however, more to this posting than the official correspondence implies. In reality, it occurred because of personal associations and contacts. A friend had written on his behalf to the high commissioner in Egypt, Field Marshal Viscount Allenby, but received an initial rebuff: "There was a long waiting list, and I had little chance." Then Col. R. M. Darwall, assistant adjutant general in Khartoum, visited Deal, staying at the depot with the chief instructor (Col. Maurice C. Festing) and giving a lecture on a punitive expedition he had commanded against the Aliab Dinken in the Sudan.[5] Chater expressed his interest to Darwall, and through his personal intervention[6] the Royal Marine Corps was informed that the Egyptian Army had applied for Chater's services.[7] At just under the age of twenty-five, Chater, now a combat-experienced veteran, twice wounded in action, holder of two gallantry medals, a brevet major, and still single, set off for Egypt in February 1921. Unbeknownst to him he would not return to Britain and Royal Marine duty till 1931. Thus commenced his service in Africa, which would eventually total more than sixteen years in Egypt, the Sudan, and Somalia. Not for Chater the dull routine of rotation between administrative division (barracks) duty and unchallenging and unrewarding sea assignments.

One factor in his decision was that some of this time counting double for retirement purposes and other pay allowances (e.g., for language proficiency). And, as he later candidly recalled, "I applied to be seconded to get more independent command on active service."[8] This did indeed occur, ensuring Chater had a very different interwar duty than almost all of his peers.[9]

COLONIAL CONSTABULARY SOLDIER—
I: 14TH SUDANESE BATTALION

When Arthur Chater departed Britain on 3 February, he was just underage for service in the Egyptian army, but on 7 February while at sea he reached the required twenty-five years of age for such duty. In opting for such an assignment, Chater avoided the routine duty and hierarchical shipboard structure of service afloat alternating with administrative postings to barracks ashore. Rather, he not only would be in a different locality than most of his peers but also would perform duties that required independence, self-confidence, astute judgment, a different type of professionalism, adaptability, and cross-cultural sensitivity. These challenges he confronted immediately after his initial welcome in Egypt by his sister and her husband, and then by Colonel Darwall at Khartoum.

Independent duty Chater sought, and this he promptly received—in mid-February, the young marine was posted to the 14th Sudanese Battalion at Omdurman, just across the Nile from Khartoum.[10] He was one of three British officers assigned to it, but within forty-eight hours was the only one remaining! The day after he arrived the battalion's commanding officer was medically evacuated to hospital in Khartoum and the other officer departed on four months' leave. Chater had time to check the safe, try to count the money in it, and then sign for it. As he recalled, "My hands soon got dirty trying to count the different coins of a strange currency, and I gave up the unequal task." With the departure that day of his two fellow British officers, Chater confronted a new and unique challenge: "[I] found myself in command of a Battalion of more than [a] thousand officers and men."[11] He was also unable to speak any of their languages.[12]

Chater well realized he had much to learn. In addition to a dozen Egyptian officers, Chater now worked with troops from another culture and race, Sudanese who had enlisted for life. This presented an initial challenge, which he candidly recalled: "At first when riding on to parade, and being confronted by a sea of a thousand black faces, all looked exactly alike; but before long, one came to see every variety of feature, and to recognise just the same characteristics as one had known on one's British troops." As the acting commander of the battalion he became involved in their lives, from marriage and divorce to granting circumcision requests and determining punishments.

Discipline especially reflected the differing customs of the British forces and an indigenous force, such as when a Sudanese soldier was charged with having entered "his comrade's house." Chater now confronted a cross-cultural dilemma, as recalling that he had been raised in a tradition where, "under no circumstances must a soldier be struck—not even by an officer." One of his Egyptian subordinates provided appropriate counsel, but decades later this still troubled him. "The Egyptian Bimashi advised me that I must sentence the man to be flogged, as otherwise his 'comrade' might knife him. . . . When the sentence was carried out, I felt like the proverbial schoolmaster who said to the boy he was beating 'It hurts me more than it hurts you.'"[13]

Chater could and did candidly assess his command. He enjoyed the 14th Sudanese Battalion's music, which he found loud but not tuneful. More significant, he was critical of the battalion's overall professional skills. He perceived that two cultural negatives had been merged, saying, "I did not rate the fighting value of the troops high. They had been pampered and spoilt. They were a bad imitation of poor British troops. They had lost the attributes of African natives, without gaining the qualities of British soldiers."[14]

Duty with the 14th Sudanese Battalion was generally routine. Parade commenced at 0630 unless weapons firing was scheduled. On days of live firing parade began an hour earlier. When on parade, officers wore boots, breeches, and jackets and carried drawn swords. Early in his tour Chater was queried by the sirdar (the British commander in chief of the Egyptian army) as to why he was drilling his troops on foot. He replied that he was learning by doing training, giving the command in Turkish, the command language, thus ensuring he learned more quickly. His senior accepted this but emphasized that medal ribbons were to be worn. Presumably this ensured the officer's psychological ascendancy over the troops by conveying that he had been under fire, acknowledging his courage and combat experience. Chater also learned to play and enjoy polo.

This increased his personal expenses, for in addition to his uniforms and other kit it necessitated the purchase of two polo ponies.

Still, there were moments when routine was interrupted. Shortly after his arrival in the Sudan, one thousand disgruntled Yemeni workmen employed in building the Blue Nile Dam were returned to Yemen. To Chater fell the duty of escorting and guarding them on the journey to Port Sudan on the Red Sea. As he later wrote, "That slow journey in a very long train across the desert and the time in camp at Port Sudan in May, was as hot and uncomfortable as any duty I performed before or since,"[15] an interesting comment from an officer medically evacuated from Gallipoli in the summer of 1915.

A more positive and rewarding experience occurred at Omdurman during the Muslim holiday of Bairan, just after Ramadan. Chater was again the acting commander of his battalion, and his date of rank as brevet major became the impetus for what ensued.[16] Because he was acting commander, he would be the senior British officer for a ceremonial event. He later recounted the details:

> On the second day of the holiday, it was customary for the Sirdar and Governor General to ride round a vast assembly of the Faithful gathered in the great square beside the Mahdi's tomb in Omdurman. That year the Governor General was in England, and the Acting Governor General was cut off by rains, and could not reach Khartoum. His deputy was the Chief Justice, who did not appear mounted on parade. The result of this was that the Governor General was represented by the senior officer in the Civil Administration, while the Sirdar was represented by the Senior Army Officer present—myself—As it happened, the senior officer the Civil Administration was Major Bramble, Royal Marines. So two Royal Marine officers, escorted by the Sirdar's mounted escort, and followed by the British and Egyptian flags (as Kitchener used to be) rode up from of the Nile to the great square.[17]

The exhilaration of the two officers as they dismounted and moved among the assembled multitude can be easily imagined. As Bramble commented, "What would the chaps sitting the mess at Forton think of us?"[18]

Soon after this, unrest in the province of Darfur caused unease in Sennar. The political officer there feared it would spread to his district, as many locals laboring on a new dam were from the area of turbulence. He therefore requested military protection for the Europeans working on the dam, and Chater was ordered there with a company and machine-gun section. Off to Sennar he went—but nothing happened. The incident, however, further reflected the type of posting the young marine craved. In response to his request for written orders, he received the following reply: "In this country, we do not give written orders, but expect people to do their best, and then we back them up." This was why he had come to Africa: "I thought nothing could be better."[19]

Then came orders to report to El Obeid, the end of the railway and capital of Kordofan province, another six hundred miles to the west. Here Chater found something new and different: the Sudanese Camel Corps, which had its headquarters at El Obeid. After consulting with its second in command, he requested a transfer to it for two reasons. The first was simple: it was different. As he later recounted, "I would dearly love to serve in a mounted unit. Being a Marine I had no hope of getting into the Cavalry: but the Camel Corps—why not? No British officer had experience of Camelry before coming to the Sudan."[20] The second was more professional: The troops he saw were distinctly different from his Sudanese soldiers. "I quickly saw the contrast between the Camel Corps and a Sudanese Battalion. The Camel Corps soldiers were tough lightly built Arabs, who received a high rate of pay, and fed and housed and largely clothed themselves. As a result they were very independent and highly mobile 'irregulars.' They enlisted for only three years at a time. They had none of those interminable Orderly Room cases, and no band."[21]

To this, Chater again received a bureaucratic reply. His request was noted, but a lengthy wait existed. Despite this lackluster response to his request, it was granted two weeks later. Was Darwall involved again? Chater is silent on this. He was transferred to the Camel Corps and ordered to assume command of No. 1 Company at Geneina, more than six hundred miles farther west into Africa. Geneina was located in Dar Mesalit, an area between the Sudan and French Equatorial Africa, until recently (circa. 1921) an independent area ruled by a sultan. Here Chater met an officer with whom he would develop a lifelong friendship: Col. (later Maj. Gen.) Arthur Huddleston, the commanding officer of the Sudanese Camel Corps.[22]

COLONIAL CONSTABULARY SOLDIER—
II: THE SUDANESE CAMEL CORPS, 1922–31

On 12 February 1922 Chater set off for his new command: an infantry company of 250 men and 80 animals. It consisted of four platoons and a machine-gun section, with just enough mule and camel transport to make it "fairly mobile." More important, the new assignment involved command and independence. As he later reminisced, "Each company of the Camel Corps was in itself a 'unit', the OC company enlisting, training, promoting, and discharging his own men, and having full Commanding Officer's powers."[23] The contrast with normal Royal Marine ship and barracks duty could not have been greater.

He departed for his new command accompanied by Colonel Huddleston for part of the journey. With minimal uniforms, food, and a parade pony and camel, he and fifteen troopers made their way west. After the first day, he shifted his mount from horse to camel—and soon mastered riding the latter. The day before reaching Geneina his pack camels bolted, leaving him in central Africa unmounted and with few of the necessities of life. The new company commander arrived, by his own admission, "miserably scruffy and unshaven"—an inauspicious start to what would become a most successful nine years of service.[24] Several days later the missing camels were recovered—with all of his provisions, clothing, and other equipment.

Local strife had recently occurred in the area, but a major force had restored order, although except for Chater's and one other company most of it had been withdrawn. The larger region had also been twice occupied by the French, and twice France had faced major and partially successful rebellions.[25] In 1921 the French and British agreed that Dar Mesalit would be occupied by the British, although unrest had occurred that year resulting in the deaths of two officers and the request for military assistance in Sennar. The local indigenous ruler had his own method of psychological warfare, which Chater later recalled: "The Endoka, in whose house hung the uniforms of the French officers who had been killed, used to point to the uniforms and say, 'Of course I could do the same to the English, but I am a man of peace.'" Hence, precautions were taken through the construction of a strong mud fort with all the "essentials of defence." Chater stressed, "We did not live in the fort: but my plan of defence was the fort should always be so garrisoned that, whatever might happen to individuals, the fort would be impregnable." With the summer rains forthcoming and the attendant temporary isolation of the force, rumors abounded that a revolt would occur. However, as Chater noted, "The sultan was a man of his word, and there was no rising." Did Chater recall this time and the sultan with fondness and nostalgia? Possibly, for he added, "I called on him in his 'palace' at Geneina in 1949, he was then an old man. He had been to London and was very pro-British. His son was being trained to succeed [sic] him."[26]

Chater also had contact with a nearby French garrison while at Geneina. Once he had to return a troublemaker to the French post at Adre, approximately twenty miles away. Here, in interior Africa, one of the assignment's highlights occurred while a guest of the officers there. A good time was had by all, for he recalled departing in "somewhat of a haze" owing to ample consumption of red wine and champagne. After a year of service away from the Camel Corps' headquarters, No. 1 Company was due to return to El Obeid because his troops were technically on "foreign service" and they wanted to return home. The relief occurred in November, and they returned in December to find Sir Lee Stack, governor general of the Sudan and the sirdar of the Egyptian army, there.[27] The sirdar complimented Chater's command on its martial bearing though not on the "smartness of appearance," as the troops' uniforms were in rags. As Chater commented, this certainly contrasted with the normal ceremonial preparations for the commander of the Egyptian army. With the troops returned, the feasts abounded with the "killing of bulls and the brewing of beer." Still, the non-lethal cost of service in a distant land was evident: "The most painful toothache, which I had for weeks past been suffering, was temporarily alleviated."[28]

Six months later, during the summer of 1923, Chater received command of No. 4 Company, stationed at Bara. Again the benefits of independent duty were revealed—minimal paperwork, responsibility only for his company—an almost ideal posting. He succinctly summarized this assignment: "My two and a half years in command of No. 4 Company, were the best years of my service." Superb training areas, responsive troops, 250 camels, a fully mobile company, and constant patrolling at thirty miles a day left no time for boredom. A day meant four and a half hours of travel in the morning and another such period in the evening, three hours loading and unloading, six hours during the day and six at night for rest, food, administration, and other matters.[29] During this period of command Chater had four months of leave in England in 1923, and the following year a leave period to Kenya to visit his brother. While there he also hunted, bagging two lions and several antelope.[30]

Upon his return, more turbulence loomed in the form of Egyptian nationalism: Assassins killed Sir Lee Stack, the sirdar and governor general, in Cairo. A mutiny occurred in the military school in Khartoum, bringing about its disbandment. Egyptian officers at Talodi refused to leave the town. Finally, the 10th Sudanese Battalion mutinied. The British response included pressure on the Egyptian government to withdraw all Egyptian officers and troops from the Sudan. Chater's mobile unit at Bara was a potential reaction force in case of trouble, and it was ordered moved to Talodi, 275 miles to the south. Chater kept various communications pertaining to these incidents, including messages from his commander, which provided guidance on movement, routes, food, etc. In a letter dated 1 December 1924 the commanding officer of the Camel Corps, Col. D. W. Reynolds, writing from Talodi, wanted Chater in the area and ordered him to march quickly but not at major expense to the animals. He also noted that the 10th Sudanese Battalion had mutinied, taken refuge in a building, and been fired on by artillery ("blown to blazes"). Rumors abounded that British forces were "plotting to massacre" the local troops.[31]

The 11th Sudanese Battalion also mutinied. These two battalions were later disbanded, and three companies from them were added to the Sudanese Camel Corps. When Chater's command eventually arrived they found that the Egyptian officers had departed, but the companies remained there for six weeks as a garrison. Upon their return to Kordofan province, further patrolling took the troops into regions where a representative of the government was rarely seen.

In 1924 all Egyptian army officers and troops were removed from the Sudan, and the Sudan Defence Force (with Huddleston as its commander) was created.[32] Chater then signed his second five-year contract for service in sub-Saharan Africa, but now with the Sudan Defence Force. In this new military organization, the proportion of British officers assigned to units was slightly increased; hence, Capt. J. E. H. Boustead, Gordon Highlanders, joined him at Bara. In April 1925, with the Sudan Defence Force created, routine being reestablished and the unrest abated, Chater took leave in Britain. From this leave, amid his voluminous personal papers, Chater made the most personal private comment extant in them:

> In April 1925 I went on leave to England, and it was whilst staying with Archie Craig the Adjutant of the Depot RM at Deal, that I first met Di, who nearly thirty years later became my wife. One sunny afternoon Archie took us for a drive in the country. Near Northbourne, we stopped outside a deserted house. Archie and I walked into the garden, and there I saw a bed of perfect roses. I picked some, and gave them to Di—a little incident which has been a happy memory.[33]

The following year proposed economies would have reduced the Sudanese Camel Corps companies at Bara from two to one. Then another of the unofficial and personal incidents outside of official channels occurred and affected the larger organization. While this was being considered, the Sennar dam was to be opened, with the British High Commissioner for Egypt and Sudan, Lord Lloyd, doing the honors.[34] As part of these ceremonies, the Sudanese Camel Corps came to El Obeid for a review. Simultaneously, trouble arose in the Nuba Mountains through the murder of a government representative and defiance of the district commissioner. Because of this, Chater attended the official luncheon with Lord Lloyd, and later recalled what ensued: "An urgent request for troops had been received. As the result of this, the OC Camel Corps was too busy to attend the Governor's lunch party, and I was invited in his place. I was seated next to Lord Lloyd, a dynamic personality. Of course I took the opportunity of telling him that one of the companies he had seen on parade that morning was to be disbanded. This coming at the very moment when troops were being asked for in the Nuba Mountains amazed him. The Company was not disbanded."[35]

The next day the mounted companies of the Camel Corps set off for Jebel Julud, this being only one of many such operations against a most worthy and difficult foe.[36] Chater himself kept three press reports of the ensuing operations of February 1926, which contained general details of events. One account, titled "Soudan Revolt," described the character of such warfare: "The rebels, numbering a thousand warriors, had plenty of rifles prepared in inaccessible caves in the Temein Gulad hills, and big supplies of food."[37]

How did Chater describe this type of warfare? As he later wrote,

> Fighting in the Jebels was unlike any other kind of warfare. The Nubas had many rifles, and when threatened with attack, they retreated to their rocky hills, which were honeycombed with caves, some of which were stocked with food. From the safety of their dark caves, they could shoot out at troops moving over the rocks. I had heard a lot about Jebel warfare, but this was my first experience of it.

Ultimately, nothing of significance occurred. The Nubas withdrew into the hills, used their caves as a base, and took no actions against the Camel Corps troops. Eventually their chief surrendered, leaving a disappointed Chater with mixed conclusions: "It was rather an ineffective operation, but I learnt a lot, which proved very useful to me later."[38] Unfortunately, Chater did not say what he learned.

Shortly thereafter, another expedition against the Jebel was planned and Chater was to have commanded it, though illness precluded this. Upon recovery in El Obeid, he was promoted to kaimakam (lieutenant colonel) and became second in command of the Camel Corps, dealing with administration and civil and military authorities. This was a necessary task, but one he probably did not particularly enjoy. Then further change loomed: The commander of the Camel Corps was due to depart in April 1927, and he asked Chater to take early annual leave that year. As Chater later wrote, "On my way through Khartoum, I looked in on the Senior Officer who would, I thought become the next OC Camel Corps. I made some remark about looking forward to serving under him. He smiled and replied—'I shall not stand in your way.' Until that moment it had not entered my mind that I was designated to be the next OC Camel Corps. I was thirty."[39]

Chater officially assumed command of the Camel Corps of the Sudan Defence Force on 1 April 1927. On 16 April 1930 he was granted the local British army rank of lieutenant colonel.[40] With this, he assumed more responsibility and a significant professional challenge near the end of his time in the Sudan: issues associated with airpower in irregular warfare.

CHANGES IN WARFARE: COLONIAL SOLDIERING, THE ROYAL AIR FORCE, AND THE AIR ISSUE

Chater assumed command of a unique organization.[41] The Camel Corps consisted of a headquarters (administrative staff, escort, and a garrison machine-gun section of four guns); two camel companies (each of four troops of riflemen and a two-weapon machine-gun section); one mounted infantry company (of four troops of riflemen and a two-weapon machine-gun section) mounted on horses and mules; and four dismounted companies (each consisting of two platoons of riflemen, a two-weapon machine-gun section, and a mule transport section with enough mobility for one platoon and one machine-gun crew). Companies were commanded by British officers, titled bimbashi, with subordinate Sudanese or Arab officers.[42] The Headquarters Company, three mounted companies, and one dismounted company were Arab, while the three dismounted companies were Nuba troops. The troops were locally enlisted, housed and fed themselves, and provided some of their own gear. Weapons and some equipment were centrally stored and issued as needed for various duties, training, patrolling, and operations.

More important were the command's principles, articulated by Chater in the autumn of 1927. He wrote that the Camel Corps was an "irregular" one, with infantry training and skills paramount coupled with required mobility. "Rapid mobilisation" and "mobility" were "valued higher than dress and parade drill." He demanded good marksmanship skills and men who were light weight. Chater also practiced in command what he both personally and professionally valued as a subordinate commander: Subject to supervision and general direction of the commanding officer, "Company Commanders were solely responsible for the discipline, interior economy, equipment, and preparedness for war of their companies, the training of their officers, non-commissioned officers, and men, and the condition of their animals." He issued his revised regulations, for the "information and guidance for all concerned," and stressed that "officers are expected to interpret them reasonably and with due regard for the interests of the service."[43]

With this force and operational approach, Chater's small unit was to enforce the will, or power of the government in his area.[44] Overall operations must have been routine, for Chater wrote very little about them until 1930. Then in late 1929 and early 1930 came his opportunity to command an operation against the Nuba in Jebel Eliri. Chater described these natives as a "very uncivilized tribe" who wore no clothes and whose most marked characteristic was their conceit. They were also dangerous because they were armed with rifles. As he later wrote to a friend, the operation was of no political significance, the issue initially being the capture of a noncooperative local chief. This issue later escalated to the seizure of cattle as payment for taxes. Overall, it was a somewhat routine paramilitary and police colonial constabulary mission.

From Chater's perspective it was "interesting chiefly as an example of cooperation between the ground forces and the Royal Air Force."[45] His basic plan was simple: Move to the area at night via trucks, climb to the top of the Jebel hills, surround the village, and, using surprise, seize the chief at dawn. To the Royal Air Force's initial desire to participate, Chater responded that they could do little at night, the sound of aircraft would eliminate surprise, their planned ordnance dump at Talodi would signal intent, and no bombing was needed. Using his ground force, the operation initially succeeded and Chater even flew over the area.

Then the operation changed: cattle were seen during an air reconnaissance and the local political officer wanted them seized for taxes. With a ground force in the area, this could be done. Hence, the effort was made, but the Nubas resisted and they inflicted casualties on the attacking force.[46] The air staff at Khartoum then wanted to participate, and the use of airpower in colonial conflicts dominated Chater's assessment of what occurred.[47]

This issue then and now has relevance. In 2007 the Lord Trenchard Memorial Lecture of the Royal United Services Institute was titled "Counter-Insurgency—Echoes from the Past." In announcing it, the institute wrote, "Whilst relationships between the Army and the Air Force in the 1920s might have been strained in Whitehall, at a working level it rapidly became apparent that only a strategy which used the capabilities of both air and land forces to best effect would achieve the desired results." The Royal Air Force's experiences in the early twentieth centuries in Somaliland, Iraq, and Afghanistan would be assessed.[48]

Chater's critique of what happened was not so sanguine, combining both personal irritation and professional issues: First, the Camel Corps commander was especially critical of a flight lieutenant on the air staff at Khartoum, a "RAF propagandist, who admitted that he was more interested in proving his theory that the RAF could have dealt with the situation far better by themselves than he was in winning the war." This officer articulated the views of the "moral effects of bombing, hitting the enemy without giving him an opportunity of hitting back at us, etc., etc." This advocate of bombing also stressed a new bomb that could be used with a six-hour delay fuse, and these were indeed dropped. Then, as the start of air operations approached on 24 December, Chater's irritation was directed at and reflected in his comments about a wing commander who arrived in the area on 22 December ("no one knows why"). This outsider talked to Chater only via the telephone, said the air unit was not ready, criticized Chater for not permitting a dump at Talodi, emphasized many bombs would have to be dropped, and then "left for Khartoum and England the next day."

So what happened? Chater articulated a more balanced view of the use of airpower in such colonial expeditionary operations. He stressed that the Royal Air Force was good for reconnaissance, invaluable for medical support (i.e., evacuating wounded, bringing doctors in), and helping to capture a foe, but only once the ground force surrounded the enemy before bombing commenced. If air operations started before then, the enemy would disperse "and we would never capture them." Ultimately, the bombing occurred as Chater desired and produced the surrender of noncombatants. His troops had the high ground, and they advanced under cover of this air attack with reduced chances of casualties.

Here, the ground and air views conceptually clashed, as Chater candidly wrote: "In this latter respect, I would say the Royal Air Force form a most effective kind of artillery. They bombed targets about 400 yards in front of our posts with great accuracy and I give them full marks. When, however, I compared them to Artillery, they at once took exception to such a comparison." After the ninth air raid on 2 January, Chater's troops, on his insistence, occupied the main position; airpower alone could not accomplish the mission, although he acknowledged its valuable support. The Camel Corps commander stated that on three occasions the "aircraft effectively covered the forward movement of our troops." Chater also noted that the air operations normally included one raid per day, although on one occasion there were three. The best effort was three aircraft dropping ordnance and one observing, although normally only two aircraft participated in a mission.

Significantly, on the ground reality and theory diverged. Not all the bombs exploded and these proved to be dangerous, as the force soon learned after combat operations ceased. Since the air personnel had never seen the caves used as a base by the Nubas, arrangements were made for a cave inspection on 3 January. A team advancing toward one disturbed a 112-pound bomb that detonated, killing three men and wounding several others, including a doctor who lost a leg. Six weeks later, another team accompanied by a new wing commander (presumably from Khartoum) embarked on a similar inspection when a distant bomb detonated. No one was near it, hence no injuries were incurred. Chater speculated a monkey set it off. Still, the inspection tour of the tactical area ceased.

The issue ultimately can be simply stated: the airmen articulated a theory without literal knowledge of the terrain and the alleged effects of their bombing. As Chater commented, the caves in which the Nubas sheltered ran for hundreds of feet below ground, and none of the Royal Air Force personnel had ever seen them. Later, one of his company commanders finally took an air staff officer into one and sent a report to Chater, adding he "was amused by the surprise of the Royal Air Force officer, who had not previously realized how bomb proof such caves are."[49]

Chater's assessment was indeed correct but also enlightening. The operation was of little significance in and of itself.[50] His force numbered only 475 troops of the Sudanese Camel Corps, led by six British infantry officers, a doctor from the Royal Army Medical Corps, and himself (plus the Royal Air Force personnel). The key became the proper use of aviation assets, and in this Chater could and did state the obvious: it was, he said, "essentially an infantry operation, carried out by the Camel Corps, assisted by the Royal Air Force."[51] In 1931 Chater was cited for distinguished service in this operation (along with other personnel) and was awarded an OBE in the June 1931 honors list.[52] On 3 February 1931 Brevet Maj. A. R. Chater, DSO, Royal Marines, left the Sudan Defence Force and returned to Royal Marine Corps duty, pay, and assignment. More diverse assignments were to follow, including many more years in Africa, but that lay many years into the future. On the date of his departure he was still a very young officer, aged thirty-two—with a career out of the ordinary pattern of his contemporaries and with experiences, command, and responsibilities most never had and would never have.

CONCLUSION

This paper has assessed the African service in the 1920s of Captain (later Brevet Major) Chater, DSO, for which he received the OBE in 1931. During this time, this young officer commanded African troops in their homelands in which heretofore he had had no experience. This cross-cultural environment included extensive duty in isolated areas, countering a mutiny by Sudanese forces, training local forces for their duties, developing extensive contacts with indigenous elites, participating in irregular warfare operations, and confronting the issue of the role of airpower in nontraditional combat. Indeed, Chater was an exceptional person and military officer, leader, and commander. Still, inherent abilities had to be shaped and developed. In this, Chater excelled. He related to, understood, worked for, and commanded men of exceptional abilities and diverse backgrounds in his career, be they older marines, officer and enlisted, or seniors such as Field Marshal Sir Claude Auchinleck and Lord Louis Mountbatten. His African service in the Sudan (and later in British Somalia) was both unusual for a marine and the highlight of his career. Chater embodied the best elements of the British professional military tradition: he knew his craft, understood those he led, looked after his troops, continued to learn and grow professionally, and accomplished the diverse missions assigned to him. Would that all officers, junior and senior, had such success in their careers.

NOTES

Research support from the Marine Corps University Foundation and the American Philosophical Society is gratefully acknowledged and appreciated.

The following abbreviations are used in the notes:

ARCHIVES	Archives, Royal Marines Museum, Eastney, Portsmouth, Hampshire, UK.
Chater Papers, Folder CHATER [x]	Liddle Hart Centre, King's College, University of London.
Chater, Personal Narrative	"The Personal Narrative of Arthur Reginald Chater, 1913–1927. Later Major General, ADC, CB, DSO, OBE, Royal Marines," n.d. (but written before 1966 when Chater received the CVO in the Queen's birthday honors list). Three copies of this memoir are in three Chater personal papers collections: ARCHIVES 9/2/C. Royal Marines Museum, Eastney, Portsmouth, Hampshire, England; the Liddle Hart Centre, King's College, University of London; and the Liddle Collection, Brotherton Library, University of Leeds, Leeds, UK.
Chater Official Record of Service, ADM 196/64, with appropriate page number	The National Archives (formerly the Public Record Office), Kew, Richmond, Surrey, England.

1. Marques Jacques, "The Problem with Abroad," *Weekly* [Manchester] *Guardian,* 27 August–2 September 2004.
2. This brief career summary is based on Chater's official record of service, ADM 196/64, pp. 328 and 330.
3. Chater, Personal Narrative, 26.
4. All the correspondence between Chater, the Royal Marines Office, the War Office, and Corps Depot, Deal is retained in the Chater Papers, Folder CHATER 1/3–1/4, within Folder CHATER 1/3, titled "Camel Corps. Subject: Service in Sudan. Compilation of various official documents."
5. Col. Robert Henry Darwall was born on 3 October 1879, commissioned in the Royal Marine Light Infantry, 1 January 1898, eventually lieutenant general, CBE, DSO, and retired 1 July

1937. Darwall Official Record of Service, ADM 196/63, 1. Darwall was seconded to the Egyptian Army in 1911, served in the Sudan in 1920, and eventually commanded the 14th Sudanese Battalion.

Col. Maurice Christian Festing was born on 16 September 1879, commissioned in the Royal Marine Light Infantry on 1 September 1898, eventually promoted to major (7 January 1917), brevet lieutenant colonel (31 December 1922), and transferred to the Royal Tank Corps (10 November 1923). Festing Official Record of Service, ADM 196/63, 44.

6. Utilizing personal contacts for service in the Egyptian Army had been the norm for decades. See Justin Willis, "Violence, Authority, and the State in the Nuba Mountains of Condominium Sudan," *Historical Journal* 46 (2003): 95.
7. Chater, Personal Narrative, 25–26.
8. Major General A. R. Chater letter to author, 26 January 1978 (author's possession).
9. The service of such officers posted "on detachment outside the Corps" was generally ignored in the standard history of the Royal Marines in the post–World War I decades. James D. Ladd, *The Royal Marines, 1919–1980: An Authorised History* (London: HarperCollins, 1980), 426. Stating such were "too numerous to detail," Ladd noted by name only Chater and two others: Brig. B. W. Leicester, who also served in the Sudan Camel Corps after Chater and later commanded 4 Commando Brigade during World War II, and Lt. Col. C. V. Brown, killed in France in 1940 while serving as chief of staff of the army's 3rd Division. In a revised and retitled edition, Ladd named three other officers: Lord Maurice Hankey, secretary of the Committee of Imperial Defence and later in the war cabinet, and two future commandants general of the corps, Gen. Sir Leslie Hollis (chief of staff committee and war cabinet secretariat), and Gen. Sir Dallas Brooks (deputy head of the political warfare executive). James D. Ladd, *By Sea, by Land: The Royal Marines, 1919–1997: An Authorised History* (London, 1998), 559–560.
10. The 14th Sudanese Battalion was raised in 1896, disbanded in 1902, and reactivated in 1906. A. G. Boycott, *The Elements of Imperial Defence*, 2nd ed. (Aldershot, UK: Gale & Polden, Ltd., 1936), 240. For an overview of the Sudan, see K. D. D. Henderson, *Survey of the Anglo-Egyptian Sudan, 1898–1944* (London: Longman's, Green & Co., 1946). This publication describes and has photos of places mentioned by Chater, such as the Sennar Dam.
11. Chater, Personal Narrative, 28.
12. Not till 1923 would he pass the Egyptian army's intermediate language examination in Arabic. Entry 6a, Army Form B.199A, n.d., but entries from 3 February 1921 to 3 February 1931. Enclosure, Chater Official Record of Service, ADM 196/64, 328.
13. Chater, Personal Narrative, 29. In the Egyptian army, bimbashi was the equivalent of British army major.
14. Ibid., 31.
15. Ibid., 30.
16. Owing to the nature of the corps, its officers were listed, with appropriate dates of rank, in both the army and navy lists. Chater's brevet rank of major conferred appropriate British army seniority.
17. Maj. James John Bramble was born on 11 December 1882; commissioned 2nd lieutenant, Royal Marine Light Infantry, 1 January 1902; promoted major, 1 January 1918; and retired, 24 October 1922. Bramble Official Record of Service. Bramble had service in both the Egyptian army (1913–22) and in naval intelligence. ADM 196/63, p. 183.
18. Chater, Personal Narrative, 30. Forton Barracks, located in Gosport to the west of Portsmouth, was the home of the Portsmouth Division, Royal Marine Light Infantry.

19. Ibid., 31–32.
20. Ibid., 32. Chater also stated that the train journey to El Obeid was also the last one he made in ten years of service in the Sudan.
22. Obituary, Major General Sir Arthur J. C. Huddleston, Kt., CMG, OBE, *The Times*, 3 October 1950; and Richard A. Lobban, Jr., Robert S. Kramer, and Carolyn Fluehr-Lobban, *Historical Dictionary of the Sudan*, 3rd ed. (London: Scarecrow Press, 2002), 124–125. See also *Who Was Who, Vol. IV, 1941–1950*, 5th ed. (London: Adam & Charles Black, 1980), 570.
23. Chater, Personal Narrative, 34.
24. Ibid., 34.
25. Background on this region is in M. W. Daly, *Empire on the Nile: The Anglo-Egyptian Sudan, 1898–1934* (Cambridge: Cambridge University Press, 1986), 188.
26. Chater, Personal Narrative, 34–35.
27. Maj. Gen. Sir Lee O. F. Stack, GBE, CMG. For a brief biography, see Lobban et al., *Historical Dictionary of the Sudan*, 266–267. See also *Who Was Who, Vol. II, 1916–1928*, 5th ed., 764.
28. Chater, Personal Narrative, 35–36.
29. Ibid., 36.
30. Ibid., 37. Chater, in addition to describing the long and difficult trip, commented on conditions in Kenya, compared them to what he encountered there in 1949, and concluded, "I preferred it as it was in 1924."
31. Col. D. W. Reynolds letter to Brevet Major A. R. Chater, 1 December 1924. Chater Papers, Folder CHATER 1/4.
32. Boycott, *The Elements of Imperial Defence*, 239–240.
33. Chater, Personal Narrative, 38. Archibald M. Craig, born on 5 January 1895; commissioned second lieutenant, Royal Marines (1 October 1912); promoted major general, Royal Marines (3 October 1943); retired (1 January 1944); married Dianna Daubeny, 1917; died, 23 September 1953. Craig Official Record of Service, ADM 196/64, p. 316. Chater married Craig's widow, Mrs. Dianna Craig, in 1954.
34. First Baron Lloyd of Dolobran, high commissioner for Egypt and the Sudan, 1925–29. *Who Was Who, Vol. IV, 1941–1950*.
35. Chater, Personal Narrative, 39. In 1936 a listing of the Sudan Defence Force assets notes the Camel Corps had three companies: two in the Central Area, headquarters at El Obeid, and one in the Eastern Area, headquarters at Gedaref. These were separate from mounted infantry companies. Boycott, *The Elements of Imperial Defence*, 240–241.
36. Twenty-seven such significant operations (i.e., involving more than one company) have been identified between 1903 and 1945. Willis, "Violence, Authority, and the State," *The Historical Journal*, fn 12, 91–92.
37. Chater photo album, ARCHIVES 11/14/43.
38. Chater, Personal Narrative, 39. A modern description of such operations, albeit based on sources of operations of several decades earlier, is in Willis, "Violence, Authority, and the State," 94.
39. Chater, Personal Narrative, 40. This is the end of all three copies of this manuscript end on p. 40.
40. Entry 10, Army Form B.199A, n.d., but entries from 3 February 1921 to 3 February 1931. Enclosure, Chater Official Record of Service, ADM 196/64, 328.
41. A partial history of the Camel Corps is in D. C. E. Comyn, *Service and Sport in the Sudan: A Record of Administration in the Anglo Egyptian Sudan* (London: John Lane, 1911). Extracts

from Comyn, with updated comments presumably by Chater, are in his papers, CHATER 2/2–2/4, in Folder 2/2. There is also a list of the officers commanding the Camel Corps, from its permanent formation in 1893 to 1930, although other sources date its founding in either 1883 or 1885. In Folder CHATER 2/3, there is a list of the officers commanding No. 4 Company from its inception in 1906 to 1930. Both lists end with Chater's name.
42. A picture of a deployed Camel Corps company is in Merian C. Cooper and Ernest B. Schoedsack, "Two Warring Tribes of Sudan," *The National Geographic Magazine* 56 (1929): 468. The caption partially reads, "A company of the Camel Corps formed in a square in battle position. Kordofan Province, now peacefully administered by a few lonely Britishers with the aid of native troops." A picture of the gateway into El Obeid is on page 467.
43. "Sudan Defence Force. Camel Corps Regulations and Standing Orders, 1928," Chater Papers, Folder CHATER 2/1. Chater signed these at his headquarters in El Obeid in September 1927, with the title "Miralai, Officer Commanding, Camel Corps." Miralai meant colonel (or brigadier).
44. This emphasis on showing the power of the government is emphasized in Willis, "Violence, Authority, and the State," especially 93, 94, and 96. The phrase "power of the government" is used repeatedly.
45. For an assessment of the role of airpower in colonial Africa in this era, see David Killingray, "'A Swift Agent of Government': Air Power in British Colonial Africa, 1916–39," *Journal of African History* 25 (1984): 429–444. For an assessment of operations in the Sudan, see ibid., 437–439. Killingray notes air only played a role in the December 1929–January 1930 operation discussed by Chater. More important, for the Sudan he stresses the split on the use and effectiveness of airpower in irregular war as between air officers and the civil administrators, in contrast to Chater's position of ground versus air officers' views.
46. The incident was also reported in the United States, including the name of the wounded officer (Capt. A. Low). "British in Clash in Egypt [*sic*]," *New York Times*, 21 December 1929.
47. This issue is addressed by James S. Corum and Wray R. Johnson, *Airpower in Small Wars: Fighting Insurgents and Terrorists* (Lawrence: University Press of Kansas, 2003), Chapter 2, "Colonial Air Control: The European Powers Develop New Concepts of Air Warfare." Corum and Johnson address primarily Iraq, but the Royal Air Force's theory, and its lure (inexpensive and allegedly effective) is analyzed on pages 52–66. Three press reports of the 1926 operation noted that, in addition to fighting one thousand Nuba warriors, the Royal Air Force dropped two tons of bombs on them—but did not assess the effect of this bombardment.
48. Royal United Services Institute Events, "Lord Trenchard Memorial Lecture 2007" (presented on 10 September 2007 by Air Chief Marshal Sir Glenn Torpy, Chief of the Air Staff, Royal Air Force), e-mail to distribution list, 29 August 2007.
49. Brevet Maj. A. R. Chater letter to "Tom" (not further identified), n.d. but in 1930. Chater Papers, Folder CHATER 2/2–2/4.
50. However, it was large enough to be included by Justin Willis in his list of twenty-seven significant operations in the Nuba Mountains. Willis, "Violence, Authority, and the State," footnote 12, pp. 91–92, under Lafofa. The operation was covered in *The Times*, 21 December 1929, for the initial phases, and *The Times*, 9 January 1930, for reports of the casualties from the exploding bomb attendant to the cave inspection.
51. Chater letter to "Tom", n.d. Chater Papers, Folder CHATER 2/2–2/4. Corum and Johnson, more than seven decades later, had a similar assessment of the ground and air relationship in

this era: "Most of the RAF operations in the colonies in the interwar years were in support of, and in cooperation with, ground troops." Corum and Johnson, *Airpower in Small Wars,* 61.

52. "Special Order, Sudan Defence Force Headquarters, Khartoum," 19 April 1930. Chater Photo Album. ARCHIVES 11/14/43. *The Times*, 27 June 1931. The OBE was gazetted in the *London Gazette*, 2 June 1931. Chater official record of service, ADM 196/64, 328. Flight Lt. Willett A. B. Bowen-Buscarlet (eventually Air Vice Marshal Sir Willett A. B. Bowen-Buscarlet, KBE, CB, DFC, originally Royal Artillery), whom Chater praised, received a DFC; and Capt. A. Low, wounded in the initial phase, a promotion to brevet major.

U.S. Marines' Counterinsurgency Campaigns in Nicaragua in the Early Twentieth Century

Charles Neimeyer

> There's no use sending a handful of our boys down there to get butchered. If it's war let us call it that and successfully conclude it.
> —*Mr. N. H. Dowdell, Father of a dead Marine*[1]

At the beginning of the twentieth century the involvement of the United States in Latin American affairs could be described as frequent. Time and again, the United States intervened in the internal politics of numerous Latin American states on a wide variety of pretexts. Restoration of order was usually given as the primary reason for nearly every intervention. When Depression-era President Franklin Roosevelt finally eschewed America's interventionist program with his Good Neighbor Policy in 1933, the U.S. Marine Corps (USMC), as the lead defense force for U.S. foreign policy in Latin and Central America, had been conducting various counterinsurgency and constabulary operations in this volatile region on a nearly continuous basis for more than twenty years. These "small wars" were what we would term today counterinsurgency operations. Owing to the largely expeditionary nature of such combat, the Marine Corps responded with an effective and, at the time, unique idea of providing small units operating on the ground with direct air support from above—tactics that ultimately evolved into the modern-day hallmark of the Corps, the Marine Air/Ground Task Force. Eventually, the Marine Corps refined its far-ranging counterinsurgency lessons learned and published these findings in the still widely read *Small Wars Manual* (1940).[2]

With the possible exception of Haiti, no place in Central America seemed more chaotic than Nicaragua. The internal and often confused politics of Nicaragua had long been divided between Conservative and Liberal political parties. However, such terms can be misleading as they bear little resemblance to their modern-day definitions. In essence, by the turn of the twentieth century the Liberals held to a more nationalistic line, had generally greater popular support, and adopted a more anti-American tone than their Conservative counterparts. On the other hand, the Conservatives had more support in the army and business community and could also be very anti-American at times but, on the whole, seemed willing to work with the United States in return for favorable business and political connections.

While the United States may have thought it had secured a diplomatic coup in Nicaragua with the elevation of the Conservative Estrada-Diaz faction to power in the early 1920s, the U.S. ambassador, Elliot Northcutt, ominously noted that the overwhelming majority of Nicaraguans remained openly hostile to American interests, especially in the mountainous backcountry. Thus the atmosphere was ripe for counterrevolution. In order to counteract any further outbreaks of violence in the still-volatile capital of Managua, the U.S. State Department requested and received a reinforced company of U.S. Marines to act as a legation guard.

Although not immediately recognized at the time, this large USMC presence had a double-edged effect. While the size of the U.S. legation force guaranteed some amount of calm, especially in the vicinity of the national capital of Managua, the large force served to make the Nicaraguan government complacent. Knowing full well that they could call on the Marines at a moment's notice, Nicaraguan leaders did nothing to improve their own internal security forces. To make matters worse, U.S. military officers observed that the Nicaraguan military could fill its ranks only through forced conscription. In order to compensate for an exceptionally high desertion rate, the Nicaraguan army rule of thumb was to physically impress four men for every one that might possibly remain with the army. It was not unusual to see lines of men tied by ropes being led off at gunpoint to army training camps.

Thus by the mid-1920s Americans in Nicaragua had begun to assume more and more direct responsibility for the overall security of the country. By 1925, in order to overcome the moribund state of the Nicaraguan regular army, U.S. diplomats and military officials took a page from their counterinsurgency experience in Haiti, the Dominican Republic, and even the Philippines and created an internal Nicaraguan security force called the *Guardia Nacional* (national guard), or *Guardia*.

The creation of a national guard in Central American states had long been a favorite theme of U.S. diplomats in the 1920s, as Dr. Dana G. Munro, a former chargé d'affaires in Nicaragua, noted:

> The establishment of nonpartisan constabularies in the Caribbean states was one of the chief objectives of our policy from the time it became clear that the customs collectorships wouldn't assure stability by themselves. The old armies were or seemed to be one of the principal causes of disorder and financial disorganization. They consumed

most of the government's revenue, chiefly in graft, and they gave nothing but disorder and oppression in return. We thought that a disciplined force, trained by Americans, would do away with the petty local oppression that was responsible for much of the disorder that occurred and would be an important step toward better financial administration and economic progress generally.[3]

The *Guardia* was to be trained and organized by "suitable instructors . . . with experience gained in other countries in organizing such corps."[4] In reality, this meant Marine junior officers and some noncommissioned officers would be offered commissioned officer status in the new national guard force. Most important, the *Guardia* was supposed to be nonpartisan and made up of men loyal to the nation vice a specific political party such as the Conservatives or Liberals—a major problem that had plagued past efforts to reform the Nicaraguan military. In essence, the State Department hoped that at some point the *Guardia* would ultimately supplant the corrupt and coup-prone regular army.

With their *Guardia* plan now firmly in place, the U.S. State Department began to signal their intention to withdraw the Marine legation guard as soon as possible. However, Nicaraguan president Carlos Solorzano, who had just assumed office on 1 January 1925, stated that without the Marines in the capital, revolution was "inevitable."[5] Accordingly, the State Department agreed to his request to keep the Marines in place for the present moment but informed Solorzano that once it was believed that the new *Guardia* was ready to provide internal security, the Marines would leave. As an additional incentive, the U.S. government brought in a veteran of the Philippine constabulary, U.S. Army Maj. Calvin Carter, to lead the recruiting and training effort.

However, when Carter arrived in Nicaragua in July 1925 he was shocked at the abysmal state of the *Guardia*. Finding only two hundred ragged and untrained recruits in the barracks collocated with the Nicaraguan army, Carter noted that ninety of the two hundred men failed their physical examinations. He quickly outspent his meager budget in just a few short weeks trying to provide his new recruits with even the basic military necessities. Nevertheless, within two months Carter had made tremendous progress in equipping and training the new *Guardia*, despite attempts by Solorzano's brother-in-law, Gen. Alfredo Rivas, the Conservative commandant of the fort at La Loma (located in the capital of Managua) who, true to form, tried to subvert it for his own political purposes.

While Solorzano was ostensibly a Conservative, in order to make his government more bipartisan (and thus more palatable to the U.S. high commissioner), he appointed a number of Liberals to cabinet positions, including Liberal Gen. José Maria Moncada as minister of war. The Conservatives simply would not tolerate this power-sharing arrangement. More specifically, they feared that War Minister Moncada might use the new and growing *Guardia* for his own purposes because it was what they would have done if a Conservative were to hold the office of war minister. Indeed, just three weeks after the Marine legation guard left Nicaragua, Conservative General Rivas staged an incident at a government-sponsored party held at the International Club in Managua. Most of the Nicaraguan cabinet as well as U.S. High Commissioner Roscoe Hill were present when an armed and drunken group organized by Gen. Alfredo Rivas rushed into the club and announced their purpose was to "liberate President Solorzano from the Liberal element in his government." The men then proceeded to arrest Moncada and any other Liberal ministers they could find at the time. General Rivas quickly followed up on this incident and demanded that the president purge his government of all Liberal influence. While Major Carter urged Solorzano to crush the revolt, the president demurred. Not only were members of his own family leading the coup, but also he recognized that, despite Carter's efforts, the nascent *Guardia* was still too weak to really do anything about the situation. The *Guardia* had fewer than three hundred men and was dwarfed by the size of the Nicaraguan regular army, which was still dominated by Conservatives.[6]

By October 1925 Conservative Gen. Emiliano Chamorro, who was likely behind the International Club incident, had fully consolidated his power over the old national army; he and his adherents occupied the fort at La Loma. While Carter once again stated that he was willing to use the *Guardia* against the rebels in the fort, Chamorro knew of the *Guardia*'s actual weakness and sarcastically told the president to have Major Carter phone him in advance before he attacked. In the end, Solorzano capitulated to all of Chamorro's demands, and he quickly purged the government of all Liberals. Chamorro then convinced the weak Solorzano to officially appoint him commanding general of the Nicaraguan army.

By January 1926 a dejected Solorzano was granted a permanent leave of absence for so-called health reasons, and Chamorro assumed control over the government: Liberal Vice President Sarcasa had earlier fled the country, most likely to avoid being arrested or shot by Chamorro's adherents. As predicted, by March 1926 the *Guardia* was no longer the nonpartisan force that it was initially intended to be. Thanks to the efforts of Chamorro, U.S. Minister Charles C. Eberhardt noted that the *Guardia* was "fast disintegrating into a politically controlled machine of the present regime." He observed, "It is very apparent that the time had not yet come, if it ever will, when a nonpartisan constabulary or National Guard, organized and maintained under American ideas and ideals, will be a success in Nicaragua. *It is not wanted* [italics in original]."[7]

Soon after a brief Liberal revolt in Bluefields, a seaport located on the East Coast of Nicaragua, was crushed by Chamorro's forces in May 1926, Liberal bands began attacking the railroad along the West Coast of Nicaragua. The continued fighting placed great pressure on Nicaragua's national finances and on Chamorro's Conservative regime itself. Moreover, desperate to raise money, Chamorro had been thwarted from selling the National Railroad and National Bank by the wily vice president in exile, Sarcasa, who announced that *when* he returned to power, he would not recognize the sale of either institution. The country was broke and there seemed no end to the fighting. The United States was finally able to broker a peace conference between the two warring sides, but the only thing that could be agreed to was that the reviled Chamorro must leave the presidency. There was no consensus as to who should be his successor.

The U.S. State Department asked former Conservative Vice President Adolpho Diaz to temporarily serve as president. He took office on 14 November 1926; his government was quickly recognized by the United States. Diaz seemed a logical middle choice between the two warring factions, and on the whole both sides initially seemed to be satisfied with his selection. Diaz soon requested a huge U.S. loan to continue to fight the rebellion and requested the immediate return of the Marine legation guard to Managua. The State Department assented to both requests, and by 15 March 1927 there were more than two thousand Marines and bluejackets in the capital city.[8]

However, it was at this moment that Vice President Sarcasa decided to return to the country. As vice president in exile, now that Chamorro had stepped aside he proclaimed himself the actual constitutional president. And of course, to make matters more complicated, Mexico quickly recognized the "constitutional" government of Sarcasa. However, Sarcasa's Mexican diplomatic maneuver sent shock waves through the U.S. State Department. In a confidential memorandum, Undersecretary of State Robert Olds summed up the situation for the United States: "[T]he action of Mexico in the Nicaraguan crisis is a direct challenge to the United States. . . . We must decide whether we shall tolerate the interference of any other power (i.e., Mexico) in Central American affairs or insist upon our own dominant position."[9]

This was the Roosevelt corollary writ large. Nevertheless, the U.S. situation in Nicaragua remained a difficult one since the issue boiled down to whether the United States could tolerate a Liberal victory and allow Sarcasa to assume power. Since the Liberal side was now being overtly supported by

Mexico, this would make Sarcasa's elevation to power appear to be a Mexican victory at a time when the United States was having its own problems with its southern neighbor. Conversely, if Diaz remained in office it would appear to the Liberals that the United States was intent on maintaining an unelected puppet president in office who had little popular support.

The immediate decision of the United States was to stick with Diaz and hope for the best in the 1928 elections. On 27 April 1927 President Calvin Coolidge selected former Secretary of War Henry L. Stimson, a veteran of negotiating tough deals with Filipino insurrectionists and who had previously arbitrated a settlement between the countries of Peru and Chile, to broker a deal between the still-warring Conservative and Liberal factions. Stimson was told by Coolidge himself that the only thing that was not negotiable was Diaz remaining as president until the 1928 elections. Ultimately, by May 1927 Stimson was able to get both sides to agree to peace terms on the following conditions: (1) the declaration of an immediate peace and general amnesty for all combatants, (2) inclusion of Liberals in the cabinet and a general disarmament of both sides with the arms turned over to U.S. forces, (3) retention of the Marines in Nicaragua until a new Nicaraguan *Guardia* was formed to replace them, (4) the organization of a nonpartisan *Guardia* under U.S. officers, and (5) U.S. supervision of the 1928 elections.[10]

In the final analysis, it initially appeared as if Stimson had pulled off a magnificent diplomatic triumph. Soon U.S. military commanders were collecting thousands of weapons from both sides. The agreement also provided an opportunity for the Americans to reconstitute the *Guardia* as it had been initially envisioned. Notably, while Sarcasa never officially acquiesced to the Stimson agreement (in 1928 known as the Peace of Tipitapa), only one Liberal commander, Gen. Augusto Sandino, refused to turn in his weapons— but it was heard that he commanded only two hundred men and was likely to cross over into Honduras into a sort of self-imposed exile. While diplomats and military men were lighting cigars and toasting each other's health in Managua, the brief period of peace proved to be the lull before the storm.

By 1926 Augusto Sandino was convinced he was a man on a mission to rid his long-suffering country of the influence of Conservative Gen. Emiliano Chamorro. He came from a Liberal party family but had spent a few years outside Nicaragua after a shooting incident had forced him to flee the country in 1920. Having worked for a number of U.S.-owned firms, Sandino landed a job in Tampico, Mexico, working for a U.S. oil company. At the time, Tampico was "a hotbed of radical thinking, ranging from communism to syndicalism." It was here that Sandino became imbued with the idea of "Latin American nationalism of the anti-Yanqui variety."[11]

Returning to Nicaragua in 1926, the charismatic Sandino raised his own company of twenty-nine men, and on 2 November 1926 he unsuccessfully attacked the government post at Jicaro. A short while later he moved to link up his small force with the larger Liberal army under the command of Gen. José Moncada. However, instead of being welcomed as an ally, Sandino was at arms length by Moncada. His brusque treatment by Moncada might also partially account for why Sandino decided to not lay down his arms after Moncada had agreed to the Peace of Tipitapa. Now referring to Moncada as "a traitor" to the cause, Sandino turned down his offer to make him Governor of Jinotego and instead went off with his men to the northern mountain fastness of Nuevo Segovia. He left convinced that only *he* had been "called to protest the betrayal of the Fatherland."[12]

The fallout between Sandino and Moncada in the early months of 1927 was likely little known or appreciated by the USMC commanders in Managua. In fact, since January 1927 the Marines had landed most of the 5th Marine Regiment and other assorted detachments to include the Marine Observation aviation squadron. Other squadrons were soon added and the combined squadrons were now called Aircraft Squadrons, 2nd Brigade. The 11th Marine Regiment was also eventually added, and the growing force of more than five thousand U.S. Marines was placed under the command of Brig. Gen. Logan Feland, USMC. It was the largest single deployment of Marines since World War I.[13]

One of the first locations on Feland's list to pacify was the very place to which Sandino had retreated: Nuevo Segovia. The principal city of this province was Ocotal and the local government chief, Liberal party member Arnoldo Ramirez, stated that he would not enter the town without a Marine escort. To be fair, at the time Nuevo Segovia had long had a reputation as a lawless, crime-ridden region even before the most recent revolution. Feland ordered a fifty-man patrol under the command of Maj. Harold Pierce to escort Ramirez into Ocotal and to "peaceably disarm everybody." Feland instructed Pierce to "secure information that will facilitate the coming supervision of elections, but do not fire a shot unless imperatively necessary; and conciliate with firmness, tranquilize without force of arms, avoid combat, if possible; do everything compatible with dignity and self preservation, to help the big mission of the Brigade."[14]

While there were strong indications that Sandino's men shadowed Pierce's patrol, the Marines reached Ocotal on 9 June 1927 without incident. However, Pierce was frankly shocked at what he found there and wrote to Feland in Managua that he found no civil law whatsoever in effect in Ocotal. On 30 June 1927 Sandino upped the ante in the fighting in this rugged region.

He seized the U.S.-owned San Albino gold mine, where he had once been an employee. While the loss of the mine was not all that significant, his confiscation of tons of dynamite was. Sandino would soon put his stock of dynamite to good use by making an early version of improvised explosive devices that he called dynamite bombs. He later used these weapons during ambushes of Marine or *Guardia* patrols.

After Major Pierce returned with much of his force to Matagalpa, he left behind Spanish-speaking Capt. Gilbert Hatfield, USMC, to command a mixed force of U.S. Marines and *Guardias*. Interestingly, just five days prior to the San Albino gold mine attack, Sandino, who controlled the telegraph line ten miles from Ocotal, bantered with Hatfield. Charging Hatfield with arming Conservatives (which of course he was not), Sandino closed with a taunting, "[S]hall I wait here for you or shall I go to you?" implying that he intended to attack the Marines whether they came after him or not. Hatfield immediately shot back, "[I]t is not true that I am arming Conservatives to attack you . . . as I need no other help than that of the Marines." Two days later, noting that Sandino did not seem inclined to attack Ocotal, Hatfield asked him to come into the city with assurances of safe conduct for a conference between the two commanders to discuss his surrender. Sandino responded that he had no intention of "falling like a dove deceived by a few grains of rice at the door of a trap." But he did suggest that Hatfield come with five hundred Marines into *his* mountains for the conference but warned him to make sure to "make your wills beforehand." He closed with, "I remain your most obedient servant, who ardently desires to put you in a handsome tomb with beautiful bouquets of flowers." Undeterred, Hatfield wrote back, "Bravo General! If words were bullets and phrases were soldiers, you would be a field marshal instead of a mule thief." He informed Sandino to wire him again once he had something more to say other "than the ravings of a conceited maniac."[15]

Despite the dialogue between Sandino and Hatfield, it was the gold mine raid that finally got the attention of the USN/USMC high command. On 2 July Adm. Julian Latimer, USN, ordered General Feland to move into the Nuevo Segovia region in force and disarm Sandino and his men as soon as possible. Feland wrote to Marine Commandant John A. Lejeune and explained what he was going to do: "I am not planning a campaign, in the general sense of the word, but I am trying to force him out of the country by successively occupying the towns which he claims."[16] Feland appointed Maj. Oliver Floyd, USMC, as overall commander of the combined Marine/*Guardia* force. He originally envisioned that the Nueva Segovia operation be a predominately Nicaraguan effort. However, Major Floyd was skeptical of the military prowess of native *Guardias* so recently recruited and believed that the Nicaraguans would not likely be up to the task of taking on Sandino's hardened guerillas. However, before Floyd's reinforcement column could reach Hatfield and his men in Ocotal, Sandino decided to launch an attack.

THE BATTLE OF OCOTAL

From San Albino, Sandino issued the first of his many manifestos and declared that the Marines had come not to provide stability but "to murder us in our own lands." He further stated that not only was he seeking combat with the Marines but that he himself was eager to "provoke it."[17] On 14 July Captain Hatfield once again wired Sandino and warned him that he was about to be hunted down and asked him to emulate the actions of the Philippine insurrectionist Emilio Aguinaldo, who had surrendered his revolutionaries to the U.S. Army twenty-five years earlier. But Sandino refused and notified Hatfield that his "threats seem very pale to me." He added that he hoped to have the honor of "sprinkling the soil of my native country with the blood of traitors and invaders." Clearly in reference to Sarcasa, Sandino further stated, "If the United States wants peace in Nicaragua they will have to turn the Presidency over to a true Liberal, and only then will I put down my arms peacefully."[18]

The evening of 15 July 1927 was an intense one for Captain Hatfield. It was clear from signs among the population of Ocotal that something was about to take place. Reinforcements were several days away and Hatfield believed that even the village priest was a Sandinista operative. Hatfield had thirty-nine Marines inside the city hall. Across the plaza under the command of Capt. G. C. Darnall and Capt. Victor F. Bleasdale, "a man who literally ate cold steel and fire, and enjoyed it," was the *Guardia* contingent of forty-eight Nicaraguans. Hatfield and the other officers took turns remaining on watch.[19]

Sandino had organized his own forces around a core of sixty seasoned guerrillas. Not only were they armed with rifles and at least two machine guns, but also, thanks to the San Albino mine, they now had numerous dynamite bombs at their disposal. Sandino's plan was to infiltrate Ocotal at night and, working with collaborators, attack the buildings where the Marines and *Guardia* were quartered. However, around 1:15 AM on 16 July 1927 an alert Marine sentry noticed movement down the street leading to the main plaza. His challenge was met with rifle fire and Sandino's men charged into battle shouting "Viva Sandino" and "Death to the Yankees." Almost immediately, a rebel machine gun opened fire on the buildings around the plaza. The fighting continued through the dawn hours but accurate Marine rifle and automatic weapons fire had taken its toll on the Sandinistas. The Sandinistas launched at least three frontal assaults against the city hall complex, but the Marines and *Guardias* across the plaza stopped each attack cold, killing Rufo Marin, one of Sandino's principal lieutenants. After Marin was killed, the Sandinistas temporarily halted their assaults to reorganize their forces. While the heavily outnumbered Marines and *Guardia* had thus far held their own, they were clearly on the defensive.

Around 8:10 AM a significant amount of Sandino's men had briefly drifted away from the plaza to go off on looting expeditions or to settle old scores against the homes and property of known Conservatives. At this point, believing that Hatfield and his men were low on water and had had enough of the intense combat, Sandino sent a message to Marine commander and promised that they would not be harmed if they tossed their weapons in the street within sixty minutes. But Hatfield had plenty of water and ammunition. He notified Sandino, "Marines did not know how to surrender" and told him that he would fight on no matter what. Firing in the plaza immediately resumed.[20]

A little after 10:00 AM two USMC aircraft were spotted overhead. One aircraft, flown by Lt. Hayne "Cuckoo" Boyden, USMC, landed on the rough Ocotal expeditionary airfield and immediately came under small-arms fire from nearby Sandinista riflemen. The other plane, flown by GySgt. Michael Wodarczyk, USMC, strafed the rebels with his guns, allowing Boyden to take off again. Relaying the dire situation of the Marines in Ocotal to Marine headquarters in Managua, Maj. Ross Rowell, having dodged thunderstorms and mountain peaks, had by 2:35 PM five DeHavilland bombers over the city. Hatfield used panels to communicate with Rowell's bombers to vaguely identify for the Marine airmen where the Sandinistas were concentrated. Peeling off one by one, Rowell's dive-bombers dove toward the Sandinistas from 1,500 feet. During each dive, the planes often were within three hundred feet of the ground before dropping a bomb on each run. After the plane pulled out of its dive, the rear observer would suppress the area with machine-gun fire. After forty-five minutes Rowell's aviators were out of bombs and ammunition and returned to Managua. As for the Sandinistas, the air attack caused them to scatter about the town. Rowell noted, "[S]ince the enemy had not been subjected to any form of bombing attack, other than the dynamite charges thrown from the Laird-Swallows by the [two-plane] Nicaraguan Air Force, they had no fear of us . . . we were able to inflict damage which was all out of proportion to what they might have suffered had they taken cover."[21] It was at this point that Sandino called off his assault. By this time, Hatfield's Marines and the *Guardias* had been under attack for more than sixteen hours. By 5:25 PM, except for a few snipers who were later captured, most of the rebels had left town. Hatfield immediately sent out patrols and discovered that his small arms fire and the dive-bombing attacks had taken a great toll on the Sandinistas. On one street alone, Hatfield counted more than fifty dead. His own losses were one Marine killed and one wounded. The *Guardia* had no one killed and reported three wounded and four captured.[22]

The battle of Ocotal presaged a number of things about the growing hostilities in Nicaragua. First, the Marines continued to demonstrate the combat toughness and élan for which they are so famous. Next, the *Guardia*, when properly led, had proved that it had made great strides since its inauspicious beginning just one year earlier. The USMC had also made some improvements to its own combat capability. While communication between Marine aviators and ground combat commanders still had a long way to go, Rowell's dive-bombers provided critical fire support during a decisive moment in the battle. As for the Sandinistas, it was clear when more than one hundred local townsmen joined them in the assault against the Marines and *Guardias* in the plaza that Sandino enjoyed much more local support than had been previously thought. Moreover, as evidenced by their repeated assaults against city hall and its adjoining buildings and their nearly sixteen continuous hours of combat against the Marines, Sandino's men were well armed, disciplined, courageous, and clearly willing to die for their cause. Sandino was not going to be an easy enemy to run to ground.

Throughout the campaign, Sandino used the inaccessibility of the mountains of Nuevo Segovia to good effect. Lacking roads or even barely navigable streams, the only way to get around in this rugged area was on rough trails and bull-cart paths. Eventually, Sandino established a fortified mountain base at a place he called El Chipote and it was here that the Marines now directed their efforts. However, an initial air attack against this position by Rowell's dive-bombers had proved ineffective, largely because the ordnance used by the Marines was too light.

In late December two large Marine patrols were ordered by Col. Louis Gulick, USMC, who had temporarily replaced General Feland in August owing to the latter's ill health, into the contested Quilali region. Despite the rise in guerrilla activity and the apparent increase in Sandinista strength near this village, no one in the Marine command had thought to send significantly more forces into the region. In fact, the heightened level of fighting in Nuevo Segovia had not yet registered in Washington on those responsible for monitoring the Nicaraguan crisis. This fact alone made more ambushes of Marine patrols a near inevitability. True to form, Sandino and his men ambushed Gulick's patrols and inflicted high casualties on them to include the death of *Guardia* lieutenant (1st Sgt., USMC) Thomas G. Bruce, who had earlier won the Navy Cross for his bravery at Ocotal. In fact, if it had not been for the near-constant air cover provided by Rowell's aviators, at least one patrol commanded by Lieutenant Richal, USMC, would have faced near annihilation. During the height of the combat, Lieutenant Richal was shot in the face by a rifle bullet. In this particular emergency, Rowell decided to use Quilali's main street as an expeditionary airfield and even dropped tools to the Marines below to improve the makeshift runway as best they could. One Marine aviator, 1st Lt. Christian F. Schilt, USMC, made repeated trips into Quilali bringing in ammunition, food, and water and evacuating seriously wounded Marines. The runway was short and ended in a steep ravine, so once Schilt's aircraft touched down Marines would run out from the buildings and grab onto his wings and drag themselves along the ground acting as human brakes to slow the airplane before it reached the ravine at end of the runway. Schilt did all of his landings under intense enemy fire. For his gallantry in combat at Quilali he later received the Congressional Medal of Honor.

In January 1928 the arrival of the recently reactivated 11th Marine regiment enabled the Marines to take the offensive against Sandino and his mountain stronghold of El Chipote. Interestingly, 65 percent of the 11th Marines were fresh from basic training. General Feland, who had recovered from his earlier illness, returned to replace Colonel Gulick. He immediately ordered Col. Robert Dunlap, the commanding officer of the 11th Marines, to push into the heart of the Nuevo Segovia country. On 14 January Rowell's divebombers hit El Chipote, this time with fifty-pound bombs, including phosphorous bombs that burned down the shacks and buildings on the mountaintop. This second attack on Sandino's mountain fortress was much more effective not only because Rowell dropped heavier ordnance but also because he had been able to replace his old DeHavilland's with newer, sturdier, Vought Corsairs and Curtiss Falcons. Bomb damage assessment by Rowell's pilots counted at least forty-five bodies out in the open on the Chipote mountainside. Actual casualties were likely higher. Simultaneously, a Marine column under Capt. Roger Peard advanced on the mountain. It was not long before Marine patrols in the Coco River basin were reporting small bands of guerrillas attempting to escape the air and ground assault on El Chipote.

The attacks on El Chipote had forced Sandino to break up his guerrillas into two columns. One went north toward Jalapa, but owing to the low level of activity from this column they likely crossed the Honduran border to rest and recoup. Sandino moved a second column southward toward San Rafael del Norte. Nonetheless, while the Marines and *Guardia* controlled most of the towns in Nuevo Segovia, Sandino's men still roamed much of the countryside. Perhaps because the heat was on in Nuevo Segovia, Sandino decided to spread his guerrilla activity toward the eastern part of Nicaragua known as the Mosquito Coast.

By midsummer, after an inconclusive earlier patrol, Capt. Merritt Edson, who would later receive the Medal of Honor for courage and gallantry on Guadalcanal during World War II, was ordered by Feland to take a forty-six-man patrol up the Coco River to attack one of the remaining Sandinista concentrations near Poteca. It was Edson who conceived of the idea to place a blocking force in the Coco River basin and then send a heavy patrol sweeping in behind the guerrillas and thereby catch the Sandinistas in a pincers movement. Sandino would then either have to fight the Marines at a disadvantage in the Coco River basin or fall back into Honduras. Edson spent a number of weeks slogging his way through a nearly impenetrable river and forest. Using native guides and dugouts, he doggedly made his way toward Poteca and eventually captured the town. General Feland commented, "[F]rom the standpoint of difficulty, danger, isolation from friendly ground troops, and accomplishments, this small expedition is without parallel in the hard work done by this Brigade."[23]

THE ELECTION OF 1928

The Peace of Tipitapa had stipulated that the Americans would supervise free and fair elections nationwide in 1928. Liberal Gen. José Moncada, the man referred to by Sandino as a traitor, headed up his party. While Conservative Gen. Emiliano Chamorro once again became the leader of his party, he was constitutionally ineligible to run for office. Adolpho Bernard emerged as a compromise Conservative candidate. However, the only way of ensuring a free election was to station Marines and *Guardias* in all the ballot locations. The manpower requirement for the election totaled more than nine hundred additional U.S. troops supplied by all three U.S. military departments. The entire election effort was headed up by tough and uncompromising U.S. Army Brig. Gen. Frank McCoy. An Army, Navy, or Marine officer was appointed to have overall responsibility for each of Nicaragua's thirteen election departments and there were a total of 432 polling places to guard. A main electoral concern was over repeaters—those who might try to commit election fraud by voting more than once. This was solved by requiring each voter to dip one finger in red ink.

The election registration period was scheduled to last from 23 September until 7 October. Near the town of San Marcos, Sandinistas attacked poll workers in an effort to intimidate voters from going to the polls. However, aggressive patrolling by Capt. Norman Shaw, USMC, provided the necessary protection for voter registration to continue unmolested. Thus the election of 1928 took place with relatively few incidents. Moreover, "about 133,000 votes were cast, almost 30,000 more than in 1924." And as predicted the Liberal candidate Moncada "amassed a plurality of 19,000" votes.[24]

With the election issue safely behind them, a new problem now emerged as Sandino began to shift his position. His Liberal rival, Moncada, had won the election, and at last the Liberals could lay claim to a presidency won in a free and fair election. Now, Sandino turned his ire against so-called foreign invaders (i.e., the U.S. Marines) and wrote to Moncada that he would discuss coming in—though, Moncada should not think his proposal was a sign of weakness. "What motivates us," he wrote, "is the desire that the Yankees not have a pretext for continuing to tread upon the soil of our Fatherland."[25] He told Moncada that he would not deal with intermediaries (the Americans) and would only deal with him (Moncada). Moncada, however, spurned Sandino's proposal and was more concerned with control over the *Guardia* and the formation of an auxiliary force to the *Guardia* he called *Voluntarios*—commanded, of course, by himself as president. And true to form, the *Voluntarios*, prone to execute bandits or other personas non grata on the spot, quickly got out of hand as they settled old scores. Moncada was eventually forced to disband them.

By April 1929 Brigadier General Feland was relieved by Brig. Gen. Dion Williams, USMC. Now that guerrilla activity had been substantially reduced, it was possible to begin withdrawing Marine garrisons from many towns and replacing them with the newly reinvigorated *Guardia* forces. But while the *Guardia* was better it still had problems. From 1927 until mid-1932 there were ten mutinies of *Guardia* detachments who murdered at least five Marines who had been assigned as their officers. On the whole, however, the vast majority of the *Guardia* remained loyal and trustworthy.

By August 1929 the 11th Marines was again detached from the 2nd Brigade and disbanded en route back to its home base of Quantico, Virginia. The remainder of the Marine Brigade, now at just under two thousand Marines, was concentrated around the cities of Managua and Corinto, primarily to protect the lives and property of U.S. citizens living there. The *Guardia*'s new commander was Lt. Col. Calvin B. Matthews, USMC. Matthews soon increased the *Guardia* to more than 267 officers and 2,240 enlisted men. Many of his officers were Marines who had been seconded to the *Guardia* force. In sum, the new strategy in the interior of the country was to turn over security duties to *Guardia* units as soon as possible.[26] By mid-1929 the Marines and the U.S. State Department took a further step to pacify the countryside by announcing the funding of a major road construction program.

By the spring of 1930, just as the Marines had done a year earlier, Marine-led *Guardia* forces aggressively patrolled their respective areas to keep the guerrillas off balance and on the move. *Guardia* commanders such as Capt. Evans Carlson and captain (first lieutenant, USMC) Lewis Burwell "Chesty" Puller enjoyed significant success against guerrilla bands throughout the summer of 1931 and into 1932. Puller seemed especially adept at the type of bush warfare that was primarily fought in Nicaragua. Given a roving patrol known as "M" company and seconded by a highly capable executive officer, William "Bill" Lee (gunnery sergeant, USMC), Puller soon earned the name *"el Tigre"* from the Nicaraguan *Guardia*s for the ferocity of his attacks against the guerrillas.

The Marines and *Guardia* supervised two more elections (1930 and 1932) and assisted in the recovery of government and essential services following the great 1931 earthquake that nearly leveled the capital city of Managua. Sandino and his men continued to occasionally ambush Marine and *Guardia* patrols. Except for an especially violent fight on 31 December 1930, in which eight out of ten Marines were killed repairing a telephone line, he was never able to replicate the threat he formerly posed to Nicaraguan national order as he did from 1927 to 1929. By the end of 1932 Nicaraguans had even replaced all the USMC officers in the *Guardia*.

The 6 November 1932 election in Nicaragua was also significant. The former vice president, Juan Sacasa, and ostensibly the primary reason for Sandino's continued opposition to the government, was elected over perennial Conservative candidate Adolpho Diaz. Sarcasa was inaugurated on 1 January 1933, the same day that the last 910 Marines in the country embarked aboard transports at Corinto. Their departure marked the end of the U.S. intervention in Nicaragua and signaled the end of actual violence. The intervention had cost the USMC 187 casualties (thirty-two killed in action, fifteen who later died of their wounds, eighty-nine who died from illness, and another fifty-one who were wounded).[27]

Now that the Marines were gone, as first predicted in 1926 by U.S. diplomat Charles Eberhardt, it was not long before both President Moncada and later President Sarcasa began to tamper with the *Guardia Nacional*. Since the Marines had formerly held all senior posts in the *Guardia*, their departure provided Moncada with an opportunity to place political appointees in all the choice positions. He named Liberal party member Anastasio "Tacho" Somoza as the new director of the *Guardia*. Earlier, Somoza had proved his value to the Americans thanks to his U.S.-based education and his English language skills. Moncada later named him war minister; in fact, Somoza's selection as director of the *Guardia* was seen at the time as a positive step by the Americans. While Sandino had ceased violent attacks against the *Guardia* when the last Marine left Nicaragua, he still verbally condemned his old antagonists at every opportunity. Many *Guardia* officers feared that Sandino might soon return to his former guerrilla ways. Even the election of his old mentor Sarcasa did not seem to mollify him.

Thus it was not long before plans were put into effect to rid the country of Sandino once and for all. Gathering secretly in February 1934 Tacho Somoza and other senior *Guardia* officers signed a resolution titled, "The Death of Cesar." It was actually a death warrant for Sandino and some of his key followers. On the evening of 21 February 1934 Somoza had his *Guardia*s round up Sandino after he had spent the evening with President Sarcasa. They also arrested his brother and two other senior Sandinistas and had them executed by gunfire near the military airfield. Just two years later, Somoza, thanks to his personal control over the *Guardia Nacional*, overthrew the Sarcasa regime and established his own family's direct control over Nicaragua that lasted until the modern-day Communist-led revolution of 1979 in turn overthrew the regime of his son. These Marxist modern-day revolutionaries proudly call themselves Sandinistas.

NICARAGUAN LESSONS LEARNED

Politically, the unilateral intervention by the United States in Nicaragua and other locations such as Haiti and the Dominican Republic served to poison U.S.–Latin American relations for decades to come. While the Nicaraguan intervention seemed to have initially accomplished all of the objectives of the Stimson-brokered Peace of Tipitapa, the military mission of the Marines was made immensely more difficult owning to the constantly shifting sands of Nicaraguan local politics. Furthermore, congressional critics of the Nicaraguan intervention claimed that the Marines were there only to protect U.S. business interests. In reality, however, "the actual American investment in Nicaragua totaled only $10 million dollars in 1928 and $17 million dollars in 1929, less than in any other Latin American country."[28] Nonetheless, the American intervention did demonstrate the necessity of understanding the preeminence of local politics in determining the outcomes of even "small wars."

Operationally, the Marines learned a tremendous amount of valuable information—especially the efficacy of aggressive patrolling in retaining the tactical initiative against a wily and determined enemy. For example, two of the most successful patrol leaders, Capt. Lewis "Chesty" Puller and Capt. Merritt Edson, both utilized native allies and the terrain to better advantage than their Sandinista opponents. The enemy found their tenacity absolutely unfathomable. Furthermore, for the first time in an expeditionary operation, the Marines proved the tremendous advantage that aviation assets gave to the maneuver commander on the ground. Time and again, the use of airpower against rebel formations proved decisive, especially during the battles of Ocotal and El Chipote. By mid-1928 Marine aviation had "conducted 84 attacks on bandit forces, carried tons of supplies and personnel and had an extraordinarily low accident rate."[29]

Throughout the insurgency Marines provided valuable security and assistance for various civic action programs such as the 1929 road-building effort in northern Nicaragua. This program turned many would-be Sandinistas into government workers (at least for the time being) and made it extremely difficult for Sandino to recruit more guerrillas during this time period. The Marines and *Guardia* successfully provided adequate security for the 1928 national elections despite vigorous efforts by the Sandinistas to disrupt voter registration and actual balloting.[30]

While the Marines had indeed made the difference in Nicaragua, this did not mean that they did not conduct a thorough and rigorous self-criticism on their return from the theater in the 1930s. While the Marines consistently got the better of Sandino and his forces in nearly every engagement, most ambushes were initiated by Sandino or his principal lieutenants. Moreover, either owing to arrogance or a dearth of Marines able to take the field, Marine forces sent against Sandino and his men were usually always under strength and outnumbered. Again numbers and rugged terrain denied the Marines the ability to close off the Honduran border: whenever the Sandinistas became too hard-pressed in Nuevo Segovia, they simply went across the border where Mexican and Honduran allies were willing and able to refit their forces.

Counterinsurgency operations required the Marine Corps to consider the following for the future: in such operations, numbers matter. Because of the expansiveness of the terrain to be controlled or pacified, the Marines attempted to do the near-impossible with fewer than five thousand men in the field for the entire country. Moreover, the buildup of forces was piecemeal and decidedly reactive to the level of pressure the Sandinistas were placing on the government at the time. Next, most Marines had been catapulted into combat without any training other than that provided in boot camp; an example is the deployment of the 11th Marines in late 1927. While veterans like Puller had already had significant combat experience in places like Haiti, most of the junior officers and rank and file had had none.

The Nicaraguan campaign was the last time that the Marines would be used in Latin America to support the Roosevelt corollary. From a strictly military point of view many future World War II leaders such as "Merritt Edson,

Lewis B. Puller, Evans F. Carlson, Ross E. Rowell, and Christian Schilt learned their tactics in the mountains and jungles of Central America."[31] While it certainly cannot be said that the Marine Corps was victorious in Nicaragua, it is also true that they did not lose. Nicaragua remained a troubled nation but as the United States approached potential war with the Empire of Japan in the late 1930s, the politics of Managua no longer seemed as important as that of Tokyo.

NOTES

1. Mr. N. H. Dowdell, father of a deceased Marine, quoted in "Marines' Father Bitter," in news section of the *New York Times*, 5 January 1928. See also Ivan Musicant, *The Banana Wars: A History of the United States Military Intervention in Latin America from the Spanish-American War to the Invasion of Panama* (New York: Macmillan Publishing Company, 1990), 285.
2. *Small Wars Manual*, Washington, DC: U.S. GPO, 1940.
3. Dr. Dana G. Munro, quoted in Richard Millett, *Guardians of the Dynasty: A History of the U.S. Created Guardia National de Nicaragua and the Somoza Family* (Maryknoll, NY: Orbis Books, 1977), 41.
4. Musicant, *The Banana Wars*, 287.
5. Ibid., 288.
6. Millett, *Guardians of the Dynasty*, 44–45.
7. Ibid., 47.
8. Ibid., 53.
9. Ibid., 52.
10. Ibid., 54–55.
11. Max Boot, *The Savage Wars of Peace* (New York: Basic Books, 2002), 235.
12. Ibid., 236.
13. Maj. Julian C. Smith, Maj. Lloyd L. Leech, USMC, Maj. Thomas C. Cheatham, USMC, Capt. Edward L. Burwell, USMC, Capt. H.M.H. Fleming, USMC, 1st Lt. Gregon A. Williams, USMC, SgtMaj. Charles Davis, USMC, Cpl. Emil H. Krieger, USMC et al., *A Review of the Organization and Operations of the Guardia Nacional de Nicaragua, by Direction of the Major General Commandant of the U.S. Marine Corps* (Quantico, VA, 1937), 11.
14. George B. Clark, *With the Old Corps in Nicaragua* (Novato, CA: Presidio Press, 2001), 37.
15. Neill Macaulay, *The Sandino Affair* (Durham, NC: Duke University Press, 1985), 71–72.
16. Ibid., 73.
17. Ibid., 74.
18. Ibid., 74–76.
19. Ibid.
20. Ibid., 79.
21. Robert Debs Heinl Jr., *Soldiers of the Sea* (Annapolis, MD: U.S. Naval Institute, 1963), 269.
22. Macaulay, *The Sandino Affair*, 82.
23. Heinl, *Soldiers of the Sea*, 282.

24. Marine Corps Historical Branch, *The United States Marines in Nicaragua* (Washington, DC: Historical Branch, G-3 Division, pamphlet, 1958, reprinted 1968), 27.
25. Macaulay, *The Sandino Affair*, 132.
26. Heinl, *Soldiers of the Sea*, 284.
27. James L. Pelton, *American Expeditionary Forces between the World Wars* (Carlisle, PA: U.S. Army War College, 1973), 62.
28. Ibid., 69.
29. Lt. Col. Richard J. Macak Jr., "Lessons from Yesterday's Operations Short of War: Nicaragua and the Small Wars Manual," *Marine Corps Gazette* (November 1996), 58–59.
30. Ibid., 60.
31. Marine Corps, *The United States Marines in Nicaragua*, 34.

PART VII. SOCIAL HISTORY

Hidden Lives: Elderly Cooks, Powder Boys, and Fugitive Slaves among Eighteenth-Century Anglo-American Naval Crews

Charles R. Foy

Mariners in the age of sail are typically depicted as carefree, strong, and youthful men.[1] Maritime history has often focused on these young, able-bodied seamen. While in recent years Jeffrey Bolster, Marcus Rediker, Michael Jarvis, Emma Christopher, and others have explored the lives of black mariners, and Daniel Vickers has demonstrated the importance of age in maritime labor markets, the lives of elderly mariners, adolescent seamen, and fugitive slaves who found berths on naval ships have largely remained hidden.[2] A review of naval muster rolls, Admiralty Court records, and fugitive slave advertisements demonstrates that during eighteenth-century wars the elderly, young, and enslaved found opportunities at sea, and highlights the importance the Royal Navy played in their lives.[3]

How did fugitive slaves, elderly mariners, and young boys obtain berths? And why did they go to sea? The Royal Navy's manning needs made captains willing to employ such men, and a lack of opportunities on land, along with the draw of money, adventure, and freedom combined to create opportunities for these individuals to serve in the navy.[4]

Death and desertion caused the Royal Navy difficulty manning ships in North America. The riches privateers offered enticed many naval seamen to desert. For example, in just two months in New York, HMS *Coventry* had forty-eight mariners run. Large-scale desertions caused Admiral Arbuthnot to decree in 1779 that he would press four men for every naval seaman who deserted, and two years later he ordered a hot press.[5] The Continental Navy looked to American seamen to replace naval sailors who deserted or died.

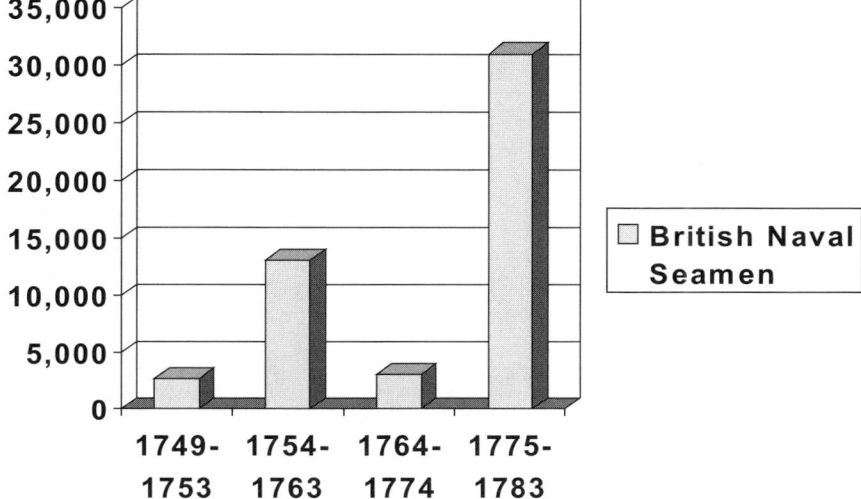

Fig. 12.1 *British Naval Seamen, North American Station, 1749–83 (ADM 8)*

Source: Payrolls and muster rolls for two ships' crew lists per year from forty-nine randomly selected warships: *Adamant, America, Beaver, Blandford, Brilliant, Brune, Captain, Centaur, Chatham, Chesterfield, Coventry, Deal Castle, Elizabeth, Eltham, Gosport, Greyhound, Guardland, Hampshire, Isis, Jason, Launceston, Lively, Lizard, Ludlow Castle, Lyme, Kennington, Mermaid, Minerva, Nightingale, Northumberland, Norwich, Otter, Phoenix, Prince George, Reserve, Robust, Romney, Rose, Savage, Scarborough, Seaford, Seahorse, Senegal, Shoreham, Soleby, Squirrel, Swan, Tartar, Vigilant.*

Unfortunately, there were a limited number of American mariners, as seafaring was for most Americans not a career, but rather "a customary apprenticeship for adult life."[6] This circumstance, of naval manning needs and American seamen's unwillingness to enlist in the Royal Navy, created opportunities for fugitive slaves, young boys, and elderly men.

As figure 12.1 shows, manning levels in North America rose and fell in direct relationship to the outbreak of wars. The onset of the Seven Years' War and the American Revolution resulted in enormous increases in the Navy's need for seamen.[7] The number of fugitive slaves seeking to flee via the sea rose and fell in a similar fashion, as shown in figure 12.2.

Similar increases were seen in elderly and adolescent individuals on British naval ships in North America during eighteenth-century wars. Fugitives, elderly men, and adolescents each had different reasons for seeking berths on naval vessels.

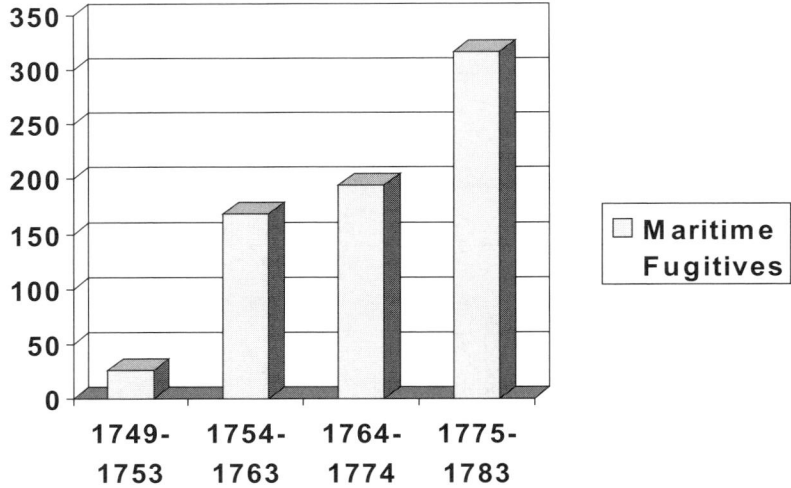

Fig. 12.2 *Maritime Fugitives, Pennsylvania, New York, and Rhode Island, 1749–83*

Note: Numbers for maritime fugitives between 1713 and 1748 are not provided owing to the limited newspaper coverage during this period. The increase in the number of maritime fugitives from 1764 to 1774 is probably the result of the substantial increase in slave imports to northern colonies during the Seven Years' War.

FUGITIVE SLAVES

For the enslaved, freedom was primary. Many slaves from northern colonies fled via the sea owing to a lack of other good alternatives to obtain permanent freedom. While West Indian runaways often sought shelter in maroon colonies, where they led what whites called a "wild and savage freedom," the geography of populated areas in northern colonies—flat with few hills—provided limited areas in which fugitives slaves could find permanent refuge.[8] Slaves who wore the striped ozenbrig clothing that marked them as bondsmen understood that a ship berth offered the possibility of permanent escape. Runaway slaves often saw the sea as their "only real shelter."[9] These men often had limited family lives in the ports from which they fled and viewed obtaining a berth as a means of escape more than the start of a naval career.[10] "Maritime fugitives," individuals who sought to flee via the sea, comprised approximately one-fifth of known northern runaways.[11] As in England, where a "significant minority"[12] of blacks were sailors, in northern maritime communities slaves could be found in all sectors of the maritime economy—on oyster boats, whaling ships, fishing boats, privateers, pirate vessels, coaster sloops, and blue sea ships.[13] Many had previous maritime experience, either from working in the maritime sector in the West Indies or Africa before coming to North America.

The Royal Navy regularly sought sailors from throughout North America. Naval captains recruited "with more of an eye to muscle than complexion."[14] When the British navy was short handed it was willing to impress in northern ports "a few negroes" such as London Lincoln, a purser's servant on HMS *St. Albans,* "to help out." The Continental Navy also employed runaways from the large number of skilled enslaved maritime workers in Virginia and South Carolina. Less likely to desert, fugitive slaves could be found on nearly every British man-of-war on the North American station. On some naval ships, 20 percent of the crew were black men. In view of the high percentage of colored crew members on captured British vessels, a conservative estimate would be five thousand maritime recruits during the war, with most drawn from New York and the northeastern seaboard.[15] My random sampling of the muster rolls for two British naval ships on the North American station for each year between 1713 and 1783 indicates that while colored sailors did not constitute "roughly a quarter of the Royal Navy" as some historians believe, the sampling does support N. A. M. Rodgers' assessment that in America there were "many black seamen, slave and free" in the Navy. Although naval musters prior to 1764 do not indicate place of birth, and most musters prior to 1783 do not provide racial identification, common slave names can readily be found in crew lists.[16] In the period between 1713 and 1739, just slightly more than 53 percent of the naval ships on the North American station had a colored seaman among their crews. These men, including Caesar Swift on HMS *Seahorse* and John Prince and John Boy on HMS *Squirrel,* tended to be clustered among the officers' servants. The bulk of these men served in the period between 1763 and 1783, during which time they made up as much as 5 percent of naval crews in North America.[17] Naval ships "chiefly manned with runaway Negroes" were reported, an indication of the stream of maritime fugitives making their way onto these vessels. For example, in 1781 two British barges with large groups of black men aboard undertook raids in Maryland, and a British barge with a largely black crew plundered the town of Lower Marlboro. Four months later, another British barge was reported to have at least twenty black men among a crew of thirty-five.[18] Many colored loyalists were Royal Navy seamen, and British ships captured by Americans were found to have between 13 and 30 percent colored crews.[19]

While colored mariners may have found freedom in the Royal Navy, their lives on naval vessels were hardly free from the racism common in North America. For example, while the *Amaranthe* sloop was in Antigua, Humphrey

Clinker, a black sailor, was sitting quietly mending his pants. Richard Cole, an English private on guard duty began abusing Clinker, calling him "a black bugger." When Clinker told Cole to leave him alone, the Englishman left only to return and confront Clinker once more. When Clinker asked him to go about his business, "the sentry then walked aft and immediately came forward again and said you black bugger how dare you talk to a white man, and ran his ramrod into [Clinker's] eye."[20]

ELDERLY COOKS

The obstacles elderly men faced to working at sea were different from those maritime fugitives confronted. For most eighteenth-century Atlantic mariners, going to sea after the age of forty was a sign of extreme dependency and poverty. Edward Barlow neatly captured the prevailing sense of most seamen, saying that if he "went to sea when I should be grown in years that then I should be little better than a slave." Naval seamen, such as fifty-two-year-old Angel Burga, were uncommon.[21] Though naval captains generally shied away from hiring elderly seamen, men over forty were frequently employed as cooks.[22] Throughout the eighteenth century, the Royal Navy used pensioners as cooks, helping to ensure sufficient numbers of healthy seamen were available to furl sails. As one sailor described his man-of-war's cook, a bullet "shot away one of his limbs, and so cut him out for a Sea-Cook."[23] Men such as Mark Anthony, a forty-eight year old on HMS *Ardents,* found respite from the physically demanding job of climbing the rigging in foul weather by serving as captain's cook.[24]

Elderly cooks were not limited to working on naval vessels. Atlantic communities also used ship cook positions to care for their elderly mariners. With mariners often required "to travel miles to pursue a [Seamen's Sixpence] claim at the Navy Office or employ a solicitor," few merchant seamen received sixpence benefits. This situation resulted in many Scarborough, England, ship captains employing elderly seamen as cooks on short collier voyages.[25] The average age of Scarborough's cooks in the period from 1748 to 1759 was just under fifty-three years of age, with not a single man under the age of forty serving as a cook on Scarborough's ships in 1759.[26] Elderly cooks, such as fifty-eight-year-old David Tristram, often served on ships of which their sons were masters.[27]

POWDER BOYS

From the beginning of European settlement in North America, young boys went to sea.[28] Onshore employment was not always attractive. Boys faced long days working on farms, or ten-hour days as apprentice ship-riggers, or, in the 1770s, fifteen-hour days in a paper mill.[29] Widows often sent young sons to sea as a means of reducing financial burdens and providing money for the entire family. Adolescents were also sent to sea to assist families in which fathers were physically incapable of earning a living.[30] Youngsters often followed the example of older boys and relatives in going to sea. In active ports such as Nantucket, New York, and Newport, adolescents heard their fathers, uncles, and cousins recount the adventures of their youth. On the other side of the Atlantic, English boys, such as Jack Cremer, also went to sea captivated by their relatives' stories of life in the Royal Navy.[31] In contrast, young blacks rarely shipped out in the company of friends or family. Instead, during the eighteenth century, these youthful souls, generally fugitives from either their parents or their slave masters, almost always came aboard by themselves.[32] Thus, unless they were able to form close relations with a young white boy on the boat, as did James Forten with Captain Bazley's son, black boys on ships were often isolated.

During the Revolution, increasing numbers of young slave boys found their way onto naval vessels, and the average age of maritime fugitives decreased considerably. The relative youth of northern maritime fugitives during the Revolution can be ascribed to the influx of large numbers of British naval ships into American ports, the new American navy's requirement for manpower, the chaos of war, and the British military's offer of freedom to those slaves who served in the king's forces.[33] Joseph King's Tom and scores of other slave boys were employed as powder boys and servants on naval vessels, as captains were less selective in their hiring in the face of increasing demands for maritime labor. These young maritime fugitives included the twelve-year-old mulatto boy Peter, whose owner believed him to "be decoyed on board the fleet" in New York harbor.[34] When they came aboard ships, these youthful runaways found young enslaved West Indians, such as Glasgow Black, serving as captains' servants, and joined other fugitives, such as Antonio Black from Virginia, a captain's servant on HMS *Robust*. The runaway boys understood that ship captains were willing to employ twelve year olds, whatever their skin color or presumed legal status.[35] Unlike white seamen who protested naval impressment in the streets of New York, Newport, and Boston, in a time when the idea of perpetual allegiance to a monarch was being replaced with the concept of voluntary allegiance to a nation of one's choosing, many young black fugitives chose to swear allegiance, albeit on perhaps a temporary basis, to King George.[36] Youthful maritime fugitives included those with and without prior maritime experience. Colored boys as young as eight or nine were also often taken to sea by ship captains to work as servants. These boys were exposed to maritime culture and learned skills that could be later used when these slaves sought to flee via the sea. Boys, such as Richard Wright's boy Alex, used their experiences on men-of-war to seek berths on other ships. Alex did so in 1778 despite having been branded with the initials "R. W." on his chest when captured running away the prior year.[37] These young runaways included those with little or no maritime experience. Dressing themselves as sailors and fleeing in stolen boats, they believed berths on ships could be obtained. Throughout the northern colonies and over the seven decades between 1713 and the end of the Revolutionary War, scores of fugitives, inexperienced in maritime work, both boys and young men, sought berths. If strong, healthy, and willing, youngsters were capable members in privateer boarding parties.

During the Revolution, scores of inexperienced fugitives were found on privateers, including an unidentified fourteen-year-old black boy and twelve-year-old Peter. The opportunities for such landlubbers to obtain a berth at sea, whether as members of boarding parties, powder boys, or servants, were particularly good during times of war.[38] The benefits naval service provided elderly, fugitive, and adolescent mariners was limited. They experienced difficult working conditions and racism, rarely received pensions, found themselves moved around the world, and, sometimes, when captured, were reenslaved. Youthful powder boys were at great risk of injury and death during naval battles, being "very much exposed to the enemy's shots," while having to contend with "shot and splinters [that] flew thick."[39] Despite such circumstances, life on board naval vessels often provided them better employment and lives than they could find ashore in colonial America. Combined with the Royal Navy's manning needs, this contrast between life ashore and life at sea drew scores of elderly, youthful, and enslaved individuals onto British men-of-war in North America.

NOTES

The following abbreviations are used in the notes:

ADM	Records of the Admiralty, TNA
CMD	Colored Mariner Database
NMM	National Maritime Museum, Greenwich, UK
TNA	The National Archives, Kew, UK

1. Jesse Lemisch, "Jack Tar in the Streets: Merchant Seamen in the Politics of Revolutionary America," *William and Mary Quarterly* 25 (1968): 371–372. Examples of images of young, healthy white male sailors include "The Fortunate Tar," PAF3791, Henry J. Richter, artist, n.d.; "Poor Mariners," NMM PAF4035, n.d.; and "Jack's Return," NMM PAF4026, n.d. Each of these images can be seen on the NMM website, www.nmm.ac.uk.
2. W. Jeffrey Bolster, *Black Jacks: African American Sailors in the Age of Sail* (Cambridge: Harvard University Press, 1997); Marcus Rediker, *Between the Devil and the Deep Blue Sea: Merchant Seaman, Pirates and the Anglo-American Maritime World, 1700–1750* (Cambridge: Cambridge University Press, 1987), 155–156, and chap. 2; Michael Jarvis, "Maritime Masters and Seafaring Slaves in Bermuda, 1680–1783," *William and Mary Quarterly* 59 (2002): 585–622; Emma Christopher, *Slave Ship Sailors and Their Captive Cargoes, 1730–1807* (New York: Cambridge University Press, 2006), chap. 2; Daniel Vickers with Vince Walsh, *Young Men and the Sea: Yankee Seafarers in the Age of Sail* (New Haven, CT: Yale University Press, 2005), 81, 297n55, Appendix B. See also Vincent Carretta, "Black Sailors in the British Navy," *Journal of Maritime Research* (November 2003), http://www.jmr.nmm.ac.uk/server/show/con.JmrArticle.102; James Baker Farr, "A Slow Boat to Nowhere: The Multi-Racial Crews of the American Whaling Industry," *Journal of Negro History* 63 (1983): 159–170. For fugitive slaves fleeing via the sea, N. A. T. Hall, "Maritime Maroons: Grand Maroonage from the Danish West Indies," *William and Mary Quarterly* 42 (1985): 476–498; and Charles R. Foy, "Seeking Freedom in the Atlantic, 1713–1783," *Early American Studies: An Interdisciplinary Journal* 4 (2006): 46–77.
3. Maritime fugitives have been identified from a review of more than four thousand New York, Pennsylvania, and Rhode Island fugitive slave advertisements. These advertisements, however, do not fully describe the world that maritime fugitives encountered when they fled slavery. To recreate that world my research included muster rolls, log books, High Court of Admiralty and Vice Admiralty records, newspaper dispatches, ship captains' journals, account books, military pension records, and secondary sources. This research resulted in the creation of the CMD, which now contains names of more than [eight] nine thousand colored mariners from throughout the Atlantic world. The CMD's colored mariners include maritime fugitives; any crew member on a ship that had a classical, African, or place name; and those lacking a surname, which typically was an indication during the eighteenth century that a man was or had been a slave. Because most eighteenth-century records do not provide racial identification and many dark-skinned mariners had been given Christian surnames, the CMD undercounts the number of eighteenth-century colored mariners, although the extent of that undercounting cannot be stated with certainty.
4. John William McElroy, "Seafaring in Seventeenth-Century New England," *New England Quarterly* 8 (September 1935): 334–335; Samuel Eliot Morison, *The Maritime History of Massachusetts* (Boston: Houghton Mifflin, 1921), 105–107, 111.
5. *New York Gazette & Mercury,* 20 September 1779; TNA, ADM 36/8816, HMS *Adamant* Muster Roll, 1781; *New York Weekly Journal,* 26 April 1740, 18 October 1742; Elphinstone Papers, 16 November 1778, letter from Admiral Elphinstone to an unknown individual, NMM KEI/2/1; HMS *Coventry,* Muster Rolls, 1763–1765, TNA ADM 36/7568.
6. Roland G. Usher Jr., "Royal Navy Impressment during the American Revolution," *Mississippi Valley Historical Review* 37 (1951): 680; Capt. A. Forrest to Lt. Gov. Spencer Phips, 26 October 1745, TNA ADM 1/1782. For the nature of America's seamen, see Vickers, *Young Men and the Sea,* 96–130; Daniel Vickers, *Farmers and Fishermen: Two Centuries*

of Work in Essex County, Massachusetts, 1630–1850 (Chapel Hill: University of North Carolina Press, 1994), 167–91, 198–203; Rediker, *Between the Devil and the Deep Blue Sea*, 295. The best analysis of impressment in North America is Denver Alexander Brunsman, "The Evil Necessity: British Naval Impressment in the Eighteenth-Century Atlantic World" (unpublished PhD dissertation, Princeton University, 2004).

7. Peter Earle has estimated that from 1738 to 1748 approximately twenty-five thousand additional men were needed annually. Peter Earle, *English Merchant Seamen* (London: Methum Publishing Ltd., 1998), 187.

8. *New York Mercury*, 16 October 1765; *Providence Gazette*, 16 August 1777; *New Jersey Gazette* (Trenton), 17 April 1782; *Pennsylvania Gazette*, 9 May 1751; *New York Mercury*, 15 March 1756; Graham Russell Hodges and Allen Brown, *Pretends to Be Free: Runaway Slave Advertisements from Colonial and Revolutionary New York and New Jersey* (New York and London: Garland Publishing, 1994), 345; Bryan Edwards, *Observations on the Disposition, Character, Manners and Habits of Life, of the Maroon Negroes of the Island of Jamaica* (London: J. Stockdale, 1796), repr. as Appendix to vol. 1, *History of the West Indies* (London: J. Stockdale, 1789), 527. I want to thank Kathleen Wilson for this reference.

The few slaves who did escape to frontier areas tended to be Native Americans and mixed race men who sought haven in remnant tribal structures in Rhode Island before attempting to pass as free or sail to England. Billy G. Smith and Richard Wojtowicz, *Blacks Who Stole Themselves: Advertisements for Runaways in the Pennsylvania Gazette* (Philadelphia: University of Pennsylvania Press, 1989), 12; John A. Sainsbury, "Indian Labor in Early Rhode Island," *New England Quarterly* 48 (1975): 391–392; *Pennsylvania Gazette*, 3 November 1763; *Newport Mercury*, 28 September 1772.

9. Lemisch, "Jack Tar in the Streets," 374–375.

10. Foy, "Seeking Freedom in the Atlantic," 77; Charles R. Foy, "Ports of Slavery, Ports of Freedom: How Slaves Used Northern Seaports' Maritime Industry to Escape and Create Transatlantic Identities, 1713–1783" (unpublished PhD dissertation, Rutgers University, 2008), chap. 5.

11. Foy, "Ports of Slavery, Ports of Freedom," chap. 3.

12. Philip D. Morgan, "The Black Experience in the British Empire, 1680–1817," in *The Oxford History of the British Empire*, Vol. II, P. J. Marshall, ed. (Oxford: Oxford University Press, 1998), 471.

13. Ibid.; Paul Gilje, *Liberty on the Waterfront: American Maritime Culture in the Age of Revolution* (Philadelphia, PA: University of Philadelphia Press, 2004), 25. Slaves were employed as mariners in northern ports in Connecticut and Massachusetts, as well as in Philadelphia, New York, and Newport. Daniel Vickers, *Farmers and Fishermen: Two Centuries of Work in Essex County* (Chapel Hill: University of North Carolina Press, 2001), 18–20, 28–29; Yang, "From Slavery to Emancipation," 177–190. Black seamen had become a "common sight" in British ports by the 1690s. Steve Murdoch, "John Brown: A Black Female Soldier in the Royal African Company," World History Connected, http://worldhistoryconnected.press.uiuc.edu/1.2/murdoch.html#edn26.

14. W. Jeffrey Bolster, "'To Feel Like a Man': Black Seamen in the Northern States: 1800–1860," *Journal of American History* 76 (1990): 1179.

15. Cassandra Pybus, "Jefferson's Faulty Math," *William and Mary Quarterly* 62 (2005): 243–264; Bolster, *Black Jacks*, 30–32; Gerald W. Mullin, *Flight and Rebellion: Slave Resistance in Eighteenth-Century Virginia* (New York: Oxford University Press, 1972), 94–98 (25 percent of Virginia fugitive slaves were maritime workers); Philip D. Morgan, "Colonial

South Carolina Runaways: Their Significance for Slave Culture," *Slavery and Abolition* 7 (1985): 65. Maritime work was the third largest occupation for South Carolinian male slaves. Included among the Royal Navy's maritime recruits were colored mariners they pressed from enemy ships. (The CMD characterizes as "colored mariners" all identifiable mariners described as "Negro," "Mulatto," "Mustee," or "Indian." It does so because the racial boundaries in the eighteenth-century Atlantic were elastic, enslaved individuals in northern colonies included members of all these groups, and intermarriages among these groups by free and enslaved mariners were not uncommon.) Anthony Mingus, an African-born able-bodied seaman, who was impressed from the Spanish ship *Friendship* and then served on a number of Royal Navy ships throughout the Atlantic, was one of scores of colored mariners impressed. Mingus's naval career can be followed in HMS *Brune* Muster, 1777, TNA ADM 36/7756; HMS *Brune* Paybook, 1778, TNA ADM 34/93; HMS *Brune* Captain's Log, TNA ADM 51/1838; HMS *Lizard* Muster, 1778–1779, TNA ADM 36/8576; HMS *Lizard* Master's Log, 1778, TNA ADM 52/1838; HMS *Courageux* Captain's Log, 1779–1781, TNA ADM 51/169; HMS *Courageux* Muster Rolls, 1779–1780, TNA ADM 36/8309–8310; HMS *Courageux* Pay Book, 1780, TNA ADM 34/189–190; HMS *Courageux* Muster Roll, 1781–1783, TNA ADM 36/8727.

16. N. A. M. Rodgers, *The Wooden World: An Anatomy of the Georgian Navy* (Annapolis, MD: Naval Institute Press, 1986), 159. Cf. Richard Pares, "The Manning of the Navy in the West Indies, 1702–63," in *The Historian's Business and Other Essays* (Oxford: Claredon Press, 1961), 32; L. P. Jackson, "Virginia Negro in the American Revolution," *Journal of Negro History* 27 (1942): 249 ("some instances of slaves giving their allegiance to the British").

17. HMS *Seahorse*, Paybook, 1719–1725, TNA ADM 33/316; HMS *Squirrel* Paybook, 1717–1720, TNA ADM 33/244. My random review of muster rolls for Royal Navy ships on the North American station indicates that 2.57 percent of the crews during the Revolution were colored mariners. With muster rolls not indicating seamen's race and many colored sailors having names commonly associated with white mariners, my tabulations clearly understate the presence of colored seamen. If one assumed two times as many colored naval sailors in the years with the highest rates of colored mariners, these men would not have totaled more than 8.2 percent of naval mariners serving in North America.

18. Benjamin Quarles, *The Negro in the American Revolution* (Chapel Hill: University of North Carolina Press, 1996), 153–155; Lemisch, "Jack Tar in the Streets," 384; *Pennsylvania Packet*, 13 May 1780; HMS *St. Albans* Pay Books, 1776–1777, TNA ADM 34/12; *Pennsylvania Ledger* 30 September 1775.

19. Quarles, *Negro in the American Revolution*, 153–155; Peter Linebaugh, *London Hanged: Crime and Civil Society in the Eighteenth Century* (Cambridge: Cambridge University Press, 1992), 134. Forty percent of British merchant mariners were black.

20. John D. Byrn Jr., *Crime and Punishment in the Royal Navy: Discipline on the Leeward Islands, 1784–1812* (Aldershot, UK: Scolar Press, 1989), 144. Clinker is listed in the *Amaranthe's* muster roll as a landsman, born in Africa, aged twenty-five at enlistment. TNA ADM 37/2993 and 37/4466.

21. Vickers, *Young Men and the Sea*, 119; Earle, *English Merchant Seamen*, 48–50; Rediker, *Between the Devil and the Deep Blue Sea*, 156, Appendix A; *Barlow's Journal of his Life at Sea in King's Ships, East & West Indiamen, & Other Merchantmen from 1659 to 1703*, ed. Basil Lubbock (London: Hurst & Blackett, 1934), 162. The demanding physical nature of work at sea resulted in few men with disabilities obtaining berths. Escape via the sea in northern British American colonies largely being a tool of resistance used by men. Foy, "Seeking

Freedom in the Atlantic," 52–53. The limited presence of colored women on North American ships was owing to their having less freedom of movement than male slaves, the masculine ethos of the maritime industry, and women's child-rearing responsibilities. Lisa Norling, *Captain Ahab Had a Wife: New England Women and the Whalefishery, 1720–1870* (Chapel Hill: University of North Carolina Press, 2000); Suzanne Stark, *Female Tars: Woman Aboard Ship in the Age of Sail* (Annapolis, MD: Naval Institute Press, 1996); Margaret S. Creighton, and Lisa Norling, ed., *Iron Men, Wooden Women: Gender and Seafaring in the Atlantic World: 1700–1920* (Baltimore, MD: John Hopkins University Press, 1996).

22. TNA HMS *Prince Edward* Pay Roll, 1776, ADM 33/348; TNA HMS *Asia* ADM 36/8079: Muster Rolls, 1774; May 30, 1743 letter from Francis Geary to the Commissioners of the Navy, NMM GC/4/31; Janet McDonald, *Feeding Nelson's Navy* (London, 2004), 104, 142–143.

23. 30 May 1743 letter from Francis Geary to the Commissioners of the Navy, NMM GC/4/31; 16 April 1776 letter from James Gambier to Navy Board, NMM POR/F16; Robinson, *The British Tar in Fact and Fiction* ("give the preference [as cooks] to such cripples and maimed persons as are pensioners"), 92; Naval Board In-Letters, 6 May 1769, TNA ADM 106/1178/128 (ordinaries who lost limbs seen as suitable to serve as naval cooks); McDonald, *Feeding Nelson's Navy*, 104, 142–143; *The Wooden World Dissected: In the Character of a Ship of War: As also, The Characters of all the Officer, From the Captain to the Common Sailor* (London: J. Skirven, 1749), 59.

24. HMS *Ardents* Pay Book, 1776, TNA ADM 33/468.

25. *The Manning of the Royal Navy: Selected Public Pamphlets, 1693–1873*, ed. J. S. Bromley, Records of the Navy Records Society, vol. 119 (London: Navy Records Society, 1974), xxxii, note 2; "Seamen's Sixpence," *Mariner's Mirror,* 70 (1984), 433–434. Whether Seamen's Sixpence was, as Conrad Dixon characterizes it, "a most successful confidence trick whereby the state used compulsory deductions from the scanty wages of naval and merchant seamen chiefly for the benefit of the former," or not, the large majority of seamen listed in Pension Registers as receiving benefits under the Seamen's Sixpence Program were naval mariners. TNA ADM 82/71–100. As *The Life and Adventures of John Nicol, Mariner*, ed. Tim Flannery (New York, 2000) so aptly depicts, disabled mariners were often shuttled from one government office to another without receiving benefits. Scarborough's town elders recognized this problem establishing its own Trinity House and building a hospital with twenty-seven apartments. Trinity House provided relief to destitute families of mariners, with almost 150 applications for assistance having been granted by 1780. However, the Society's efforts were almost exclusively focused on mariners' families, causing elderly mariners to "retire at sea." Records of Scarborough Trinity House, North Yorkshire Record Office, ZOX 10/1; James Buckley, "The Outport of Scarborough, 1650–1853," NMM PBC 6985, 22–23.

26. McDonald, *Feeding Nelson's Navy,* 104, 142–3. There are few muster rolls for eighteenth-century English merchant ships. Besides those for Scarborough, 1748–1759, and Plymouth, 1775–1776, the National Archives in Kew has only Colchester Seamen's Indentures, 1704–1757, TNA BT 167/103; Plymouth Crew Lists, 1761–1783, TNA BT 98/106–107; and Liverpool Crew Lists, 1772–1783, TNA BT 98/33–43.

27. Colored cooks such as John Cato, Augustus Thammers, Alexander Nemo, and John Snow were common on British men-of-war on the North American station. TNA HMS *Coventry* Muster Rolls, 1763–1765, ADM 36/7568; TNA HMS *Seaford,* Muster Roll, 1754–1755, ADM 36/6710; TNA HMS *Vigilant,* Pay Roll, 1746, ADM 33/4420.The pattern of employing elderly men as ship cooks was also true for nineteenth-century New London and West Indian merchant ships. Among the twenty elderly colored New London mariners for

whom crew lists indicate their positions, eleven were cooks, while fifteen out of seventy-seven identified West Indian black mariners worked as cooks. Alan Cobley, "Black West Indian Seamen in the Mid-Nineteenth Century," *History Workshop Journal* 58 (2004): 271.
28. McElroy, "Seafaring in Seventeenth-Century New England," 345.
29. Paul B. Hensley, "Time and Work in New England," *The New England Quarterly* 65 (1999): 552–553. In London during the 1750s workers generally worked between twelve to thirteen hours a day. Hans-Joachim Voth, "Time and Work in Eighteenth-Century England," *The Journal of Economic History* 58 (1998): 33.
30. Vickers, *Young Men and the Sea*, 156–160. Financial considerations led poor families and widowed mothers throughout the Atlantic to send young boys to sea. Hugh Cunningham, "The Employment and Unemployment of Children in England, c. 1680–1851," *Past and Present* 126 (1990): 122.
31. Jack Cremer, *Ramblin' Jack: The Journal of Captain John Cremer, 1700–1774*, ed. R. Reynall Bellamy (London: J. Cape, 1936), 31–40.
32. Vickers, *Young Men and the Sea*, 105.
33. Colored boys could be found on a variety of vessels. Some, like the "Swan Warner's Negro Boy of Philadelphia" or an unnamed nine-year-old Middletown, New Jersey, boy, had their maritime employment end suddenly when they accidentally drowned. *American Weekly Mercury*, June 20, 1734. Young slave runaways could be found on nineteenth- century American naval ships. Herbert Aptheker, "The Negro in the Union Navy," *Journal of Negro History*, 32 (1947): 169n1.
34. *Royal Gazette*, 10 October 1778.
35. CMD; Ship *Catherine* log, 1782–83. MC 60.43, Collection 64, vol. 2, G. W. White Blunt Library, Mystic Seaport, CT; *New York Mercury*, 13 January 1755; *New York Gazette* (Weyman's), 11 May 1761; *New York Gazette & Weekly Mercury*, 6 April 1772, 4 May 1772, 2 February 1775, 12 April 1779; *Royal Gazette*, 10 October 1778; HMS *Otter* Muster Roll, 1746–1747, TNA ADM 36/2334; HMS *Roebuck* Muster Roll, 1776, TNA ADM 36/644. From 1716 to 1783 only 6.5 percent of New York slaves fled with another slave. Hodges and Brown, *"Pretends to Be Free,"* Table 7. Gary Nash has estimated that "probably more than one thousand African Americans served in the small American navy." Gary B. Nash, *The Unknown American Revolution: The Unruly Birth of Democracy and the Struggle to Create America* (New York: Penguin Books, 2005), 227. Naval recruiting officers were "less in a position to pick and chose men than their counterparts in the army." Benjamin Quarles, *The Negro in the American Revolution* (Chapel Hill: University of North Carolina Press, 1961, reprint, 1996), 83. Despite such lack of selectivity, it is highly unlikely that one thousand colored men served in the small American navy. The majority of the fewer than two hundred colored mariners from American naval and state navy vessels listed in the CMD served on state navy ships. As the CMD includes records of colored mariners from a wide variety of sources, including secondary sources that compiled lists of blacks based on military records, it is appears the vast majority of colored mariners serving during the American Revolution found berths either on British men of war-or-privateers.
36. Lemisch, "Jack Tar in the Streets," 391–323, 402–403.
37. Vincent Carretta, *Equiano, the African: Biography of a Self-Made Man* (Athens: University of Georgia Press, 2005), 45; *Captain Graham in his Cabin*, c. 1745, NMM, BHC 2720; *Rivington's New York Loyal Gazette*, 13 October 1777; *Royal Gazette*, 7 February 1778. Examples of slave boy mariners include *Royal Gazette*, 2 September 1777; *New York Gazette & Weekly Mercury*, 7 October 1771; *New York Journal or General Advertiser*, 4 June 1772.

38. *American Weekly Mercury,* 10 November 1737; *Pennsylvania Gazette,* 10 April 1740; *Newport Mercury,* 9 October 1759; *New York Gazette & Weekly Mercury,* 2 June 1777; *Rivington's New York Gazetteer,* 13 October 1777; *Royal Gazette,* 2 January, 17 October 1778; and *Pennsylvania Gazette,* 17 October 1778.
39. Olaudah Equiano, *The Interesting Narrative of Olaudah Equiano, or Gustavus Vassa, the African: An Authoritative Text/Written by Himself; Contexts, Criticism,* ed. Werner Sollers (New York: Norton, 1794, reprint 2001), 83–84; *Pennsylvania Gazette,* 31 December 1741.

Navy Women's Pioneering Experiences at Sea

Catherine A. Leahey

Of course, there are some pessimists who will say: "Women on shipboard with the Fleet? It can't be done!" It *can* and *is* being done successfully. . . . We [women] look upon this as very serious work—not as a pleasure trip—and the dignity of our position is of great consequence to us.[1]

Who was the author who proudly penned these words? A woman who reported for sea duty on naval auxiliaries under the Women in Ships Program in 1978? A woman assigned to the hospital ship USS *Sanctuary* (AH 17) as part of the 1973 pilot program to assign women to sea duty? A Women Accepted for Volunteer Emergency Services (WAVES) hospital corpsman serving aboard a transport ship in the 1950s? A nurse aboard a hospital ship during World War II? In fact, it was Chief Nurse J. Beatrice Bowman, writing in 1921 onboard USS *Relief* (AH 1), the first U.S. Navy ship built with women's quarters. But *Relief* was not the first ship to have Navy women serving aboard, nor was it Beatrice Bowman's first time on sea duty.

The nineteenth-century *Navy Regulations* prohibited ship captains from taking women to sea unless they had the approval of the secretary of the Navy or a squadron commander.[2] That proviso enabled Commo. Stephen Decatur to enlist the wives of two of his sailors to act as nurses on his flagship *United States* in the War of 1812. During the Civil War the crew of the Union hospital ship *Red Rover* included women nurses, laundresses, and chambermaids. Her captain circumvented regulations because *Red Rover* operated on the Mississippi River and never went to sea. In the Spanish-American War, women nurses served aboard the Army hospital ship *Relief*, which did not come under Navy jurisdiction.

With the creation of the Navy Nurse Corps in 1908, the Navy broke its one hundred–year tradition. The enacting legislation specifically stated that nurses could serve onboard hospital and ambulance ships.[3] Before World War I, however, assignments to sea duty for Navy nurses were extremely rare. Surgeon-General Rear Adm. Presley M. Rixey believed women nurses were more valuable at hospitals ashore training male hospital corpsmen. His successor, Rear Adm. Charles F. Stokes, also indicated that he had no plans to send nurses to sea.[4] As a consequence, the first assignments of nurses to ships were not on hospital or ambulance ships, as might be expected, but on USS *Supply* (the Guam station ship) in 1911, USS *Mayflower* (the presidential yacht) in 1913, and USS *Dolphin* (the secretary of the Navy's dispatch boat), also in 1913. In each case, the assignment was temporary, and it was the nurses' duty to care for civilian women and children passengers.

Nurses were not assigned to hospital ships during World War I, ostensibly because there was no adequate berthing for them. The medical corps officers commanding hospital ships unreasonably believed that every woman had to have a private stateroom and convinced Surgeon General Rear Adm. William C. Braisted that those staterooms would be better used for additional surgeons and chaplains. After the war, forty-five nurses received orders to sea duty aboard the transport ships, bringing the American Expeditionary Force home and returning prisoners of war and refugees to Europe. For most, the assignment was temporary but the nurses assigned to USS *Leviathan*, USS *George Washington*, and USS *Imperator* had permanent orders to their ships. In his annual report for 1919, Braisted admitted the concerns about women nurses adapting to the confined life aboard ship "were unfounded."[5]

FIRST PERMANENT SEA DUTY

In December 1920 a new hospital ship joined the fleet. Unlike previous hospital ships, USS *Relief* (AH 1) was not a converted passenger liner but a ship designed and built by the Navy. With a five hundred–bed capacity, she counted among the largest hospitals of the day in the United States. Notably, *Relief* had private quarters for eleven women nurses secluded in the superstructure, as far away as possible from the 340 men in the crew. The chief nurse had a single stateroom and the other nurses slept in double staterooms that opened onto the nurses' wardroom. These quarters were fitted out much the same as the officers' but the nurses personalized their wardroom with a Persian carpet on the deck, fresh flowers on the dining table, and a full length mirror on the bulkhead. The nurses ran their own mess and seldom entered the officers' wardroom. Reportedly, the food was better in the nurses' mess and a few officers applied unsuccessfully to join.[6]

Chief Nurse Beatrice Bowman volunteered for the senior nursing position on *Relief*. She was no stranger to sea duty, having made a two-month cruise aboard *Supply* in 1916. She and the other nurses were personally selected by the Superintendent of the Navy Nurse Corps and the Surgeon-General of the Navy. Early on, Beatrice Bowman dismissed the notion that women were physically unable to endure life at sea: "When we first set sail, bulletins were carried by word of mouth to all parts of the ship when one or more of us looked pale, but these bulletins have ceased and all the nurses are proving themselves as good sailors as can be found."[7]

Relief operated as an integral part of the Battle Fleet, accompanying it wherever it sailed. Being so close to the fleet, the nurses had many opportunities to observe naval maneuvers. "We followed the Fleet out of this Bay.... We saw them maneuvering that evening and the next morning ... the Destroyers were scampering around us to the Starboard. The 'Battle wagons' that is the big ones were on the Port side. It seems that they had been successfully torpedoed and were sinking.... It was all intensely interesting."[8]

Each day, the nurses saw about 245 patients and soon learned that aboard ship there was no such thing as an eight-hour day: "Life on a Hospital Ship is entirely different for, as we have so often heard in the Navy but never fully understood until now, when you are aboard you are always on duty. And there is no exception made of the Nurse."[9]

Nurse Thomasina Libby reported to *Relief* in September 1922. Fleet operations were in full swing, and she left the ship only once during her first month aboard, to get into a boat for an abandon ship drill. Unfamiliar Navy lingo was her first challenge. She was laughed at "for not knowing starboard from port, fore from aft, abeam from abaft, a chief with gold chevrons from a captain with gold stripes."[10]

A nurse's sea bag had only two uniforms: an ankle-length white ward uniform and a dark blue wool outdoor duty uniform that only nurses serving at sea and overseas were authorized to wear. The latter was a government-issued uniform, unlike the white uniform, which nurses had to purchase themselves. During the 1920s, as a cost-savings measure, the Navy assigned nurses who already had this uniform to sea duty so the Navy would not have to buy a new one.

Superintendent of the Navy Nurse Corps Lenah S. Higbee was delighted with not only reports that the nurses seemed happy on the ship but that they also enjoyed their work: "[I]t would seem that the shortage in the Nurse Corps could be quite quickly filled if all the applicants could be assigned to the USS RELIEF [*sic*]."[11] Not only did nurses like working in the fleet, but the travel opportunities were especially attractive. In 1921 four nurses on the hospital ship *Mercy* became the Navy's first women shellbacks, on a cruise to South America. In 1925 *Relief* deployed with the fleet to Hawaii, Samoa, Australia, and New Zealand.

During the interwar years opportunities for sea duty were plentiful aboard naval transports carrying VIPs and Navy and Marine Corps families to overseas bases. These voyages often lasted for several months at a time. Transiting the Panama Canal was the most interesting part of Chief Nurse Susie I. Fitzgerald's assignment to USS *Henderson* in 1922. She logged more than 15,000 miles at sea, sailing from Norfolk, Virginia, to Bremerton, Washington, and back to New York via California, Mexico, Panama, and Haiti.[12] Nurses' duties included conducting dependents' sick call and supervising the children's mess. They also assisted with special details, such as acting as mustering officer for Abandon Ship and roving the ship to inspect for stowaways during Special Sea and Anchor Detail. They ate with the other officers in the wardroom, but their staterooms were conveniently located adjacent to the passengers' sick bay.

BAPTISM OF FIRE

On the morning of 7 December 1941, the hospital ship USS *Solace* (AH 5) lay at anchor near Battleship Row in Pearl Harbor. Explosions around the ship nearly knocked Nurse Anna Danyo out of her bunk. Other nurses awoke thinking some ships must be holding gunnery drills. Nurse Ruth Cohen, on duty as the night nurse, looked out a porthole and saw USS *Arizona* (BB 39) erupt into fire and billowing smoke like "a million Roman candles."[13] Chief Nurse Grace B. Lally recognized immediately what was happening because she had witnessed the Japanese bombing of Shanghai in 1937.

Within minutes, *Solace*'s boats were in the water recovering burned and wounded men and bringing them back to the ship. Inside the ship, the thirteen nurses worked nonstop for three days, tending to more than three hundred burn cases.[14] Never before had a hospital ship been a participant in a naval battle. *Solace* had the distinction of being the first hospital ship awarded a battle star. Every nurse aboard *Solace* received a citation from the fleet commander in chief for her outstanding performance of duty under fire.

For the next year, *Solace* was the only hospital ship in the Pacific theater. Ships from the combat zone rendezvoused with her in rear areas and transferred their patients. *Solace* then evacuated the wounded men to hospitals in Australia and New Zealand. Pacific Fleet sailors dubbed *Solace* the "lollypop ship" and her crewmen sissies because their ship was always in the rear area.[15] As the war progressed and more hospital ships came on line, the Navy moved hospital ships closer to the combat zone until their primary mission became the treatment of casualties sent directly from the battlefield.

Sometimes the fighting was uncomfortably close. During the battle of Saipan, a dogfight between a B-24 and a Japanese Zero took place overhead USS *Bountiful* (AH 9). Enemy shells landed within one hundred yards of *Solace* at Iwo Jima, forcing her to move farther out to sea. *Relief* barely escaped being bombed in Okinawa harbor while she was evacuating casualties; antiaircraft fire from a nearby destroyer drove off the Japanese planes. Three weeks later at Okinawa, a kamikaze plane crashed into USS *Comfort* (AH 6) killing twenty-eight, among them six Army nurses. Surprisingly, nurses had very little damage control training before reporting to their ships. They took a short survival swimming course, and a few attended fleet fire-fighting school in Pearl Harbor. The majority simply watched a couple of Navy training films.

Shipboard life for women had not changed much since 1921. Following the model of *Relief*, the new hospital ships had self-contained quarters for nurses, a cloister where no man dared enter and from which women descended daily into the men's world. Sailors on *Solace* called the nurses' quarters the "holy of holies."[16] On *Relief*, sentries patrolled the deck of "Nurses' Country" from 2200 to 0700 to ensure the nurses' privacy.[17] The captain of USS *Benevolence* (AH 13) armed his nurses with .45-caliber pistols and instructed them to shoot any intruder in their quarters between 2100 and 0700. The nurses obediently hung their pistols by their bunks but never revealed to the crew that the captain had not issued them ammunition.[18]

Hemlines had risen but otherwise nurses' uniforms were impractical for shipboard conditions, especially in wartime. The indoor duty white uniform had no option for slacks, was uncomfortable in the tropics, and was notoriously difficult to keep clean. The nurses on *Solace* had to wear the oil-stained uniforms they had worn on 7 December for months because they could not get replacements in the South Pacific. To make their uniforms more comfortable, some nurses shortened the sleeves and wore them without belts. Later in the war, some captains authorized their nurses to wear enlisted WAVES aviation coveralls, Army nurses' uniforms (khaki shirt and slacks), or men's khaki clothing.

Nurses viewed sea duty as a unique experience, one that made them feel truly part of the Navy and direct contributors to the war at sea. For Ens. Frances Quebbeman, duty aboard *Solace* in 1942–43 was "the most memorable of my Navy career."[19] Lt. Charlotte I. Bailey described her "outstanding year" on USS *Consolation* (AH 15) as one that gave her "respect and appreciation of the Navy—for you can't really know it, until you've been aboard ship."[20] Lt. (junior grade) Georgia Reynolds, assigned to *Bountiful* in the central Pacific in 1945, was proud of her time at sea, writing, "We expect to see further action and perhaps take part in the final invasion before victory. When back ashore we shall be able to look back at our sea duty and have the satisfaction of work well done."[21]

WAVES GO TO SEA

Thus far, nurses were the only women assigned to sea duty because Congress had prohibited WAVES from serving on ships during World War II. After the war, the Navy sought legislation to integrate women into the regular forces. Carl Vinson (D-GA), the ranking minority member of the House Armed Services Committee, adamantly opposed having women in the military except as reservists. He did his best to limit what women could do, famously ordering, "Just fix it so that they cannot go to sea at all."[22] Vinson relented slightly to allow women aboard hospital ships and transports because of the historical precedent of nurses' service on those ships. The resulting legislation, Title 10 U.S. Code, Section 6015, prohibited Navy women—but not those from other services—from serving on any other Navy vessel.

Capt. Joy Bright Hancock, director of the WAVES, wasted little time in proposing to send WAVES to sea. In particular, she believed that enlisted WAVES in the hospital corps could be useful on naval transports. This, in turn, could eventually lead to their assignment on hospital ships.[23] Enlisted women had never been assigned to hospital ships because those ships lacked appropriate berthing. Berthing modifications on transports, though, were unnecessary since the enlisted women could sleep in a passenger cabin. Many transports already had a nurse onboard who could supervise the enlisted women. Disappointingly, it took some years to convince the naval hierarchy to assign enlisted women to sea duty.

It was not until 30 July 1953, the eleventh anniversary of the establishment of the WAVES, that the Navy announced that women of the Hospital Corps could volunteer for duty on naval transports, with thirty-five billets in the Pacific Fleet and twenty-eight in the Atlantic Fleet. Their principal duties were preparing baby formula for infant passengers, a job many male corpsmen had found disagreeable, and assisting with passenger sick call. Volunteers had to be at least twenty-one years of age and have served in the Navy at least two years: in essence, a woman had to be a petty officer to go to sea. Their normal tour of duty was twenty-one months, generally with two WAVES per ship. If there were no dependents embarked on the ship, the WAVES were detached and assigned quarters ashore. If the ship was going to be in port a long time, they were given temporary orders to a nearby base.

Two WAVES reported for duty on USNS *General George W. Goethals* (T-AP 182) and two on USNS *General H. F. Hodges* (T-AP 144) in September 1953. More than sixty others served at sea until the Navy decommissioned the last of its transports in 1966.[24] Ironically, some of these WAVES had more sea time and visited more foreign ports than many Navy men because of the nature of a transport ship's operations.

The case for WAVES officers at sea was not as straightforward. In accordance with secretary of the Navy policy, women officers could only supervise other women, effectively disqualifying them for division officer or shore patrol officer duties. Furthermore, *Navy Regulations* barred women from succeeding to command afloat, making them ineligible to be navigators or command duty officers.[25] Women officers on a ship who could neither take their place on the watch bill nor perform division officer duties would place an unfair and unnecessary burden on the male officers. Nevertheless, commanding officers of transport ships were eager to have WAVES officers aboard—as long as their assignment did not mean one fewer male officer—to attend to "the peculiar problems of women" passengers.[26]

The Bureau of Naval Personnel (BUPERS) was not as enthusiastic and limited sea duty for WAVES officers to those in the Naval Reserve who volunteered for the assignment for their annual two weeks' active duty training. Lt. (junior grade) Clarice L. Pierson was the first to volunteer, reporting to USS *General H. W. Butner* (AP 113) in April 1949. *All Hands*, a magazine published by BUPERS, assured its readers "lady officers" would not stand deck watches or perform any military duties while at sea. They would only assist with office work and with the administration of passengers.[27]

In 1961 the Navy assigned Lt. Charlene Suneson to USS *General W. A. Mann* (AP 112) for permanent duty. Suneson described herself as a trial balloon and reported aboard believing that as a line officer she would stand watches under way on the bridge or in the engine room. Once onboard the ship, she was quickly disabused of that idea. The chief engineer ordered her to stay out of the engine room, and the captain declared he didn't want her on the bridge.[28] The captain also made it clear she would not command a lifeboat unless no male officers were available. As the assistant transportation officer, she was responsible for the 325 women and children who traveled as cabin passengers, nothing more.

Lieutenant Suneson's sea-duty assignment lasted one year, after which she transferred ashore to recruiting duty. At her departure, *Mann*'s captain complimented her on her performance. He presented her with a commendation letter from the Navy that explained that the Navy wasn't ready for women at sea yet. Charlene Suneson's trial balloon had not floated. No other

WAVES officers went to sea duty. Before long, Suneson realized she had no future in the Navy and resigned her commission in 1968. After sea duty, how could shore duty compare?

JOINING SHIP'S COMPANY

During the Vietnam War, Navy recruiters reaped a bountiful harvest from draft-eligible men seeking to avoid Army service. When the United States finally withdrew from Vietnam in 1972 and the draft ended, the Navy immediately experienced recruiting shortfalls. Add to that a declining population of military-eligible young males plus an all-time low of 10 percent first-term reenlistments and the situation looked bleak for manning the Navy.[29] The Navy tried several schemes to meet the crisis, including lowering military entry requirements, reducing personnel on ships, and rotating crews among ships. These measures met with limited success. As predicted, the manning situation got worse. On some ships manning was so reduced that they were placed in the C-4 category, "not combat ready," unable to get under way because there were not enough skilled sailors onboard to steam ships safely.[30]

One solution to the personnel shortage was to recruit more women to fill noncombat positions. Of all the services, this was most difficult for the Navy because of the added factor of sea/shore rotation. Women in the Navy concentrated almost exclusively in the medical, administrative, communications, supply, and data-processing fields. Adding more women in those ratings would negatively impact the sea/shore rotation for men in the same ratings while doing nothing to alleviate the more critical shortages in nontraditional ratings. Only if the Navy could assign women to ships in a wide variety of ratings could it expand the ranks of women without jeopardizing shore duty opportunities for men.

Chief of Naval Operations Adm. Elmo Zumwalt had a specific ship in mind to initiate his plan to open sea duty to women. USS *Sanctuary* (AH 17) was in overhaul to convert her into a dependent support ship for the six ships home ported in Piraeus, Greece. For her new mission she would have a much-reduced sixty-bed family-oriented hospital, commissary, and exchange facilities, and a child-care center (staffed by civilians, not sailors). Because *Sanctuary* was a hospital ship, Admiral Zumwalt did not need congressional consent to assign women to her crew. The pilot program on *Sanctuary* had billets for one line officer (later increased to three), a Supply Corps officer, seven nurses, and fifty-eight enlisted women of various ratings. This time, there were no special age or time in service requirements for female sailors. Most would be volunteers but that was not a requirement. There was no special screening of the women except that the initial group of women were unmarried.

With respect to the jobs women would have on the ship, the chief of naval personnel directed *Sanctuary*'s commanding officer to assign women to normal in port and underway military duties as he deemed appropriate. "Women are not, however, to be assigned as underway Officer of the Deck [OOD] or Command Duty Officer pending changes to the current legislation."[31]

By the end of 1973 *Sanctuary* had fifty-three enlisted women in the crew. Of these, twenty-one hospital corpsmen and dental technicians worked in the medical department. The remainder worked in other departments of the ship, with the exception of engineering. Integrating women into the crew was a learning process with policies evolving as the need arose. Some issues were minor, as when Capt. Thomas A. Rodgers told reporters, "I never thought I'd see stuffed animals on board a Navy ship; but so what, it's not all that important."[32] He relied on "people's good sense and discretion" to keep out of berthing spaces of members of the opposite sex.[33] Other issues required direct leadership involvement. Public displays of affection blossomed during a goodwill cruise to Colombia because crew members had more recreational activities on deck in the warm weather. The captain solved the problem by making public displays of affection subject to punishment. When two crew members married, the secretary of the Navy ruled that husband and wife would not be allowed to serve on the same ship.

The enlisted women faced a steep learning curve in their new duties as their training to date had been quite different from their male shipmates. At an all-female boot camp they received comparatively little instruction in seamanship and ship operations. After boot camp, they did not go to seaman or fireman apprenticeship schools because those schools were closed to women. What the women lacked in training they made up with enthusiasm and diligence. Within a year, *Sanctuary*'s crew boasted the first women in the Navy rated as boatswain's mates.

Not surprisingly, the women's uniforms proved wholly inadequate for shipboard duty. The enlisted women's working uniform was not sturdy enough for either shipboard work or the ship's laundry. Most women resorted to wearing men's dungarees. Women officers had no working uniform. Their uniforms were designed for office work, parades, and social occasions, and none had an option for slacks. Of necessity, they wore men's khakis.

In January 1974 Lt. (junior grade) Ann Kerr, the administrative officer, formally requested a transfer, citing her frustration at being restricted from becoming an OOD under way even though she had completed all the qualifications. After some investigation, Navy lawyers could find no statutory or regulatory provision prohibiting women line officers from standing underway OOD watches.[34] This finding came too late for Ann Kerr: she was given her OOD qualification letter at her farewell party. Nevertheless, it opened the door for Lt. Susan B. Canfield, the operations officer. She qualified OOD underway in November 1974, becoming the first woman in the Navy to stand that watch.

Sue Canfield's next goal was to qualify surface warfare officer (SWO). The major stumbling block was *Sanctuary*'s rudimentary combat information center, which was "about the size of a telephone booth."[35] It had a radar repeater, a status board, and barely enough room for one person. Canfield would have to train on other ships in order to qualify SWO. Matters were complicated by a Navy policy restricting Navy women from getting under way on ships except for "daylight cruises."[36] Few ships were willing to expend precious fuel for just one day under way. SWO qualification remained elusive.

Meanwhile, events in Greece sealed *Sanctuary*'s fate. The ruling military junta, which had encouraged a U.S. military presence in Greece, returned the country to civilian rule in August 1974. The new government asked the United States to withdraw most of its military bases. *Sanctuary* was no longer needed as a dependent support ship, nor did the Navy have a need to maintain an active hospital ship. For budgetary reasons, the Navy decommissioned her for the last time on 28 March 1975, bringing the pilot program to an end because there were no other ships in the Navy inventory on which women could legally serve.

The Navy declared the *Sanctuary* pilot program a success. Nineteen women officers, including fourteen nurses and ninety-seven enlisted women had been a part of the crew for more than two years. Women stood in port and underway watches and served on general quarters repair parties, special sea and anchor detail, and underway replenishment detail. They had performed every assigned shipboard function with the same ease, expertise, and dedication as men. Captain Rodgers reported that enlisted women had performed on a par or superior to their male shipmates. "The striking difference," he noted, "is that women perform their assigned tasks with inspiring enthusiasm which invites a man to do his best."[37]

Sanctuary's operational schedule made it difficult to truly assess how women would perform at sea. She spent the first ten months of the pilot program in the shipyard. After that, she had only sixty-two days under way, the longest at-sea period being twelve days. Significantly, the pilot program had not evaluated women in the engineering ratings. Nevertheless, the Navy concluded women were capable of serving aboard ships.

FULL INTEGRATION ON AUXILIARIES

In 1977 the status quo for Navy women was under attack. Congress was considering no fewer than eight bills to amend or repeal Section 6015. The year prior, it had passed legislation granting women admission to the service academies. If that weren't enough, seven Navy women had filed a class-action suit against the Navy (*Owens v. Brown*) alleging gender discrimination because they were barred from sea duty.[38] Rather than let Congress or a federal judge dictate how to man its ships, the Navy submitted its own proposal to amend Section 6015 to allow the assignment of women to permanent duty on noncombatant auxiliary ships and to temporary duty on combatant ships not engaged in a combat mission.

While Congress debated the proposed amendment, the Navy began its implementation planning for the Women in Ships Program. Of the 556 ships in the active Navy, Naval Reserve force, and the Military Sealift Command, sixty-nine met the noncombatant criteria of the proposed amendment. Scheduled decommissionings of several ships, expensive or impractical berthing modifications on others, plus the objections from the submarine community that was unwilling to give up some billets to women, reduced the list to forty-nine. Of those, only fourteen could provide ample berthing and varied job assignments for a range of enlisted ratings and officer specialties. The missile test ship USS *Norton Sound* (AVM 1) and the deep submergence support ship USS *Point Loma* (AGDS 2) were medium-size ships with potential billets for about seventy women each. The vast majority of sea-duty billets for women would be on four repair ships and eight newer tenders, with crews ranging from 750 to 1,200.

In determining how many women could be assigned to sea duty, BUPERS had several desired manning criteria. First, at least one-third of the women assigned to a ship would be in nontraditional ratings in order to avoid concentrating women in areas traditionally considered "women's work." Second, at least 30 percent would be petty officers in order to maintain the overall experience base of the ship, provide role models for junior enlisted women, and prevent an inordinate number of women in the junior ranks.[39] Finally, enlisted women would not exceed half of any work center or half of a ship's crew.[40] These ambitious goals proved impossible to reach. More than 60 percent of all enlisted women were in traditional ratings and only about 5 percent were petty officers.[41] BUPERS calculated that only 398 enlisted women would be qualified and available for sea duty in fiscal year 1978, far too few to have women on all fourteen ships.[42] The first year embarkation plan had to be trimmed to five ships at a ratio of 10 percent of the crew, for 375 women in twenty-eight ratings.[43]

There was a similar skill mismatch with women officers. Nurses accounted for more than half the women officers in the Navy, but for the first time in the history of women on Navy ships, there were no sea-duty billets for nurses. Of the 881 potential billets for women officers, almost 80 percent (702) were for restricted line, staff corps, and warrant officers. Women in these designators made up just 10 percent of the women officer inventory. Another 4 percent of billets were for limited duty officers, a type of commission prohibited by law for women. Unrestricted line officers, the second-largest community of women in the Navy (38 percent), were left with 16 percent (139) of the billets. More than one-third of those billets, however, required prior experience at sea. BUPERS settled on fifty-five billets on fourteen ships for the first year: thirty-five unrestricted line, eighteen staff corps, one restricted line, and one warrant officer.[44]

Motivation and desire for sea duty was high among the unrestricted line officers who recognized it as a means to improve their competitiveness for promotion and command ashore. Roughly six volunteered for every available sea-duty billet. Staff corps women, however, showed lukewarm enthusiasm for sea duty, volunteering at a rate of one for every two billets. Medical Corps and Dental Corps officers, especially, saw no apparent advantage to sea duty. They could have fulfilling twenty- to thirty-year careers at hospitals and clinics ashore.

The initial group of enlisted women volunteers was a bit discouraging. Of the 284 volunteers, only 135 matched the ratings and pay grades needed.[45] As expected, there was no shortage in the traditional ratings but women in nontraditional ratings volunteered in very low numbers or not at all.[46] Critically, volunteers supplied only half of the 179 petty officers needed. Simply using the remaining volunteers to boost the women petty officer population on ships would inevitably concentrate them in areas traditionally considered women's work. BUPERS opted instead for fewer petty officers but spread across all departments.[47]

On 20 October 1978 President Carter signed the 1979 Defense Authorization Act, which included the Navy-sponsored amendment to Section 6015. Twelve days later, eight women officers reported to USS *Vulcan* (AR 5), USS *Puget Sound* (AD 38), USS *L. Y. Spear* (AS 36), USS *Dixon* (AS 37), and USS *Norton Sound* (AVM 1). The women wore their service dress blues with slacks, finally an authorized part of a woman's uniform. The Navy still did not have khakis for women and would not until almost a year later.

Capt. Harry A. Spencer, *Vulcan*'s commanding officer, predicted that women at sea would have a positive effect on his ship. "Men will work hard not to be out done by women, and women will work hard to prove themselves."[48]

Vulcan sailors told reporters they had been ordered to get rid of their dirty magazines and clean up their language but, for the most part, were accepting: "I don't care if women come on board or not, as long as they don't get in front of me in the mess line."[49]

The first enlisted women reported aboard *Vulcan* in December, with more arriving in January and February. Of the sixty-two women in the crew, only five were nonvolunteers. Unlike their predecessors on *Sanctuary*, these women were better trained, having attended damage control and fire-fighting schools en route to the ship. The most junior among them benefited from changes made to recruit training in 1976. The women's curriculum was now almost the same as men's, and women could to attend seaman apprenticeship school.

Vulcan's crew converted a male berthing compartment to accommodate their new shipmates. Alterations were minimal: installing locks on doors leading to male berthing areas, removing urinals, and covering portholes and ventilation shafts to thwart Peeping Toms. The only extra feature in women's berthing was more electrical outlets for hair dryers. Other modifications included an obstetric/gynecological examination table in sickbay and the addition of women's toiletry and hair-care items in the ship's store. The total cost for the conversion was a mere $3,000.[50]

Barely two weeks after the women reported aboard, two male sailors tried to sneak into women's berthing. To reporters, the captain and commanding officer downplayed the incident as a prank, comparing it to a college panty raid, but at captain's mast Captain Spencer meted out the maximum nonjudicial punishment. Three other men, after drinking ashore, tried to get into women's berthing in February and were court-martialed. Captain Spencer was making it clear that he would not tolerate "nonmilitary behavior" on his ship. To prevent further incidents, he instituted security watches at night to keep men out of women's berthing.[51]

In February *Vulcan* got under way for the first time with the enlisted women. She spent four days off the coast of Virginia to train the new crewmembers. As with the nurses on *Relief* in 1921, many men assumed women were somehow more susceptible than men to seasickness, a traditional mark of distinction between landsmen and seamen. Just as in 1921, this proved not to be the case. Rough seas brought men and women alike to the railings. One woman later recalled, "When I got sick . . . there were three guys standing right beside me, heads hanging over the rail. One of them asked me if I was all right. When I said yeah, he said, 'Well then help me, because I'm not.'"[52]

Vulcan departed for a six-month deployment on 11 September 1979, her first in twenty years and the first time a Navy ship deployed with women sailors. Her first port of call was Palma de Mallorca for a turnover of duties with

USS *Shenandoah* (AD 26). Instead of a friendly welcome, *Shenandoah*'s sailors greeted *Vulcan* with demeaning and unmistakably sexual banners. The largest read, "Welcome Love Boat, Are your women turn'n over, too?" A second sign hinted that the women were not up to doing the job: "Lots of luck—You're going to need it!" Pictured on this sign was a threaded screw with the caption "Bend over, I'll drive it in."[53]

In Genoa, Italians unaccustomed to women working in the waterfront area on legitimate business assumed the worst. One *Vulcan* woman was approached to sell her services. Another was nearly arrested for prostitution. The real prostitutes and bar girls threatened violence against the female sailors, fearing a loss of business. It was quite a shock for Italians to see uniformed women on shore patrol. People on the street stared, pointed fingers, and even took photographs.

In Naples, the enlisted women were the object of attention from American sailors seeking an English-speaking companion in a foreign port. Most men just wanted to talk to someone new, but a handful seemed to think the women were on *Vulcan* to satisfy the sexual needs of sailors. The women found wearing wedding bands discouraged most overeager sailors. Despite these incidents, the women assured reporters that they were enjoying the deployment. "I'm having the time of my life, just seeing different places, meeting the people, eating different foods."[54] In Barcelona, the enlisted women had a party to celebrate their one-year anniversary onboard.

Vulcan returned to Norfolk on 1 March 1980. Only a handful of reporters and photographers waited on the pier. The novelty was beginning to wear thin, but amid the banners and balloons raised by the crowd was one never before seen by a returning deployer: "Welcome Home Mom." Captain Spencer declared the deployment a success. *Vulcan* had tended twenty ships, ranging from an aircraft carrier to a small salvage ship, and had helped install a satellite antenna at a communications station ashore. "As a whole," he affirmed, "the women performed as well as the men professionally."[55] By and large, *Vulcan*'s women agreed. One observed, "The cruise couldn't have been any better. All the things everybody told us to worry about, like sex and chauvinism, were just exaggerations."[56] Another added, "We all want to make it [the Women in Ships Program] work. Everyone goes out of her way to do her job and make sure it's done right."[57]

Of course, not everyone painted a rosy picture. One man grumbled, "Women have no place on our ship. In my opinion, they're worthless. But don't use my name."[58] Another man thought women had jinxed the ship since there had been an increase in accidents after they arrived.[59] Officially, this was attributed to the women's initial lack of training and experience.

To commemorate her role as the lead ship in the integration of enlisted women on Navy ships, *Vulcan* redesigned her ship's seal. The original seal, devised in 1945, depicted the Roman god of fire and metallurgy working at his forge. On the new seal, Vulcan still toils at his anvil, but the setting is at sea and a Navy enlisted woman, wearing blue dungarees and leather gloves, assists him with his work. At the same time, the ship also changed its motto from "Service to the Fleet," which had been a source of sexual innuendo on the waterfront after the women arrived, to "We Tend to Be Better."

BREAKING THE FINAL BARRIER

At the end of the first year of the Women in Ships Program, fifty-three women officers were serving on fourteen ships and 307 enlisted women on four of those ships. These numbers gradually increased as the Navy converted more ships to mixed-gender crews. Over the next few years, women achieved significant milestones: In January 1980 Ens. Roberta L. McIntyre became the first woman to qualify SWO. In September 1980 Lt. (junior grade) Colleen Nevius and Lt. Karen Thornton were the first women to fly vertical replenishment missions at sea. In 1981 the first woman qualified enlisted surface warfare specialist. In June 1984 Lt. (junior grade) Susan Cowan, a special operations officer (diver), became the first woman executive officer afloat on USS *Quapaw* (ATF 110). In 1985 the first woman qualified surface warfare Supply Corps officer. And in 1986 Lt. Roberta Spillane qualified for command at sea.

Despite these achievements, sea duty for women remained static for the next thirteen years. Women served primarily on tenders with little underway time or operational experience. The lack of command afloat opportunity discouraged women SWOs. Further contributing to a sense of dissatisfaction among women was that the rules for sea duty pay had changed in 1976, making most tender sailors—and therefore almost all women—ineligible to collect the special pay. Navy leadership indicated it had no desire or need to further amend or repeal Section 6015. With no other prospect than tender duty, many women chose not to go to sea again.

The first meaningful change came in 1988 when the Navy, under pressure from Congress and the Defense Advisory Committee on Women in the Service, opened twenty-five replenishment ships of the Combat Logistics Force to women. This action more than doubled the number of women's sea-duty billets, opened engineering ratings that had been closed, and provided a viable path to command for women SWOs. An unexpected consequence was that twenty-five ships with women in their crews, almost all Combat Logistics

Force, participated in Operations Desert Shield and Desert Storm (1990–91) in the Persian Gulf and Red Sea. Notable among them was Lt. Commander Darlene Iskra, the first Navy woman to command a ship, on USS *Opportune* (ARS 41). Never before had women been so involved in naval operations.

With thousands of military women in Southeast Asia working in conditions very near to combat, Americans began to question why women were excluded from combat positions. After the war, change was swift. In December 1991 Congress authorized women to fly combat missions and in 1993 repealed Section 6015 opening sea duty on combatant ships to women. Today, Navy women proudly serve on every class of ships except submarines. Their assignment no longer depends on the presence of civilian women and children. They no longer fill shore-duty billets so that men can be sent to sea. They no longer fill billets on auxiliary ships in order to prevent manning shortfalls on combatants. They are an integral part of the fighting Navy. (And I'm jealous!)

NOTES

The following abbreviations are used in the notes:

BUPERS	Bureau of Naval Personnel
NAVPERS	Navy Personnel
NC	Nurse Corps
NHC	Naval Historical Center
OA	Operational Archive
OPNAVINST	Office of the Chief of Naval Operations Instructions
PERS (or Pers)	Personnel

1. J[osephine] B[eatrice] B[owman] [Chief Nurse, USN], "A Letter from a Navy Nurse—from the U.S.S. *Relief*," *American Journal of Nursing* 21 (1921): 644.
2. Department of the Navy, *Naval Regulations Issued by Command of the President, 1802*, reprint (Annapolis, MD: U.S. Naval Institute, 1970), 9.
3. *The Statutes at Large of the United States of America from December, 1907, to March, 1909*, 35, pt. 1 (Washington, DC: GPO, 1909), 146.
4. Department of the Navy, *Annual Report of the Surgeon-General of the U.S. Navy 1910* (Washington, DC: GPO, 1910), 19.
5. Dermott Vincent Hickey, "The First Ladies in the Navy: A History of the Navy Nurse Corps, 1908–39," (unpublished master's thesis, George Washington University, Washington, DC, 1963), 79.
6. J. Beatrice Bowman, letter to Superintendent Lenah S. Higbee, 31 March 1921; Bowman Papers, Correspondence 1920–21 (Higbee); Navy Nurse Corps Records, Box 1; OA, NHC.
7. Bowman, "A Letter from a Navy Nurse," 644.
8. J. Beatrice Bowman, letter to Lenah S. Higbee, 16 April 1921; Bowman Papers, Correspondence 1920–21 (Higbee); Navy Nurse Corps Records, Box 1; OA, NHC.

9. J. Beatrice Bowman, letter to Lenah S. Higbee, 20 April 1921; Bowman Papers, Correspondence 1920–21 (Higbee); Navy Nurse Corps Records, Box 1; OA, NHC.
10. Thomasina Libby, Nurse, USN, "My First Duty Aboard Ship, the U.S.S. '*Relief*,'" *United States Naval Medical Bulletin* 20 (1924): 741.
11. Lenah S. Higbee, Superintendent, Navy Nurse Corps, letter to Beatrice Bowman, 24 February 1921; Bowman Papers, Correspondence 1920–21 (Higbee); Navy Nurse Corps Records, Box 1; OA, NHC.
12. Susie I. Fitzgerald, Chief Nurse, USN, "A Transport Ship," *American Journal of Nursing* 23 (1922): 222–225.
13. Ruth M. Cohen, Lieutenant (junior grade), NC, USN, "I Was a Navy Nurse," *Life Story* (October 1943): 65, 103.
14. "The Task Force in White," *All Hands*, no. 336 (March 1944): 23.
15. Page Cooper, *Navy Nurse* (New York: McGraw Hill, 1946), 79–80.
16. Sarah Lorimer, "Life Line," *Ladies Home Journal* 60 (1943): 59.
17. Ruth B. Scott, "Women Who Nurse: Lt. Norma D. Chamers," *R.N.* (September 1945): 166.
18. Jan K. Herman, *Battle Station Sick Bay: Navy Medicine in World War II* (Annapolis, MD: Naval Institute Press, 1997), 174–175.
19. Doris M. Sterner, Captain, NC, USN (Ret), *In and Out of Harm's Way: A History of the Navy Nurse Corps* (Seattle, WA: Peanut Butter Publishing, 1997), 133.
20. Charlotte I. Bailey, Lieutenant, NC, USN, "Aboard a Hospital Ship;" Miscellaneous Articles, Folder 13; Navy Nurse Corps Records, Box 21; OA; NHC.
21. Georgia Reynolds, Lieutenant (junior grade), NC, USN, "On a Navy Hospital Ship," *American Journal of Nursing* 45 (1945): 235.
22. U.S. Congress, House Committee on Armed Services Subcommittee 3, Organization and Mobilization, *Hearings on S. 1641, To Establish the Women's Army Corps*, 80th Congress, vol. 1173-A, 5712.
23. Joy Bright Hancock, Captain, USN (Ret), *Lady in the Navy: A Personal Reminiscence* (Annapolis, MD: Naval Institute Press, 1972), 169.
24. Susan H. Godson, *Serving Proudly: A History of the Women in the U.S. Navy* (Annapolis, MD: Naval Institute Press, 2001), 191.
25. Department of the Navy, *Policies for the Administration of Women in the Regular Navy and Naval Reserve*, NavPers 15,085 (1 April 1949), 11, 13.
26. Paul S. Maguire, Captain, USN, undated postcard; Folder I–66 Officer Policies, Plans, etc. 1950–53; ACNP for Women Series I, Box 9; OA, NHC.
27. "Two Wave Officers Serve in Ships during Cruises," *All Hands* 388 (June 1949): 7.
28. Beverly Beyette, "She Went to Sea to See What She Could See," *Los Angeles Times*, 26 February 1979, Part IV, 6.
29. Godson, *Serving Proudly*, 222.
30. "Ships Lacking Key Personnel Set to Sail, Congressman Says," *Washington Post*, 1 July 1980, A2.
31. (Pers B 1104), Chief of Naval Personnel, letter to PCO USS *Sanctuary*, 26 October 1972; Folder 1 of 2, USS *Sanctuary*, Evaluation of Women Aboard 1972–3; BUPERS Special Assistant for Women's Policy (PERS 00W) Series III Subject File Women Assigned to Sea Duty—Section 6015 of Title 10, Box 10 of 22; OA, NHC.
32. Jack Viets, "The Women at Sea: How the Navy Did It," *San Francisco Chronicle*, 22 September 1973, 4.
33. Viets, "The Women at Sea," 4.

34. Charles R. Davis, Captain, JAGC, USN, (Pers 14b), Memorandum for Director, Equal Opportunity (Pers 61) of 27 February 1974; Folder 2 of 2, USS *Sanctuary*, Evaluation of Women Aboard 1974–75; BUPERS Special Assistant for Women's Policy (PERS 00W) Series III Women Assigned to Sea Duty—Section 6015 of Title 10, Box 10 of 22; OA, NHC.
35. Susan Canfield, Captain, USN (Ret), "Panel 2: The Early Years: Roundtable Discussion," *Women at Sea: 25 Years and Counting*, unpublished transcript of symposium held at Navy Memorial, Washington, DC, on 20 November 2003 (Washington, DC: Naval Historical Foundation, 2005), 36.
36. Department of the Navy, "Embarkation in U.S. Naval Ships," OPNAVINST 5720.2G, 27 September 1973.
37. Sandra Harley Carey, Lieutenant, USN, Ulysses James, Commander, USN, and Marnee L. Finch, Lieutenant, USN, *Women in the Navy Information Handbook*, NAVPERS 155169 (Bureau of Naval Personnel, Washington, DC), 49; Folder 7, Box 1 CNO Study Group; OA; NHC.
38. On 27 July 1978, Judge John Sirica ruled that Title 10 U.S. Code, Section 6015 was unconstitutional. However, he did not order the Navy to amend the law.
39. Memorandum, "U.S. Navy's Women in Ships Program"; Folder 5, CNO Study Group—Women in Navy Misc.; CNO Study Group—Women in Navy, Box 4 of 11; OA, NHC.
40. U.S. Congress House Committee on Armed Services, *Hearings on Military Posture*, 95th Congress, 2nd Session, Part 5 of 7, 21 March 1978 (Washington, DC: GPO, 1978), 1183–1185.
41. Ibid., 1195.
42. Ibid., 1184.
43. Rosemary Purcell, "Navy Details Plan on Women at Sea," *Navy Times* 27 (1978): 1.
44. U.S. Congress, *Hearings on Military Posture*, 1185–1186.
45. "Navy Seeking More Women for Sea Duty," *Navy Times* 28 (1978): 3.
46. "Enlisted Manning SITREP (Requirements/Volunteers);" Folder 1 of 2, Women Assigned to Sea Duty—Section 6015 of Title 10, 1977–78; BUPERS Special Assistant for Women's Policy (PERS 00W) Series III, Box 14 of 22; OA, NHC.
47. "Women in the Navy at Sea Plans" prepared by P. D. Butcher, Deputy Assistant Chief for Personnel, Planning and Programming (PERS 2B), 12 September 1978; Folder 2 of 2, Section 6015, Women Assigned to Sea Duty—Section 6015 of Title 10, 1977–78; BUPERS Special Assistant for Women's Policy (PERS 00W) Series III, Box 14 of 22; OA, NHC.
48. Sandy Banisky, "Navy History Made as 5 Woman Officers Become the First of Their Sex to Join Ships," *Baltimore Sun*, 2 November 1978, A11.
49. Katherine Calos, "Sailing, Sailing—at Last!" *Richmond News Leader*, 2 November 1978, 15.
50. Marlene Cimons, "Navy Women at the Helm of History," *Los Angeles Times*, 26 February 1979, View Part IV, 1.
51. Ibid., 5.
52. Ibid., 5.
53. *Vulcan* cruise book, 1979–80.
54. John Stevenson, "Traditions Yield to Navy's Women," *Virginian-Pilot and Ledger-Star*, 18 November 1979, A6.
55. "*Vulcan*'s Coed Deployment a Success," *Navy Times* 29 (1980): 20.
56. "57 Women Prove Mettle in Cruise to Mediterranean," *Los Angeles Times*, 2 March 1980, Part I, 20.
57. "*Vulcan*'s Coed Deployment a Success," 20.
58. "Love Boat," *Stars and Stripes*, 2 March 1980, 1.
59. Rosemary Purcell, "Mixed Crew Set for Deployment," *Navy Times* 28 (1979): 4.

ABOUT THE EDITOR

Maochun Miles Yu is professor of East Asia and military history at the U.S. Naval Academy in Annapolis, Maryland. He holds a doctorate degree from the University of California at Berkeley (1994), a master's degree from Swarthmore College (1987), and a bachelor's degree from Nankai University, Tianjin, China (1983). He is the author of *The Dragon's War: Allied Operations and the Fate of China, 1937–1947* (Naval Institute Press, 2006), *OSS in China—Prelude to Cold War* (Yale University Press, 1997), and numerous articles on modern China and the military and intelligence history of World War II and the Cold War.

ABOUT THE CONTRIBUTORS

Dr. Donald F. Bittner is professor of history at the Marine Corps Command and Staff College, Quantico, Virginia. He received his BS, MA, and doctorate in history from the University of Missouri. From 1963 to 1989 he served in the Marine Corps as a regular officer and reserve officer. Since 1975 he has been on the faculty of the Command and Staff College. His publications include *The Lion and the White Falcon: Britain and Iceland in the World War II Era* (Archon Books, 1983) and *Officers of Royal Marines in the Age of Sail: Professional and Personal Life in His and Her Majesty's "Soldiers of the Sea* (2002). In 1992 he was chairman of the annual meeting of the Society for Military History and edited a book of selected papers from that meeting as part of the Marine Corps University series *Perspectives on Warfighting: Volume III—Selected Papers from the 1992 (59th) Annual Meeting of the Society for Military History* (1994). His current research focuses on a social and professional history of the officer corps of Britain's Royal Marines between 1815 and 1914; he is also editing the memoirs of Lt. Col. C. F. Jerram, DSO, CMG, Royal Marines.

Charles R. Foy is an assistant professor of early American and Atlantic history at Eastern Illinois University. He is the author of "Seeking Freedom in the Atlantic, 1713–1783," *Early American Studies: An Interdisciplinary Journal* 4:1 (Spring 2006): 46–77, and "Possibilities & Limits for Freedom: Maritime Fugitives in British North America, ca. 1713–1783" in the forthcoming *Gender, Race, Ethnicity and Power in Maritime America* (Mystic Seaport, 2009). His research focuses on slavery in colonial British North America and the Black Atlantic.

Willard C. Frank Jr. received his doctorate in 1969 from the University of Pittsburgh and is an emeritus professor of history at Old Dominion University and a Fleet Seminar professor in strategy and policy and strategy and war at the Naval War College. He has published the books *The Sources of Soviet Naval Conduct* (Lexington Books, 1989) and *Soviet Military Doctrine from Lenin to Gorbachev* (Greenwood, 1992), as well as articles in seven countries on the Spanish Civil War at sea (1936–39), for which he is preparing a large-scale study.

Kenneth P. Hansen received his BS (Honors) in zoology from the University of Alberta in Edmonton and his MA (Honors) in war studies from the Royal Military College in Kingston, Ontario. He is currently the Defense Fellow with the Centre for Foreign Policy Studies at Dalhousie University in Halifax, Nova Scotia. He is the editor for the Centre for Foreign Policy Studies series *The Maritime Security Occasional Papers*. His current research interests include joint and naval doctrine, expeditionary warfare, and operational logistics. Commander Hansen's thesis, "Fuel Endurance and Replenishment at Sea in the Royal Canadian Navy, 1935–1945," was awarded the 2005 Jacques Cartier Prize by the Canadian Nautical Research Society as the year's best graduate thesis on a nautical subject in Canada. His other literary awards include the Hannington Millennium Essay Prize and the Bruce S. Oland Prize. He has published articles in *Canadian Military Journal, Canadian Naval Review, Frontline, Maritime Affairs, Naval War College Review,* and *The Northern Mariner*. He has also written book reviews for *Canadian Naval Review, Maritime Affairs, The International Journal of Maritime History,* and *The Northern Mariner*. Commander Hansen, his wife Cynthia Plant-Hansen, and their sons, Thomas and Peter, reside in Halifax, Nova Scotia.

Catherine A. Leahey, USN (Ret.), received her commission through the NROTC program at Purdue University in 1977. The following year she was among the first women to volunteer for sea duty under the Women in Ships Program. A qualified surface warfare officer, her sea-duty assignments included USS *Point Loma* (AGDS 2), USS *Shenandoah* (AD 44), USS *Simon Lake* (AS 33), and USS *Pyro* (AE 24). She retired from the Navy in 1997. She holds MA degrees from the Naval War College and Savannah College of Art and Design.

Chris Madsen is an associate professor in the Department of Defence Studies at the Canadian Forces College in Toronto, Ontario, and the Royal Military College of Canada in Kingston, Ontario. He holds a doctorate in history from the University of Victoria. He was the academic cochair of maritime studies in joint operations and planning and teaches courses in strategy, military law, and naval history to senior and mid-rank officers. His publications include the legal loose-leaf service *Military Law and Operations* (Canada Law Book, 2008), the coedited documentary collection *Kurt Meyer on Trial* (Canadian Defence Academy Press, 2007), *Another Kind of Justice: Canadian Military Law from Confederation to Somalia* (UBC Press, 1999), *The Royal Navy and German Naval Disarmament 1942–1947* (Frank Cass, 1998), "Strategy, Fleet Logistics and the Lethbridge Mission to the Pacific and Indian Oceans 1943–44" (*Journal of Strategic Studies*), "John Maynard Keynes and Stage II Naval Requirements for the War against Japan" (*International Journal of Maritime History*), "Continuous Production in British Columbia Shipyards during the Second World War" (*The Northern Mariner*), and "Limits of Generosity and Trust: The Naval

Side of the Combined Munitions Assignment Board 1942–45" (*War & Society*). He is presently writing a book on wartime shipbuilding along the Pacific coast, 1937–1946, with a standard research grant from the Social Sciences and Humanities Research Council of Canada.

Charles Neimeyer is currently the director and chief of Marine Corps history at Marine Corps University, Quantico, Virginia. He was the former dean of academics at the Naval War College and Forrest Sherman Chair of public diplomacy in Newport, Rhode Island, and served for a short period as vice president for academic affairs at Valley Forge Military Academy and College in Wayne, Pennsylvania. Prior to his stint as academic dean at the Naval War College, he was a full-time professor of national security affairs from 1997 to 2002. He also previously served as an award-winning history professor at the U.S. Naval Academy and the University of Central Oklahoma, where he was named Liberal Arts Outstanding Professor of the Year. Prior to his academic career, Dr. Neimeyer served as an officer of the Marines and retired at the rank of lieutenant colonel in 1996. He was awarded a doctorate and MA degree in history from Georgetown University with distinction and was also awarded an MA degree with highest distinction from the Naval War College.

Neimeyer has written a variety of history and national security affairs articles and has published the widely acclaimed monograph, *America Goes to War: A Social History of the Continental Army, 1775–1783* (New York University Press, 1996). He most recently published a second monograph, *The Revolutionary War* (Greenwood Press, 2007).

Katherine K. Reist is an associate professor and head of the Department of History at the University of Pittsburgh at Johnstown. A graduate of Muskingum College and the Ohio State University, she is a specialist in East Asian history. Her research interest is U.S. military forces in China in the first half of the twentieth century. Her most recent publications include articles in the *Encyclopedia of Chinese-American Relations*, edited by Yuwu Song.

Alexandre Sheldon-Duplaix graduated from the Paris Institute of Political Science and holds an MA degree in history and has completed two predoctoral dissertations in history and political science from the Sorbonne. From 1987 to 1999 he worked as a civilian analyst under contract with the French Ministry of Defense. He then joined the research unit of the French Navy Historical Service in Vincennes (Service Historique de la Defense) and lectured at the Joint Defense College (Collège interarmées de défense) on the history of Russian and Asian navies. He is the author of a general history of aircraft carriers (ETAI, 2006) and coauthor of two general histories of submarines (ETAI, 2002; Gallimard, 2006). With the late Capt. Peter Huchthausen, USN, he cowrote *Hide and Seek*, a book on naval intelligence during the Cold War (John Wiley and Sons, 2008).

Chuck Stanton is a retired naval aviator and retired Northwest Airlines pilot who pursued a late-in-life doctorate in medieval European history at the University of Cambridge with a focus on Norman naval power in the Mediterranean. He received a BA in political science from the University of California at Riverside (1971), an MA in history at the University of West Florida (1975), and a master of philosophy degree in medieval history at the University of Cambridge (2005). He received his doctorate in medieval history at the University of Cambridge in October 2008.

Kenneth M. Swope earned his BA at the College of Wooster (Ohio) in history, spending a semester abroad in Hong Kong. He then pursued graduate studies at the University of Michigan, earning his MA in Chinese studies (1995) and a doctorate in history (2001). After graduating from the University of Michigan in 2001, he taught for three years at Marist College in New York. Since 2004 he has been at Ball State University, where he teaches courses on all eras of East Asian history, world history, World War II, and the history of baseball. His primary area of specialty is early modern East Asian military and political history, with a focus on comparative history. He is a board member of the Chinese Military History Society and belongs to numerous other scholarly organizations, including the Society for Qing History, the Society for Ming Studies, and the Society for Military History. He edited *Warfare in China since 1600* (Ashgate's International Library of Essays in Military History, 2005). He is the author of *A Dragon's Head and a Serpent's Tail: Ming China and the First Greater East Asian War, 1592–1598* (University of Oklahoma Press, 2008). He is currently in the early stages of research for his next project, *The Military Collapse of China's Ming Dynasty, 1620–1644*, which is under contract with Routledge.

David P. Werlich is professor emeritus at Southern Illinois University–Carbondale, where he has taught Latin American history for four decades. He is a specialist on the history of Peru, with a particular interest in the Amazon portion of that country. His books include *Peru: A Short History* (Southern Illinois University Press, 1978) and *Admiral of the Amazon: John Randolph Tucker, His Confederate Colleagues, and Peru* (University of Virginia Press, 1990). His essay in the present volume won a Best Paper award at the 2007 Naval History Symposium.

Jorit Wintjes is an assistant professor at the Department of Ancient History at Julius-Maximilians-Universität Würzburg, Germany, and he is involved in a major research project on Roman naval operations. He holds MA degrees in contemporary history, Latin, and Greek, and a doctorate in ancient history.

The Naval Institute Press is the book-publishing arm of the U.S. Naval Institute, a private, nonprofit, membership society for sea service professionals and others who share an interest in naval and maritime affairs. Established in 1873 at the U.S. Naval Academy in Annapolis, Maryland, where its offices remain today, the Naval Institute has members worldwide.

Members of the Naval Institute support the education programs of the society and receive the influential monthly magazine *Proceedings* or the colorful bimonthly magazine *Naval History* and discounts on fine nautical prints and on ship and aircraft photos. They also have access to the transcripts of the Institute's Oral History Program and get discounted admission to any of the Institute-sponsored seminars offered around the country.

The Naval Institute's book-publishing program, begun in 1898 with basic guides to naval practices, has broadened its scope to include books of more general interest. Now the Naval Institute Press publishes about seventy titles each year, ranging from how-to books on boating and navigation to battle histories, biographies, ship and aircraft guides, and novels. Institute members receive significant discounts on the Press's more than eight hundred books in print.

Full-time students are eligible for special half-price membership rates. Life memberships are also available.

For a free catalog describing Naval Institute Press books currently available, and for further information about joining the U.S. Naval Institute, please write to:

Member Services
U.S. Naval Institute
291 Wood Road
Annapolis, MD 21402-5034
Telephone: (800) 233-8764
Fax: (410) 571-1703
Web address: www.usni.org